Meter in English

A Critical Engagement

METER IN ENGLISH

A CRITICAL ENGAGEMENT

edited by

David Baker

The University of Arkansas Press
Fayetteville 1996

oo   99   98   97   96   5   4   3   2   1

Designed by Gail Carter and Liz Lester

⊚ The paper used in this publication meets the minimum requirements of the American
National Standard for Permanence of Paper for Printed Library Materials Z39.48-1984.

Library of Congress Cataloging-in-Publication Data

Meter in English : a critical engagement / edited by David Baker.
       p.   cm.
       Includes bibliographical references and indexes.
       ISBN 1-55728-422-9 (alk. paper). —ISBN 1-55728-444-X (pbk. : alk. paper)
       1. English language—Versification. 2. Poetics. I. Baker, David, 1954–   .
PE1505.M48   1996
821.009—dc20   96–27935
                                                                 CIP

Excerpts from "Burnt Norton" in *Four Quartets,* copyright 1943 by T. S. Eliot and renewed 1971 by Esme Valerie Eliot, reprinted by permission of Harcourt Brace & Company.

"Rhythm and Rhyme" will appear in *The Collected Poetry of Robinson Jeffers, Volume IV,* edited by Tim Hunt, forthcoming from Stanford University Press. No portion of it may be reproduced without the express permission of Stanford University Press.

John Logan: "On Reading Camus in Early March" copyright © 1989 by The John Logan Literary Estate, Inc. Reprinted from *John Logan: The Collected Poems* with the permission of BOA Editions, Ltd., 92 Park Ave., Brockport, NY 14420.

"Poetry" reprinted with the permission of Simon & Shuster from *The Collected Poems of Marianne Moore.* Copyright © 1935 by Marianne Moore, renewed 1963 by Marianne Moore and T. S. Eliot.

"Poetry" by Marianne Moore reprinted with the permission of Faber & Faber Ltd. from *The Complete Poems.* Copyright 1935 by Marianne Moore, renewed 1963 by Marianne Moore and T. S. Eliot.

"The Waking," copyright 1953 by Theodore Roethke from *The Collected Poems of Theodore Roethke* by Theodore Roethke. Used by permission of Doubleday, a division of Bantam Doubleday Dell Publishing Group, Inc.

"The Waking" by Theodore Roethke reprinted with the permission of Faber & Faber Ltd. Copyright 1953 by Theodore Roethke.

Soft is the strain when zephyr gently blows,
And the smooth stream in smoother numbers flows;
But when loud surges lash the sounding shore,
The hoarse, rough verse should like the torrent roar:
When Ajax strives some rock's vast weight to throw,
The line too labors, and the words move slow:
Not so when swift Camilla scours the plain,
Flies o'er th' unbending corn, and skims along the main.

—ALEXANDER POPE

Contenting myself with the certainty that music, in its various
modes of meter, rhythm, and rhyme, is of so vast a moment in
poetry as never to be wisely rejected—is so vitally important an
adjunct, that he is simply silly who declines its assistance—
I will not now pause to maintain its absolute essentiality.

—EDGAR ALLAN POE

CONTENTS

INTRODUCTION

David Baker

Poetry is an art of repetitions. Images and ideas repeat and combine into metaphors; metaphors in turn may recur and further extend into patterns of conceit, into symbols, into epic similes. A poet's rehearsal of ideas may become his or her theme, and the recurrence of themes, or of a theme's tropes, may develop into a convention. Rhyme is the repetition of sounds at the ends of lines, and within lines many other duplications of sound are recognized as alliteration, consonance, and assonance. When details accumulate in a pattern, we have the catalogue; when the beginnings of parallel phrases or clauses repeat, in pattern, we have anaphora; when a scheme of whole lines returns, we may have the refrain of a villanelle or a ballade. And when entire stanzas are repeated, the chorus is born, and the poem turns around again.

Consider the accumulating power and grace of repetitions in these first three stanzas of Theodore Roethke's great villanelle:

> I wake to sleep, and take my waking slow.
> I feel my fate in what I cannot fear.
> I learn by going where I have to go.

We think by feeling. What is there to know?
I hear my being dance from ear to ear.
I wake to sleep, and take my waking slow.

Of those so close beside me, which are you?
God bless the Ground! I shall walk softly there,
And learn by going where I have to go.

The results of poetic repetitions are manifold: a returning phrase may enchant, a repeated line may emphasize, a pattern of rhymes or repetitions may hold itself longer in the memory. The recurrent sounds of poetry embody the music of the language itself. The final stanzas of Roethke's "The Waking" enact the fascination as well as the imperative, the absolute instruction, of poetic repetition:

Light takes the Tree; but who can tell us how?
The lowly worm climbs up a winding stair;
I wake to sleep, and take my waking slow.

Great Nature has another thing to do
To you and me; so take the lively air,
And, lovely, learn by going where to go.

This shaking keeps me steady. I should know.
What falls away is always. And is near.
I wake to sleep, and take my waking slow.
I learn by going where I have to go.

Rhythm is the one of poetry's most haunting and abiding forms of repetition. In *The New Book of Forms,* Lewis Putnam Turco calls rhythm the "movement of cadences in language." It is the pace, the pitch and fall, of language, the breathing, walking, tumbling, pulsing dynamic of our words interacting with each other. Rhythm gives poetry an essential component—the movement of music in the human voice. Edgar Allan Poe, in "The Poetic Principle," describes poetry's most essential "province" to be "Beauty" and asserts that the poet's method of constructing the beautiful is to combine the aspects of language and music: "I would define, in brief, the Poetry of words as the Rhythmical Creation of Beauty." This union of the body and meaning, of music and words, is what Roethke suggests, too: "I hear my being dance from ear to ear."

Meter is created when rhythm assumes and holds a recognizable pattern. It is, to be more precise, the abstract method by which we *measure* those regular, real patterns of rhythm. *Meter's* Greek origin is, after all, *metron:* a thing by which to measure. Meter is one fundamental tool for poets as they seek to exploit the manifold possibilities of repetition. Some say that meter makes language's cadences utterly familiar to the body, an essence as physical and primary as the heartbeat, which is itself (depending on the position of the cardiologist's stethoscope) either a trochee, *LUB-dub,* or an iamb, *lub-DUB.* Others claim that meter is the ultimate *de*familiarization of rhythm, by making highly regular, and thereby artificial, the naturally less even rhythms of our words. Meter is at once a source of beauty and of debate for poets and for the readers of poetry . . . and meter—*flowing, lashing, roaring, laboring, flying* meter, as Pope says in "An Essay on Criticism"—is the subject of this symposium.

HOW THE BOOK GOT STARTED

In the summer of 1993 Robert Wallace circulated to a few friends the initial draft of an essay, "Meter in English." Among those friends were Miller Williams, the director of the University of Arkansas Press, myself, and some of the contributors to the present volume. Wallace wanted to know what we thought about his ideas, whose central aspirations, he said, were clarity and simplicity: to clarify some of the methods of scansion, to simplify (or make more appropriate) some of the vocabulary of metrics, and to streamline our ways of thinking about the fundamental structure of meter in English. Even in its early, shorter draft, Wallace's essay elicited from this small audience a vociferous response, one which ranged from considerable agreement to point-by-point and rousing discord.

The current dialogue about metrics is eclectic, at best. Few critics or poets write about it at length, and those who do often disagree utterly about even the most basic terms, methods, uses, and meanings of meter. X. J. Kennedy has rather playfully referred to the last few decades, when free verse has been the primary prosodic method of most poets, as "the *Howl*-dominated Dark Ages of American poetry," and the New Formalists with their dedication to meter and rhyme have suggested that their school, along with the New Narrative poetry, may be the two significant movements in contemporary American poetry. At the same time, Los Angeles poet Kate Braverman, among others, has declared that "Form is dead. . . . [Formalism] is a kind of intellectual game, but it doesn't serve the purpose of women. It doesn't serve the purposes of, oh, shall we call them issues of freedom that have defined this century."

There is no doubt that issues of prosody and poetic form are not just personal, but yes, cultural issues. The choices we make as writers and as readers are grounded in systems of value embedded in our language itself. This should not be news to us. And yet the rich, inclusive possibilities of contemporary poetry may also be jeopardized by proprietary claims limiting its formal, its aesthetic, and its social range. Would our poetry be more representative, more flexible, without the spacious capacities of free verse? Would it be better without the formal tensions and intricacies particular to metrical verse? Either singular direction is the reductionist's solution. "Why shouldn't a poet," as Dana Gioia has written, "explore the full resources the English language offers?"

I suspect these kinds of concerns first informed Miller Williams's idea that Wallace's essay could serve more fully as the centerpiece of a new book about meter. Indeed, the passion of the original responding letters and the continued crossfire of debate and discussion resulted in our first notion that this book be composed of Wallace's essay and the letters themselves. But it became clear to us that these letters—and subsequent others from additional interested writers—were only prologue to each potential respondent's fuller, more studied expression of his or her convictions. *Meter in English: A Critical Engagement* is the result of the need we saw for a book of essay-responses, all based on issues of meter in English and all based, more particularly, on Wallace's primary article "Meter in English." Wallace's initial goals of clarity and simplicity remained as guideposts in his own ensuing drafts and resulted in the ambitious essay which serves as part 1 of this book and the impetus for the rest of it.

Part 2 of *Meter in English* opens up the critical engagement which gives this book its subtitle and its unique character. We wanted to offer a rich, diverse articulation of the state of metrical analysis today. Each contributor to part 2 received a copy of Robert Wallace's "Meter in English," along with two guidelines: that each contribution specifically address, in full or in brief, all ten of Wallace's main propositions and that any more general discussion of meter should still remain focused on Wallace's concerns. This component of the book is particularly exciting: every contribution was written for this book and is heretofore unpublished. I invited the contributors to shape and frame their work in whatever way they found most appealing or sensible—as a complete essay, as a series of separable responses to each of Wallace's ten proposals, or as a combination of these two stylistic choices. Part of the flexible character of this symposium is embodied by the rhetorical variety of the contributions, from the formal to the casual, from the scholarly to the personal. Even with this range, Wallace's essay serves as the common ground for the entire book.

The variety of part 2 also stems from the authors' widely differing specialties and backgrounds. While all fourteen contributors (a sonnet's worth!) are accomplished prosodists and metrists, some are more nearly at the beginnings of their careers while others are long-distinguished. Several are or have been literary editors—of books, journals, anthologies—and many have written about meter and poetics in books of their own. Most, but not all, are practicing, indeed masterful, poets; most, not all, are or have been full-time teachers. Many have considerable experience as translators, from a great variety of languages, and often this experience lends a distinctive perspective on metrics. For instance, much of John Frederick Nims's orientation is guided by his knowledge of Greek meters; so too Dana Gioia's and Rachel Hadas's experience in Latin. Represented here are experts in classical prosody, in Old and Middle English versification, in Renaissance metrics, in British, Irish, and American poetics; and while none of the contributors is, strictly speaking, a linguist, several bring extensive backgrounds in linguistics to their prosodic study. In short, our contributors are diversely prepared but singularly concerned about poetry and its metrical properties.

The final section, part 3, is once again Robert Wallace's work. It seemed right—in fact necessary—to end where we began, with the congruity of his single perspective, as a debate returns to the affirmative for its rebuttal. Indeed, Wallace's afterword, "Completing the Circle," is more extensive an argument than his "Meter in English." Here he is able himself to engage and assess the specific and often adverse opinions of his respondents in their analyses of his ten propositions; he focuses sharply the lively issues of this discussion which, we hope, will continue beyond these pages. Here too he widens the scope, surveying what he sees as a crisis, "the incoherence of the present understanding of meter."

SOME OF THE ISSUES AND QUESTIONS

Readers will find that one of the debates throughout these discussions revolves around the nature of meter itself, about what we mean when we say "meter." As I mentioned previously, the root of meter suggests that a meter is a kind of measurement. But *what* is being measured, and *by what means* the measurement occurs— these are some of the sticky questions.

Our colleague mathematicians have solved the issue of metrics for themselves. In mathematics, of course, a meter is not a loose and varying set of measurements as it is in poetry. It is quite exact. In eighteenth-century France a meter was first defined as one ten-millionth of the distance from the equator to the North Pole, just over a yard in length to us, or approximately 39.37 inches. Today, more precisely, we measure a meter according to a frequency of atomic vibrations; since we know that light travels 299,792,458 meters per second, a standard single meter is defined as the distance a beam of light will travel during 1/299,792,458 of a second.

The specific entity of "a meter" is quite different in poetry. But this illustration leads me to a useful, if rough, analogy. To determine what a meter is, mathematicians measure a *quantity* of time or, equally, a quantity of distance. They measure an amount of something. In the standard poetry handbooks, too, the measurement of quantities is one kind of poetic meter, inherited from and based on the quantitative patterns of classical prosody. In Greek poetry, for instance, a meter is the measurement of certain patterns of short and long syllables—that is, a meter based on the duration of time (and sometimes, on the related pitch) of each syllable's utterance. We can see at least a rough illustration in English, where a short vowel sound often corresponds to a shorter utterance, as in "bĭt," while a long vowel results in a lengthier duration, as in "bīte." "Bite" is a longer quantity than "bit." But where Greek meter measures the length of syllables, English meter more usually measures the relative, audible stress—the accents and emphases—of those syllables.

In addition to *quantitative* meter, the handbooks typically list *syllabic, accentual,* and *accentual-syllabic* as the four basic meters in English. These subsequent three classifications are not based on the durations of single syllables. A poem in syllabics simply counts the number of syllables in a line; a poem in accentuals counts the number of heavy beats, or accents, in a line; and a poem in accentual-syllabics counts both the number of syllables and the number of heavy stresses.

One of the most hotly debated issues in *Meter in English: A Critical Engagement* is Wallace's contention that the accentual-syllabic method constitutes the only viable or true meter in our language. Fully half of his initial proposals, and much of the ensuing discussion in part 2, probe the reasons for and implications of this assertion. Wallace does not want to discard syllabics as an important compositional method, but he wishes to exclude both it and accentuals from the category of real meters. Meter, to Wallace, must be auditory, and hereby he argues that one cannot hear any consistent or predictable pattern in an accentual arrangement of words in a line, much less a syllabic one.

Meter is an even more basic element to Lewis Putnam Turco. It is, he argues, the single aspect which distinguishes all poetry, or verse, from all prose. To Dana Gioia meter must have a predictive quality: meter is not only a rhythmic method by which we can identify a pattern, in scansion, but also predict what rhythmic pattern will follow—hence his agreement that syllabics is not a meter. John Frederick Nims holds that meter is a viable denotation not just at the level of the poem, or the line, but at each foot itself. Each of these and other theories herein describe both the flexible and the highly arguable nature of our shared subject.

Wallace further extends his prosodic strategy by proposing that iambic rhythm is the exclusive basis of his one meter, accentual-syllabic. This component recalls Robert Frost's similar assertion about rhythm that "In English the meter is either strict iambic or loose iambic." And yet, taken with his proposals about the singularity of accentual-syllabic meter, Wallace's conviction about iambics describes nothing less than a paradigm shift in metrics, a potentially dramatic redirection of our study of meter and prosody. This stance elicits some of the book's most inflamed but educative debate. In defining anapestic, trochaic, and dactylic rhythms as useful metrical feet within the iambic accentual-syllabic norm, but not as meters in their own rights, Wallace both clarifies and simplifies the system. Some of his respondents are adamant to maintain the fuller range of equal meters. Some too disagree with Wallace's proposal that a two-degree system of stresses in scansion is sufficient, indeed is preferable to a three- or four-value system. The reader will find everywhere the search for the line dividing valuable simplification and over-simplified reduction.

A related point of order involves the marks our writers have employed in their scansions. When I received all of the initial drafts of these contributions, I saw that the contributors identified their preferred mark for a stressed syllable as either an ictus ′ or a virgule / and their generally preferred mark for the weak syllable as the breve ◡. I wrote to everyone, then, asking whether all the contributors would agree to use consistent marks, and all agreed to apply the ictus to stresses. But a note here still seems useful. I think the discrepancy between the ictus ′ and the virgule / to indicate a strong stress derives, at least in part, from the typewriter's insufficiency. The ictus is of course the classical mark for accents and strong stresses, but many typewriters and keyboards (like my own) do not make this mark available, while the virgule is present below the right little finger. Habit and ease may persuade or force some to employ this longer mark; still, a ready problem arises for its use to mark accents, since its traditional application is to divide lines of poetry when they are written out as prose, as in "A poem should not mean / But be."

In addition, both Charles O. Hartman and Susanne Woods employ this mark × rather than the ◡ to indicate an unstressed syllable. Both reminded me that the breve ◡ originally indicated, in quantitative verse, a short syllable rather than an unstressed one. Remaining consistent, both use the ictus to indicate a stressed syllable, abandoning the quantitative mark of the macron ‾ used to indicate a long syllable. (We still use these marks, ◡ and ‾, to show the short and long pronunciations of our English vowels.) In the essays of Hartman and Woods I have not changed the × to the ◡, in order to be faithful to these writers' preferred historical frame of reference.

Dana Gioia employs two different sets of scansion marks, applying the standard ictus and breve when scanning by regular accentual-syllabics. But when he scans by dipodics—that is, pairs of feet considered together—he uses the macron, the breve, and a third mark ∠ to indicate the strongest stresses. Like Gioia, Timothy Steele and Susanne Woods do not find a two-degree system of stresses sufficient to mark the subtleties of poetic rhythm, and so employ numerical notations of 1 to 4 to indicate metric relationships of as many rhythmic degrees. Following Otto Jespersen's method, they mark the heaviest stress with 4 (though Woods, in her book *Natural Emphasis,* uses Trager and Smith's method of marking the heaviest beat as 1). At times Steele also uses a graphic system of mountains and valleys, a kind of contour map to designate the rising or falling of rhythms. These occasional variations in marking should be clear as readers see them applied, appropriately, in context.

Some of the proposals in this book will seem central to one reader and not to another. Each reader will find merit where he or she will—in the large issues or in the particular, in theory or in application, and perhaps in them all. The same has been true for the contributors themselves, who variously focus on the issues most compelling to themselves. To be sure, Wallace's propositions range from the terminological to the theoretical. But every serious reader of poetry will agree that even the simple, single choice of a word can make a world of difference.

HOW TO READ THE BOOK, AND WHAT IT WILL AND WON'T TELL YOU

A symposium, to the Greeks, was a drinking party where intellectual ideas were discussed. While I like to imagine that similar festive occasions might be born from this book, I know certainly that it comprises a vigorous discussion. Like our language itself, the practice and meaning of meter evolve with use and with developing theories of poetry, rhetoric, and critical theory. Just so, *Meter in English: A Critical Engagement* is not a closed argument but rather a forum for such discussion, debate, and sometimes heated contention among experts. It is designed to seek out and investigate these writers' points of dissension about meter as well as to illuminate their important agreements in the making. Readers will find an abundance of both. Gerald Graff has urged us all to teach the problems of literary study to our students instead of presuming to teach them the answers only, as if "answers" are universal and complete. Meter is not a problem to be "solved" at all, but a set of formal applications to be chosen, adjusted, and constantly reviewed. Here, the points of loudest dissension are among the points we most need to study. The interplay of illustrations and critical analyses, from a wide range of poetic texts, provides an invaluable look at the different ways the contributors' theoretical stances actually operate.

There exist a number of useful handbooks and reference sources for poetry and metrics. *Meter in English: A Critical Engagement* does not intend to serve as such a handbook. It does not offer extensive listings, tables, or definitions with illustrations of those definitions. Here, instead, the reader will find many of the central issues of metrics probed *in context* as these writers undertake their critical exchange. In other words, the present book discusses what the handbooks imply, what they take for granted, and what kinds of arguable definitions and usages they sometimes take as generally accepted.

Readers will find at the end of these essay-responses a bibliography of sources for their further reading in metrics. Again, this is a collective enterprise. Invited to nominate any titles they felt central to their own understanding of meter and to the present project, the respondents have appointed to this bibliography a range of sources, from general histories of prosody to critical studies of the metrical practices of particular poets. Readers will also find a table of metrical feet, following this introduction, and two indices at the back of the book. The index of proposals allows the reader to locate and follow the developing debate about each of Wallace's ten propositions, while the index of authors identifies the location of any discussion of a specific critic or poet.

Something that readers will find absent from *Meter in English: A Critical Engagement* is any extensive consideration of the merits of studying formal prosody and writing in meter, as compared to the relative merits of studying or writing free verse. That debate continues elsewhere. Too often the argument fixes itself at the predictable poles of a familiar dialectic: free verse is aligned with the Romantic values of self-discovery and rebellion, while metrical poetry is seen as more sympathetic to the neoclassical belief in the knowledge and forms of the established historical conventions. Alan Shapiro has intelligently and more fully examined some of these issues in his recent *In Praise of the Impure*. In "Some Notes on Free Verse and Meter," Shapiro agrees that each prosodic system does indeed carry inevitable and implicit convictions:

> The poet writing in meter is always the belated one . . . the bearer of other lives. . . . And his metrical symmetries . . . are the persistent echoes of the gate of Eden closing shut behind him.
>
> The poet writing in free verse . . . claims for himself the Adamic privilege of starting over.

Underlying every free-verse poem, Shapiro asserts, is the belief that "the mind can return to the originating moment of its own emergence," while the metrical poem is borne from a mind that is "unredeemably historical, and can only look back, as it were, with longing and relief, at what it had to give up to get where it is."

For myself and for the purposes of this book, the issue is more like this: Many poets today write in meter, many poets today do not write in meter, and many do both; and while the cultural and aesthetic reverberations of such choices for poets are fascinating, the simple fact is that one's decision to write in meter, or not to write in meter, is not the same as one's decision to *understand* meter. After all, *Meter in English: A Critical Engagement* is for the readers of poetry, not the writers—or perhaps more accurately, for all readers of poetry, only some of whom are its writers.

But, much more to the point, poets for millennia have employed meter as a method. The serious reader of poetry must always regard meter as a fundamental property of poetry, one of its central, defining devices—whether or not any particular poem at hand is metrical, whether poetry becomes more meter-based in the future, as some argue, or whether poets eventually will abandon that formal strategy altogether, as others predict. Each formal and rhetorical choice has its effects, its consequences, and its particular graces. To disregard the study of meter in poetry is like teaching students of abstract art that a study of figures is irrelevant.

The contributors to this symposium do not especially argue against free verse. But of course the implicit and clear statement made here is that meter is not only a valid but an invaluable method in poetry—then as now.

CONCLUSION

The nature of poetry in English changed in the middle of the nineteenth century. A few scattered examples of open-form poetry existed in English before this time—the King James Psalms, a poem here and there by Christopher Smart or William Blake. These are rare examples, though, isolated exceptions to the steadfast metrical standard. But something tremendously important happened between the Walt Whitman of the 1840s, among whose early poems appear stanzas like these from "Time to Come":

> O, Death! a black and pierceless pall
> > Hangs round thee, and the future state;
> No eye may see, no mind may grasp
> > That mystery of Fate.

This brain, which now alternate throbs
    With swelling hope and gloomy fear;
This heart, with all the changing hues,
    That mortal passions bear—

This curious frame of human mould,
    Where unrequited cravings play,
This brain, and heart, and wondrous form
    Must all alike decay . . .

and the democratic, optimistic enthusiast for whom, only a decade later, poetic form would become an essential articulation of the future. His poetry assumed the rhetorical and visible shape of an audacious American liberty. What he wrote in 1874 could describe the shocking mettle of his 1855 edition of *Leaves of Grass:*

> [concerning] the measurement-rules of iambic, spondee, dactyl, &c., . . . even if rhyme and those measurements continue to furnish the medium for inferior writers and themes, (especially for persiflage and the comic, as there seems henceforth, to the perfect taste, something inevitably comic in rhyme . . .), the truest and greatest *Poetry,* (while subtly and necessarily always rhythmic, and distinguishable easily enough,) can never again, in the English language, be express'd in arbitrary and rhyming metre.

It was time to declare the poetic independence of the still-young country. And always we must retain the imperative to newness and ingenuity in our poetry. This Whitmanian spirit—of rebellion, of equity—is what Kate Braverman taps into, I think, by her assertion that "Form is dead."

But of course form is never dead. All poetry is formal poetry. It has shape, and meaning, and nuance, and layers of technique. And eventually one age's successful experiment will become another age's daily practice. Surely we have arrived at and passed the historical moment when free verse is *in itself* a radical, progressive, and heretical prosodic choice. Indeed, many critics and poets today— from the Language Poets to the New Formalists—argue that free verse is our predominant orthodoxy.

All poets must claim the language for their own, metered or

free, and not allow the receding past merely to sustain its own political framework. In "Owning the Masters," Marilyn Nelson Waniek has written about issues of tradition, form, and history: "Form itself is communal. . . . Yes, writing in traditional form is taxing. But it is also liberating. . . . Why don't we instead take possession of, why don't we own, the tradition?" Such has been the project of poets, and the audiences of poetry, from the beginning. We have come around to it again.

ACKNOWLEDGMENTS

I am grateful to Miller Williams, of the University of Arkansas Press, for his early belief in this project and for his guiding support. I am particularly grateful to the authors of these essays for their various, enthusiastic, and intelligent passions about our gathered subject of poetic meter, and grateful as well for their patience and help as we put this book together. To Bob Wallace, without whom this project would never have been born or grown, I owe special thanks for his wisdom, dedication, and friendship. In awarding me a Robert C. Good Faculty Research Fellowship, Denison University allowed me some welcome time to work and concentrate, for which I am grateful. And mostly, to Ann, my continuing love, and to Katie, *who fills the air / with gladness and involuntary songs.*

A TABLE OF METRICAL FEET

Here is a table of the metrical feet discussed or mentioned in this book. Several of these are not normally available in English, but are instead features of classical prosody, where quantitative measurements of short and long syllables—rather than of stressed and unstressed ones—make possible such triple and dipodic varieties. The metrical feet are called the

iamb ⌣ /
trochee / ⌣
anapest ⌣ ⌣ /
dactyl / ⌣ ⌣
spondee / /
pyrrhic ⌣ ⌣
amphibrach ⌣ / ⌣
cretic (or amphimacer) / ⌣ /
bacchic ⌣ / /
antibacchic / / ⌣
tribrach ⌣ ⌣ ⌣
molossus / / /
ionic major / / ⌣ ⌣
ionic minor (or double-iamb) ⌣ ⌣ / /

PART
ONE

METER IN ENGLISH

Robert Wallace

In English, the poetry makes the rules, not the rules the poetry.

—GEORGE SAINTSBURY,
A History of English Prosody

An outsider would be startled at the lack of consensus among poets and metrists about the nature of metrical verse in English. Those of us interested in meter have perhaps grown accustomed to the confusion, and therefore careless. The poetry matters, after all, not the theory. But it cannot be argued safely that our understanding is irrelevant to our practice nor, I hope, that our teaching is irrelevant to the future of poems written in meter.

My aim, therefore, is to question our assumptions and differences of opinion. To make a beginning, I will go over what seems safe and familiar ground.

It is the unit of line that distinguishes verse from prose or speech. Line introduces into the sentences of verse a further set of breaks or pauses complementary to those already present in the syntactical organization. When line-ends coincide with and so reinforce them, these syntactical breaks are in effect promoted, while others are in effect demoted. We call such effects, respectively, end-stopped lines and caesuras. Line-ends may also occur where there are no syntactical breaks or only very slight ones, thus in effect creating breaks or pauses. Such effects we call run-on lines. Together, these modulations control the special character of verse. How far such effects of line-end are aural (affecting pauses in performance) or merely visual (that is, perceptual) depends on individual practice.

In free verse, the units of line are, or appear to be, arbitrary; that is, relatively unpredictable. In metered verse, the units of line are relatively regular or predictable, measured (metered) by the counting of some quality or qualities of the language that seem natural for this purpose. In English, for instance, a normative line is

$$\cup \ \ / \ \ \cup \ \ / \ \ \cup \ \ / \ \ \ \cup \ \ / \ \ \ \cup \ \ /$$
When I | consid | er how | my light | is spent.

By convention, following the terminology of classical prosody, this line is rationalized as pentameter ("five-measure"), each unit of measure being a "foot," here specifically an iambic foot or iamb: an unstressed syllable followed by a stressed one. There may also be tetrameter ("four-measure") lines, and so on.

Two things should be noticed. Greek and Latin meters were based on vowel duration (long/short) rather than on accent (stress/unstress), and the adaptation of classical terms to cover English practice thus introduced the possibility of confusion in terminology. Entities may seem to exist in English (e.g., the cretic foot: $/\cup/$), when they do not in actuality or, to put it differently, when they might be rationalized in a different or simpler way. The pyrrhic foot ($\cup\cup$) is puzzling. Lacking any stress, it makes little sense in a language where we count or hear primarily stresses. Probably it does not exist in English, except in one isolated configuration. I will return to this point in section 3, "Coming to Terms."

Metrical counting in English is binary. Despite the wide range of levels of stress occurring in speech, syllables are counted as either stressed or unstressed. That determination is made *relative* to the stress of neighboring syllables; that is, by comparison, and not absolutely, as was the case in determining long/short duration in classical prosody. In the line,

$$\cup \quad / \quad \cup (/) \quad \cup \quad / \quad \cup \quad / \quad \quad \cup \quad /$$
Nor ser | vices | to do | till you | require

the third syllable of "services," which is almost unaccented in speech, counts fully, so that the line is regular iambic. If we are scanning merely to determine the meter (aha, this line is pentameter), there will be little difficulty. But when we scan—as we do more often—to inspect the rhythm of a line or passage, there is enormous room for difference of opinion or, less charitably, for confusion.

Three further conventions complete the metrical system: An unstressed syllable at the end of a line, as in

$$\cup \quad / \quad \cup \quad / \quad \cup \quad / \quad \cup / \quad \quad \cup \quad / \quad \cup$$
And yet | it may | be said | I loved | her dear | *ly*

is metrically *uncounted.* That is, the line remains regularly iambic. We need a fresh term for this, and I suggest that **(1) Instead of the term "feminine ending," we should say simply extra-syllable ending**, which may be abbreviated as e-s ending. (Equally, we may speak of extra-syllable or e-s rhymes.)

Conversely, an unstressed syllable at the beginning of a line may be omitted without changing the normative scansion, as in

$$x \quad / \quad \cup \quad / \quad \quad \cup \quad / \quad \cup \quad /$$
Fif | ty springs | are lit | tle room

The first foot here is counted as if it were an iamb rather than an irregular or "lame" foot, which elsewhere in a line would mark a noteworthy rhythmic interruption. A common variation, this omission of an initial syllable appears in the seventeenth century:

$$x \quad / \quad \quad \cup \quad / \quad \cup / \quad \cup \quad /$$
Come, | and trip | it as | ye go

as in the fourteenth century:

$$x \quad / \quad \cup \quad / \quad \cup \quad / \quad \cup \quad / \quad \cup \quad /$$
Twen | ty book | es, clad | in blak | or reed

Several terms for this convention are current, among them *acephalous line* (from Greek, meaning "headless"), *decapitation,* and *initial truncation* (from the Latin verb meaning "to shorten by cutting off, as limbs from trunk or torso; to maim or mutilate"). As these terms both overstate and seem pejorative, I suggest that **(2) For an omitted first syllable of a line, we should use the term anacrusis** (from Greek, meaning "the striking up of a tune") which Saintsbury allows in this sense (vol. 1, 64, 78, 170).

The third convention is the *substitution,* for an iamb in the normative line, of any of several other feet: trochee (/⌣), pyrrhic (⌣⌣), spondee (//), anapest (⌣⌣/), or dactyl (/⌣⌣). The point is to accommodate in the metrical norm certain other frequent rhythmic patterns of English, as well as to avoid metronomic rigidity.

<pre>
 / ⌣   ⌣ /   ⌣   ⌣   / / ⌣   /
When to | the ses | sions of | sweet si | lent thought.
</pre>

Despite substitutions of trochee, pyrrhic, and spondee in the first, third, and fourth places, the line remains iambic pentameter.

There has been, and remains now, some prejudice against the legitimacy of trisyllabic substitutions, that is, anapests and dactyls. Historically, however, as Saintsbury argues (vol. 1, 402), the anapest made its appearance "practically at once" in English meter, and has persisted with enough frequency for him to conclude that it is "omnipresent." An example from about 1500 is

<pre>
⌣ / ⌣ ⌣   / ⌣ /
And I | in my bed | again
</pre>

The musical notation in the manuscript makes the foot unmistakable. Instances exist even in the verse of poets as syllabically rigorous as Pope. The naturalness of the anapest derives, if for no other reason, from the structure of simple prepositional phrases. That structure can also be accommodated by allowing the meter to point up a light stress on syllables that would be virtually unaccented in speech, as in

<pre>
⌣ (/)   ⌣ /   ⌣ (/) ⌣   /   ⌣ /
That on | the ash | es of | his youth | doth lie
</pre>

or by contriving a trochaic substitution to fit, as in the first two feet of

```
  /  ⌣  ⌣  /  ⌣  /  ⌣  /  ⌣  /
But, of | the two, | less dang | 'rous is | th' offence
```

But it is plainly simpler, and entirely natural, to use an anapest as the anonymous poet does in "And I in my bed again" or as appears in

```
  ⌣  /   ⌣ /   ⌣ ⌣ /  ⌣   /
Two roads | diverged | in a yel | low wood
```

The convention of trisyllabic substitution replaces another convention, which no one would now wish to revive, practiced most notably in those periods when anapestic substitution was least in favor. I mean elision, as in

```
  ⌣   /   ⌣   /   ⌣  /  ⌣  /   ⌣   /
And moan | th' expense | of man | y a van | ished sight
```

In order to maintain the regularity of syllables, one is required to mouth or imagine such barbarous, artificial syllables as "th' ex-" and "-y a." Similarly, in the Pope, "th' of-" avoids "the offence." The anapest is a good, and frequent, foot in English verse.

Meter is thus a system of measurement, conventional but natural to the language, which makes the rhythmic units of line more or less predictable to a reader or hearer of verse.

What meter measures is speech. We tend to speak in clothesline-looping phrases, with one primary stress per phrase, the other syllables (secondary stresses or unstressed) being spoken rapidly so that normally we scarcely distinguish among them. Playing over the metrical expectation, this speech-run produces what we may call poetic rhythm. The process may be figured

$$\frac{\text{speech-run}}{\text{meter}} = \text{rhythm}$$

We read a poem neither as we would say its sentences in speech nor by the rigid te TUM te TUM of meter, but in a way somewhere in between the two. The speech-run is slowed, made more distinct—so that, for instance, we may hear the light stresses on "on" and "of" in the line "That on the ashes of his youth doth lie." Subtleties we may be unaware of in speech are thus magnified into perception. Conversely, the rigidity of meter (an inch is an inch) is given a more flexible embodiment. No two lines of iambic pentameter, therefore, can ever be quite the same.

In reading metered verse, we hear its rhythmic approximation of the underlying metrical pattern. Divergences that are conventional are felt as regularities. Reading unmetered verse, by contrast, we are not aware of any fixed or predictable underlying pattern. In free verse, there will of course be natural patterns and probably significant repetitions of them, but we have no consistent sense of predictability or expectation. (An oddity is, as free verse has claim to having become the predominant verse form in the twentieth century, how little curiosity there has been to sort out the different kinds of it or the variety of patterns and conventions that operate in it.)

In thinking about poetic rhythm in meter, we may be aware of two sorts of effect. The subtler occurs in the relative levels of unstress and stress in the paradigmatic iambs of a line. In Shakespeare's "And yet it may be said I loved her dearly," though all the feet are clearly iambic, the unstressed syllables "I" and "her" carry somewhat more accent than the other unstressed syllables, making the line seem to slow or become more emphatic at the end. This sort of effect may be very expressive, as in Wilbur's "A ball will bounce, but less and less."

A more obvious sort of rhythmic effect occurs when, in whatever form, substitution displaces the paradigmatic iamb, by adding a syllable as the anapest does in "*in a yel*low wood," by reversing the expected unstress/stress as the trochee does in "*But, of* the two," or by replacing an unstressed syllable with a stressed, as the spondee does in "*sweet sil*ent thought."

Both sorts of effect contribute to what we may feel as expressive or imitative rhythms, as in

$$\cup \quad / \quad \cup \quad / \quad (/) \quad / \quad \quad / \quad / \quad \cup \quad /$$
When A | jax strives | some rock's | vast weight | to throw

The two spondees suggest heaviness. An impression of difficulty or strain, though, has already begun to register in the relatively heavy or hard-to-enunciate unstressed syllables of the iambs in the first two feet, "When" and "-jax." The line, thus, builds to the release in the final iamb, "to throw," where the distinct contrast between the unstressed syllable and the stressed one seems to let us feel the physical gesture. This extremely clever line depends of course on the inversion. If we restore "to throw" to its place in normal word order, Ajax is left standing there with the rock sagging in his grip:

$$\smile \quad / \quad \smile \quad / \quad \smile \quad / \quad (/) \quad / \quad / \quad /$$
When A | jax strives | to throw | some rock's | vast weight

The particular value of the spondee is that it can damp or modulate the regular alternations in the flow of a passage. Its effects may be of lightness or stasis as well as of weight, as in Keats's third line here:

No stir of air was there,
Not so much life as on a summer's day
$$/ \quad / \quad / \quad / \quad / \quad \smile \quad \smile \quad / \quad \smile \quad /$$
Robs not | one light | seed from | the feath | ered grass

The suggestion is, in the unruffled evenness of the five level stresses, an absence of such breeze as might dislodge even a single poised bit of dandelion fluff. The metrical stress—the counting stress—is made to fall on "not" and "light," thus muting an emphasis we are perhaps readier to hear. Consider this clumsy alternative scansion:

$$x \quad / \quad (/) \quad / \quad (/) \quad / \quad \smile \quad \smile \quad / \quad \smile \quad /$$
Robs | not one | light seed | from the feath | ered grass

Keats plays masterfully on the foot-structure of the line. His spondees resist the natural flow, as if debating within themselves whether to accept it; and that slight indecisiveness of stress makes the line's rhythm expressive. The little tug of quickness in "from the feathered grass" cannot overcome it.

Meter is useful for its predictability, which keeps reader or hearer tuned to even fine variations of rhythm. Actual lines are interesting for their approach to, as well as their divergence from, the iambic norm.

I have been discussing what is called accentual-syllabic meter, because in theory both stresses and syllables are counted. As to both, however, the counting may be rather flexible in practice. A pentameter with anacrusis will have nine syllables. A pentameter with e-s ending will have eleven syllables—or perhaps with an anapest or two as many as thirteen syllables or so. The number of stresses carried by a line is even more variable. With spondees, we may count as many as nine stresses in

> /   /   /   /   /   /   ᴗ   (/) /   /
> Slow, slow, | fresh fount, | keep time | with my | salt tears

or as few as three speech stresses in

> /   /   /
> Advantage on the kingdom of the shore

Timothy Steele ("On Meter," 298) points out a pentameter with only two speech stresses:

> /   /
> In our competitive humility

In such cases, by fine-tuning our response, meter supplies the light stresses that fill out the pattern; expectation in effect makes up the lack. Nor is any contrivance needed to somehow reduce Jonson's spondees to iambs for us to sense the line's pattern properly.

This meter, accentual-syllabic, as described, *is* English meter. There is no other.

It evolved from the accentual-alliterative meter of Old English, influenced probably by changes taking place in the language itself, by the syllabic meter of French, and by efforts to adapt classical prosody to the vernacular. Historical puzzles remain—if it was Chaucer's meter, for instance, why were there uncertainties about it for another century and a half? But, unquestionably, sometime just before 1600 English meter as we understand it was fully in place.

II. ONE METER

My purpose in this essay is to clarify our understanding of meter in English. So far, I have tried to lay out the system succinctly;

and except for the two minor propositions about terminology (e-s ending and anacrusis), there is no novelty in that outline, though it will have provoked disagreement about this or that. I must turn now to those areas of disagreement—or to what I see as the confusions and unexamined contradictions in the various accounts of English meter at present, in which those of us who are interested often seem to be talking past one another. In arguing for the propositions embedded in this and the next two sections, I will be as quick and frugal as I can, although the discussion must be specific and exacting.

Recent authoritative accounts, such as Paul Fussell's in *Poetic Meter and Poetic Form* (1965), hold that there are four meters in English: syllabic, accentual, accentual-syllabic, and quantitative. Most critics seem agreed to put aside the last as unworkable, or primarily of historical interest, though there have been attempts (as late as Robert Bridges's) to imitate in English the counting of duration from Greek and Latin. The problem is that the strong accents of English tend to override, for all but the most classically trained readers, the pattern of vowel-lengths. As X. J. Kennedy remarks (*An Introduction to Poetry,* 7th ed., 1990, 166), "Campion's 'Rose-Cheeked Laura, Come' was an attempt to demonstrate [quantitative meter] in English, but probably we enjoy the rhythm of the poem's well-placed stresses whether or not we notice its vowel sounds." As the poem is scannable as accentual-syllabic, no metrical question arises:

> Rose-cheeked Laura, come,
> Sing thou smoothly with thy beauty's
> Silent music, either other
>   Sweetly gracing.

Sidney's "O sweet woods, the delight of solitariness," also recommended as a lovely poem in quantitative meter, is a harder case. Except for a line or two (like "Such wisdom, that in her lives speculation"), it would be regularly scannable only with great awkwardness:

> Nought disturbs thy quiet, all to thy service yield,
> Each sight draws on a thought, thought mother of science,
> Sweet birds kindly do grant harmony unto thee,

> Fair trees' shade is enough fortification,
> Nor danger to thy self if be not in thy self.

As William A. Ringler, Jr. (editor of *The Poems of Sir Philip Sidney,* 1962) notes, the poem is one of only thirteen "experiments" in quantitative verse by Sidney; and "the meter is exceedingly imperfect, for the rules of quantity are broken in one or more places in 16 of the 42 lines" (404). More generally, Ringler says (392), Sidney's "application [of quantities] results in patterns of scansion that continually clash with Elizabethan pronunciation. Since Sidney measures his lines by artificial rules that are divorced from phonetic actualities, [a passage] may have the appearance of, but cannot be read aloud to sound like verse."

Such experiments, especially in the period of the founding of English meter, are both understandable and admirable. But as they hardly amount to a body of work in quantitative meter, or prove its workability in English, it will be economical and clarifying to drop the term from our list. **(3) Quantities are not a basis for meter in English.** Odd cases can be valued as odd cases. Even successful imitations of sapphics or alcaics needn't be seen as establishing a meter in English.

Fussell also has misgivings about syllabics, noting that "syllabism is not a natural measuring system in a language so Germanic and thus so accentual as English." Given contemporary poems in the form, especially by Marianne Moore, however, textbooks and other accounts continue unquestioningly to include it.

Let's be firmer. **(4) Syllabics is not a meter in English.** We do not *hear* the count of syllables. By itself, and taking no account of where accents occur, a line's number of syllables in no significant way determines its rhythm. There is no interplay or tension between sentences and a pattern of sound, no predictability—any syllables, stressed or unstressed, in any order will do. Syllabics is a kind of free verse. For the poet constructing lines by syllable-count, it is only a trellis, like shaped stanzas, William Carlos Williams's variable-foot indentings, or (say) the counting of the number of *letters* as the basis for line. The actual rhythm is determined freely, line by line, according to whatever mixtures of stressed and unstressed syllables may be natural in speech, as in other free verse. Variations in such syllabic norms, as in Moore's "Critics and Connoisseurs" or "Poetry," cannot be rhythmically meaningful in themselves. Even locating variations is painstaking and usually without point.

The two poems by Moore are good, if not exactly fair, examples. "Poetry" has claim to be the most famous poem in syllabics in English—if it is in syllabics at all, which is a question open to a good deal of doubt.

Both poems were written, as appears to have been Moore's practice, in stanzas of which the corresponding lines have an exactly identical number of syllables. The first line in each stanza of "Critics and Connoisseurs," for instance, has fourteen syllables, the second line in each has eight syllables, and so on. In revising the poems between appearances in print, however, Moore made excisions in several lines *without bothering to re-regularize the syllable-count.* So, technically, in the versions we are likely to be familiar with, neither poem is in syllabic meter. However useful Moore found syllable-count in composition, it is clear at least that she placed no very great formal value on it in the finished poem.

Although there is some merit in that debating-point, my reason for calling it to your attention is to make you uncertain, when I quote corresponding lines from the four stanzas of "Critics and Connoisseurs," whether they are syllabically exact or inexact. Please read the lines and, before you count on your fingers, decide whether they are syllabically identical or not:

similar determination to make a pup

proclivity to more fully appraise such bits

itself, struck out from the flower-bed into the lawn

in proving that one has had the experience

If you are still not sure after having counted on your fingers, you will see the difficulty of treating syllabics as a meter. Whatever the French are able to do, it is plain that in English we cannot really hear syllable-count; and that there is no perceptible, or discussable, rhythmic similarity in syllabically equal lines.

I invite any reader still unconvinced to spend an hour studying the texts of these two poems in two or three printed versions, including those in the 1951 *Collected Poems* and the 1967 *Complete Poems* (and, for "Poetry," in Moore's 1921 version which may be found in *Marianne Moore: An Introduction to the Poetry* by George W. Nitchie, 1969, 37–38). Given printers' difficulties with the longer lines, it is not easy even to decide, or to keep in mind, how many *lines* the stanzas have. In one of the very best books about Moore, a fine critic says that "Poetry" in its most familiar version is a poem of thirty-eight lines when in fact it has only twenty-nine lines; and that Moore's final, very abbreviated version has four lines, when in fact it has only three.

The claim that, in English, syllabics is a meter rests in quicksand.

Accentual meter is, alas, even more problematic. In the obvious sense, like syllabics, it does not exist; that is, it is not a meter. As I will argue, counting only stresses offers no meaningful predictability and is, ultimately, hopelessly subjective. Moreover, the accounts invariably describe one thing but mean something else entirely, causing terminological confusion. Moreover again, that something else turns out to be only accentual-syllabic meter *allowing trisyllabic substitution.* Consider

> [Accentual meter] maintains a more or less regular number of stresses within the line; there is no fixed number of unstressed syllables. This is the *strong-stress meter* of Old English poetry.
> (Harvey Gross, *Sound and Form in Modern Poetry,* 24)

> While in syllabic meter only the syllables are counted, in accentual meter only the accents are. Syllables may vary in number per line, it being assumed that three or four short syllables can be uttered in the same time that one or two long ones can.
> (Fussell, 9)

> [In accentual meter] the poet does not write in feet (as in other meters) but instead counts accents (stresses). The idea is to have the same number of stresses in every line. The poet may place them anywhere in the line and may include practically any number of unstressed syllables, which do not count.
> (Kennedy, 157)

Noting that what is described is *not* Old English meter (lacking both the alliteration and the strong medial caesuras), let's begin with the obvious sense of these definitions. Only Gross and John Frederick Nims (in *Western Wind,* 2nd ed., 1983) discuss examples that reflect this obvious sense of the term. Gross (37–38, 187) cites the opening eighteen lines of "The Waste Land" as four-beat accentual meter. As "even in Old English verse we encounter lines of three or five stresses" (25), Gross notes, the line

   /   /   /
Memory with desire, stirring

is an acceptable variation in the four-stress norm.

Even so, at its most regular, we are required to hear as *metrically identical*

   / /   /   /
Dull roots with spring rain

and

   /   /   /   /
I read, much of the night, and go south in the winter

Nims (258) cites

    rough roads, rock-strewn

and "the unlikely but possible"

    due to the *ru*thlessness of the *ru*morings, due to the Pe*ru*vians' incommunica*bi*lity. . . .

There are clearly two problems with accentual meter in this sense. It may be plausible enough, given the metrical norm TUM TUM TUM TUM, to accept TUM TUM te TUM TUM ("Dull roots with spring rain") as a rhythmic variation. But it seems exceedingly implausible to take as also metrically *equal:* te TUM te te te TUM te te TUM te te TUM te ("I read, much of the night . . .") or: te te te TUM te te te te TUM te te te te te te TUM te te te te te te te TUM te te (the line about the Peruvians). On the face of it, this meter offers no predictability at all; and I do not see how we might even begin to discuss the rhythm of such lines if "the number of syllables does not matter" (Nims) and we do not count the unaccented syllables or notice where they occur.

The second problem is that what we may count as a stress seems extremely subjective. Nothing in theory prevents that determination from being arbitrary. The very existence in speech of any number of levels of stress makes it impossible to tell exactly which stresses should count as the *metrical* stresses. Why, for instance, in

    /   /   /   /   /   /   ´
I read, | much of | the night, | and go | south in | the winter

do we not find six stresses? (The line is scannable iambic hexameter with trochees as the second and fifth feet?) In the line about the Peruvians, why don't we also hear as stresses "Due," "due," and—as necessary to the meaning—the first syllable of "incommunicability"? Whereas accentual-syllabic meter has evolved a roughly workable way of bringing the wide variety of stress-levels in speech into its binary counting, accentual meter offers no way at all. Anything that might seem a stress in speech might equally be a stress in accentual meter—*or not.* Hence, of course, the need for the *defining* alliteration and caesuras of Old English meter.

I do not see how a poet, setting out to write in this meter, would be guided in any useful way; or how a reader, suspecting the meter, could ever be sure it was operating. There is, obviously, no body of work written in this supposed meter. Like syllabics, accentuals in this sense is not a meter but a form of free verse. (Gross's otherwise elegant analysis of Eliot's verse, and Robert Hass's "Listening and Making" in *Twentieth Century Pleasures,* however, show the usefulness of studying free verse by examining its accentual patterning.)

As I said, what Fussell, Kennedy, and Nims and Gross elsewhere —along with others such as Miller Williams in *Patterns of Poetry: An Encyclopedia of Forms* and Timothy Steele in *Missing Measures*—mean by the term accentual verse is accentual-syllabic meter that allows trisyllabic—dactyls being rare, anapestic—substitution. We can arrive at this understanding, however, only by inference from the poems they offer as exemplary of accentual meter, since the descriptions seem almost deliberately misleading.

In the illustrative poems or passages, there is scarcely any irregularity, other than anapests, that we might not expect to encounter in Robert Herrick. The student will search in vain for the strings of three or four unstressed syllables suggested by Fussell's comment or, for that matter, for stressed syllables clumped or otherwise not regularly spaced by unstressed ones. The poems are all written in metrical feet. Here is a tabulation of substitutions and variations:

	iambs	anapests	trochees	spondees	other
Yeats, "Easter 1916" lines 1–4, 13–16, 51–56 [Gross]	23	15	3		monosyllabic foot: 1
Yeats, "Why Should Not Old Men Be Mad?" lines 1–8 [Fussell]*	24	1	3	3	anacrusis: 2
Auden, "September 1, 1939" lines 1–9 [Fussell] *	17	6	3		pyrrhic: 1 e-s ending: 1
Anon., "I Have Labored Sore" 6 lines [Nims]*	19	2	1	1	anacrusis: 1
Coleridge, "Christabel" lines 48–52 [Kennedy]	10	7	1	1	pyrrhic: 1
William Meredith, "About Opera" 12 lines [Williams]*	43	10	4		anacrusis: 1 dactyl: 1 e-s ending: 1. anomalous foot: 1
Hardy, "Neutral Tones" lines 9–12 [Steele]	8	7			

* *My scansion.*

I assume that the reader is familiar with these poems or can look them up, but as it contains an arguable exception to my point, take as an example Meredith's "About Opera." Williams comments that the lines all have five stresses, and he confirms my marking of "on" as stressed in line 12. (Line 3 might optionally be scanned with anapest and iamb in the third and fourth places.)

　　　　ᵕ　／　ᵕ　／　　ᵕ　／　　ᵕ ／ ᵕ ／　ᵕ
It's not | the tunes, | although | as I | get old | er

X | ／　ᵕ(／)　ᵕ　　／　ᵕ ／　　ᵕ　　／　ᵕ
A | rias | are what | I hum | and whis | tle.

　　　ᵕ　／　　ᵕ　　／　　　／　ᵕ　／ᵕ ᵕ　ᵕ／　ᵕ
It's not | the plots |—they con| tinue to | bewild | er

　　ᵕ ᵕ　／　　ᵕ　／　　ᵕ ᵕ　／ ᵕᵕ　／ ᵕ　／ᵕ
In the tongue | I speak | and in sev | eral that | I wrestle.

　　　ᵕ ／　ᵕ　ᵕ ᵕ／　ᵕ ᵕ （／）　ᵕ　　／ ᵕ／
An im | age of artic | ulateness | is what | it is:

／ ᵕ　　ᵕ　／　ᵕ　／　ᵕ　／　　ᵕ ／
Isn't | this how | we've al | ways longed | to talk?

　／　ᵕ　　ᵕ　／　ᵕ　／　ᵕ／　　ᵕ　／　ᵕ
Words as | they fall | are mon | otone | and blood | less

　ᵕ　ᵕ　／　　ᵕ ／　ᵕ　／　ᵕ　／ ᵕ ／
But they yearn | to take | the risk | these nois | es take.

　　ᵕ　／　ᵕ ／ ᵕ ᵕ　／　ᵕ　／　ᵕ ／
What danc | ing is | to the slight | ly spas | tic way

　／　ᵕ　ᵕ ／　ᵕ　　／　　ᵕ ／ ᵕᵕ ／
Most of | us teet | er through | our bod | ily life

　ᵕ　ᵕ　／　　ᵕ　／　ᵕ ᵕ　／ ᵕ ／　　ᵕ ／
Are these meas | ured cries | to the clum | sy things | we say,

　ᵕ ᵕ　／　　ᵕ ／ ᵕ （／） ᵕ　／　　ᵕ ／
In the heart's | dures | ses, on | the heart's | behalf.

In line 5, the second foot seems anomalous: "-age of artic-."
Counting a light accent on "-age of," a possible reading, avoids the
anomaly, but would give the line six feet and make it seem overlong,
suggesting a wooden, unconvincing interpretation, given the light-
accented anapest of "-ulateness" and the anapestic looseness of the
poem in general. The poem remains, I think, plainly scannable with
trisyllabic substitution.

One other of the examples merits comment, the anonymous "I
Have Labored Sore" from the fifteenth century:

　ᵕ ᵕ　／　ᵕ　／　　ᵕ　／　ᵕ　　／
I have la | bored sore　|　and suf | fered death,

　ᵕ　／　ᵕ ／　　ᵕ　／　ᵕ　／
and now | I rest　|　and draw | my breath;

```
 ∪  /   ∪    /              ∪    /    (/)    /
but I | shall come    |    and call | right soon
  /  ∪    ∪   /             ∪    /   ∪    /
heaven | and earth    |    and hell | to doom;
  ∪    /    ∪      /           ∪    /   ∪ ∪    /
and then | shall know    |    both dev | il and man,
 x    /  ∪  /         ∪      /   ∪ /
what | I was    |    and what | I am.
```

Routinely scannable, it nonetheless retains clear signs of the Old English meter—the spaced, distinct medial caesuras and residual indications of formal alliteration, although the rhyme belongs to the new accentual-syllabic metric. The poem thus seems to illustrate the transformation of the old meter into the new. The Old English accentual meter did not disappear, only to burst forth again several centuries later, as we have been told (Burton Raffel, *From Stress to Stress,* 1992). It long ago *changed* into the tetrameter and pentameter of accentual-syllabics, a meter far more flexible and adaptable to the variety of the language.

In *all* of the examples, iambs predominate, though only narrowly in the stanza of "Neutral Tones." Steele notes

> A metrician might say that the rhythm of the poem is "iambic-anapestic"; or since the iambs outnumber the anapests by a slight margin, he or she might call the rhythm "iambic with frequent anapestic substitutions." But such terms do not entirely suit a poem like Hardy's, which approaches the condition of a sort of rhymed accentual verse. (23)

It seems clear here that accentual meter is only an *alternative term* to be used instead of accentual-syllabic meter *in some cases,* those where trisyllabic substitution appears. Fussell (49), distinguishing between scanning Pope and scanning Browning, notes that "by the nineteenth century trisyllabic substitution had become a metrical convention," though he does not explain why he nonetheless attributes accentual meter to Yeats and Auden. But of course, despite the definitions with their guff about all those unstressed syllables we needn't count, accentual meter in this sense isn't a separate meter at all.

I don't see the advantage of having two different systems for describing the same thing, especially if they are presented as describing two different things. Nor do I see the greater precision of saying that Hardy's stanza "approaches the condition of a sort of rhymed accentual verse" as against saying that it is "iambic with frequent anapestic substitutions." It isn't even clear how a student might be expected to recognize a poem in accentual meter. At the appearance of one anapest, as Fussell's example from Yeats implies? Or with something more than "frequent anapestic substitutions," as Steele's "approaches" seems to suggest? Nor is there anywhere in the accounts even a hint as to how, having determined that a poem is in accentual meter, we might then insightfully discuss its rhythm—not bothering of course with the unaccented syllables.

Far from aiding in understanding, the attribution of accentual meter to such a poem appears likely to plunge us into confusion . . . from which we can rescue ourselves only by returning to accentual-syllabic scansion, recognizing trisyllabic feet. We may as well do so openly, thus regaining the simplicity and elegance of the evolved metrical system in English, strict or loose iambic, in Frost's phrase. Trisyllabic substitution may be more or less frequent, as well as more or less to our taste, but the fact cannot be blinked away, whether quarantined out of some snobbish purism or promoted, as Coleridge claimed, as "a new principle."

The source of all the confusion about "accentual meter" is of course Coleridge's brief, grossly inaccurate note about the meter of "Christabel":

> I have only to add that the metre of the Christabel is not, properly speaking, irregular, though it may seem so from its being founded on a new principle; namely, that of counting in each line the accents, not the syllables. Though the latter may vary from seven to twelve, yet in each line the accents will be found to be only four. Nevertheless, this occasional variation in number of syllables is not introduced wantonly, or for the mere ends of convenience, but in correspondence with some transition in the nature of the imagery or passion.

This, in its entirety, is the seed from which both of the kudzu-like notions hiding in the term "accentual meter" have grown. No new principle at all is involved in the poem's practice; Saintsbury tartly remarks (vol. 3, 56) that it is "inconceivable" that Coleridge thought there was. The poem scans regularly, without anomaly, having among its 2665 feet: 2210 iambs (83 percent), 201 anapests and one dactyl (7.8 percent), 174 spondees, 46 trochees, and 33 lines with anacrusis. In that, then, is the source of the idea that trisyllabic substitution somehow means a separate meter.

As to the other sense of the term, the unaccented syllables in "Christabel" are all unquestionably counted, and they space the metrical accents with undeviating regularity. There is nothing about "practically any number of unstressed syllables," whether few or many, nor about nearly innumerable silent Peruvians. That is merely gossip, changing as it gets passed along. Nor is it even true that Coleridge counted only speech accents. As Robert Bridges points out (*Milton's Prosody,* 1901, appendix F, 73): "Now the primary law of pure stressed verse is, that there shall never be a conventional or imaginary stress: that is, *the verse cannot make the stress, because it is the stress that makes the verse.*" "Christabel" is littered with such light accents, like that in

   ᴗ   /   ᴗ /   ᴗ (/) ᴗ   /
   The gems I entang I led in I her hair

As to what's left, Saintsbury remarks (55): "Now, there is no piece of Coleridge's celebrated 'f-f-f-f-fun' which is more complicatedly and dangerously funny than this." The muddle of our textbooks demonstrates how dangerous.

Let's put "accentual meter" into the dustbin. The term has no legitimacy even in regard to Old English verse (or to contemporary imitations such as Pound's "The Seafarer" and Wilbur's "Junk"), as stress is only one of its essential characteristics. The more common terms "alliterative meter" or "Old English meter" will do.

(5) In modern English, accentual meter does not exist. The term, for prosody, like the breath-measure of Charles Olson, is denotatively empty.

(6) Anapests and dactyls are legitimate substitutions in the iambic norm of English meter.

There is one meter in English: accentual-syllabic, and its base is always iambic.

III. COMING TO TERMS

Our prosody has all along been pestered by the terminology of classical prosody. The metrical system in English verse, as it has developed, is in fact simple, elegant, and comprehensive. Our descriptions of it, however, and in some measure our understanding of it, have been continually thwarted by error and obfuscation brought over from classical prosody. We need, for instance, as Fussell notes (21), only six feet to account for everything that occurs in English verse, but he then adds, "it does no harm to be acquainted with the following . . ." and lists in tabular format: amphibrach; antispast; bacchic; choriamb; cretic; first, second, third, and fourth epitrite; ionic a majore; ionic a minore; first, second, third, and fourth paeon; molossus; and tribrach.

The harm is in intimidation and in a sort of general obfuscation, as if someone might figure out something to do with these Greek terms. And of course someones do. In *The Public Poet* (1991, 53), Lewis Turco scans a line by Dana Gioia, "The flickering lights reflected from the city," as ending in an amphibrach ($\cup/\cup$), rather than in an iamb and extra-syllable ending.

The notion that, as none of our watches goes just alike, we may each keep time as we please, fails Saintsbury's great touchstone (vol. 1, 403): "The only safe and philosophical rule in prosody, as in other things, is not to multiply your entities." Until someone offers a convincing, totally new account of English meter (which probably will dispense with the classical concept of feet altogether), those of us interested in the future of meter must take care to be precise and frugal in our terms. It is risky to make meter seem, to our students, more complex, cumbersome, or esoteric than need be.

If Turco's attribution of an amphibrach is merely gratuitous, a serious claim has been made for that foot's advantage in scanning Auden's "'O where are you going?' said reader to rider," the suggestion being that it forms the basis for the poem's meter. I will scan the poem here in that way, though it seems to me a sufficient difficulty that the poem is obviously and entirely scannable in the traditional way with anapests (35), iambs (27), trochees (2), and extra-syllable endings. Most readers, even most very experienced ones, will read the poem in that way. So the question perhaps is whether a metrical expectation can significantly influence the way we hear the identical poem. Italics show those places where the amphibrachic norm fails.

```
    ∪    /   ∪   ∪   / ∪     ∪   /  ∪   ∪  / ∪
"O where are | you going?" | said reader | to rider,
       ∪    /  ∪    ∪  / ∪     ∪    / ∪   ∪   /    ×
"That valley | is fatal | when furna | ces burn,
  ×   /  ∪   ∪   / ∪      ∪   / ∪     ∪     / ∪
 Yonder's | the midden | whose odours | will madden,
    ∪   / ∪  ∪   /     ∪     ∪  / ∪   /    ×
That gap is | the grave where | the tall re | turn."

    ∪   /  ∪   ∪  / ∪     ∪   /  ∪   ∪  / ∪
"O do you | imagine," | said fearer | to farer,
    ∪   /    ∪   ∪ / ∪   ∪    /   ∪   ∪   /   ×
"That dusk will | delay on | your path to | the pass,
   ∪   / ∪  ∪    /    ∪    ∪  / ∪    ∪  /  ∪
Your dili | gent looking | discover | the lacking,
    ∪   /  (∪)    /    ∪   / ∪   ∪   /   ×
Your footsteps | feel | from granite | to grass?"

   ∪    /   ∪    ∪   /     ∪   / ∪   ∪   / ∪
"O what was | that bird," | said horror | to hearer,
    ∪   /  (∪)  ∪    /   ∪   ∪   / ∪     /   ×
"Did you see | that shape in | the twisted | trees?
  ∪ /    ∪     /  ∪  ∪  / ∪     ∪    / ∪
Behind you | swiftly | the figure | comes softly,
     ∪   / ∪    ∪   / ∪ ∪  / ∪   ∪ /   ×
The spot on | your skin is | a shocking | disease."

 ×   /  ∪  ∪   /      ∪   / ∪   ∪  / ∪
 "Out of | this house"|—said rider | to reader,
    ∪    / ∪     /     ∪   / ∪  ∪  / ∪
"Yours never | will"|—said farer | to fearer,
      ∪    /  ∪   ∪   /     ∪   / ∪  ∪  / ∪
"They're looking | for you"|—said hearer | to horror,
```

∪ / (∪) ∪ /   ∪ / (∪) ∪ /   x
As he left | them there, | as he left | them there.

Lines 1, 5, and 7 are regular; and with only the minor variations of anacrusis or omitted final syllable, 2, 3, 6, and 12 are nearly so. Omission of a syllable at the caesura isn't disturbing in lines 9 and 15, nor in 13 where (with anacrusis as well) the syllabic tightening is felt but seems suitably emphatic. The trochee "swiftly" in line 11, far from disrupting, helps make it the sleekest line in the poem.

Five lines, however, seem problematic. Monosyllabic feet— "-turn" in 4, "feel" in 8, and "will" in 14—are rhythmic jolts, for which I sense no expressive purpose. Nearest to working is "feel," but after the rattling amphibrachs of the preceding lines, it seems almost bathos to focus so intently on blind feet seeking the softer grass. In all three instances, an iambic reading would be superior; and in the last two, the possibility of spondees would allow a useful rhythmic modulation. The three nearly equal stresses in

∪ /   (/) /   ∪ / ∪ ∪ /
Your foot | steps feel | from gran | ite to grass

would give the line a subtler expressive gesture. So, too, in

/   / ∪ /   ∪ / ∪ ∪ / ∪
"Yours nev | er will" |—said far | er to fear | er

I take it that the first three lines in stanza 4 are responding to the questions and statements in the first three stanzas respectively. That is, "'Out of this house'" answers "'O where are you going?'" If then "'Yours never will'" answers "'O do you imagine . . . That . . . Your diligent looking [will] discover,'" and so on, the strong rhetorical emphasis should be on "'Yours.'" My looking may not discover, but *yours* never will, because you do not search at all. Perhaps it is only that we are so unaccustomed to reading amphibrachs that we inevitably miss the subtlety. Nonetheless, the monosyllabic emphasis on "will" appears quite unhelpful.

The two remaining lines, read with amphibrachs, involve distortions of speech stress. Line 10 is doubly troubling, showing yet another jolting monosyllabic foot, "trees." But the main problem is the false amphibrach, "Did you see," needed to keep the meter.

Only the need for a *very* strong rhetorical stress on "you" could justify this reading, but it seems clear that the meaning focuses at least equally on the *seeing,* noticing, being aware of the shape. A traditional scansion causes no real loss:

⏑ ⏑ / ⏑ / ⏑ ⏑ / ⏑ /
Did you see | that shape | in the twist | ed trees

Nor can I justify the distorting "Ăs hé left" in line 16. As Anthony Hecht correctly argues (*The Hidden Law,* 1993, 455), Auden is fudging with the pronoun "he," uniting the trio of rider, farer, and hearer into a single figure. But marking "he" for special stress in no way clarifies the matter; and in any case, the adventurous *leaving* is at least equally important to the meaning. The traditional scansion, with its slightly less strong stress on "there," gives a rhythm that, rising, then falling—repeated in the second half of the line—seems cogently plaintive:

⏑ ⏑ / ⏑ / ⏑ ⏑ / ⏑ /
As he left | them there, | as he left | them there

Tempting as it may seem for the poem's first line, an amphibrachic scansion is not advantageous.

In general, the difficulty with trisyllabic feet, anapests or amphibrachs, is that they cannot really carry stress on more than one of the three syllables. A forced muting of a speech stress, as here in "Did you see" or as in Browning's

⏑ / ⏑ ⏑ / ⏑ ⏑ / ⏑ (⏑) /
I turned | in my sad | dle and made | *its girths tight*

will invariably seem a flaw—for which the term "false anapest" seems handy. A poet may risk false anapests if, say, a galloping rhythm seems worth overriding sense for; and they may be acceptable in comic forms like the limerick. Otherwise, however, they are blemishes.

Conceivably, somewhere, a poem will show a foot-pattern ⏑/⏑ that can't be avoided as a substitution. If so, such a case will be rare; and we needn't preserve the term amphibrach to refer to it. We will do as well to call it an anomalous foot, as I did of the pattern ⏑⏑⏑/ in "About Opera." Strictly, that could be called a "fourth paeon," but I see no wisdom in being able to invoke that term.

We can, therefore, accept Fussell's limitation to six feet for scanning English meter, with one modification. **(7) We should drop the pyrrhic foot (⌣⌣) and accept in its place the double-iamb (⌣⌣//), as one of the six foot-terms necessary: iamb, trochee, anapest, dactyl, spondee, double-iamb.**

This change was suggested by John Crown Ransom (in "The Strange Music of English Verse," *Kenyon Review,* vol. 18, 1956, 471). He noted its utility in scanning, for example, "the mar*riăge ŏf trúe mínds.*" "I have computed hastily," he says, "that there is an average of more than one [such] foot in the Shakespearian sonnet, and at least as good an average (of one in each fourteen lines) in the pentameter verse of Milton, Shelley, Keats, Tennyson, and many other poets." Ransom uses the Greek term "ionic foot," but plain English seems preferable, carrying with it a reminder that a *double-iamb* counts as two feet, and having the advantage (double-*iamb*) of suggesting that this pattern is quite normal to the iambic base. A traditional scansion of Marvell's line would show *four* substitutions (two pyrrhics, two spondees):

```
      ⌣  ⌣     /      /       ⌣  ⌣     /      /
To a | green thought | in a | green shade
```

The line in context, however, seems smooth and we will be closer to the character of the language in thinking of it as two double-iambs and so fairly regular.

Having the double-iamb at hand, I believe, will also give us a reliable scansion of the much discussed first line of Yeats's "After Long Silence":

```
  x     /     ⌣ ⌣   /    /   ⌣   (/)  ⌣  /
Speech | after long si | lence; it | is right
```

Anacrusis (followed by two unstressed syllables) accounts for the sense of abruptness we feel in the rhythm; and the caesura dividing the fourth foot registers the sense of awkward stopping and starting up again. The line is really much more regular than some have supposed.

Other than in the double-iamb sequence, I believe, the pyrrhic foot will always be scannable as iamb or trochee, taking a stress, however light, on one or the other syllable, as in "Nor ser*vices* to do till you require." For example, consider in this line by Keats the foot scanned as pyrrhic by W. Jackson Bate and David Perkins (in *British and American Poets: Chaucer to the Present*):

∪　／　／　　　／　∪　　∪　　∪　／　∪　／
The hare | limped trem | *bling through* | the froz | en grass

No difficulty occurs if we accept the foot as iambic. Indeed, iambic seems, as to performance, more accurate.

I said earlier (5) that sometimes in scanning there may be differences of opinion or confusion. It is, I think, confusion when the interpretation results from different assumptions about the way meter works. Not one of the four feet of Marvell's line as scanned above is scanned in the same way by Donald Hall (in *The Pleasures of Poetry*, 38):

／∪　∪　／　　　／∪　∪　／
To a | green thought | in a | green shade

Hall's logic seems impeccable but is not:

> No one could deny that "green" is louder than "To"; but the difference is metrically irrelevant. What is metrically relevant is that each group of two syllables contains one syllable that is louder than the other.

It is dubious to assume that, since the meter is iambic, relative stress is to be weighed exclusively as to "each group of *two* syllables." We do parse stressed/unstressed syllables relative to those adjacent (I would prefer to say "neighboring," to allow more flexibility when a line's pattern isn't obvious at once). But "green" is also adjacent; and the anapestic possibility (∪∪／) ought to keep the interpretation open. Suppose the line turned out to go, "To a green*est* thought. . . ."

Hall, albeit grudgingly, accepts anapestic substitution; so he might equally hear "Tŏ ă gréen-" or "Tó ă grĕen." As to "Tó ă" and "Tŏ ă," there is precious little difference in their levels of unstress; and meter can supply the lack in the right context:

(／)∪　∪·／　　　∪　／　　∪　／
Into | my hands | themselves | do reach

What is startling in Hall's view, then, is the divergent reading of "grĕen" and "grée̒n-," to which he seems forced by his assumption in contexts only slightly different.

The explanation perhaps lies in his holding that meter and rhythm are "wholly different things" (30):

> Rhythm is a large, loose, and inclusive word. Rhythm is things like fast and slow, staccato and smooth. . . . Meter, on the other hand, is a repeated number of something. . . . Meter indicates a form of arithmetic; we add something, and we find the same number of it in another line.

Excluding pyrrhics and spondees as feet in English (45–46), he adds, "In English, these effects are rhythmic and not metrical." So—if I understand Hall's view—the *meter* of "To a green thought" is /∪|∪/, but the *rhythm* could be ∪∪|//. Speaking of a substituted anapest, however, he says (36), "It is a common metrical variation, which makes us take a little rhythmic quick step in saying the line." Saying that, though, seems to void the distinction between meter and rhythm as "wholly different." I am puzzled.

Scansion, it seems to me, does two things. It shows a line's sufficient *approximation* of the metrical norm; and, more important, it shows those *divergences* from the norm (as in Hall's comment about the anapest) that let us begin to discuss the line's characteristic rhythm, its musical qualities, which of course also include such effects as alliteration, assonance, or syntactical balance/imbalance.

Hall's assumption about each group of two syllables arises because he is discussing iambic meter. He suggests (31–32) that there are other meters in English, and means at least anapestic, trochaic, and dactylic. To these we may now turn.

Testing again with Saintsbury's touchstone, I conclude that **(8) Anapestic, trochaic, and dactylic meters do not exist in English**. In theory, I suppose, though I have never seen it stated this way, these are (along with iambic meter) *sub*-meters of accentual-syllabic meter. Even with the sub-meter distinction carefully made, however, these seem to be multiplied entities that may be confusing.

Poems in accentual-syllabics are overwhelmingly iambic, so it makes sense to see iambic as the metrical base; and, given substitution, the other so-called sub-meters obviously all lie somewhere along a *continuous* spectrum of variations. At some point iambic meter with anapestic substitutions turns into anapestic meter with iambic substitutions—and the distinction is, thus, needless. One could hardly claim, to any purpose, if the balance in the stanza of Hardy's "Neutral Tones" shifted from eight iambs/seven anapests to seven iambs/eight anapests, that the *meter* had changed. It seems clear that when we are tempted by terms like "anapestic meter," what is involved is not meter (the system) but variations in rhythm. These we can discuss usefully by speaking of "frequent anapestic substitutions" or, if we want to be precise, by quantifying the proportion of anapests (or whatever) to iambs in any poem or passage. (I count the first stanza of "How They Brought the Good News from Ghent to Aix" as comprising eighteen anapests, four iambs, two spondees. So, "heavily anapestic.")

I hope we agree that, properly, meter refers to *poems,* not lines *per se.* We do not, for instance, if we find three spondees and perhaps only one iamb in "And with old woes new wail my dear time's waste," conclude that the line is spondaic.

So-called trochaic meter is merely a mirror image of iambic, so this is another case of having two quite different ways of describing the same thing:

```
 x    /    | ᴗ   / | ᴗ / | ᴗ    /      [as iambic]
   Come, and trip it as ye go
   /    ᴗ  | /  ᴗ | / ᴗ | /   x    [as trochaic]
```

Often, as here, the iambic reading is faithful to the pattern of the wording. Buckets of ink and spittle might have been spared over "L'Allegro" alone, which has fully iambic lines like "To live with her, and live with thee." Whatever we may want to say of the syncopation of rhythm in such lines as "Come, and trip it as ye go" in Milton, or in Larkin's "First Sight," or in Herrick's "Here she lies, a pretty bud, / Lately made of flesh and blood"—which ends, "The earth, that lightly covers her"—the *meter* is iambic tetrameter. Poems do not change meter from line to line; and Milton's "Then to come in spite of sorrow," even in a poem entirely of such lines— that is, with no lines ending in a stressed syllable—would remain iambic, scannable with anacrusis and extra-syllable ending; as it would seem odd to say that a line can be in iambic meter in one poem and in trochaic meter in another. Also, we cannot be consistent about extra-syllable endings if, in trochaic meter, we do count the syllable as belonging to a foot.

What I am urging in this proposition is of course fully implicit in Frost's comment about strict and loose iambic. Our loss, in having multiplied entities, is the failure to see clearly how splendidly unitary English meter is.

IV. TWO LEVELS OF STRESS

In our century, in an illusion of greater precision, linguistics has multiplied entities for prosody. In 1900 ("Notes on Metre," reprinted in *The Structure of Verse,* Gross, ed., 1966), Otto Jespersen first applied *four* levels of stress to English verse, rather than the conventional two levels. Marked numerically, they are: 4 = "strong," 3 = "half-strong," 2 = "half-weak," 1 = "weak." He comments (115) that "in reality there are infinite gradations of stress . . . but it will be sufficient to recognize four degrees." In 1951, in *An Outline of English Structure,* George L. Trager and Henry Lee Smith, Jr., offered a comparable system of four levels of stress ("primary" = /, "secondary" = ∧, "tertiary" = \, and "weak" = ◡), which has been employed by metrists Harold Whitehall, Seymour Chatman, and others.

Useful as linguistic analysis may be in other ways, let me be emphatic: **(9) We should *never* use four degrees of speech stress for scanning.** It will be sufficient for prosody to recognize two degrees of stress, as Shakespeare, Pope, Keats, and Frost have done. As to poetry, persons in white lab coats will bring not help, but confusion. The term *isochronic,* for instance, is merest jargon. It is simply not true that meter (or English, for that matter) is stress-timed, each foot taking exactly the same time to articulate (so that we hurry the unaccented syllables of an anapest to make them fit). If we are then told that, although this may not be true in fact, it is nonetheless true perceptually, we are only back where we started: a foot is a foot. So never mind isochronism.

The use of Trager-Smith stress-levels is meant to complement regular binary foot-scansion; that is, as Chatman says ("Robert Frost's 'Mowing': An Inquiry into Prosodic Structure," *Kenyon Review,* vol. 18, 1956, 422), "to account for the phonological complexity of verse by envisaging a tension between *two* systems: the abstract metrical pattern . . . and the ordinary stress-pitch-juncture system of spoken English." Harold Whitehall ("From Linguistics to Criticism," *Kenyon Review,* vol. 18, 1956, 418) speaks of an "orchestration" of the meter and the varied stress-levels of speech. This formulation is essentially what I described (7) as the interrelationship of speech-run and meter that produces the individual rhythm of a line or passage of verse. The implicit claim is that using *four* levels of stress will produce a finer discrimination of the rhythm than is possible conventionally.

On the evidence of the model applications by Chatman and Whitehall, however, the claim is untrue. On the contrary, if we occasionally have difficulty ascribing unstress or stress in a two-valued system, the four-valued system almost predictably results in further disagreement and still more elaborate confusion. Moreover, Chatman and Whitehall seem to see the linguistic rules that apply to speech as *overriding* any special character meter may have; and so their accounts in fact fail to explore the special relationship (tension or orchestration) it was their intention to examine.

Whitehall (418-19) marks only two lines to exemplify the Trager-Smith scoring (the vertical lines are phrase markers); I have added a regular scansion below the lines:

```
      ∪   /  \     ∧   ∪    /   \   ∧ ∪    /
The curfew | tolls the knell | of parting day
      ∪   / | ∪     /    | ∪    /  | ∪  / | ∪   /
```

and

```
      ∪  \  ∪    /     \     ∧ ∪   \  ∪   /
The lowing herd | winds slowly | o'er the lea ||
      ∪   / | ∪   /    |  |  /     / | ∪   /  | ∪   /
```

The Trager-Smith scoring of the iambically regular first line is unobjectionable, though one may wonder what insight we can draw from the "orchestration" shown in ascribing secondary stresses to "tolls" and "part-" or tertiary stresses to "-few" and "of." The information doesn't seem very helpful.

The other line, however, is a calamity. I assume that Whitehall has correctly performed whatever linguistics operations give this result, but the result is unacceptable for scanning English meter. That "low-" and "winds" (the verb!) get only tertiary stresses like that on "o'er" and (in the other line) "of" is clearly disputable. I *hear* no such major difference from the stresses on "herd," "slow-," and "lea." The stresses of "winds slow-" seem virtually level and the foot is a spondee. Predictably, Whitehall's discussion focuses, not on the indicated rhythm or orchestration and what it may tell us about Gray's moo-cows, but on the way the English language works.

I will return to the spondee hereafter, but Chatman (in *A Theory of Meter,* 98–99) reports why in Trager-Smith scoring we will never find one. Like pyrrhics, spondees "are declared impossible, one of the two syllables being considered allophonically louder than the other." Before you shrug and accept this, however, let me say that it means only that, given suprasegmentals, *no two actual stresses in all of English* are ever exactly alike to the nth degree—like snowflakes! This is a matter of faith, not evidence. In the practical world, guided by what we hear, we can confidently find spondees. If, as seems likely, "winds" got demoted to tertiary stress because, with "slow-" scored as secondary, it had to be kept at a lower level of stress, the system is rule-bound. (Allophones are, for instance, the very slight differences in the two k-sounds in "King Kong.")

Seymour Chatman in "Robert Frost's 'Mowing' . . . ," though he later appears to have abandoned scoring by Trager-Smith stresses, affords several other useful glimpses of the endemic confusion. As Ransom points out (466), Chatman gets the *regular* scansion of three of the Frost poem's thirteen lines wrong. Here, for the flavor, is the complete presentation of line 2 (427). Chatman tabulates the scoring of performances by eight random readers, A through H (Frost is H). The numerals and vertical lines show intonation patterns. "Theoretical metrical stress points"—the foot markers—are shown by underlined vowels in the text:

A	2	3	' 3|2	3	^	2	'	2||3	'	2|2	2	'	I#
B	2	4	' 4|2	3	^	2	'	|3	'I	#I		'	I#
C	2	3	^		^		'	2|3	'	2|2	3	'	I#
D	2	3	' 3|2		^	3	'	2|3	'	2|2	3	'	I#
E	2	3	'		^	^		I#2	^		`	'	I#
F	2	3	'	`	^	^		2|3	'		^		I#
G	2	3	^		^		'	2|3	'	I|I		2	^	I#
H	2	3	' 3|2	3	^		'	3|3	^			'	I#

2. And that was my long scythe whispering to the ground.

Putting aside the silly notion that there can be any gain in precision in the scoring of a committee, what does this data come to? Everyone scored a primary or secondary stress on "that," "long," "scythe," "whis-," and "ground." The only surprise is that reader E, bless him or her, gave a secondary stress to "to." We need this stress if the line is to be heard as iambic pentameter; "scythe whis-" is of course a spondee. Here is the line again with, above it, what I take from Chatman's underlinings to be his conventional scansion, and with my scansion underneath:

⏑ / ⏑ ⏑ / / / ⏑ ⏑ ⏑ ⏑ /
And that was my long scythe whispering to the ground
⏑ / | ⏑ ⏑ / | / / | ⏑ ⏑ (/)| ⏑ /

This divergence of pentameter and spoken language is surely an instance of the tension Chatman wants to account for, but in the many pages of commentary that follow the data, line 2 never rates a mention. Its expressive rhythm goes unremarked.

By contrast, Chatman discusses at length (431–32) "an inappropriate intonation pattern" which might result in a poor reading of line 13: "The fact is the sweetest dream that labor knows."

> the locution "The fact is. . . ." is an extremely common way of beginning utterances like "The fact is, my dear, that we don't have any more money." Confronted with the written sequence, "The fact is . . . ," the ordinary speaker of English will almost automatically use the pattern ² *The* ³ *fact is* ². . . or even ² *The* ³ *fact is* ². . . .

Two of the eight readers in the data get caught in the first, milder version of this misreading. All of which has *nothing* to do with the advantage or disadvantage of Trager-Smith scoring. The proper emphasis is already encoded in the *metrical* norm of the line. Intonations belong to the language, not to Trager-Smith scoring, which would in no way prevent the error, though Chatman seems pleased to be pointing it out.

Or consider this muddle, where the Trager-Smith scoring is Chatman's own (424):

```
    ^        ^  /    ^   \  \      /
The course of true love | never did run smooth
```

Turning Shakespeare's pentameter into a *tetrameter,* Chatman has missed the necessary foot stresses on both "true" and "nev-" and supplied an incorrect one on "love." The point is that even *true* love doesn't go easily; we know how the other kind goes. For comparison, here is a regular scansion:

```
  ∪   /    ∪   /   (/)  /   ∪  /   /     /
The course | of true | love nev | er did | run smooth
```

Chatman overrides the meter by insisting on a speech-rhythm that ignores the plain emphasis in the meaning of the passage. It is an error quite as egregious as mistaking "The fact is."

The overlay of Trager-Smith scoring on regular scansion is just too much machinery even for a good linguist to keep track of; and ordinary readers, and poets, I hope, will be forgiven if we just struggle on with conventional binary scansion, relying on common sense and a good ear.

Turn now to the use of Jespersen's four levels of stress. The ride will be similarly bumpy, albeit with a difference. As to the difficulty of having four sorts of choice we can make, instead of just two, Jespersen himself comments (116):

> It is not always easy to apply these numbers to actually occurring syllables and it is particularly difficult in many instances to distinguish between 3 and 2. Unfortunately, we have no means of measuring stress objectively by instruments.

(That was 1900. By now, I fancy, electronics could at low cost equip us, our students, and poetry readers everywhere with elegant, portable Metermeters.)

The difference I mentioned is important. Jespersen's purpose in introducing four levels of stress, recall, is to *replace* foot-scansion—which he concludes is absurd—by a new system (118) involving the regular alternation of "an upward and a downward movement, a rise and a fall, an ascent and a descent, at fixed places," that is, from each syllable to the next. A pentameter is figured in this way, with *a* and *b* representing syllables and the slashes representing the required ascent (/) or descent (\):

a / b \ a / b \ a / b \ a / b \ a / b \ a / b

The *relationship* of each stressed syllable (*b*) to the next unstressed syllable (*a*) is fully as important as the relationship between an unstressed and a stressed—hence, the irrelevance of feet.

This isn't the place for a full critique of Jespersen's system. However interesting, it is complicated, and plausible only up to a point. It is also incomplete, making no provision whatever for tri-syllabic substitutions (or meter). And it is finally a mess, collapsing in the face of actual lines Jespersen is at a loss to explain without great contrivance and some deliberate misreading of levels of speech stress. As he confesses (123), "In spite of all this there will remain some instances in which the second syllable cannot easily be made stronger than the third. Metrics is no exact science aimed at finding out natural laws that are valid everywhere." Whatever may be others' view of Jespersen's system, no recent metrist has chosen to adopt it.

The difficulty with using Jespersen's four stresses for scanning, then, is that there is nowhere to go with the result *except back to the conventional system of feet,* and so, by translating, skewing the wonderfully adaptive system of binary unstress/stress. Consider a scansion of Marvell's line with Jespersen stress-scoring, to which I have added below the line the resulting foot-relationships marked conventionally:

```
 2 1  3     4    2 1  3    4
To a green thought in a green shade
 / ∪|  ∪     /    |/ ∪ | ∪    /
```

The binary result, coincidentally, is the same as Hall's scansion (27); and if we are translating Jespersen-stress into breve and ictus—what else might we do?—we may ask the same questions. Suppose the line went, "To a green*est* thought. . . ." How would we then parse "To a green" into a foot? Is it an anapest, or must we decide that it is a weak cretic foot? Does a 2 count as unstressed or stressed? Or what? Will all similar phrases, like "And live alone *in the bee*-loud glade," be counted as 2 1 3? We are making trouble for ourselves by translating from one system into the other.

Given that we will encounter in reality far more actual levels of stress than four, assigning Jespersen's levels of stress will often be even more arbitrary than in a binary system. "To" is perhaps more strongly stressed that "a," though not by much; neither is anywhere near the adjective and noun that follow. Why might we not scan "To a" as 1 1? Further, to my ear "green," which is the surprising word and is, moreover, surprisingly repeated, rings at least as strong as either the expected "thought" or "shade." When I try to read the line, the pitch *drops* on the nouns:

To a green thought in a green shade

Why not, then, 1 1 4 4 1 1 4 4 or, conceivably, 1 1 4 3 1 1 4 3? The answer, if we are following Jespersen, will turn out to be *not* that we are listening very carefully and accurately, but that a mistaken theory is afoot.

Consider a line of Frost cited by Steele (*Missing Measures,* 61), which he scans elsewhere by Jespersen stresses:

3   4 1   2   3   4 1   4   2   4
Snow falling and night falling fast, oh, fast

Here is the line again, with above it the Jespersen stresses translated into breve and ictus, and below it a commonsense scansion (with double-iamb):

˘ / | ˘ / | ˘   / | ˘ / | ˘ /
Snow falling and night falling fast, oh, fast
/ / | ˘ ˘   /   / | ˘ / | (/) /

The Jespersen-based translation (above the line) shows it as being entirely iambs, and has lost the subtlety registered in the numerical and traditional scansions. Steele would affirm the iambic reading here, I think. In "On Meter" (298–99) he cites a number of lines including the following which, he says, "appears to have seven notable speech stresses" (his italics):

> *Kind pity chokes* my *spleen; brave scorn* for *bids*

I would agree so far, seeing spondees as the first and fourth feet. Steele, however, sums up:

> Despite their rhythmical differences, all the lines quoted above are metrically identical. All the lines conform in one way or another to the lighter-to-heavier movement. All the feet in the lines are iambic, in that the second syllable is more emphatic than the first.

The puzzle is, what is *gained* by thus insisting on the absolute iambic regularity? There is at least a risk of loss, or of being misunderstood.

An issue lurking in much of the foregoing must now be focused on: the spondee. It seems odd that we need to discuss at this late date whether there is or is not a spondee in English meter; and our students—or a physicist who happened into our classrooms—might well be puzzled at the disorder about something so basic. But, as some authoritative accounts firmly declare that the spondee doesn't exist in English (Hall, 45) or that it is extremely rare (Yvor Winters, "The Audible Reading of Poetry," in *The Function of Criticism*, 1957, 90), let me assert **(10) The spondee is a good, and fairly frequent, foot in English.**

Insofar as rejection of the spondee may depend on the Trager-Smith schema, I have suggested that we not worry about snowflakes. Let's pursue the question as to the Jespersen system.

Steele (305–6) is among those who consider "true" spondees rare in English verse. Discussing a line of Keats, scanned by Bate and Perkins as having an iamb and a spondee as the first two feet—

ᵕ / / / ᵕ ᵕ ᵕ / ᵕ /
The hare | limped tremb | ling through | the froz | en grass

—Steele offers instead this Jespersen-stress reading:

1 2 / 3 4
The hare limped trembling. . . .

Steele's slash shows foot-division, the feet being iambs of course.

In following the trail here back to Jespersen, let me go the long way around. Steele's reading of "hare" as a 2 is astonishing. Without question, Jespersen would have scored the Keats fragment as 1 4 3 4, or 1 4 2 4, rather than as 1 2 3 4, on the model of his reading of "*The still sad mu*sic of humanity" (116)—a reading that would preserve the normal "descent" from the second to the third syllable.

Steele's 2 for "hare" is not a typo, however. He introduces his reading of the fragment by saying that "we appear to have, in these two feet, one of those cases of four successive syllables representing four rising degrees of stress." Just before (301) he has mentioned this as a "special case." "From time to time, in iambic English verse, one will encounter two adjacent feet whose four syllables represent four rising degrees of stress," and he cites the beginning of Sidney's line:

 1   2 / 3   4
With how sad steps O moon thou climbst the skies

This points us correctly to the place in "Notes on Metre" (125) where Jespersen is struggling unsuccessfully to reconcile to his system a number of lines such as *"In the sweet pangs* of it remember me." Of this pattern Jespersen then comments

> I incline to read it with 1 2 3 4 and thus to say that the ascent is normal between the first and the second as well as between the third and the fourth syllable, so that there is only the one small anomaly of a slight ascent instead of a descent between the second and the third syllable. It is worth noting how frequently this figure contains an adjective (stressed 3) before a substantive (stressed 4).

With startling nonchalance—"I incline to read it"—Jespersen chooses to ignore actual speech stress to favor his theory, as he also does on page 122 to deal with another difficulty.

Steele's 1 2 3 4 for "The hare limped trembling," we see, then, is an attempt (albeit mistaken) to follow a doctrine. And here, in Jespersen, we see the doctrine being created. He needs a 1 2 for "In the"—as he does for "And the," "But the," and even "are the"—in order to make the lines he is considering even *almost* fit his system. A reading of 2 1, as in Hall's reading of "To a green thought," would of course be more like what we hear; or a 1 1. But Jespersen is not listening, he is making dogma.

Here, too, is the doctrine of 3 4 for "sweet pangs"—or for "green thought," "brave scorn," "Snow falling," or "limped trembling," no matter what we may hear. Requiring alternating ascent/descent for his system, Jespersen will not admit a 4 4; and those who scan by Jespersen-scoring will not admit a spondee.

But there is no necessity about this. Go back to what Jespersen has said (116) just before he outlines the system:

> Verse rhythm is based on the same alternation between stronger and weaker syllables as that found in natural everyday speech. Even in the most prosaic speech, which is in no way dictated by artistic feeling, this alternation is not completely irregular: everywhere we observe a natural tendency towards making a weak syllable follow after a strong one and inversely.

In speech, two equal or virtually equal stresses may occur together; so a spondee is plainly possible in meter. The refusal to accept it is mere dogma, borrowed from the failed theory of Jespersen's system. Even Winters, in his striptease about the extremely rare "truly spondaic foot" (139), one of which he ultimately uncovers in Barnabe Googe, is following the dogma, as his comment about "When to the ses*sions of sweet si*lent thought" suggests (94): "we have in effect a series of four degrees of accent within two successive feet." The point of talking mysteriously about "true" spondees has always been one-upsmanship. Meter cannot depend on discriminations too fine for ordinary mortals, poets or readers, to make out pretty easily.

Meter is not a seismograph, but a binary system of conventional *approximations* of the language's rapid and complex levels of stress. We know, from "To a," that "green thought" counts as two stresses; as we know, from "green thought," that "To a" counts as a pair of unstressed syllables. The binary nature of English meter, which requires that we resolve everything into its two values, means that we must be at once flexible and precise.

In scanning, a simple method of noting possibly ambiguous

cases is to show the breve or ictus in parentheses, as I have often done in this paper. In marking

ᵕ / ᵕ / (/) / / / ᵕ /
When A | jax strives | some rock's | vast weight | to throw

I mark "some rock's" as spondee, for instance, but suggest that hearing it as an iamb is also plausible. In this way, we can moot some disagreements as well as make our scanning somewhat more finely responsive. The device will give us, in effect, a way to register an intermediate level of stress when, occasionally, that may aid in interpretation.

In scanning, we often show such tact rather than rigor. For instance, we allow as stressed a syllable that in speech is virtually unaccented, as in Frost's

ᵕ / ᵕ (/) ᵕ / ᵕ / ᵕ /
That gath | ers on | the pane | in emp | ty rooms

As Miller Williams says deftly, "Any set of three unaccented syllables will nearly always be read with a perceptibly greater force on the middle one." But—notice—we ignore this effect in other cases, as in Housman's

/ ᵕ ᵕ ᵕ / ᵕ / ᵕ /
Loveliest | of trees, | the cher | ry now

where, I think, the tetrameter context of the line determines what we register as metrically relevant. In a passage of pentameters, however, we might properly hear:

x / ᵕ(/) ᵕ / ᵕ / ᵕ /
Love | liest | of trees, | the cher | ry now

Underlying tact is what might be called the LCD rule (lowest common denominator). In scanning, when more than one interpretation of a line is possible, we should usually opt for the simpler or closer to the metrical norm. "Loveliest of trees" might be read as either dactyl/iamb or trochee/anapest, but the former is preferable, as showing only one substitution. Similarly, a less than preferable reading of the Yeats line, which is scannable as anacrusis/double-iamb/iamb/iamb (26), would be

```
  /    ◡   ◡   /    /  ◡    ×(/) ◡  /
Speech af | ter long | silence; |   it | is right
```

which shows two trochaic substitutions and a lame foot. Equally awkward would be reading "it is right" as an anapest, thus giving the line only four feet though the poem is clearly otherwise pentameter. Any of these alternative interpretations can be rationalized as emphasizing expressive effects, but none seems necessary for that purpose. Turco's amphibrach (22) violates the LCD rule.

A scansion in a textbook, cited by Steele—

```
 ◡   ◡  /    /  ◡   /◡  ◡ ◡    /   /
To the land | vaguely | rea | lizing | westward
```

—manages to read a pentameter with no iambs at all, though it is in fact fairly regular:

```
 ◡   ◡   /   /    ◡  / ◡(/)  ◡   /    ◡
To the land vague | ly re | aliz | ing west | ward
```

An anapestic reading of "To the land" would be correct if the next syllable was unstressed,

```
 ◡   ◡   /    ◡   /    ◡
To the land | *that* vague | ly . . .
```

But it is incorrect for the line as it reads. That error leads to the mistaken attribution of trochees in the next places, and so to a mishearing of the plain secondary stress on "-liz-" and to a false stress on "-ward."

My aim in all of the foregoing has been to urge that we simplify our accounts of meter in English. Hereafter, we should expect that any new or revised account will be *simpler* than what we have. Hoping for and confidently predicting such a "synthesis" in 1907, T. S. Omond (*English Metrists,* 240) noted, "When it does come, I suspect it will be found less and not more complex than its many predecessors."

Unworkable complexity, I think, defeats both Jespersen and the theory offered by Morris Halle and Samuel Jay Keyser (in *English Stress: Its Form, Its Growth, and Its Role in Verse,* 139–46 and 164–80). I am unaware that anyone on the literary side has adopted

Halle and Keyser's account, but it appears still to have currency on the linguistics side, so a comment seems in order. Their process of scansion strikes me as hugely cumbersome. We might, I suppose, grow accustomed to that. But consider the results produced. This line by Keats—

How many bards gild the lapses of time

—is judged (171) "unmetrical since it has a stress maximum in the fourth W position in violation of the last alternative of (52bii)." *But* the following (invented) line would, by their system, be metrical, scanning as iambic pentameter (178):

> Billows, billows, serene mirror of the marine boroughs,
> remote willow

Smokey Stover, thou shouldst be living at this hour!

Perhaps Omond's expectation is doomed to be forlorn. If, however, a truly new synthesis appears, we will know it by the ease and clarity with which it accounts for the roughly regular use of unstressed syllables (and sometimes stressed ones, as in spondees) as spacers between countable stresses. It will be simpler than the system of native footnotes wild we have now. Meanwhile, let us carefully strip away the inessentials from this homemade prosody and make do. It is, I think, seen properly, both simple and elegant.

Going by recent authoritative accounts, however, the situation hasn't improved since 1907 when Omond concluded

> This, for certain, that we have as yet no established system of prosody. . . . It is a strange fact so late in the history of our literature; Greek metrists would have viewed it with surprise.

PART TWO

METER IN ENGLISH

A RESPONSE

Eavan Boland

(1) "Instead of the term 'feminine ending,' we should say simply extra-syllable ending, which may be abbreviated as e-s ending."

As a working poet I am often struck by how abstract the discussion of meter is; how scientific and customary. In one sense it may well be that it needs to be, since it is making a catalogue of an historic usage. Yet that usage remains ambiguous, governed by variables and hard to define. In one of his masterly asides in *Biographia Literaria* Coleridge referred to metrical stresses as— I quote this from memory—"at first the offspring of passion and then the adopted children of power." Any discussion of meter seems to run the risk of concentrating on the adoption and forgetting the passionate origin. No doubt this is because the range of such discussions is always divided between practice and effect. The first has names and fixed measurements; the second is elusive and subject to change.

Therefore giving a new name to an old fixity fills me with doubt and unease. I can see the need for it, while recognizing that changing the terms does not always clarify the effect. Certainly the term extra-syllable ending, in the most downright and practical way, is clearer than "feminine ending." But somehow the new name makes it sound like a take-it-or-leave it and once-over usage. Whereas the way in which the final syllable is swallowed by the end of the line has, of course, to do with the composition of the previous sounds. I understand that the intention is to re-name the usage rather than describe it. But it might be useful to look at it more closely. Take the example given:

> And yet it may be said I loved her dearly.

In this instance the actual metrical arrangement of the lines is at variance with their effect. The scansion suggests an iambic count. In fact, the decisive favouring of two words by assonance—"yet" and "said"—means that the ear moves backward rather than forward, buttonholed by the sound-relation of the vowels, so that by the end of the line a ledge of music and emphasis has been made over which the final syllable falls into an emotional silence made by the earlier noise.

Neither is this a chance arrangement. The exemplary line comes from Sonnet 92 by Shakespeare. This is the second line of the opening quatrain. The quatrain itself gains its effect by alternating loud and muted lines. The first and third lines, which end with what is termed the e-s ending here, are more logically constructed when you see their context, in which they are very definitely playing second fiddle to the lines immediately before them. I have put what I consider the loud lines in bold type.

> **That thou hast her, it is not all my grief,**
> And yet it may be said I loved her dearly;
> **That she hath thee, is of my wailing chief,**
> A loss in love that touches me more nearly.

This so-called feminine ending or, as in the proposed revision here, e-s ending marks the second of the exceptions which John Crowe Ransom quotes in "The Strange Music of English Verse." He states there, "an extra unstressed syllable after the tenth made 'a feminine ending' and did not count." Ransom in turn notes these exceptions as being codified by Bridges in his book *Milton's Prosody*—"the best handbook we have," he adds, "on iambic pentameters."

The e-s ending may be a licensed exception. It is also interesting to observe that it is not simply a neutral convention, a silent partner at the edge of sound. It is in fact a usage which finds disfavour with some critics, not so much perhaps because it constitutes an exception to the iambic norm, as that it appears to be a soft option. In his illuminating discussion of the early influences on John Keats's versification, Walter Jackson Bate mentions feminine endings as a regrettable and weak element of versification, derived mainly from Leigh Hunt. He characterized the writing of "Isabella" in 1818 as a technical advance for Keats, partly because it marked a departure from such practise. "Meanwhile," he states, "he (Keats) has completely dropped most of what he had taken over from Hunt's versification two years before. Feminine endings so abundant in the 1817 volume (about 25 percent) have now been cut to about 3 percent."

However, the issue here is not so much the choice of line as the actual naming of the choice. And that naming I understand is to indicate that the feminine or e-s ending is metrically uncounted as well as emotionally unheard. It is certainly true that the naming of meter has an unfortunate history in poetry. Inasmuch as young poets and students find it the most intimidating and disheartening part of their work, to read and remember this old and seemingly arbitrary catalogue, then this more accurate and explanatory term seems preferable.

(2) "For an omitted first syllable of a line, we should use the term anacrusis."

Once again, from the viewpoint of the naming of parts, "anacrusis" is probably better than the other terms. The unstressed syllable which is not consciously heard or counted, is still just enough of a presence to give resonance to the line, while maintaining the norm of the scansion.

(3) "Quantities are not a basis for meter in English."

If quantities are not a basis for meter in English, then the inference is that there is another, more authentic basis. This in turn raises the complex and vast question of the origins of meter. Therefore I want to consider the precise question about quantities in the more imprecise context of the nature of meter itself.

"The purpose of rhythm," wrote Yeats, "is to prolong the moment of contemplation, the moment when we are both asleep and awake, which is the one moment of creation, by hushing us with an alluring monotony, while it holds us waking by variety." I see the metrical system as an ambitious attempt to regularize this power and this effect. It legislates for that moment when perception is alerted by musical variety while simultaneously relaxed and made less vigilant by cadence and repetition. Such a subtle effect would have no authority if meter was not itself the map of a lost kingdom of perception. I say "lost" only in the figurative sense. But certainly a powerful musical statement, metrically designed and achieved, gains access to areas of perception which are more often closed than not.

But musical variety and lulling repetition are not things in themselves. They can only work if they are abstracts of sounds which are familiar enough in their concrete and everyday version so that the abstract is both orderly and moving. Therefore meter, it seems to me, cannot work if it is predicated on a relation to those everyday sounds, which is neither organic nor easily recognizable.

Quantities do not provide such a relation. Therefore they do not provide a basis for meter in English.

(4) "Syllabics is not a meter in English."

At this point I confess to some difficulty with the conventional discussion of meter. There is a need for names and labels. There is a historic catalogue of usage and convention which needs to be respected, if only because from that respect, in turn, comes further convention and usage. But the cut-and-dried and well-patrolled definitions miss some important points. Take this one for instance. Syllabics is not, in the strict sense, a meter in English. At face value this is a reasonable and sustainable proposition. Take it further, however, into Robert Wallace's argument about Marianne Moore's poem "Poetry" and it becomes flawed and exclusive. Let me first of all quote the poem:

I, too, dislike it: there are things that are important beyond all
this fiddle.
Reading it, however, with a perfect contempt for it, one
discovers in
it after all, a place for the genuine.
Hands that can grasp, eyes
that can dilate, hair that can rise
if it must, these things are important not because a

high-sounding interpretation can be put upon them but because
they are
useful. When they become so derivative as to become
unintelligible
the same thing may be said for all of us, that we
do not admire what
we cannot understand: the bat
holding on upside down or in quest of something to

eat, elephants pushing, a wild horse taking a roll, a tireless wolf
under
a tree, the immovable critic twitching his skin like a horse
that feels a flea, the base-
ball fan, the statistician—
nor is it valid
to discriminate against 'business documents and

school-books'; all these phenomena are important. One must
make a distinction
however: when dragged into prominence by half poets, the
result is not poetry,
nor till the poets among us can be
'literalists of
the imagination'—above
insolence and triviality and can present

for inspection, imaginary gardens with real toads in them, shall
we have
it. In the meantime, if you demand on the one hand,
the raw material of poetry in
all its rawness and
that which is on the other hand
genuine, then you are interested in poetry.

Randall Jarrell said, "Miss Moore's forms have the lacy, mathematical extravagance of snowflakes and seem as arbitrary as the prohibitions in fairy tales." But in fact there is nothing arbitrary about the formal intensity here. If its construction were merely a matter of syllabics, then the point that syllabics is not a meter in English would be ironclad. But whereas I accept Robert Wallace's point that Marianne Moore herself may have placed no great formal value on this method, that in itself does not seem to me the essential point about her choice of cadence. Under its quirky and beautiful surface, this poem is an aggressive and disruptive dialogue with historic iambic meter. It constitutes a dissonance which is something like atonal music: a quarrel with historic expectation is at its heart. I think we read Marianne Moore's poem with a shadow metrical catalogue in our mind. I think her dissonances outrage our sense of metrical decorum and therefore radically refresh it.

This is not the only decorum it flaunts, but it is an important one. Nor is she the only poet to do this. In the age of the Elizabethan lyric John Donne conducted a dialogue with the meters of the sixteenth century which cannot be excluded from any final sense of his achievement.

What troubles me about historic definitions of meter is their tendency to overlook the powerful shaping presence which such disruptive dialogues can be and have been in the history of poetry. I give a real and particular weight to such dialogues in a metrical and not simply a contextual sense. By that I mean something fairly precise. I believe as we read such dialogues we engage in them. We add and subtract, we colour and revise, we make more musical or less musical the construct before us as we supply the missing metrical system it engages and addresses. Therefore, although I understand the need to dismiss syllabics from a definition of metrical practise which seeks to grow more accurate by such exclusion, I believe the dialogue which such practises establish needs to be an integral part of metrical definition.

(5) "In modern English, accentual meter does not exist."

Contemporary poetry has emerged from a tangle of influences, some of them visible, some well hidden. I understand that accentual meter—despite some wishful post-war thinking—does not really exist in modern English. Therefore I agree that it is not a useful element in the definition of meter and needs to be excluded from such definition. But it is fascinating to speculate at what point the powerful stresses of the Old English line lost their force and were absorbed into a new line-shape. *The Princeton Encyclopedia of Poetry and Poetics* gives a partial answer: "Although it persisted for a time in the new language, the Old English accentual line, with its varying number of unaccented syllables, is gradually abandoned in favour of a line in which syllabic numeration becomes, for the first time, one of the structural criteria. One can observe the phenomenon of the two hemistichs of the OE line transforming themselves into the 4- and 3-stress lines of the ballad meter."

I mention this because the absorption of the old accentual line into some of the energies of the ballad meter seems important. Meter is so often defined purely according to the practise of the poets of the English tradition that the vitality of the street-corner and the gallows singer and the flower-seller can be discounted. They should not be. The accentual line may be gone. The erosion of Germanic dialect by Norman French saw to that many centuries ago. But the sense-to-sound spectrum which remains a vital consideration in any broad consideration of meter is part of the bequest from those ballad traditions which swallowed accentual meters. As such, it needs to be looked at.

The discussion of meter is properly concerned with systems and titles. But the effect of meter is wider and deeper than any of these names can suggest. Most poets, whether the meter they use is regular or various, have a distinctive sense-to-sound spectrum across which their customary line describes itself. In the most plain-speaking language this means that a poet like Dylan Thomas uses a line which tends to make more sound than sense. Yeats on the other hand, in his last poems, makes so much urgent and complicated sense that the sound is at times hard to hear. Yet both poets, in some of their best and most characteristic poems, were using the iambic pentameter.

This sense-to-sound spectrum seems to me the fossil aftermath of poetry's old relation to song. Anglo-Saxon poetry may or may not have been accented by the harp. But the shadow of song across metrical usage is persistent. And the division of the line from the intense musical simplifications which lie deep in the origins of all poetry has made a certain amount of meter—no matter what language we use in defining its separation—a visible scar tissue. I take this to be what Yvor Winters meant when he remarked, "The correlation between sound and feeling may have its origin in some historical relationship between music and language."

I do not offer these general remarks to contest in any way Robert Wallace's admirable and sensible attempt to clear away impostor-systems from the definition of meter. I merely suggest that over-and-done-with definitions can make a history of cadence which is deceptive. They exclude the slow, irrational makings and unmakings which go into the mapping of that zone between sleep and waking which Yeats wrote about. Therefore, although accentual meter can no longer be considered as a meter in English, it must be a subtle part of what we are left with. Indeed, the meter we have—and the definitions we give it—seem to me like the smooth exterior of a shark which, when opened, proves to have another fish and an old boot and a wedding ring inside it. As in so many other things so also in meter: the origin is restless in the outcome.

(6) "Anapests and dactyls are legitimate substitutions in the iambic norm of English meter."

I agree with Robert Wallace's general point here—and indeed his analysis of the mischief Coleridge did with his note on "Christabel." I accept that anapests and dactyls are substitutions within the iambic norm and that trisyllabic substitution in general does not constitute a separate meter.

(7) **"We should drop the pyrrhic foot (⌣⌣) and accept in its place the double-iamb (⌣⌣//), as one of the six foot-terms necessary: iamb, trochee, anapest, dactyl, spondee, double-iamb."**

The pyrrhic foot was an odd term. Double-iamb is a better one. It suggests the strength and conviction which this particular measure acquires in certain contexts. John Crowe Ransom's reference to "the marriage of true minds" is a good example. There the double-iamb allows "minds" to remain strong enough to pick up the alliteration from "marriage" which is crucial in making a forceful, bright enjambment with a singing assonance, and a perfect caesura, which follows hard on it.

> Let me not to the marriage of true minds
> Admit impediments.

Jerome Beaty and William Matchett in *Poetry: From Statement to Meaning* make a note of four feet "that account for accentual poetry." They list these four as iamb, anapest, trochee, and dactyl. They also list four substitute feet. These are given as spondee, pyrrhic, cretic, and rocking foot. This seems to me to lose the importance of the double-iamb. I agree with Robert Wallace that giving it this name identifies its strength and importance. I also believe that strength entitles it to be part of the expanded list he suggests of six feet for scanning.

In Shakespeare's sonnet, as in other instances, the double-iamb at the end of the line creates a slight hesitation which levels out into a small but important musical delay. The dissonance of such a measure can acquire an unusual and definite emotional colour which is effective in making a mood which is just perceptibly off the note. In other words the double-iamb is an attention-seeking unit of scansion.

Take, for instance, this stanza from "Wessex Heights" by Thomas Hardy. The poem was written in 1896. It has the off-key brio of some of Hardy's defiantly local poems. Nevertheless, despite the long balladeering line, despite the attack and jingle of the stresses, there is something open-ended and hesitant about the ending of the stanza, an effect in which the double-iamb plays a decisive part:

There are some heights in Wessex, shaped as if by a kindly hand,
For thinking, dreaming, dying on, and at crises when I stand,
Say, on Ingpen Beacon eastward, or on Wylls-Neck westwardly,
I seem where I was before my birth, and after death may be.

(8) "Anapestic, trochaic, and dactylic meters do not exist in English."

It has been one of the most intense debates of the century, as to whether the normative base of meter is iambic. When Eliot qualified modernism as "not a revolt against form but against dead form," I have no doubt that this was part of what was in his mind. Arnold Stein in his essay on George Herbert's prosody speaks of the momentum and emphasis of poetry in these terms: "A movement forward that did not remember as it paused could neither repeat nor vary; to this extent every means of ordering movement forward depends on listening backward."

The forward movement of poetry in English is largely organized according to iambic principles. This seems clear although it is by no means uncontentious. Therefore it seems sensible, as Robert Wallace suggests, to take the iamb as the defining presence in the metrical structure of English poetry, and to consider trochaic and anapestic and dactylic variations as just that: variants but not meters. If there is to be a science of meter at all, if there is to be a codified series of propositions which continues to define and hand on the practice of meter, then it is essential that it clarifies its tenets and does not simply clutter them with possibilities and alternates. The anapestic and dactylic can certainly be submeters. But the metrical base remains iambic.

(9) "We should *never* use four degrees of speech stress for scanning."

Jespersen's system seems fussy and unnecessary. The making of codes and systems for scansion is difficult enough without adding to it an untried and untested type of measurement. Meter is not, as Jespersen has said, an exact science. But it is a customary language. It has been used and reused and has more or less stood the test of time, at least until this century. But Jespersen's system, by canvassing an alternative which may or may not be unworkable, raises the wider question of what metrical systems achieve by their existence and clarification.

When I was a young poet in Ireland—this happened twenty years ago more than it happens now—it was quite usual to be approached after a reading by someone whose comments were thinly disguised complaints. Whether they approved or disapproved of your own poetry, they wanted to talk about a more general sense of disaffection and disappointment in modern poetry. They didn't like its language. They couldn't understand its subject matter. But above all, and this came up over and over again, it no longer sounded like poetry.

Ireland is a country where poetry finds an engaged and opinionated constituency. And I learned to listen with real interest and respect to these members of that constituency. I did not regard them as reactionary or obscurantist. I could detect a feeling of pain and even a small grief in their remarks. Their demographic profile was of interest also. They tended not to be young; they were more rural than urban. The poetry they remembered was the poetry they had committed to memory: in small schoolrooms, in gas-lit parlours where a piano stood in the corner and a portrait of Robert Emmett hung on the wall. They looked to poetry to make emotional sense when they read it and musical sense when they heard it. That it no longer did, in their view, had caused them—in this confined but important sense—to be disenfranchised.

In the light of this symposium what they were saying—or more accurately implying—is of real interest. Essentially what they were complaining about was that modern poetry had broken the metrical contract they understood and accepted. And, of course, to a certain extent it had; and to a certain extent it sought to.

I raise this here because the idea of the metrical contract which readers feel they have understood and entered into is of vital importance. It has a bearing on the reading of meter. It has a crucial bearing on the interpretation of it. It is that metrical contract, held in the head and heart from as far back as childhood, which is unwritten by the attack and surprise of Marianne Moore's syllabics and then written afresh.

There has to be a metrical contract. There has to be a system of coding it and describing it. That system should be as clear and amenable to understanding as is possible. It should not become a series of ornamental mysteries which few can understand except those who devised them. Scansion should proceed by clear rules and with clear results. And the present system, with all its faults, seems the best.

(10) "The spondee is a good, and fairly frequent, foot in English."

I accept Robert Wallace's proposition about the spondee, but I would have to say it is a subjective matter. On this fringe of scansion, there can be differing interpretations and variations from reading to performance, and from reading to hearing. The reading of a spondee is not always easy. It is possible to mistake it for something else, even to read it as a double-iamb. I can see Robert Wallace's enthusiasm for reintegrating it in the codes and systems of meter. It has been his intention to make clear rules and stable ones. However, I do not expect that enthusiasm to reach the classroom or to accompany the poet's midnight oil. As a young poet, with quite a zest for metrical changes and games, I could understand iambic structure, and I enjoyed trochaic variation. But a spondee to this day fills me with unease and anxiety, and on these grounds alone, I might end up in agreement with Yvor Winters.

WORKS CITED

Bate, Walter Jackson. *John Keats.* Cambridge: Harvard University Press, 1963.

Beaty, Jerome and William Matchett. "Pattern and Form: Meter." *Poetry: From Statement to Meaning.* New York and Oxford: Oxford University Press, 1965.

Coleridge, Samuel Taylor. *Biographia Literaria.* Ed. James Engell and W. Jackson Bate. Princeton: Princeton University Press, 1983.

Jarrell, Randall. "The Humble Animal." *Poetry and the Age.* New York: Knopf, 1953.

Ransom, John Crowe. "The Strange Music of English Verse." *Kenyon Review* 18.3 (1956): 460-77.

Yeats, William Butler. "The Symbolism of Poetry." *Selected Criticism and Prose.* Ed. A. Norman Jeffares. New York: MacMillan, 1980.

METRICAL DIVERSITY

A DEFENSE OF THE NON-IAMBIC METERS

Annie Finch

When I began work on a critical study of the changing connotations of iambic pentameter in American poetry, I didn't expect
that I would devote so much attention to dactyls. In free verse from
Whitman, Stephen Crane, and Eliot through Anne Sexton and
Audre Lorde, I noticed the consistent presence of triple rhythms,
usually falling triple rhythms. Studying these poets' prosodic practice,
I found that for each of them the triple rhythm presented an aesthetic, emotional, and ideological alternative to iambic pentameter—
the standard meter for centuries by the mid-nineteenth century, and
the meter which Robert Wallace now proposes to normalize even
further.

Because I enjoyed the non-iambic passages I was analyzing, I
began to experiment with non-iambic meters in my own poetry. At

first I found it extraordinarily difficult to conceive of a poem of indeterminate shape in a non-iambic meter (though I had written some sapphics), much less to sustain the rhythm; the poems would transform themselves into iambic pentameter or die on the page. I spent several years in the process of training my poetic ear (which had originally been trained in free verse and then in iambs) in meters other than iambic. Recently, I was asked to produce a series of poems for use in celebrations of the seasons. The project required me to produce eight poems, conveying very different moods, for the same audience at six-week intervals. I wrote each poem in a different non-iambic meter: trochees, alternating dactylic and anapestic stanzas, dipodic meter, cretics, and so on. In writing these poems, I found myself challenged and inspired by my rhythmical raw material, and the supposedly arcane meters provided pleasure to the audience as well.

Robert Wallace might argue that, rather than bringing non-iambic meters into the discussion, I could just as easily refer to this series of poems as using a variety of "rhythms" overlaid on the basic iambic meter of English. The use of the single label "iambic" to include lines in other meters, however, may prove to erase what it assumes to include.[1] John Thompson establishes in *The Founding of English Meter* that the early history of the iambic pentameter in English was characterized by no substitution at all, clumsy substitution, and "forcing" the meter. As I discuss in *The Ghost of Meter,* only over the past two centuries have non-iambic meters become a barely accepted presence in English-language written poetry. Perhaps the early history of non-iambic meters in English is now developing analogously with the early history of the iambic pentameter. If so, Wallace's proposed relabeling would surely stunt that development.

If Wallace's labeling were widely adopted, non-iambic meters would be seen at the very least as less legitimate than they are now. They would be subcategories of the iambic meter rather than sub-categories of accentual-syllabic verse. Our ears already are losing touch with the most basic metrical distinctions, let alone subtler or more complex patterns such as the dipodic. The proposed step would be likely to numb our hearing even further. The loss would be especially sad at a time when the long hegemony of free verse has finally cleared our ears of the stifling and artificial associations that haunted metrical verse, particularly non-iambic verse, at the beginning of our century. The field is, in a sense, clearer for metrical verse, especially non-iambic verse, than it has been for many generations.

It is important to recognize that the iambic pentameter is not a neutral or essentially "natural" meter. Its connotations are distinct and culturally defined. Each of the non-iambic meters, also, has its own character, music, and history, however subtle or intermittent. As I notice throughout *The Ghost of Meter,* the dactylic rhythm carries connotations of irrationality, violent or beautiful. Trochaic poems, from Macbeth's witches to "The Tyger" to "The Raven" and even "Hiawatha," have a history of supernatural and exotic subject matter. If it is true that, as Martin Halpern posits, the non-iambic meters are a more direct legacy of Anglo-Saxon poetic rhythms than the iambic, it will be valuable to see what kind of energy a new connection with that legacy might bring into our metrical poetry and how the connotations of non-iambic meters will play out in the imagery, the mood, and the cultural role of future poems. Poets in English need the full support of the prosodic system for whatever kinds of music they want to write, whatever rhythm they want to use as a metrical base from which to modulate.

Wallace writes, "meter is useful for its predictability, which keeps reader or hearer tuned to even fine variations of rhythm. Actual lines are interesting for their approach to as well as their divergence from the iambic norm." In other words, meter differs from rhythm insofar as it constitutes a predictable base that can be rhythmically varied. When the audience, reading my poems aloud, was able to predict which syllables to stress in spite of variations in the non-iambic meter, prosodic agreements between poet and reader were certainly in evidence, albeit non-iambic ones. Wallace's proposed system would deny any rhythm other than the iambic the privilege of such predictability, consigning all non-iambic meters to an absurd limbo of perpetual substitution status.

I suspect that an all-iambic system would substitute a manufactured and arbitrary confusion for a confusion that has some basis in the human ear and in common sense. On the surface it may seem more complicated to keep the different meters. Some lines have rhythms that are half anapestic and half iambic, but whose metrical base we call one or the other depending on the poetic context. Occasionally there are poems whose meter we are unable to classify with certainty, except perhaps by the useful term "mixed meter" (once called "logaoedaic")—rising, falling, triple, or duple mixed meter, as the case may be. The prosodic situation is more complex than if all meters were called iambic, but our tools for understanding the rhythm of individual poems are also more complex, and potentially more flexible and sensitive. I use the adverb "potentially" here, however, because I find our prosody still unable adequately to acknowledge substitution and modulation in non-iambic meters.

Perhaps because of their roots in the rhythms of the oral verse tradition in English, non-iambic meters have been restricted to popular poetry for so long that their consignment there has become something of a self-fulfilling prophecy. It is no coincidence that the examples of poems I discuss in this piece are virtually all drawn from "low" poetry. The last time that non-iambic meters peered out into the world of high culture, during the late nineteenth century, the declamatory recitation style of such poets as Poe, Longfellow, and Tennyson gave them the reputation of being inherently artificial, particularly in contrast to the emerging free-verse aesthetic. Few if any poets in our own century have written non-iambic meters that are subtly modulated and meant to be read aloud with natural speech stress, according to our twentieth-century preference. That fact, however, does not necessarily mean it cannot be done. In closing off the possibilities for non-iambic meters, Robert Wallace's system would close doors that have barely been opened.

The main source of difficulty with the non-iambic meters is the assumption that they are not "natural" to English. This view appears to have originated in the nineteenth-century reactions to dactylic verse in English.[2] It has held strong from Yvor Winters's conviction that the "iambic movement . . . appears to be natural to the language" (91) through most contemporary accounts. I have of course been taught, repeatedly, in the words of a poet who instructed me in graduate school, that "English falls naturally into iambics." To my ear, this sentence has a distinct triple rhythm. I would scan it as dactyls, ending in a trochee as many dactylic lines do, with one secondary stress or "cretic" substitution in the first foot: "Énglish fálls | nátu̯rally̆ | ínto ῐ | ámbĭcs." I find this the simplest scansion and the one that best embodies the actual music of the line. I am well aware, however, that according to the most common system—whereby a line is accepted as innocent (i.e., iambic) until proven guilty (non-iambic)—the line should scan as an iambic pentameter with initial trochaic substitution and a falling ending, a reading I find jerky and decidedly "forced."

Is iambic meter the only natural meter? Though some contemporary poets believe that we no longer speak in iambic pentameter, others enjoy citing everyday examples of the meter to prove how ubiquitous and innate it really is.[3] One of my favorite such examples, Marilyn Hacker's "a glass of California chardonnay," was quoted at a recent conference. On the flight home, I began idly to wonder if the non-iambic meters could also be found easily in everyday speech. Only four or five minutes later, a flight attendant announced, "pléase retu̯rn | to̯ yŏur séats | ănd mắke súre | thăt yŏur séat | bèlts ăre fás | tĕned sĕcúre | ly̆(ῐ)." Robert Wallace writes that "the anapest is a good, and frequent, foot in English." Perhaps, along with dactyls and trochees, it forms a "natural" rhythm as well.

Certainly both anapestic and dactylic rhythms can be scanned away into elaborate versions of iambs, like the amphibrachic rhythm of Auden's "Where Are You Going." I see no advantage in such manipulations. The amphibrachic reading is more efficient, more delightfully stomach-churning, and ultimately more satisfying to my ear than the alternative scansion: "⁽⌣⁾Whére are | yŏu gŏíng, | sặid réadĕr | to̯ rídĕr. . . ." Even though these are not the tidiest amphibrachs, Auden, a poet who reportedly said that his ideal reader "keeps a look out for curious prosodic fauna like bacchics and choriambs," deserves better than to have them obscured by an ill-fitting anapestic scansion.[4] As for the monosyllabic feet, for the record I do sense an expressive purpose in each of them: unmediated finality in "re | turn," intense perception in "feel," suspense in "trees," and defiance in "will." Furthermore, I find Wallace's "false amphibrach" in line 10 ("dĭd yŏu sĕe | thăt shápe ĭn | thĕ twistĕd | trées") a true amphibrach; it stresses the "you" just as a horrified speaker would, to my ear, and, preceding the light stress on "see," the stress on "you" breaks and jerks the line quite effectively. At any rate, even if one chose to scan that foot as an anapest in an amphibrachic context, should Auden be denied the skill of his substitution simply because he is composing in amphibrachs? Would we call all of Wordsworth's initial trochaic substitutions actually "false iambs"?

Of the many questions yet to be answered about the nature of non-iambic meters, one of the most essential is the question of their hospitality to metrical substitution. The prosodist Martin Halpern formalized in 1962 the idea, now a truism, that iambic meter is different from all the other meters because it alone can absorb substitutions with varying degrees of stress. As Timothy Steele puts it, "trochaics and triple meters . . . haven't the suppleness and the capacity for fluid modulation that iambic measures have, nor do they tolerate the sorts of variations (e.g., inverted feet at line beginnings or after mid-line pauses) that the texture of iambic verse readily absorbs" (242). Steele gives as an example a line from Longfellow: "The blue heron, the Shuh-shuh-gah," and comments, "it is unlikely that we would emphasize the two definite articles . . . but that is what Longfellow wishes us to do, since he is writing in trochaic tetrameter" (242). This line of reasoning constitutes a tautological trap in which to catch non-iambic meters; because the meter is trochaic, we assume the pronunciation is meant to be unnatural; then we damn the trochaic meter for forcing unnatural pronunciations. According to this common conception, "substitutions" in a non-iambic meter do not substitute at all, but actually demand that we "force" the pronunciation of certain words to fit the meter. Non-iambic meters are held to be so overbearing that they can't allow word-stresses an independent and counterpointing rhythm.

To me, the idea that non-iambic meters can't be modulated through substitution is a prejudice analogous to the Renaissance scholar Gascoigne's belief—described by John Thompson in *The Founding of English Meter*—that the iambic meter in the line, "your meaning I understand by your eye," is faulty because it forces us to stress "der" (72). To cite a well-known example, Clement Moore's line "As dry leaves that before the wild hurricane fly" in *The Night Before Christmas* employs two expressive substitutions of the pattern unstress-stress-stress in the anapestic base. These beautiful changes can be accepted as substitutions, not explained away as "false anapests." Similarly, the line "the moon on the breast of the new-fallen snow" substitutes an iambic foot and a foot of the pattern stress-unstress-stress (it might be called a cretic) in the anapestic base. Isn't the counterpoint between speech and meter in such lines just as enjoyable as the counterpoint in iambic lines that employ substitution?

The distinctions between meters add immeasurably not only to accuracy in scanning individual poems, but also to the aesthetic pleasure the ear finds in metrical substitutions. The movement of metrical counterpoint, from which the beauty of accentual-syllabic prosody—in all meters—largely emerges, depends on the existence of distinct metrical norms that can play off of each other and stretch each other's limits, but never overtake each other completely. Metrically skillful poets play with the reader's perception of meter, testing and pushing it but never letting it lapse entirely, as when Shakespeare follows two lines with trochaic-spondaic substitutions with a strictly iambic one, in the very nick of time: "Let me not to the marriage of true minds | Admit impediments. Love is not love | Which alters when it alteration finds." The power of effective substitution arises not from rhythmical variation alone but from the dangerously close presence of a conflicting meter which would, if indulged too excessively, undermine the poem's actual meter. Wallace would forestall the danger of metrically ambiguous lines by making all feet scannable as iambs, but it is the fault of the poet, not of the prosodic system, if excessive or careless substitution causes the metrical undercurrent of a poem to be lost on a reader. The tension between conflicting meters, a source of beauty and excitement, would disappear in a monodimensional prosodic system with only one metrical base.

Wallace argues that since the various metrical feet are already interchangeable, we are already acting as if there is only one English meter. But metrical feet are not all equally interchangeable. Dactyls and trochees, for instance, can't be substituted into a line of iambs (except after a caesura or line-break) without ruining the meter. That is why the trained ear finds the line "Ode to | the West | Wind by | Percy | Bysshe Shel | ley," to use a hypothetical example from

Halle and Keyser, unrecognizable as iambic pentameter. But dactyls and trochees can easily be substituted, of course, in lines of falling meter. The kinds of substitutions the ear will accept in a line depend entirely on the line's metrical context. For this reason alone, it is necessary to preserve distinctions between meters.

The elaborate contortions of all-iambic scansions may be as damaging as the terminology that would downgrade all non-iambic meters to the status of "rhythms." Though I agree in preferring the term "anacrusis" to "acephalous" and its kin, when and if such a term is necessary, I take strong issue with the assumption that lines like "Come, and trip it as ye go"—particularly when they are the norm of the poem and not a variation in an iambic context—are iambic lines in disguise. As James McAuley puts it in *Versification* (in a passage I will quote in full because the book has been out of print for some time):

> The reluctance to treat as a trochaic line one that occurs in an iambic passage is abated if one reflects that the two disyllabic meters can and do cooperate easily together, just as the three trisyllabic ones do. It is just the fact that the line begins with an accented syllable that makes the difference; unless the line reimposes an iambic pattern by the characteristic /xx/, the trochaic scansion will prevail. The real proof that this is the sound way of looking at it comes from reading those tetrameter poems that intermingle iambic and trochaic lines frequently. The two metres combine together in a unified texture, but the alternation of an iambic and a trochaic option is quite evident and should not be belied by unnecessary metrical subterfuges. Milton's "L'Allegro" and "Il Penseroso" illustrate the truth of this; and so do Crashaw's alternations in "An Epitaph upon a Young Married Couple":
>
> > They, sweet /Turtles,/folded/ly/
> > In the/last knot/love could/ty./
> > And though/they ly/as they/were dead,/
> > Their Pil/low stone,/their sheetes/of lead/
> > (Pillow/hard, and/sheetes not/warm)/
> > Love made/the bed;/they'l take/no harm./
>
> Though such variation of metre is much less common with pentameters than it is with tetrameters, the same holds true: the

line is trochaic, tends to be felt as such, but fits into the iambic texture by reason of its disyllabic kinship, as once more, in Chaucer, the second of these lines referring to the Clerk:

> For hym/was le/vere have/at his bed/des head/
> Twenty/bokes/clad in/black or/reed./ (27)

Obviously the current hybrid system causes confusion. It is difficult to explain why a line which is "trochaic" in one context is "iambic with anacrusis" in another. I find McAuley's solution to the problem simpler than Wallace's, however. I would rather remark that trochaic lines do occur in iambic passages—an easily accepted explanation, according to my experience teaching prosody—than to argue that the students' ears are wrong and that a line with a distinct trochaic rhythm is actually iambic. The final catalexis necessary to scan lines such as "come and trip it as ye go" as trochaic rather than as beheaded iambs is the mirror-image of the extra-syllable ending (to use Wallace's new term) on an iambic line. In both cases, something is changed at the end of the line in order to modify the verse's texture and to facilitate the appropriately metrical beginning of the next line.

As for accentual poetry, which Fussell and others have defined as poetry whose lines consist of any number of unaccented syllables interspersed with a predictable number of accents, Robert Wallace does a convincing job of explaining many examples of such poetry as actually accentual-syllabic. Even if all such poetry is discounted, however (and I am still not convinced that there is not some genuinely accentual poetry according to that definition), there is another kind of poetry which can conveniently and accurately be scanned as accentual. Unless one believes that accentual-syllabic meter is restricted to iambs, the term "accentual meter" efficiently describes those poems which unite lines in conflicting accentual-syllabic meters, such as the following passage from Robert Louis Stevenson's "From a Railway Carriage":

> And charging along like troops in a battle,
> All through the meadows the horses and cattle:
> All of the sights of the hill and the plain
> Fly as thick as driving rain;

And ever again, in the wink of an eye,
Painted stations whistle by.

The first and fifth lines quoted are anapestic, the second and third dactylic, the fourth and sixth trochaic. All have four stresses. A poem combining two duple feet could be scanned as "mixed duple meter," one with two triple feet as "mixed triple meter," one with two rising feet as "mixed rising meter," and so on; but this passage combines three different meters that could not *by definition* coexist in any one accentual-syllabic meter. Nonetheless, the ear can make sense of the pattern and predict the number of stresses in each line, since the poem's audible rhythm draws on the power of stress to override syllable-count in the heavily accentual oral tradition. Such a passage, lines of which can be predicted to carry metrically contradictory audible stresses, is most simply and accurately scanned as accentual meter.

The essential feature of such accentual poetry is that it combines lines and/or feet that would not be able to coexist in one of the regular accentual-syllabic meters. A primarily iambic accentual poem, for instance, can include metrical variations, such as dactylic or trochaic feet not preceded by a caesura or line-break, that would render an iambic poem unmetrical. These substitutions, incidentally, should be distinguished from the simple trisyllabic substitution of anapests in iambic lines or dactyls in trochaic lines, which have been acceptable metrical variations since the mid-nineteenth century. The general effect of accentual meter to my ear is one of propelled movement, distinctly different from the controlled modulation of a single clearly established rhythm that characterizes an accentual-syllabic poem. Unless one believes that different metrical feet can be substituted anywhere at will without hurting the rhythm of an accentual-syllabic poem, accentual meter is a necessary possibility in our prosody.

It is sometimes difficult to determine the number of accents in isolated lines of accentual poetry, because their number of accents depends in part on the context of other lines in the poem. This fact in no way undermines the integrity of accentual scansion. In the rhymes and nursery songs of accentual tradition, it is common to "favor the meter" based on context: "There wére three coóks of Cólebroók/and théy fell oút with oúr coók/and áll was fór a púdding he toók." "Óh dear óh, my cáke is all doúgh/and hów to make it bétter I dó not knów." Part of the special charm of such poems is that they encourage (or allow) the reader or speaker to stress words differently than would be done in normal speech. There is no reason that a line of accentual poetry should be deemed unscannable simply because its scansion is affected by that of the other lines in the poem.

Wallace's reductive system may be useful for teaching prosody to beginning readers of poetry, but aspiring poets and creative writing students need to learn the full range of English prosodic possibilities. They will gain fluency and resourcefulness as writers, flexibility and sophistication as readers, from learning to hear the many different metrical patterns in English and the rhythmical variations on those patterns. My own prosody students—mostly beginning undergraduate poets—hear anapestic, dactylic, and trochaic rhythms as different from the iambic. If I were to try to persuade them that "Evangeline"—or, for that matter, a popular triple-meter rap tune—has an iambic base, I would convince them once and for all that prosody as a discipline is either deaf or terminally arcane. Exposing beginning poets to a spectrum of metrical options helps them to become more aware of their own inclinations toward certain rhythms, including but not limited to the iambic. By maintaining that only iambs can form a metrical base for substitution, Wallace's system would deny those students who might enjoy other meters the chance to develop skill in modulating them.

My current image of English prosody is a compass, with the duple and triple, rising and falling, rhythms constituting four primary compass points: trochaic, anapestic, iambic, dactylic. Interspersed among these fall the other meters and combinations of meters, accentual-syllabic and accentual, many possible ideals in relation to which poets and readers can situate the shifting and relative rhythms of actual poems. Rather than abandoning the non-iambic directions of the metrical compass, we can allow time for further experimentation to develop and refine these less-used meters through poetry and prosodic theory. Time may prove the falling and triple rhythms in written English to be sophisticated metrical idioms in their own right, worthy counterparts to the rising duple rhythm with which we are already so familiar.

Contemporary poetry has much to gain by investigating the very prosodic knowledge that Robert Wallace's proposal suggests we jettison. As the contributors to and readers of this book know, poetry is an art as difficult and complex as any other. Prosody's goal is not to become an efficient, easy-to-learn system at all costs, but to nurture and inspire the complex strategies of poetic music. To many of us, starved by decades of flat free verse and monodimensional iambic pentameter, the more complex those strategies, the better for the integrity and beauty of our art at this literary moment.

∽

[Discussion of Wallace's proposals not covered in my essay above.]

(1) **"Instead of the term 'feminine ending,' we should say simply extra-syllable ending, which may be abbreviated as e-s ending."**

Changing the term "feminine ending" is a good idea. I would suggest the term "falling ending" rather than "e-s ending," for several reasons: (a) It is a more graceful and convenient term than "extra-syllable ending" and will not need to be abbreviated into initials. (b) The term "falling ending," consisting of two words in falling rhythm, has the virtue of embodying its own meaning. (c) The accompanying term "falling rhyme" is more versatile than "extra-syllable rhyme," since it is a useful description in cases where the final syllable is not "extra" at all (trochaic poems, for example).

(3) **"Quantities are not a basis for meter in English."**

Quantities are not a basis for meter in English, and the special cases can always be considered as such.

(4) "Syllabics is not a meter in English."

Meter is aural in nature, and meter in English (including accentual meter) counts the most conspicuous feature in English-language poetry and in the English language, which is accent. Some poets have assured me that they do hear subtle aural patterns in their own and others' syllabic poetry, but this probably occurs because certain configurations of accents are more likely to repeat when the number of syllables is held constant. I accept syllabics as a fine and useful form, a regular pattern that can shape a poem through structural repetition, but I see no reason to call it a meter.

(5) "In modern English, accentual meter does not exist."

Since the caesura and alliterating stressed syllables are integral to the meter of Old English poetry, I have no problem with the term "alliterative meter." It should not be used interchangeably with "accentual meter," which does exist, which I define in my long essay above.

(6) "Anapests and dactyls are legitimate substitutions in the iambic norm of English meter."

Only by allowing random dactylic or trochaic substitutions in iambic lines can one posit iambs as a true "norm." In fact, however, misplaced dactylic or trochaic substitution renders a line of iambic pentameter unmetrical and ruins it to the educated reader's ear. Halle and Keyser's example of a nonmetrical decasyllablic phrase, "Óde tŏ | thĕ Wést | Wínd bў | Pércў | Býsshe Shél | lĕў," with its trochees in the third and fourth feet, illustrates this point.

As Halle and Keyser explain, dactyls and trochees occur in only three places in lines of iambic pentameter: line initially; after a major syntactic break (or caesura); and after a stressed syllable (187). If these restrictions were thrown over, *any* grouping at all of ten to fifteen syllables would scan as iambic pentameter. The metrical distinction between such pairs of decasyllables as "Th'expense of spirit in a waste of shame" and "English falls naturally into iambics" would then be inaudible to our prosodic system.

(7) **"We should drop the pyrrhic foot ($\cup\cup$) and accept in its place the double-iamb ($\cup\cup//$), as one of the six foot-terms necessary: iamb, trochee, anapest, dactyl, spondee, double-iamb."**

No, we should not drop the pyrrhic foot and recognize in its place only the double-iamb. Many pyrrhics are followed by a spondee, but not all of them. This maneuver would needlessly render our scansion system deaf, for instance, to the sharp and expressive increase in accent apparent in the fourth word of Shakespeare's, "Ĭt ĭs | thĕ stár | tŏ év' | rў wán | dĕrĭng bárk." The first foot here is not a trochee; to scan it as such would obscure the earnest, hopeful, thwarted stretch of the second syllable towards a stress, and the consequent increase in energy that finally accompanies the awaited stress on "star." Only the pyrrhic-iamb combination could embody this dynamic.

(9) **"We should *never* use four degrees of speech stress for scanning."**

I agree that the four-level system renders essential distinctions meaningless. But I find great use for the secondary stress, which I mark as a reverse accent. It is not only useful in making fine distinctions in scansion, but also in reaching consensus or compromise between different interpretations in the classroom. (I prefer to reserve parentheses for hypermetrical unstressed syllables at the end of an iambic line or the beginning of a trochaic or dactylic line.)

(10) **"The spondee is a good, and fairly frequent, foot in English."**

My favorite remark on the spondee comes from Stanford linguist Paul Kiparsky: "The question is purely terminological: do we want spondee to refer to a foot with two stresses? or with two equal stresses?"[5] I am happy to agree with Robert Wallace that the spondee refers to two stresses, not necessarily equal, and to accept it as "a good, and fairly frequent, foot in English." The belief that spondees don't exist in English, by the way, predates Jespersen by some time, since it dates back at least to Southey's 1821 preface to *A Vision of Judgement.*

As one of those on the literary side who happen to find Halle and Keyser useful, I would like to put in a word in defense of their essay on "The Iambic Pentameter." Halle and Keyser, very responsibly, introduce the two lines quoted by Wallace in order to demonstrate that their system of generating metrical lines, like any system, should not be taken to undue extremes. To print these quotes out of context in an attempt to discredit their theory is to do their essay an injustice.

The "willows" line is a purposefully ridiculous example which Halle and Keyser have concocted in order to demonstrate the limits of their own theory by reminding us that poets have a sense of metrical taste that cannot fully be accounted for by any system. Halle and Keyser quote Keats's line "How many bards gild the lapses of time" not to give us an example of a bad line but to call attention to a powerful and expressive break in the anticipated metrical pattern on Keats's part. No one would dispute that the line has a fine rhythm, but it is obviously closer to a tetrameter than to an iambic pentameter. By drawing fine and accurate distinctions between "metrical" and "unmetrical" (iambic pentameter and non-iambic pentameter) decasyllabics, Halle and Keyser acknowledge the parameters of Keats's normal practice and are able to recognize his lapse for what it is, a self-reflexive break from that normal practice. Their principles of scansion lead us to appreciate the full impact of this metrical anomaly within the poem's literary as well as prosodic context. We should expect no less a degree of accuracy and sensitivity from our prosodic system.

NOTES

1. A useful analogy might be the English language's traditional use of the masculine pronoun to refer to females, which has indeed been proven to erase what it assumes to include in many cases.

2. I discuss these reactions at some length in *The Ghost of Meter*.

3. Galway Kinnell, during a workshop held at the Poetry Society of America in 1980, told me that people no longer speak iambic pentameter.

4. Quoted in Fussell, page 3. Auden also once remarked to William Packard that "the one thing I am vain about is my knowledge of meters" ("Craft Interview," 9).

5. Paul Kiparsky, unpublished comment on draft of *The Ghost of Meter,* 1990.

WORKS CITED

Auden, W. H. "Craft Interview With W. H. Auden." *The Craft of Poetry: Interviews from the New York Quarterly*. Ed. William Packard. New York: Doubleday, 1974.

Finch, Annie. *The Ghost of Meter: Culture and Prosody in American Free Verse.* Ann Arbor: University of Michigan Press, 1993.

Fussell, Paul. *Poetic Meter and Poetic Form*. New York: Random House, 1965.

Halle, Morris, and Samuel J. Keyser. "The Iambic Pentameter." *The Structure of Verse: Modern Essays on Prosody*. Ed. Harvey Gross. New York: Ecco Press, 1979.

Halpern, Martin. "On the Two Chief Metrical Modes in English." *PMLA* 77.3 (1962): 177–86.

McAuley, James. *Versification: A Short Introduction*. Detroit: Michigan State University Press, 1966.

Southey, Robert. Preface. *A Vision of Judgement*. 1821. Vol. 10 of *The Poetical Works of Robert Southey*. London: Longman, Orme, Brown, Greer, and Longmans, 1838. 422–36. 10 vols.

Steele, Timothy. "Staunch Meter, Great Song." *Meter in English: A Critical Engagement*. Ed. David Baker. Fayetteville: University of Arkansas Press, 1996.

Thompson, John. *The Founding of English Meter*. New York: Columbia University Press, 1961.

Winters, Yvor. "The Audible Reading of Poetry." *The Function of Criticism*. Denver: Alan Swallow, 1957.

METER-MAKING
ARGUMENTS

Dana Gioia

Literary etiquette demands that in mixed company poets pretend prosody is a dull subject. What genuine artist could possibly take those dusty Greek terms and mechanistic scansions seriously? Only pedants reduce art to arithmetic. Among their own kind, however, poets find prosody anything but boring. I have watched poets argue intemperately over a detail of scansion and witnessed others exhaust an evening disputing theories of versification. Free-verse poets display surprisingly little immunity from these fevers; no one, after all, likes to debate religion more than an atheist. Has any recent topic raised tempers in the poetry world so high as the revival of rhyme and meter?

The passions that rage over versification puzzle and even perhaps embarrass the common reader. Poets should be noble creatures of intuition, not car mechanics trading greasy-fisted blows over how to rebuild an engine. But isn't a religious fervor for technique the deepest difference between the artist and the poseur? Artists know, as Gustave Flaubert observed, that "God is in the details." Anyone who finds the poet's obsession with prosody mysterious should listen to opera singers talk about techniques of vocal production. These conversations, too, are remarkable for their passionate concern with detail. Singers understand that the physical production of sound is not a theoretical issue: it is the raw material of their art. Every detail of technique may open or close some expressive possibility. Superb technique may not create a great singer, but one cannot sustain a career without it, and bad technique can incontestably ruin a voice. Words are the poet's only material, and prosody determines how they are arranged into poems. If vocal technique affects every note a singer produces, prosody shapes—consciously or intuitively—every line a poet writes.

I confess that I am one of those disputatious poets with a shameful passion for prosody. My mania takes many forms; the least annoying is book collecting. Over the past quarter century I have slowly acquired nearly every study of English versification published since 1900. Building my reference library was a bibliophile's dream—each volume proved both hard to locate and inexpensive to buy. I could reminisce about the dusty corner where I first spied some obscure monograph or recount a bizarre theory from my library's most lunatic treatise, but the relevant fact is something more depressingly concrete: my entire collection occupies only two shelves on my bookcase. A similar accumulation of modern books and pamphlets on a single poet like Emily Dickinson or T. S. Eliot, might easily fill the entire wall. Prosody has not been a popular subject lately, although our age has left almost every principle of versification tantalizingly open to question.

Robert Wallace's "Meter in English" is, therefore, a welcome addition to contemporary prosody. He does not merely repackage traditional ideas but offers a radical revision of metrical theory. I find as much to debate as endorse in Wallace's revisionist system, and yet his treatise impresses me as a significant contribution to the field. Iconoclastic, lucid, and informed, "Meter in English" is the work of a practicing poet engaged with the literary tradition. He writes with the insider's view of the artist as well as the historical perspective of a scholar. He consistently focuses on real issues of scansion and description. Wallace's piece belongs to an encouraging recent trend—

along with other works by Annie Finch, John Hollander, Robert McDowell, Timothy Steele, Lewis Turco, and Miller Williams—of poets recapturing the critical discourse about versification. Poets bring special insights to discussions of prosody. They understand that versification is not merely a retrospective discipline but one that influences how new poetry comes to be written.

Now let me respond to each of Wallace's propositions.

(1) "Instead of the term 'feminine ending,' we should say simply extra-syllable ending."

Wallace's new term, "extra-syllable ending," is clear and precise, but I favor keeping the traditional term unless there is a compelling reason for revision. Contemporary sensitivity to gender issues makes some people reflexively uncomfortable with prosodic terms like *masculine* and *feminine*, but I suspect that sensitivity over these innocent terms borrowed from Romance philology will prove short-lived. (Romance language nouns divide by gender, a common feature of most Indo-European languages other than English.) Like any specialized subject, prosody possesses a technical vocabulary, most of which like *dactyl, caesura,* and *feminine ending* originate in foreign literary traditions. One of Wallace's stated objectives is to simplify the theory of English prosody. While his suggestion here is unobjectionable, it seems simpler to maintain the status quo since the proposed change offers no conspicuous advantage.

(2) "For an omitted first syllable of a line, we should use the term anacrusis."

This suggestion seems even less compelling than the first. Why change the conventional meaning of *anacrusis* when a concrete English term, *headless,* and an equivalent Greek term, *acephalous,* already exist? I would not worry about the pejorative connotations of *headless* or the overstatement of *acephalous.* Moreover, in traditional usage *anacrusis* means just the opposite of Wallace's intended use; it describes the *addition* of a syllable at the beginning of the line. The current terminology remains preferable.

(3) "Quantities are not a basis for meter in English."

Wallace is right in making this categorical judgment. Quantity is not a reliable basis for English meter. The prosody of any language grows out of the immediately apprehensible features of its physical sound. Scansion makes metrical schemes appear abstract and intellectual—language rarefied to the level of mathematics—but scansion is not meter, only one method of describing it. Meter itself is sensory and immediate. An auditor must intuitively recognize a meter as a regular physical rhythm; otherwise, the metrical system is ineffective.

Since languages differ in the ways they organize the sounds the human body can produce, they also exploit different acoustic elements in their prosody. T'ang poets, for example, used contrasting tone patterns in shaping their lines because native Chinese speakers naturally apprehend that essential feature of the language. Anglo-Saxon poets used accentual stress patterns their audience could hear. The Greeks and Romans apparently heard the temporal duration of syllables as an overt feature of their speech. Grammarians standardized this element into a codified system of quantities, and poets reinforced it by artistic convention. Even if quantity began in ancient literature as an imprecise linguistic feature, the classical tradition soon transformed it into a universally recognized system. When Roman students learned a Latin word, they also learned its quantities just as modern students of English learn the accents of a word as part of its pronunciation.

Such a system has never existed in English, despite the effort of many capable theorists and poets, because quantity is not a sonic feature we easily hear. A poet can contrive quantities for English words, as Robert Bridges and others did, but the feature remains an abstraction. Another poet might assign different quantities to many words. One may learn intellectually to construe such verse on the page, but one cannot hear it unambiguously when the poem is read aloud. One occasionally finds a passage in a poet like Thomas Campion where quantity speaks effectively, but these successes remain rare. Quantity is not a workable structural principle in organizing English verse but only a secondary musical resource (like tempo, pitch, and timbre) that helps shape the local effects of a poem.

(4) "Syllabics is not a meter in English."

Wallace's observations on syllabic verse are essential reading for students of prosody, but his boldly revisionist dictum banishing syllabics to the outer darkness needs some qualification. Meter merely means a measure. Any linguistic feature that both the writer and reader can accurately recognize and count can serve as the basis of a legitimate meter. One can establish meters by counting stresses, syllables, words, visual line lengths, and numerous other items. (The problem with quantities is not counting but recognizing them: native speakers of English cannot consistently and accurately apprehend them; if identifiable, they could be counted.) Syllable count is easy to recognize in English. Students learn it as Romans once learned quantities. Our dictionaries illustrate the syllabification of a word as a standard part of its pronunciation. Syllable count is, therefore, an available English meter, and fine poems by Marianne Moore, W.H. Auden, Dylan Thomas, Donald Justice, Thom Gunn, and others demonstrate the meter's viability.

What Wallace's analysis really suggests is something more specific—namely, that syllabics are not an *auditory* meter in English. As he himself observes, "we do not *hear* the count of syllables." A syllabic pattern of any complexity is impossible to follow by the ear alone, and the intricate syllabic stanza patterns devised by Moore and Thomas lie beyond the furthest potential of human hearing. Surely it is significant that so many of the best syllabic poems in English are rhymed; how else can an auditor recognize the line endings? In a vowel-centered language like French, an audience can accurately hear the syllabic length of a line. It is worth noting, however, that even the French have traditionally relied on rhyme to underscore their line endings; no other European language has traditionally considered end rhyme so indispensable. In English syllabic verse, end rhyme is usually the only sonic element one can consistently hear.

Wallace later claims that "syllabics is a kind of free verse." While this statement is wrong in the narrow sense, its deeper implications are correct. Syllabics cannot be strictly considered free verse because they are composed according to a regular pattern. In practice, however, syllabic poems usually sound unmetered. Like much free verse, the formal principle of syllabic verse is visual not auditory. A reader usually recognizes the syllabic pattern of a poem only by seeing it on the page. Syllabic meters can effectively provide a poem (or stanza) with visual shape, but they give it no apprehensible auditory structure.

Finally, speaking as a poet, I must admit that I consider syllabics to be as much a compositional technique as a meter. Adapting a strict syllable count for each line assists the author in shaping a poem, but the metrical system provides little sensory pleasure for the audience—unless the author contrives an elaborate visual form on the page. (Of course, other elements like rhyme or assonance may provide acoustic pleasure—as in free verse.) What the reader gets is the assurance (if the syllable count is noted) that the author took trouble to shape each line.

(5) "In modern English, accentual meter does not exist."

Wallace is hopelessly wrong in asserting that accentual meter does not exist in contemporary English, but his analysis of the subject is nonetheless illuminating. By skeptically examining statements and scansions by Paul Fussell, Samuel Taylor Coleridge, and Harvey Gross, he correctly points out the vagueness and inconsistency of most critical discussions of accentual meter. No metrical system has been so poorly explained in prosodic literature. The case for the existence of accentual meter, however, does not rest on the performance of prosodists, but on the actual practice of poets, and even a quick survey of English verse reveals many poems that can only be scanned satisfactorily as accentual.

While prosodists have struggled with accentual meter, audiences immediately hear the organizing principle. They don't worry about the syllable count (which Wallace himself notes, they cannot hear independently of the stresses anyway); they just count the beats.

Anyone who doubts the existence of accentual meter should attend a rap concert. Or, if that excursion is too much trouble, they might try reading nursery rhymes aloud to a child who has not yet learned to read. Every child knows how to perform the stress pattern of the following poem whose lineation defies the rules of any accentual-syllabic system.

<pre>
   /   /   /   /
Star light, ‖ star bright,
   /   /   /   /
First star ‖ I see tonight.
   /   /   /   /
I wish I may, ‖ I wish I might
   /   /   /   /
Have the wish ‖ I wish tonight.
</pre>

One might, of course, contrive some tortuously complicated theory of iambic substitutions and headless lines to explain the meter of this famous rhyme, but the real system is utterly simple—four beats per line with an audible medial pause, just like Anglo-Saxon, just like rap. Why complicate the obvious?

One reason why accentual verse has fared so badly in critical literature is that most prosodists habitually try to make sense of it in terms of metrical feet. Trained in the quantitative systems of classical Greek and Latin as well as the dominant accentual-syllabic system of English poetry, they naturally consider the foot as the basic analytical unit of prosody. Wallace repeats this mistake by trying to force-fit accentual verse into a series of loosely iambic feet. The problem, however, is that the concept of a foot is meaningless in accentual verse. What relevance do foot divisions have when their identity constantly shifts into unpredictable entities? Metrical feet can be applied *post-factum* as an analytical device, but they do not reveal the generative principle of an accentual composition. The basic unit of accentual verse is the line. No matter how the syllable count shifts, the accentual line will have a constant number of strong stresses. To divide an accentual line into feet is mostly an exercise in futility—like analyzing Shakespeare's blank verse for quantities; one may do so, but the operation will not reveal the true governing structure.

The number and arrangement of syllables that occur in an accentual line are inconsequential to the meter (though they do, of course, affect the rhythm). Flexibility is indeed a chief virtue of this system. Anglo-Saxon lines can vary from eight to twenty-one syllables. Some rap lyrics and Mother Goose rhymes display similar syllabic range. What determines the line's length, however, is only the number of *strong* stresses. The word *strong* is a necessary qualifier here because secondary stresses are not counted. In fact, the chief technical challenge of writing accentual verse is arranging secondary stresses so that they do not make the metrical stresses ambiguous. Anglo-Saxon poets solved this problem by alliterating most of the strong stresses. Modern poets have adopted a variety of strategies—often by keeping the syntax simple and the line lengths short as in the great accentual trimeter poems of Yeats and Auden.

The difference between strong and secondary stress has, incidentally, not been lost on poets working in the accentual-syllabic tradition. That distinction is the basis of dipodic verse—another metrical system poorly explained and skimpily documented in prosodic literature. Dipodic verse sets up three levels of accent—strong stress, secondary stress, and no stress. (It is crucial, however, to note that although there are three levels of stress, syllables are arranged only in binary combinations of stressed and unstressed.) Here are some famous dipodic lines of Rudyard Kipling:

$$- \cup \; \acute{\angle} \cup \; | - \cup \; \acute{\angle} \; \cup \; | - \cup \; \acute{\angle} \cup \; | - \cup \; \acute{\angle}$$
To the legions of the lost ones, to the cohort of the damned,
$$- \cup \; \acute{\angle} \cup \; | - \cup \; \acute{\angle} \cup \; | - \cup \acute{\angle}$$
To my brethren in their sorrows overseas

These lines can be scanned either as trochees or—more accurately—as dipodic trochees in which the poet alternates feet beginning with secondary stresses with those starting with strong stresses. The poet is in effect, creating a double-foot of four syllables ($\cup \cup \acute{\angle} \cup$) with the third syllable receiving the heaviest beat. Each fifteen syllable line, for example, has four strong stresses, four secondary stresses, and seven unstressed syllables.

Once one understands the principles of dipodic verse, one finds the system throughout English verse, especially in Victorian poets like Robert Browning, George Meredith, and A. E. Housman. One also sees it frequently in song lyrics like "Waltzing Matilda" or W. S. Gilbert's "I Am the Very Model of a Modern Major General." Prosodists may grumble about the unnecessary complexity of the dipodic system, but any musician would recognize it as the conventional means of metrical organization in any measure longer than three beats. The most-widely used time measure in Western music is 4/4 time, which arranges the four-beat unit into two binary pairs—one with a strong stress, the other with a secondary stress— ONE, two, THREE, four. (This metric is so frequent it is called common time or common measure.) Every English poet for centuries has heard this musical meter from infancy on. Is it any wonder it entered poetry?

I make this digression on dipodic meter to point out that not only is there a distinction in English verse between stress and strong stress, but that exploiting the distinction has become the organizing principle of at least one variety of accentual-syllabic verse. I also mention dipodics to emphasize the importance of looking to music for both the conceptual framework to analyze English meter as well as the experiential framework to apprehend it. Metrical systems are not only organizational schemes; they are performative instructions. They both tell a reader or auditor how to hear a poem, and they guide a reciter in speaking a poem aloud. Any system that makes those instructions difficult to decipher has significant limitations for both the artist and audience, and accentual verse has exactly such limitations.

The practical issue of controlling secondary stresses in relation to the metrical scheme is not a trivial one for a poet. Metrical ambiguity can confuse a reader and upset an author's control of the rhythm. These issues beset all poets who work in stress meter. One finds such problems even in *Mother Goose's Melodies* (1765). The first three lines of the following nursery rhyme bounce along with two strong stresses each, but the final line seems awkwardly ambiguous. The only way to say it satisfactorily in the meter is to ignore the possibility of a secondary stress on *one* or *by* and to punch *wear* and *side* with unnatural zeal.

If wishes were horses
Beggars would ride;
If turnips were watches
I would wear one by my side.

Such ambiguity does not necessarily exist when the verses are spoken. The reciter provides the stresses—correctly or not—and the auditor hears, in effect, a scansion of the line. Most reciters will crudely stylize the language to illustrate the base meter; that is, after all, the only way that the line *sounds* right. Seeing the text however, one cannot escape its inherent metrical ambiguity. Accentual verse's inherent inability to guide a reader through rhythmically complicated passages limits its utility for many poets.

To my recollection, I have never seen a critic make the crucial observation that accentual meters seem generally the most common prosody for popular poetry while accentual-syllabics are almost inevitably the choice for high-art poetry. This distinction might be phrased even more sharply by saying that accentual meter is the preferred form for popular *spoken* verse whereas accentual-syllabic meters dominate in *written* literary poetry. Popular verse forms like nursery rhymes, limericks, comic doggerel, cowboy poetry, and rap, all of which are primarily heard rather than read, tend to favor the simplicity of accentual systems. Meanwhile accentual-syllabic verse dominates canonic literary poetry, though poets like Hardy, Auden, or MacNeice wishing to strike a demotic tone often return to the simpler system. It is obvious why English-language poets have generally preferred accentual-syllabic meters to pure stress systems. The tighter framework of accentual-syllabic meters give an author better control over most aspects of language; properly used, it incorporates secondary stresses unambiguously; and it allows a wider range of rhythmic effects. For literary poems that invite close and repeated textual scrutiny, the advantages of accentual syllabic meters became quickly apparent.

There is no doubt that individual lines of accentual verse will often fall into accentual-syllabic measures. After all, strictly speaking, accentual-syllabic verse is merely a subset of the accentual system. Scansion, however, should identify the system that accounts for the entire poem rather than merely a few individual lines. The last two lines of the following poem are iambic, but that isolated scansion does not account for the measure of the entire passage, which is, once again, the four beat accentual line that English has favored from the *Beowulf* bard to the Beastie Boys.

> /　　/　　∪　/ ∪　　/
> Tom, Tom, the piper's son.
> /　∪　/　∪　∪　/　∪　/
> Stole a pig and away did run;
> ∪　/　∪　/　∪　　/　∪　/
> The pig was eat, and Tom was beat,
> ∪　/ ∪　　/∪　/　∪　　/
> Till he run crying down the street.

In science the best theory is the one that provides the simplest explanation of past data and offers the most reliable predictions of future data. The application of a metrical system should explain how a particular poem (or set of poems) works, and, given part of a poem, it should reliably predict how the rest of that poem will operate metrically. Simplicity and reliability are virtues conspicuously absent from Wallace's reclassification of accentual verse into the accentual-syllabic category. If one examines a representative poem from his list, Auden's "September 1, 1939," one sees the problems with Wallace's system. Here is the poem's most famous stanza with the strong stresses scanned and the syllable count indicated in parentheses at the end of each line:

> /　∪　/　∪∪　/
> All I have is a voice.　　　　　(6)
> ∪　∪　/　∪　/　∪　/
> To undo the folded lie,　　　　(7)
> ∪　∪　/　∪　/　∪∪　　/
> The romantic lie in the brain　　(8)
> ∪　∪　/　∪∪　　/　∪　∪　　/
> Of the sensual man-in-the-street　(9)
> ∪　∪　/　∪　∪　/∪/
> And the lie of Authority　　　　(8)
> ∪　　/　∪　　/　∪　　/
> Whose buildings grope the sky:　(6)

˘ ˘ / ˘ / ˘ ˘ /
There is no such thing as the state   (8)

˘ / ˘ ˘/ ˘/
And no one exists alone;   (7)

/ ˘ ˘ / ˘ /
Hunger allows no choice   (6)

˘ ˘ /˘˘ / ˘ ˘ /
To the citizens or the police;   (9)

˘ ˘ / ˘ ˘/ ˘ ˘ /
We must love one another or die.   (9)

If one tries to scan this passage as iambic trimeter, one is faced with a significant problem. Only one line in eleven is altogether regular! Even if we accept the inverted first foot of line 8 as a normal variation for iambic trimeter, we still have only 18 percent of the stanza following the base meter. The syllable count also provides no indication that the passage is regularly accentual-syllabic. Auden's lines range unpredictably from six to nine syllables each. On close scrutiny almost every line differs from the one before and after in its arrangement of stressed and unstressed syllables. Exception, therefore, becomes the main rule. No metrical system operates this loosely. An accentual-syllabic scansion of "September 1, 1939" is neither simple nor predictive. If, however, one scans the passage as accentual meter, every line is absolutely regular with three strong stresses and a rhyme scheme that reinforces the final stress in each case. Meters rarely get simpler than this one.

Wallace states he wants to simplify the theory of English meter. In some cases he achieves this goal, but not here. His revisionist account of accentual verse substitutes a complicated and unreliable system for a straight-forward one. "I don't see the advantage of having two different systems for describing the same thing," he comments wisely. Neither do I. Let us keep the simpler and more reliable one—accentual meter.

(6) "Anapests and dactyls are legitimate substitutions in the iambic norm of English meter."

Yes and no—but mostly no. Anapestic substitution does

work in iambic verse, though historically the overwhelming number of *soi disant* triple feet involve the elision of open vowels, variations in regional pronunciation, compressed diphthongs, and other common speech contractions that the poets presumably scanned as strictly metrical. Once one makes those allowances, even Shakespeare's late blank verse becomes extremely regular. Nonetheless anapestic substitution does occur in our poetry, especially in modern authors like Frost. Wallace's zeal to scan all of English verse as some variant of iambic, however, leads him to ignore the unavoidable, defining issue—how much variation can a metrical scheme support before the norm is lost, and the poem becomes free verse?

Wallace's system is too vague to be of much practical use—for either the poet or the prosodist. His definition of iambic meter is so permissive that it provides, for example, no dividing line between free and formal verse. Surely, not every poem with occasional iambic feet is iambic. Much free verse is haunted, as Eliot noted, by "the ghost of some simple metre." In much of Wallace Stevens's later work, for example, the blank verse scheme becomes so loose that the poem relaxes into *vers libre*. We hear echoes of pentameter, but the poem is no longer truly metrical because no predictive norm now shapes the line lengths. The musical effect of these poems differs significantly from Stevens's regular blank verse. What is gained by lumping both methods together as iambic? Why not recognize the unique qualities of each procedure? Wallace would be better off lobbying for reinstatement of the term *vers libre* as a variety of free verse that consciously echoes a familiar metrical norm. Prosodic analysis should illuminate the tangible differences between different systems of rhythmic organization, not blur them. Once too many anapests are added to an "iambic" poem, the overall measure changes into something else—*vers libre*, anapestic verse, or accentual verse, depending on the arrangement.

Dactyls are more troublesome, though open admission of them into iambic verse is necessary for Wallace's declaration that accentual verse does not exist. Having scanned tens of thousands of lines of iambic poetry, I cannot recall a single passage in which dactyls are prominent—unless Wallace means the inverted first foot, as in Marlowe's line:

<pre>
  /   ᴗ ᴗ   /   ᴗ   /   ᴗ   /   ᴗ   /
</pre>
Cut is | the branch | that might | have grown | full straight.

The inverted first foot is common to all English iambic measures and has been universally accepted by prosodically conservative
poets like Ben Jonson or Alexander Pope, who abhor triple feet and
allow themselves few other metrical liberties. No, I think Wallace
is seriously mistaken about dactyls. By trying to label accentual verse
and other meters as iambic, he has created a chimera.

(7)   **"We should drop the pyrrhic foot (ᴗᴗ) and accept in
      its place the double-iamb (ᴗᴗ//), as one of the six
      foot-terms necessary: iamb, trochee, anapest, dactyl,
      spondee, double-iamb."**

Wallace makes three different suggestions here, and I shall
comment on them separately. First, he states that the pyrrhic foot
has no utility as an independent metrical concept in English verse
because it exists only in combination with spondees to form a sort
of double-foot. Wallace's observation is valid. Pyrrhic feet hardly
exist as independent entities in English accentual-syllabic verse,
though to understand the rationale for their nonexistence, one needs
to accept the theory of relative stress. Innumerable lines of verse contain pyrrhic feet, if one scans only for strong speech stress. Take, for
instance, the following line from Siegfried Sassoon's "The Hero."
Scanned only for strong speech stresses, it contains two pyrrhics:

<pre>
  ᴗ ᴗ   /   /   ᴗ   /   ᴗ   ᴗ ᴗ   /
</pre>
In the | tired voice | that qua | vered to | a choke

But, of course, a metrical scansion eliminates the second pyrrhic
and positions the first pyrrhic as part of a double foot.

<pre>
  ᴗ ᴗ   /   /   ᴗ   /   ᴗ   / ᴗ   /
</pre>
In the | tired voice | that qua | vered to | a choke.

Lines like Sassoon's illustrate the utility of Wallace's observation. Relative stress explains away the second set of pyrrhics, but it
does not account for the opening double foot. A separate concept
is necessary to explain that configuration.

I am not convinced, however, by Wallace's second suggestion that we name this common metrical occurrence the "double-iamb." We already have a conventional name for this double foot, the ionic *a minore*, which has been used since classical times. If we need to simplify the terminology of English prosody, I would suggest only that we drop the "minor" appellation since the ionic *a majore* ($//\smile\smile$) is an extremely uncommon configuration in English accentual-syllabic verse.

Finally, I agree with Wallace that six terms suffice to identify the most common metrical feet in English, but I would list them as iamb, trochee, anapest, dactyl, spondee, and *ionic*. I would also suggest that the poor pyrrhic be added to the list for its analytical utility. Like four-degree scansion (see point 9), the pyrrhic helps illustrate the principle of relative stress. Whether or not the pyrrhic exists as an independent metrical entity, it remains an essential heuristic concept for scansion. Surely seven basic terms are not too many for such an important field of literary study.

(8) "Anapestic, trochaic, and dactylic meters do not exist in English."

This assertion constitutes Wallace's most radical simplification of English prosody. Unfortunately, it also represents the final *reductio ad absurdum* of his argument. Wallace's system grants infinite flexibility to iambic verse; he allows it to make any variation small or large without losing its identity. Other meters, however, must show complete regularity or be declared nonexistent. This double standard undermines his reasoning. Ironically, it also blinds him to some critical distinctions between trochaic and triple meters that might have supported certain elements in his own argument.

Wallace dismisses trochaic meter as a separate entity because it is "merely a mirror image of iambic." In his simplified system, trochaic and iambic meters become two names applied to the same underlying phenomenon. After all, what is trochaic meter except an iambic pattern missing its initial unstressed syllable? Small differences in artistic organization, however, cause immense differences in effect. The C-major and A-minor musical scales, for example, appear identical in most respects, but by using different tones as their tonic (or starting point), they create unmistakably different patterns of sound. Even untutored ears can distinguish the two scales, and composers consciously exploit those differences for expressive effect. While no one doubts the abstract similarity of iambic and trochaic patterns—both of which alternate stressed and unstressed syllables—anyone who focuses on actual poems rather than metrical schemata immediately notices two profoundly significant differences between the two meters. First, they sound recognizably different; second, the two meters handle metrical substitution in irreconcilable ways.

Critics prefer complex and subtle arguments; such elaborate reasoning makes us look intelligent. But sometimes a rationale of bone-headed simplicity is unavoidable. In addressing Wallace's proposed merger of trochaic and iambic meters, I cannot refrain from replying that trochaic verse is not the same as iambic because it sounds utterly different. This observation may not be subtly reasoned, but trochees are not a subtle meter. Intrusive, incantory, and notoriously mnemonic, trochees have an unmistakable swing. Accentual meters organize sound into immediately apprehensible patterns, and no English meter is more easily recognizable than trochaic. It represents the most extreme stylization of English speech rhythms. Trochaic meter, especially at long stretches, lacks the conversational feel of most iambic measures; it often seems curiously heightened, and is traditionally the measure for magic spells and visions:

> Tyger! Tyger! burning bright
> In the forests of the night,
> What immortal hand or eye
> Could frame thy fearful symmetry?

Or:

> And the silken sad uncertain rustling of each purple curtain
> Thrilled me—filled me with fantastic terrors never felt before . . .

The same oddly heightened qualities that make trochaic meter so intrusive and memorable, however, also seem to limit its flexibility. Anyone who scans substantial amounts of trochaic verse soon notices that it is—without any close competition—the most regular meter in English. If iambic meters accommodate all sorts of variation and substitution (though not quite as much as Wallace maintains), trochaic meters accept virtually none. The strict alternation of stress and unstressed syllables is too prominent to be varied without destroying the hypnotic swing of the line.

There are only two common variations in English trochaic verse—iambic lines and elided triple feet. When trochaic poems want a small variation in the rhythm, they temporarily substitute an iambic line (as in the fourth line of Blake's "The Tyger"). Two things need to be noted about these substitutions. First, the resulting iambic line is always perfectly regular with strict alternation of stressed and unstressed syllables. None of the usual variants that iambic poems display are allowed. Second, the entire line becomes iambic, never just a foot. Trochees are too fragile a meter to allow internal variation in the line. The iambic line, therefore, behaves differently in a trochaic context than on its native ground—a significant piece of evidence for the unique nature of the trochaic beat. The other common technique of rhythmic variation in trochaic verse is an elided triple foot, that is, the insertion of a three syllable foot, which would usually be pronounced in speech as two syllables, such as in the fourth line of Longfellow's stanza:

> Art is long, and Time is fleeting,
> > And our hearts, though stout and brave,
> Still, like muffled drums, are beating
> > Funeral marches to the grave.

Even such a small liberty as "funeral," however, remains surprisingly rare in trochaic verse. The flexibility that typifies iambic verse is absent here. The incantory spell must not be broken by inversions or substitutions. Trochaic meters sound different and operate differently from iambic meters because they are different.

Triple meters present a more complicated situation, and Wallace is surely correct in asserting that many supposedly anapestic poems are actually loose iambics. The subject of English triple meters is vast, and almost no one since Saintsbury has examined it open-mindedly. If one scans a significant number of poems in triple meter, one quickly notices how few show an unvarying anapestic or dactylic pattern. For every regular dactylic poem like *Evangeline*, there are a dozen—or perhaps several dozen—irregular ones. If English trochees are notably regular, the common behavior of dactyls and anapests is astonishingly loose.

The inherent instability of English triple meters creates too many variations to catalogue here, but most of the permutations fall into two categories—sudden shifts between the basic meter of the line and random substitution of double feet. Writing in anapests or dactyls, poets seem instinctively drawn to mixing meters—either alternating between rising and falling triple feet or else randomly mixing anapests and iambs. Judging from the evidence of centuries of verse, one must conclude that poets instinctively feel these variations sound right in English, however confusing the results appear to the prosodist trying to classify them in accentual-syllabic categories like dactylic, anapestic, or iambic. Here are two lines from Swinburne's "Hesperia" which begin in dactylic hexameter but then shift into anapestic hexameter. Swinburne obviously hears the two metrical schemes as interchangeable:

> / ⏑ ⏑ | / ⏑ ⏑ | / ⏑ ⏑ | / ⏑ ⏑ | / ⏑ ⏑ | /
> Filled as with shadow of sound with the pulse of invisible fear
> ⏑ / | ⏑ ⏑ / | ⏑ ⏑ / | ⏑ ⏑ / | ⏑ ⏑ / |
> Far out to the shallows and straits of the future by rough
> ⏑ ⏑ / ⏑
> ways or pleasant

Or later in the same poem:

> / ⏑ ⏑ | / ⏑ ⏑ | / ⏑ ⏑ | / ⏑ ⏑ | / ⏑ ⏑ | /
> Labour and listen and pant not or pause for the peril that nears
> ⏑ ⏑ / | ⏑ ⏑ / | ⏑ ⏑ / | ⏑ / |
> And the sound of them trampling the way cleaves night
> ⏑ ⏑ / | ⏑ ⏑ / ⏑
> as an arrow asunder.

This constant shifting between dactylic and anapestic bases is so common in English as to constitute some sort of norm. For reasons not adequately explained in prosodic literature, English triple meters sound fine when they are mixed, which was not the case in Latin. Sometimes the intermingling of meters becomes so promiscuous that the poem no longer seems governed by a consistent accentual-syllabic pattern but can only be considered accentual since the number of strong beats per line is the only predictable constant. One sees this principle clearly in Tennyson's "Break, Break, Break":

> /   /   /
> Break, break, break,
>   ᴗ ᴗ / ᴗ / ᴗ /
>   On thy cold gray stones, O Sea!
> ᴗ ᴗ /   ᴗ ᴗ /   ᴗ / ᴗ
> And I would that my tongue could utter
>   ᴗ /   ᴗ ᴗ / ᴗ /
>   The thoughts that arise in me.
> ᴗ / ᴗ ᴗ / ᴗ ᴗ   /
> O, well, for the fisherman's boy,
>   ᴗ ᴗ /   ᴗ ᴗ / ᴗ ᴗ /
>   That he shouts with his sister at play!
> ᴗ / ᴗ ᴗ / ᴗ /
> O, well for the sailor lad,
>   ᴗ ᴗ /   ᴗ ᴗ / ᴗ ᴗ /
>   That he sings in his boat on the bay!

What is the meter of Tennyson's poem? A traditionalist might label it anapestic, but that scansion does not adequately account for the opening line, which can only be explained as stress meter. The lines range from three to nine syllables in length, and, if one divides them into accentual-syllabic feet, one discovers as many iambs as anapests (not to mention the recurring monosyllabic feet). To label this poem iambic or anapestic, therefore, is misleading since almost every line would then, to some degree, be irregular. Yet the poem is tangibly metrical—one hears a steady beat common to both the three syllable and nine syllable line. What regular metrical principle unifies the poem's disparate line-lengths?

The only consistent and comprehensive explanation of Tennyson's base meter in these two stanzas is a three-stress accentual measure. Every line unfailingly fulfills this norm. Furthermore, the lines consistently move in a rising rhythm of either iambs or anapests, although they show no clear preference for either foot. To claim that the stanzas display any greater accentual-syllabic organization would be a fiction. A prosodist should claim no more regularity than really exists. The basic meter of a poem is the system that accurately and consistently accounts for its rhythmic movement. If all one can accurately predict about a poem is that every line has three strong stresses, then it is absurd to pretend the norm is anapestic, dactylic, or iambic. False precision is the besetting vice of prosody.

The examples from Swinburne and Tennyson suggest the difficulty in satisfactorily assigning poems containing predominately triple feet into either anapestic or dactylic meters. Wallace's analysis is helpful in challenging the traditional classifications for triple meters; Graeco-Roman metrical models do not accurately account for how loosely such verse works in English. Wallace's conclusions that English triple meters inevitably have an iambic "metrical base," however, is reductive. He replaces one inadequate model with another when a more flexible theory is required. Wallace is right that strict anapestic or dactylic verse hardly exists in English, but it does not necessarily follow that the phenomena traditionally classified under those terms is really a variety of iambic verse. Certainly much "anapestic" poetry is loose iambic, but many other poems operate in ways irreconcilable with iambs; the triple feet and shifting base beat do not seem like iambic variation but a different metrical norm. I suspect that in English anapests are an inherently mixed meter quite distinct from iambs. Borrowing features from both pure accentual verse and stricter iambic accentual syllabics, anapests occupy an interesting middle ground—more flexible than accentual-syllabics and more tightly organized than stress verse. In any event, English triple meters are too complex and dynamic for the static categories of conventional accentual-syllabic prosody. A cogent descriptive and theoretical account of the phenomena remains to be written.

(9) "We should *never* use four degrees of speech stress for scanning."

Wallace makes another valuable observation here. Accentual and accentual-syllabic meters are necessarily binary. This principle may seem arbitrary until one recognizes that binary opposition is the point of the entire system. The rules of art, like those of sports, rest on clearly understood but arbitrary principles from which everything else derives. The basic rule of English auditory meter is simple and divinely arbitrary—to arrange the nearly infinite degrees of speech stress into a satisfying and apprehensible binary shape. Meter must be a convention shared by poet and audience. Any degree of classification beyond binary would be too complex and ambiguous for poets to manage with the expectation that an audience could consistently follow it. Given the arguments over scanning our binary system, imagine what confusion four steps would cause. Moreover, a four-degree system is not appreciably more accurate in measuring the inexhaustible variety of speech stress. Nor does it reflect the binary methods in which poems are actually composed. Has any significant poet used a four-degree system in writing?

The four-stress system, however, offers practical advantages in the classroom as a supplementary technique to the binary system. It is particularly useful in teaching the essential concept of relative stress: that is, the metrical value of a syllable has no fixed value but depends on its position within the foot or line. Temporarily relaxing the conventional system allows students to recognize the many degrees of speech stress and eventually apply that heightened sensitivity to their binary scansions.

(10) "The spondee is a good, and fairly frequent, foot in English."

The spondee is not only a legitimate foot in English; it is a necessary one. Inverted feet and substitutions can often upset an iambic meter, but well-placed spondees fit in easily. They are easy ways to achieve rhythmic variation without confusing the meter. They also allow the poet to pack a line with meaningful words (for stress underscores meaning) while having fun with the rhythm. Even metrically conservative poets like Tennyson use such syncopation habitually. One could fill a small anthology with lines whose special musicality depends on spondees.

As Wallace notes, spondees often combine with pyrrhics to achieve beautiful ionic effects without derailing the iambic meter. Listen to Marvell's famous lines, which I would scan:

∪ ∪| /   / |∪ ∪| /   /
To a green thought in a green shade

Or Stevens's languorous line, which perhaps contains two ionics:

∪ ∪| /   / | ∪   ∪| (/)   /|∪   /
As a calm darkens among water-lights

I am pleased to end on a note of calm accord because, despite my many disagreements, I found Wallace's "Meter in English" invaluably provocative. The discussion it engenders will enrich and enliven contemporary prosody. We need more such "meter-making arguments."

"COME, AND TRIP IT"

A RESPONSE TO ROBERT WALLACE

Rachel Hadas

My discussion will take the form of comments on Wallace's separate propositions, which I number as he does.

(1) "Instead of the term 'feminine ending,' we should say simply extra-syllable ending."

There may be—probably are—excellent cultural, political, or semantic reasons for finding an alternative term. But other than the fact that "extra-syllable ending" seems a bit flat-footed (though clear), the terminological problem seems relatively minor to me. Wallace makes his first proposition in the context of discussing iambic meter; and I happen to agree with his point that an unstressed final syllable in an iambic line (he cites the line "And yet it may be said I loved her dearly") is metrically uncounted—that is, does not render the line irregular. I'd never thought the term "feminine ending" signified irregularity—only that it meant a certain rather frequent kind of variation. The wealth of such variations is part of what makes iambic pentameter splendidly flexible and expressive—a point Wallace and I agree on, I'm sure.

(2) "For an omitted first syllable of a line, we should use the term anacrusis."

How is this an improvement? Perhaps terms like "decapitation" and "truncation" do savor a bit of the abattoir; but they (and especially the elegant Greek version, "acephalous") have the merit of vividness. Wallace seems to dislike prosodic terminology which refers, or can be remotely understood to refer, to the human body—feminine, decapitated. But such terms come very naturally, and why not use them, if they prove helpful? (James Merrill puts it well: "How can a person not personify?")

Wallace's preferred new term, "anacrusis," seems to me precisely the kind of unneeded classical term Wallace himself complains of on page 22, where he mentions "intimidation and . . . a sort of general obfuscation, as if we might figure out something to do with these Greek terms."

And beyond the choice of terms (for one could argue endlessly and not very profitably about terminology) comes the more interesting question of how the headless line is *heard*—how the ear divides it up. "Come, and trip it as ye go" Wallace hears as omitting the unstressed syllable at the start of the line—in other words, it, like "Fifty springs are little room" and many such lines, is really iambic, not trochaic. If, like me, one hears these lines as trochaic, then the omitted syllable pops up (or doesn't) not at the beginning but at the end of the line. At the risk of sounding simple-minded, I think Wallace is making very heavy weather over lines we will almost all hear the same way (there's no mistaking the rapid skip of the stressed syllables) even if we name them differently. A tune is being struck up (anacrusis) either way.

This might be a good time to mention that I rarely disagree with Wallace about how a line of verse sounds. Furthermore, his approach to terminology is generally sensible; he wants to simplify our prosodic armamentarium (!) not only for elegance's and clarity's sake, but to show what he believes, that iambic meter is really a much simpler, more consistent creature than some scholars of versification would have us think. Again, by and large I agree with Wallace. I also admire his equable tone. These are matters about which the tiny handful of people who dispute them often wax very hot under the collar, but more light than heat emanates from Wallace's essay. In this connection, his propositions 3, 4, and 5 are among my favorites—points that needed making much more than any readjustment of feminine-ending terminology.

(3) "Quantities are not a basis for meter in English."

Yup. As Wallace well puts it, the problem is that the strong accents of English tend to override, for all but the most classically trained readers, the pattern of vowel-lengths. For such readers too, I'd say. John Hollander in his excellent *Rhyme's Reason* remarks that quantitative verse in English is usually "grotesque and failed"—though, like Paul Fussell in *Poetic Meter and Poetic Form* (cited by Wallace), Hollander does, perhaps confusingly, include quantitative meter in his list of possible English meters. This kind of inconsistency doesn't raise my blood-pressure, but—like almost anything I can think of that has been written about English prosody—it can very easily mislead.

(4) "Syllabics is not a meter in English."

I would go along with this too, with the same cavil expressed above, that Fussell, Hollander, and many others seem to keep including it in their discussions of prosody. Perhaps Marianne Moore is the culprit, since her poems so frequently provide examples of syllabic verse. Wallace's discussion of this whole matter (12–14) and of the problems of accentual meter (14–21) seems to me the most useful, not to mention enjoyable, portion of his entire essay.

The matter of syllabics bears further attention. Wallace follows his proposition with the correct assertion that "we do not hear the count of syllables." But the statement to which he is soon thereafter led, "syllabics is a kind of free verse," opens up a question Wallace is not in this essay concerned to answer—that is, what free verse is. A recent review by Glyn Maxwell *(Times Literary Supplement,*

3/18/94) of Thom Gunn's new *Collected Poems* and book of essays *Shelf Life* luckily sheds some light on this murky subject, for Maxwell pays a good deal of attention to Gunn's work in syllabics. Maxwell feels the need to quote Gunn on his own syllabic poetry in full, "even if it is unlikely to dent the mass production of this perilous and usually ill-advised verse scheme." The point is that when Gunn, arriving in America in 1954, discovered Pound and Williams, he recognized, according to Maxwell, "the difficulty of writing free verse when one's poetic hearing has been pulsing metrically through formative years." Gunn writes,

> My way of teaching myself to write free verse was to work with syllabics. They aren't very interesting in themselves. They're really there for the sake of the writer rather than the reader. But they were a way of getting iambics out of my ears. Around the time of *My Sad Captains* (1961) I wrote about thirty poems in syllabics but I haven't worked with them since about 1964. I bother to say this because some people are under the impression that I am still writing them because they don't know the difference between free verse and syllabics.

If syllabics are "there for the writer rather than the reader," this is both because they cannot be heard in themselves and because for the writer they have a function. For Gunn that function is "to get iambics out of my ears"; one wonders how many younger poets, American especially, have iambics in their ears in the first place. For any poet, however, syllabics may have a function of what Wallace well calls a trellis—a kind of formal framework or scaffolding over which to train one's ideas, as arbitrary (as Wallace also well says) as counting the number of *letters* as the basis of a line of verse might be.

Both Wallace, writing trenchantly about the attempts of critics to show that Marianne Moore's "Poetry" is in syllabics, and Maxwell, writing about Gunn, have more that is of interest about syllabics. Maxwell observes that "My Sad Captains" (the title poem of the 1961 collection)

> is one of contemporary poetry's few successful syllabic works, but only because particular properties of the form are so valuable to Gunn's purpose *in this poem*. Above all must be placed the quali-

ties of breathlessness—which is, simply, all that syllabics can do better than metrics because they are, essentially, verse minus breath. . . .

The point is double: syllabics in general have a quality of breathlessness (an excellent *aperçu* I have not seen anywhere else) and that quality is well adapted *to this particular poem.* I'm not sure either point would occur to Wallace. For him, syllabics are a neutral form of scaffolding, not specifically equipped to do anything in particular, let alone anything metrics cannot do better. As for the point about syllabic-specific breathlessness (or any quality) being well adapted to a particular poem—well, it's a regrettable but probably inevitable feature of Wallace's whole essay that his practice is to scoop individual lines out of their poetic context, rarely if ever considering the poem as a whole. Hence Maxwell's pithy remark (one which all formal handbooks, prosodic guides, etc., would do well to reproduce) that "no form can compensate for its lack of content" fails to resonate in the context of an argument wholly focused, as Wallace's is, on form to the exclusion of content. (It's fair to add that the various critics Wallace courteously takes on tend to practice precisely the same form of surgical strike, focusing on the words and syllables in a given line, almost never the nature of the poem from which that line has been extracted as by forceps.)

(5) "In modern English, accentual meter does not exist."

I enjoyed Wallace's entertainingly absurd and for me convincing examples of the havoc wrought among prosodists by a so-called accentual meter in which we are told to pay no attention to the unstressed syllables in a line whether those syllables are four or twenty-four in number. I won't rehash the wonderful examples of the "Peruvians' incommunicability" or the discussion of "Christabel"— rather, I recommend them to students of prosody who are as confused as I came to realize I had always been by the notion of accentual verse. All that stuck in my mind on this subject was, for years, the notion of nursery rhymes. And it may well be that the baby being bounced effortlessly grasps the essential principle of accentual verse—to count only the stressed syllables. But Wallace seems to be on the side of clarity, and a foe to obfuscation, when he writes

> this meter offers no predictability at all; and I do not see how we might even begin to discuss the rhythm of [certain] lines if "the number of syllables does not matter" (Nims) and we do not count the unaccented syllables or notice when they occur.
>
> The second problem is that what we may count as a stress seems extremely subjective. Nothing in theory prevents that determination from being arbitrary. (15–16)

The confusion of terminology in the authorities Wallace quotes in this section, writers including John Frederick Nims, Paul Fussell, Harvey Gross, and Timothy Steele—hardly a nest of ninnies—is an antic spectacle indeed. I was very grateful for this proposition and the discussion that precedes it.

(6) "Anapests and dactyls are legitimate substitutions in the iambic norm of English meter."

I agree. This point is really part of Wallace's argument about so-called accentual meter, since it turns out, as Wallace clearly shows, that "accentual meter is only an *alternative term* to be used instead of accentual-syllabic meter *in some cases*, those where trisyllabic substitution appears" (19). It's a little confusing for this proposition to appear separately; like the points about feminine endings and anacrusis, it seems more of a quibble than a clarification, though I understand the context of the quibble is the awful mare's nest of accentual meter. Still, Wallace jolts us disconcertingly from large to niggling points.

(7) "We should drop the pyrrhic foot (∪∪) and accept in its place the double-iamb (∪∪//), as one of the six foot-terms necessary: iamb, trochee, anapest, dactyl, spondee, double-iamb."

I have some trouble here following Wallace's train of thought, an attempt which may be mistaken—maybe I should only think about the propositions as they come rolling along. Anyway,

Wallace's preceding four pages have been devoted to an exhaustive demonstration that the amphibrach is not a useful or necessary foot for scanning Auden's ballad "O What Is That Sound." This demonstration is for the sake of the point that the terminology of classical terminology "pesters" us when we attempt to apply it to the metrical system of English verse.

I am perfectly ready to agree with Wallace here. Talk of long and short syllables never fails to puzzle students (see proposition 3 on quantities). To plague students with paeonics, molossians, and so on is probably at least as absurd as claiming that accentual verse exists and is readily identifiable and even scannable.

Wallace succeeds in showing that although Auden's poem contains plenty of amphibrachs if one is on the lookout for them, the poem is at least equally scannable without the use of this imported foot. My thought was that Wallace was here building up to a blanket condemnation of all metrical feet other than the familiar ones mentioned in proposition 7 or to a specific condemnation of such "complex, cumbersome, and esoteric" imports as the amphibrach. Rereading the passage, I see that Wallace's bias is towards simplicity and against importing unnecessary terms, but I am not quite clear as to what the discussion on pages 22–28 is getting at.

In more general terms—and to get away from my embarrassment at failing to follow Wallace's argument here—I find myself torn, at this point in the essay, between agreement and exasperation. I am in sympathy with Wallace's no-nonsense impatience with exotic terminology, metrical systems that do not quite fit, prosodic units that become beds of Procrustes. On the other hand, I am bothered by what seems to me Wallace's misplaced emphasis on finding an alternative term (preferably a domestic one, but then consider "anacrusis") for every esoteric one he rejects. To be sure, "double-iamb" is easier to remember than "pyrrhic," and it accounts for many places where pyrrhics have formerly been spotted. But do we need any new term for the readily recognizable phenomenon of two unstressed syllables in a row? I pine at this point for Robert Frost's statement that all English meter is either strict iambic or loose iambic. Wallace quotes this with approval at least once, and I can see why; he's making the same point himself. Yet even as he makes the point, he seems to feel compelled to fiddle with details. Perhaps what troubles me is that Wallace doesn't sufficiently trust the sense of the reader. Yet in fairness it is hard to fault him for this lack of confidence in common sense; look at what critics have done with accentual verse.

Wallace's scruples, in short, both sustain and exasperate me. English meter, as he points out on page 22, is "simple, elegant, and comprehensive." Yet he seems reluctant to entrust readers to this simplicity without the help of crutches like the double-iamb.

I recently had the pleasure of meeting Annie Finch for the first time. Annie, a reader as little in need of metrical crutches as anyone I can think of, leafed through the copy of my book of translations I had just given her, and paused at my rendering of an elegy of Tibullus, the last line of which reads "Don't burn your harvest in your rage at me!" Annie pounced on the line as clearly containing a pyrrhic—as clear an example, she remarked, as that in the line "Let me not to the marriage of true minds."

A pyrrhic? Or merely a double-iamb? Who cares? Certainly not I as I wrote the line. Can't we simply allow that in the elegant, simple, and infinitely varied (now light, now stately; now skipping, now stomping) measure that is iambics in English, unstressed syllables frequently appear in pairs—or even in threes? Whether such a pair is scanned as a separate metrical foot or as part of a specially invented double foot is merely a matter of terminology; I have trouble believing it affects how we hear the line. Whether "The hare limp'd trembling through the frozen grass" is scanned by Bate and Perkins as containing a pyrrhic or by Wallace as iambic, surely what we hear is the same line. I don't buy Wallace's claim that in scanning this line "iambic seems, as to performance, more accurate."

Granted, some famous lines of English verse, from Marvell's green thought to the astonishing openings of Frost's "Mending Wall" or "Directive," are capable of many nuances of emphasis—and hence of interpretation, for we ought to keep in mind Maxwell's point about content. But whether two consecutive unstressed syllables should be termed a pyrrhic or part of a double-iamb is unlikely to change either how we hear a line or what we think it means.

(8) "Anapestic, trochaic, and dactylic meters do not exist in English."

We are still caught in the toils of terminology. I think it's clear that we can *hear* triple or trochaic meters in innumerable poems. Two examples that come to mind are *Old Possum's Book of Practical Cats,* whose mesmerizing skipping rhythms are a chief part of its spell, and Vikram Seth's delightful trochaic (or do I mean headless iambic?) beast fables. Wallace grants that we can hear triple meter, but he is nonetheless eager to tuck it under the sober and capacious umbrella of iambics. In the shade of that umbrella, anapests and dactyls are clearly perceived as substitutions for iambs, just as the pyrrhic is seen for what it really is, part of a double-iamb. This begins to be a looking-glass world.

As long as there is some agreement among native speakers of English as to what is recognizably heard, Wallace's points are pleasurably open to debate. I agree with him, for example, that "trochaic meter is merely a mirror image of iambic" (perhaps this is what put the looking glass into my head); but I do not see that that's a reason to expunge the term "trochaic" from our vocabularies. I agree with him that "at some point iambic meter with anapestic substitutions turns into anapestic meter with iambic substitutions." But I don't follow him in regarding the term "anapestic meter" as offensive or erroneous, while the periphrasis (or euphemism?) "frequent anapestic substitution" is somehow seen as accurate and safe.

The reason Wallace gives for his objection is that a term like "anapestic meter" is a misnomer; properly speaking, we are discussing not meter, in the sense of overall metrical system, but variations in rhythm: "Meter refers to *poems,* not lines *per se*... Poems do not change meter from line to line" (29). And arguing for an overall sense of metrical consistency, no matter how great the rhythmic variation may be, he adds "Our loss, in having multiplied entities, is the failure to see clearly how splendidly unitary English meter is." Again, I agree—though "unitary" seems an odd word to describe something as endlessly inflected as English meter. Surely it should be possible to multiply entities and to continue to see *and hear* the overall consistency of English poetry at the same time.

(9) "We should *never* use four degrees of speech stress for scanning."

Despite a lamentable ignorance of linguistics, I'm sufficiently convinced by Wallace's argument in the adjacent passages, particularly his reasonable assertion that if we occasionally have difficulty ascribing stress or unstress in a two-valued system, then the four-valued system almost predictably results in further disagreement and still more elaborate confusion. In its tendency to go for a lowest common denominator, a level of prosodic articulation that can be clearly heard and agreed upon, this sensible point has an obvious family resemblance to Wallace's less specifically linguistic points about prosody.

(10) "The spondee is a good, and fairly frequent, foot in English."

Certainly we hear many spondees, though where they occur is probably a matter of a bit more dispute than the whereabouts of trochees or anapests or dactyls. So I agree with this, though I'm a bit surprised Wallace doesn't choose to call the spondee something like an intensified iamb, in order to eschew confusing terminology and too great a multiplication of entities!

Why is the point about the spondee made in the neighborhood of a discussion about linguistics? For a good reason, as I was a bit startled to see. For not only do some experts (Hall, Winters) apparently declare that spondees are either nonexistent or very rare; some of them depend on linguistic speech stress theories to back up readings which bear surprisingly little relation to what one thinks one is actually hearing (see Steele's scansion of the "trembling hare" line on page 236).

Lack of common sense; instruments which seem badly adapted to the stuff they are supposed to be analyzing; unnecessarily complex terminology—these are Wallace's enemies, and he battles them with admirable good humor, and more often than not with a clarity for which I am grateful. If I do not always follow his thread or agree with his every reading, those are minor quibbles in a battlefield spattered with gall. Have a look, for example, at the correspondence between Vladimir Nabokov and Edmund Wilson. The friendship between these two great men of letters finally foundered on the rocks of their disagreement about Nabokov's translation of *Eugene Onegin;* and among the sharpest clashes were disputes about meter.

The systems and handbooks we now have for describing, analyzing, and teaching meter are obviously confusing and contradictory. Does that mean they are inadequate, destructive, worse than nothing? Absolutely not. Something is conveyed by the very idea of analyzing meter—some kind of understanding of poetry of the past, of very ancient links between genre and meter, and of the energizing properties of constraint. I'm very glad to have Wallace more or less under my belt as I try to go about teaching meter; he certainly hasn't convinced me that the whole business is hopeless.

SOME RESPONSES TO ROBERT WALLACE

Charles O. Hartman

Reforming English metrics seems nearly as quixotic a project as reforming English spelling. The motives are similar: a rationalist instinct that rebels against the efflorescence of idiosyncrasy, and a pedagogical desire for a system streamlined and informative enough to be taught. While the conventions of spelling are subscribed to by a great many more people—an inertial body too big to move—the adherents of various metrical systems compensate for small numbers by being more rabid. Yet metrics is a conventional system, and therefore *can* be reformed, like sexist language, however large the effort required. We have to remember, though, that two layers are involved: the conventions of scansion are epiphenomena of the conventions of meter, which are much less negotiable because they are shared not just by analytical critics (the community forgathered here to discuss reform) but by poets and readers as well.

The aim of scansion is to describe meter; it is a system of useful simplifications, and the metrical analyst cannot change the metrical phenomena themselves for the sake of convenience. As Robert Wallace says, "The poetry matters, after all, not the theory."

I hear more danger to this distinction, however, when he hopes "that our teaching is [not] irrelevant to the future of poems written in meter." Scansion is unnecessary to meter; our teaching—of either scansion or the writing and reading of metrical poetry—is unnecessary to poetry, though we do it in the hope of having some beneficent influence on readers and with a healthy fear of having too much influence on young writers. Wallace says that "those of us interested in the future of meter must take care to be precise and frugal in our terms." Hubris lurks here. While teachers of metrics do participate in sustaining the tradition of metrical poetry, that tradition *has* managed to survive quite a few centuries of what Wallace, often rightly, considers imprecise and profligate terminology. It is a very recent delusion that poetry would perish without poetry courses.

Still, if we are going to do it, we should do it right, and the "precise and frugal" deployment of terminology is the right basis for the project. The theoretical metrist's job, in short, is to split the difference between clarity and accuracy. But the claims of precision and frugality compete. To shoehorn too many meanings into too few terms fuzzes distinctions that are important because they are among the aural experiences we are trying to describe. I share Wallace's suspicion of jargon, of esoteric terminology for its own sake or the sake of power. But my chief reservations about his essay derive from his zeal for theoretical unification at the expense of an accurate description of phenomena and principles.

The most startling example is his assertion that the basis of English accentual-syllabic meters is always iambic (proposition 8: **"Anapestic, trochaic, and dactylic meters do not exist in English."**). It is true that one could arbitrarily scan Blake's "Ah Sun-flower" as iambic trimeter that happens to have an awfully large number of trisyllabic substitutions, just as one could scan "Leda and the Swan" as anapestic pentameter with a surprisingly large number of disyllabic substitutions. The latter scansion is not *more* wrong-headed simply because more English poems are iambic than anapestic. Both scansions are wrong-headed because they minimize the significant difference that any reader feels and hears, consciously or not, between the two poems. A system of metrical description that made it awkward to name this difference would be failing in its pedagogical and analytic task. To instruct students in an exclusively iambic regime, and then hand them "Ah Sun-flower," is simply sadistic. To describe the first stanza of "How They Brought the Good News from Ghent to Aix" as merely "heavily anapestic" seems like a kind of euphemism.

Wallace suggests that we classify a line like Milton's "Then to come in spite of sorrow" as iambic tetrameter with (consistent) "anacrusis" and (consistent) "extra-syllable ending." But to shift from that cumbersome handle to "trochaic tetrameter" is *illuminating*, in rather the same way as translating "MCMIL" to "1949." "L'Allegro" is a complicated example. But Walter Scott clearly wrote "Lucy Ashton's Song" ("Look thou not on beauty's charming; / Sit thou still when kings are arming") under the impression that he was using trochaic tetrameter, and expected his readers to hear it that way. That traditional designation incorporates systematic constancies of the poem that Wallace's description treats as added features. To put it another way, the number of marks required to scan Scott's poem under the trochaic understanding is significantly smaller than the iambic. Wallace complains that "Our loss, in having multiplied entities, is the failure to see clearly how splendidly unitary English meter is." What he does not adequately acknowledge—it is always a delicate balance—is how splendidly *diverse* English meter is. The diversity goes deeper than substitute feet. Statistical facts, such as that most animals are insects, most corporate CEO's are male, most human DNA is identical to that of chimpanzees, do not constitute rules. Most English metrical poems are iambic, not all.

Perhaps what is at issue here is the nature of the "laws" or "rules" of accentual-syllabic meter embodied in our terminology and methods of scansion. In deriving these rules, are we seeking descriptions of what *usually* happens, or what *can* happen? Wallace's bent is toward the simplest possible description of normal phenomena, and that is a valuable impulse. But metrics, considered from the poet's point of view rather than from the peripheral point of view of the theorist, is a body of rules that are valuable because they define *fields of possible action,* like the rules of chess, not restrictions like traffic laws. If we conceive metrical principles (and the entities needed to describe them) in that way, we must attend to rare cases as well as normal ones. Subatomic particles other than protons, neutrons, electrons, neutrinos, and photons are extremely rare—they have to be manufactured in accelerators and last tiny fractions of a second—but they have turned out to be essential to our understanding of how *all* particles hang together to make the universe.

Wallace's Procrustean suggestion that all meters be reduced to the iambic amounts to a claim that one continuum joins "Leda and the Swan" and "Ah Sun-flower" and "Lucy Ashton's Song": different poems simply use more or fewer anapests, headless lines, and terminal slack syllables. This view, while it invites interesting statistical studies, obscures important patterns in the *overall* structures of poems. Iambic poems tend to resolve passages of rhythmic complication in strongly iambic lines, anapestic poems resolve on anapestic lines, and trochaic poems on trochaic lines. Whether we can identify these points of resolution or release of metrical tension in a poem partly determines whether we can grasp its movement as a whole—which is surely the ultimate goal of metrical and rhythmic analysis and training.

One final demonstration of the fundamental difference between iambic and anapestic poems may convince some scholars more than others: It is possible to write a computer program that accurately scans iambic poems, even those of such metrical complexity as "The Second Coming." That program (which I have implemented in several forms) breaks down completely when confronted with a poem like "Ah Sun-flower." Of course one can add more to the program to handle these cases; but in doing so one is specifically accommodating the habits of *anapestic* verse. (The program must choose, on a crude but adequate statistical basis, whether to treat a given input as anapestic or iambic before it knows how to begin processing individual lines.) The distinction is, in this sense, procedural and deterministic, not a matter of degree or style or taste in metrical systems.

If I am right that we must acknowledge the existence of anapestically-based poems, then we must also recognize that such poems tend to invite different kinds of foot substitution from iambic ones. Wallace announces that the cretic (or amphimacer—we can postpone the secondary question of what to *call* these things) does not exist in English ("or, to put it differently . . . [it] might be rationalized in a different or simpler way"). But in Blake's third line, for instance, "Seeking after that sweet golden clime," no reader can fail to hear the stresses on the first syllables of "Seeking" and "golden," and so the first and third feet are cretics, pure and simple. To "rationalize" them differently seems as perverse as, in iambic verse, rationalizing spondees as iambs—a streamlining that Wallace rejects. Similarly, in the line from Browning that Wallace quotes, "I turned in my saddle and made its girths tight," the last foot (×//, a bacchius) neatly images the jerking effort with which the rider cinches the girth. Is it useless or improper to have available a name for this deliberate effect? The cretic and the bacchius are natural substitutions in anapestic verse, just as the spondee and trochee are in iambic verse.

Metrics needs to describe the phenomena of metrical reading (and writing). What a reader hears, metrics serves its purpose by naming. This is the only, and sufficient, justification for inventing or adopting or retaining any term like "iamb," "cretic," "caesura," or "enjambment." (Also, the available terms help train us to hear what they designate; but this is always an argument for *more* terms, not fewer.) Wallace's case against the amphibrach (at the end of an iambic line) is worth examining in detail (proposition 1: **"Instead of the term 'feminine ending,' we should say simply extrasyllable ending, which may be abbreviated as e-s ending."**). He quotes Saintsbury's invocation of Occam's razor, "not to multiply your entities." Now, "extra-syllable ending" is just as much an entity as "amphibrach." I have long argued for the latter description. At issue is the *kind* of simplification we want. Traditionally we have agreed to fit everything into a foot; Wallace wants to minimize the number of feet. Making everything in the line a foot seems important if we are to have a foot-based prosody. But here I concede the need for change. The traditional rule—use the amphibrach only, and always, at the end of a line that terminates in a single slack syllable—leads to two problems. First, the amphibrach turns out to be pedagogically pernicious: given the amphibrach as a possible foot, students in desperation tend to use it in the middles of lines, where it prevents them from seeing the solutions that depend on iambs and anapests and spondees. Second, if we add the amphibrach (for iamb-plus-slack), we must *also* add the second paeon (for anapest-plus-slack) and the palimbacchius (for spondee-plus-slack). This begins to feel like genuine excrescence. The system is ultimately better simplified by way of a rule that an iambic line can end with an added unstressed syllable; and "extra-syllable ending" is at least a better name for this phenomenon than "feminine ending."

Wallace's stricture against the pyrrhic seems to me exactly in accord with the facts (proposition 7: **"We should drop the pyrrhic foot (‿‿) and accept in its place the double-iamb (‿‿//), as one of the six foot-terms necessary: iamb, trochee, anapest, dactyl, spondee, double-iamb."**). Examining a very large body of English iambic verse, with the concept of the pyrrhic in mind, one begins to infer a rule: that every possible pyrrhic either (1) is heard as an iamb (through "promoted stress," as in the third and fifth feet of "A sight so touching in its majesty"), or (2) occurs immediately before a spondee (as in "In a dark time"). Here is a real opportunity to prune back the terminological thicket. The two rhythmic effects feel quite different, and to give them the single name "pyrrhic" is misleading. Whether we call the pyrrhic-and-spondee pair a "double-iamb" or a "rising Ionic" seems to me a matter of relative indifference, and here I agree that "plain English seems preferable."

Wallace's suggestion that "For an omitted first syllable of a line, we should use the term anacrusis" is perplexing (proposition 2: **"For an omitted first syllable of a line, we should use the term anacrusis."**). "Anacrusis" has always meant the *addition* of syllables to the beginning of a line. This corresponds to its meaning in music, for which "up-beat" is a rough synonym—an unaccented note preparatory to a downbeat. The traditional way to name the omission of an initial syllable (there need hardly be a name for the omitted syllable itself) is to call the line "acephalous" or, in keeping with Wallace's preference for plain English, "headless." This has the additional advantage of locating the metrical context for this act of omitting in the line, where it belongs, not in the syllable or the foot.

Some other points of detail within iambic meter—the legitimacy of anapests, dactyls, and spondees as substitutions in iambic verse—should by now be wholly uncontroversial (proposition 6: **"Anapests and dactyls are legitimate substitutions in the iambic norm of English meter"** and proposition 10: **"The spondee is a good, and fairly frequent, foot in English."**). Getting rid of spondees would again be needless and uninformative wielding of the ax; to describe the metrical and rhythmic habits of "Leda and the Swan" without access to the term "spondee" is mere arbitrary hobbling. As for the old debate over trisyllabic substitution, it should have been settled by Saintsbury a century ago, and I agree entirely with Wallace that attempts to revive it are misguided. The debate grew out of a misconception of poetic history: Milton does not use trisyllabics and Pope rarely does, but Wordsworth and Frost use them all the time. Stylistic norms change, both poet by poet and century by century; elevating one over another demonstrates either pure prejudice or a discomfort with the historical dynamism of metrics, like the French Academy's rigid fussiness about correctness of diction. It is true that the dactyl can *almost* always be treated otherwise: $/ \times \times \times /$ becomes $/ \times | \times \times /$ just as readily as $/ \times \times | \times$, as Wallace notes; though he prefers the latter "as showing only one substitution," one could as easily prefer the former as showing only more ordinary substitutions. Still, "dactyl" is another category we need to keep handy for the rare case.

I agree with Wallace's rejection of quantitative meter, but for somewhat different reasons (proposition 3: **"Quantities are not a basis for meter in English."**). He argues that "The problem is that the strong accents of English tend to override, for all but the most classically trained readers, the pattern of vowel-lengths." Rather, the problem is that quantity is not a *conventionalized* aspect of syllables in English. Stress and syllable division can be looked up in an English dictionary; duration of syllables cannot. In Greek and Latin, a set of conventional rules divides all syllables (or almost all) into short and long, and quantity therefore becomes available for the further conventions of metrical patterning. It is worth wondering for a moment why classical languages conventionalized quantity while English does not. One might speculate that it has to do with the sound of those languages. As a parallel example, tones (patterns of intonation, rising, falling, low, or high) determine the meanings of Chinese syllables; Saussurean linguistic principles therefore dictate that for speakers of Chinese the continuum of intonational possibilities is conceptually divided into four discrete categories; these "four tones" therefore readily enter into the conventions of prosody. English uses intonation to determine meaning too, but the contours of pitch govern whole phrases and sentences, not single words out of context. As for classical Greek and Latin, we know relatively little about their original sound (though W. B. Stanford offers a persuasive reconstruction of the Greek). But we do know—and this may better account for the role of quantity—that Greek poetry was governed by reverence for Homer, whose preliterate work was performed musically, and that music universally tends to regiment the durations of sounds. (Modern Western music, for instance, is understood as consisting of entities such as half, quarter, and eighth notes, though in actual performance a quarter note's mechanically measurable duration may range from over two beats down to less than a half beat.) In any case, English syllables' duration is not regularized, and so no basis for a quantitative meter is shared by poet and reader. This has little to do with classical training or lack of it. It means, though, that the most careful *English* reader hears syllable durations as a free, expressive resource in the rhythms of lines ("swathe" has a different rhythmic effect from "cut"), but not as a metrical principle. (It is perfectly safe, by the way, to rationalize our notation. Though Wallace notes the confusion engendered by our taking metrical terminology from the alien, quantitative Greek system, and follows the tradition of using the virgule (/) to replace the macron (−), he misses a bet by perpetuating the breve (◡) for unstressed (not "short") syllables. Here is a reform we could all try to agree on, using some other arbitrary sign such as an "✕" for slack syllables).

Wallace's objection to syllabic meter is more problematic (proposition 4: **"Syllabics is not a meter in English."**). He is right that we do not hear syllable counts (as French readers do, undoubtedly because of the minor role of word-stress in French). But whether an aspect of sound is available for metrical use depends, again, on conventions of various sorts—linguistic, stylistic, and even personal. If a poet subjects syllable counts to a rule, and the reader has some reason to know this (if, for instance, that poet's practice becomes famous), then a syllabic meter is possible. Wallace, I think, is confused by too local a definition of "rhythm," by which he usually means the interplay of stress and syllable count that does indeed form the basis of the dominant meter in English. But rhythm, understood in a way that is applicable to various languages and traditions, is simply the distribution in time of foregrounded, commensurable events. Different languages, and different poetries, count and measure different events. The choice of events depends in part on the nature of the language (hence, again, the impossibility of quantitative meters in English). But syllable divisions are important to English, as their role in the definition of the dominant meter shows, and can in some circumstances be made the sole basis for the meter. (A few English words are indefinite in syllable count, partly for dialectal reasons; "flower" and its rhymes are prominent examples, and account for the only uncertainties in the four lines Wallace quotes as evidence that syllabic regularity is indeterminate.) We know, for reasons partly external to the poem itself, that a poem by Marianne Moore may well be based on syllable counts; this knowledge leads us to recognize, either in detail (by counting on our fingers) or in general (by recognizing visually the regularities of length in the corresponding lines in different stanzas), the metrical basis of the poem. It is true that Moore was blithe about revising her poems with far more attention to diction than to preservation of the original syllable counts, as examination of earlier drafts of a poem like "Bird-Witted" demonstrates; but this has little bearing on the question of whether syllabic verse is *possible*.

Wallace asks the right questions: "I do not see how a poet, setting out to write in this meter, would be guided in any useful way; or how a reader, suspecting the meter, could ever be sure it was operating." But when the meter is strictly kept—the strictness made necessary by the system's unfamiliarity is its main drawback—the reader who wants confirmation has only to count. The reader who suspects or confirms the meter is then aware, though farther in the background than in accentual-syllabic meter, of a rule-governed regularity, and of the rhythms of the lines playing against that regularity, with every other degree of freedom. As for its utility to the poet, syllabic meter, like any other, may offer at least the kind of fruitful resistance provided by other arbitrary formal limitations— the acrostic, the alphabet poem, or for that matter the sestina or the rhyme.

Accentual meter, by the same argument, is quite possible (proposition 5: **"In modern English, accentual meter does not exist."**). Wallace is right, I think, that clear examples of it in modern English are rare. Accent is more various than syllable count, and far more subject to alteration by context. As Wallace says, "what we may count as a stress seems excessively subjective" in most speech and in most verse. To make an accentual meter clear, therefore, demands a constant, strict and even exaggerated distinction between stressed and unstressed syllables. Such a meter can be so handled as to be unambiguous—

> Dark as the night falls
> the winter falls darker
> still: yields stars
> innumerable, fierce and clear

—but its requirements are for the most part too excessively rigid to let the poet sustain the *rhythmic* flexibility which is, from one point of view, the splendid pay-off for following the rules of a *meter*. Constraints may be useful, while imprisonment may impoverish, but one poet's love of detail is another's claustrophobia.

It seems to me that Wallace again extends his strictures against accentual meter too far, because of the same misunderstanding of "rhythm" as besets his discussion of syllabic meter. "I do not see," he says, "how we might even begin to discuss the rhythm of such lines if 'the number of syllables does not matter' and we do not count the unaccented syllables or notice where they occur." If we do not notice such prominent features in a line of English words as the number and position of stressed and unstressed syllables, we are indeed barred from discussing their rhythm. But meter is not rhythm—meter is an abstract pattern underlying varying rhythms— and the aural features on which a meter is based never exhaust the features a reader hears, or, therefore, the rhythms we can discuss. Alliterative meters are rare in modern English, assonantal ones are unheard of; yet patterns of alliteration and assonance strongly influence our sense of the rhythms of countless lines. Just so, the rhythm we hear in a strict syllabic poem will undoubtedly depend on the number and placement of accents (and, since they are not being regularized by metrical rule, also on the various degrees of accent, which the conventions of accentual-syllabic meter bid us half-ignore). The rhythm we hear in a strict accentual poem will depend also on the number and placement of intervening unstressed syllables. To argue that the term "accentual meter" "has no legitimacy even in regard to Old English verse . . . as stress is only one of its essential characteristics," is again to confuse meter (a consistent set of numerical rules governing one or a few aural characteristics of the poem's language) with rhythm (a various phenomenon including aural features whose number is indefinite and depends in part on the skill and attention of the poet and the reader). Wallace is certainly right to identify Old English meter not as simple accentuals but as accentual meter with some flexible but essential rules governing alliteration; but this is an historical consideration, not an indication of what possibilities poets can exploit. No muddle more commonly besets discussions of metrics, I believe, than the failure to distinguish when we are describing meter and metrical variations, and when we are going on (as we should) to analyze rhythm. The role of scansion is to diagram the interaction between the two. The influence of rhythm on meter emerges as substituted feet. The influence of meter on rhythm emerges as "promoted stress"—most commonly, turning what might be a pyrrhic into an iamb. I have sometimes used parentheses around a virgule to indicate a promotion, and so to underscore the interplay with rhythm that is central to the *functioning* of meter. This usage differs from Wallace's suggestion that we use parentheses to note "possibly ambiguous cases." That too can be worth doing—though, given the rough diagrammatic nature of scansion, it will be hard to draw a firm line between what is "possibly ambiguous" and what is unarguable.

This argument clarifies the real foundation of Wallace's rejection of the "four levels of stress" proposed by Chatman, Jespersen, and Trager and Smith (proposition 9: **"We should *never* use four degrees of speech stress for scanning."**). It is not only, as he says, that the system is needlessly complicated; it is not only that the system is arbitrary and its application to a particular line endlessly and fruitlessly arguable, as Wallace also rightly points out. Rather, the theory of stress levels misapprehends the whole nature of meter. There are several ways to put this point. First, a meter is an abstract set of rules, not a description of the sound (or rhythm) of a line. Second, the rules are conventional—shared by poet and reader—and any "discovery" of what is "really" going on in a line, outside of the awareness of poets and readers, is irrelevant to a formulation of the system of rules that constitutes the meter. This is *why* "Meter cannot depend on discriminations too fine for ordinary mortals, poets or readers, to make out pretty easily," as Wallace says. Yet his rejection of elision may evince a similar misunderstanding of the relation between metrical sound and metrical knowledge. We do not "mouth" the awkward elisions, we understand them, rather as we understand the stress on a "promoted" iamb, more than we actually hear it. Certainly Donne meant us to understand elision in a line like "Yet dearely I love you and would be loved fain"; the contrast between an apparent rhythmic wilderness—all those anapests—and a potentially resolvable regularity is part of how the poem's rhythm helps make its theological point. In this sense elision does not, as Wallace puts it, "replace" trisyllabic substitution, but constitutes a different kind of liberty in the treatment of the iambic line, fashionable at different times.

Third, and more subtly, the stress-level theory inverts the relation between the poem and its performance. (I discussed this "performative fallacy" in *Free Verse: An Essay on Prosody*). Chatman et al. could only "discover" their levels of stress by analyzing their own or others' vocalization of particular lines. This makes the horse follow the cart. We do not *deduce* the meter in each line, as their method pretends; after initially identifying the meter, we enter the reading of a line already knowing what its meter will be. The metrical pattern preexists its expression in particular lines: it precedes and partly shapes their rhythmic structures. As Wallace puts it, "the proper emphasis is already encoded in the *metrical* norm of the line."

Furthermore, though we may all agree that some performances of a line are better than others, we will never agree on a "best" performance (Shall we prefer Gielgud's *Hamlet* or Burton's?) to use as the basis of measurement. Worse still is any measurement based on an averaging of performances. Asking a class to read a line in unison can be very useful in helping students hear where the stresses fall, but it reveals almost nothing about their relative "levels."

Where does this leave us? Regarding the metrical system as a whole, I agree with Wallace that the intriguing qualities of Halle and Keyser's system (inspired by generative linguistics) should not turn us away from the traditional system of scansion. Wallace argues this point on the basis of the clumsiness and inaccurate (or at least counterintuitive) results of their approach. One might go on to champion the traditional system because it is traditional—not from a reactionary impulse, but from a recognition that meter is a body of conventions, a more or less conscious contract among poets and readers, to which a conventional description, passed on from generation to generation, is appropriate. Wallace is also surely right that the conventional system can be clarified, streamlined to some extent (though I have disagreed about the extent), and made more consistent, without destroying its traditional, contractual character, and with some gain in explanatory power.

Within the traditional system of metrics, large theoretical questions remain. Why, for instance, when the large majority of English disyllabic words are accented on the first syllable, does English poetry so overwhelmingly prefer iambic meters? The answer to this question—which is probably to be sought not strictly in historical linguistics but in the contrapuntal relation of rhythm and meter—would shed light on the rarity of trochaic poems, but its relation to the rarity of anapestic ones is unclear. Why is trochaic inversion of the first foot so common in iambic poems? What rhythmic effects does the coincidence (or disjunction) of word-boundary and foot-boundary produce, and how independent of context are those effects? Many similar puzzles are raised by almost any survey of English.

Ultimately, though, we will need to go farther. Meter cannot finally be clarified until we perceive it as a system that operates among other systems, notably syntax and intonation. The rhythm of a poem, in any adequately large sense, depends on these other, more or less separate patterning forces, and the poet's manipulation of them, as much as it depends on the formal metrical structure. Trying to describe the rhythm of a poem through metrics alone is like trying to describe driving a car by analyzing the movements of the steering wheel without reference to the clutch or the accelerator. Driving comprises all three; and indeed each depends in part on the others, as the different experiences of highway cruising and parallel parking quickly show. Metrics itself is falsified when we make it colonize too much, like the social-Darwinist determinism that results from assigning all influence on human behavior to genetics and none to environment. The pure metrist comes to resemble the historian who tries to explain a particular war by strictly political analysis, ignoring economics and technology.

The task is one of integration; but we also need more basic work on the separate pieces. Syntax is well understood linguistically, but too little attention is paid to its phenomenology in poetry. Intonation has had little extended treatment since Kenneth Pike's *Intonation of American English* appeared, obscurely, in 1956. In discussing Marvell's "To a green thought in a green shade," Wallace acknowledges such an impingement of two systems: "When I try to read the line, the pitch *drops* on the nouns." Yet even here he seems—at least by his choice of which word to italicize—to lump pitch together with stress. In fact the two are quite separate, just as they are in Latin (whence the old confusion about "ictus" and "accent"). A line embodying a certain metrical norm (with variations in substituted feet) will also embody a certain tune governed by the intonational patterns native to English speech. This is one of several reasons why metrically identical lines remain distinct rhythmically. If we then add a consideration of the syntactical structure of the line, and its relation through enjambment to the lines that bracket it, we begin to have a fairly complete account of the line's rhythmic character—though still other features such as assonance, the incidence of polysyllables, and even diction and dramatic context, can also have important influence.

Carried further, this kind of synthesis would clarify a number of arguments within the narrower field of metrics. Pike, for instance, in the course of his work on intonation, notes the tendency in American speech toward isochrony; that is, equal temporal intervals between stresses. (The isochrony, as Wallace notes in passing, is not exact; it is a tendency. If it were or could be made exact, a meter based on it would be indistinguishable from "meter" in the sense in which the term is used in music.) This helps explain why the lengths of syllables—more or fewer being crammed into roughly equal times—depend on context, and hence why quantitative meters are impossible in English. Similarly, the study of enjambment (as in John Hollander's "'Sense Variously Drawn Out': on English Enjambment," in *Vision and Resonance,* or in the central chapters of my *Free Verse*) shows how strongly the interaction of syntax and meter influences our perception of both. There is plenty of room for research here, and ultimately great promise for teaching.

PROSODY

A NEW FOOTING

Robert Hass

Robert Wallace's basic argument in "Meter in English" is that all metrical poetry in the language is composed in iambic meter. The first interest of this proposition is its simplicity. The second is that it involves a paradigm shift. In current pedagogy there are four kinds of meters, quantitative, accentual, syllabic, and accentual-syllabic. And then there is something called free verse. In Wallace's system there are two kinds of verse in English: metrical and accentual. All metrical verse is iambic, or has an implicit iambic base, and among accentual verse practices—both older and more recent—there are several kinds, including syllabics and what we now call free verse. The appeal of this system of classification—to some extent arbitrary like all systems of classification—is that this one seems intuitively right in the way that it reconnects accentual and syllabic verse to the other nonmetrical practices that have come into existence in the twentieth century. And this begins to make possible what we do not now have, a prosody of free verse, a useful technical account of the main practice of poetry in the English language for the past hundred years.

This is why Wallace's essay is so interesting. It has something new to say, and it introduces a new order into the messy, not-much-visited precincts of a subject intimate to the art of poetry. Not that intellectual orderliness is always a virtue. For the purposes of poets, a messier lumber room for the storage of the various received prosodies may be a more useful place, fuller of oddities and discoveries, bearing as it does so many of the traces of previous attitudes and practices. More new things might happen, if poets who take an interest continued to potter around, say, in George Saintsbury's great and ramshackle three-volume *History of English Prosody* with its poulter's measures and fourteeners and anapestic trimeters. But for teaching prosody to students and for thinking about it, Wallace's proposition has much to recommend it, including elegance.

I'm going to comment on what seem to be the central issues. Several of his other proposals are housekeeping. On his propositions 1 and 2, I take no position; legislating nomenclature has never been one of the successes of scholarship. As far as propositions 6, 7, and 10, it is certainly the case that there are anapestic, dactylic, spondaic as well as trochaic substitutions in iambic verse, and it is useful to mark a double-iamb and to do without pyrrhic feet. He seems also to want to ban the one-syllable foot; I think this is wise and cunning: it is the best way to interdict the more tortured attempts to subsume accentual verse to metrical norms. Jespersen's system of marking speech stress, discussed in proposition 9, is too complicated to be of use in teaching prosody, whatever its use to poets might be; besides, it misunderstands meter—it is really an attempt to describe rhythm, not to isolate the effects of metrical regularity.

And so, to the main points—

(1) "THERE IS NO QUANTITATIVE MEASURE IN ENGLISH."

George Saintsbury, 1908: "The fact simply is, postponing full enquiries into the reason of it, that classical scansion, as regards *metres,* not *feet,* and attempted in special reference to the hexameter and elegiac measures, has always been, must always be, a failure and an absurdity in English."

Probably the most interesting poem in the English language written in what is announced as a quantitative meter is William Cowper's "Lines Written in a Period of Insanity." It's worth examining here as a test case, if only to pay some attention to a remarkable and neglected poem. Here it is:

Hatred and vengeance, my eternal portion,
Scarce can endure delay of execution,
Wait with impatient readiness to seize my
        Soul in a moment.

Damned below Judas: more abhorred than he was,
Who for a few pence sold his holy Master.
Twice betrayed Jesus me, the last delinquent,
        Deems the profanest.

Man disavows, and diety disowns me:
Hell might afford my miseries a shelter;
Therefore hell keeps her ever hungry mouths all
        Bolted against me.

Hard lot! encompassed with a thousand dangers;
Weary, faint, trembling with a thousand terrors;
I'm called, if vanquished, to receive a sentence
        Worse than Abiram's.

Him the vindictive rod of angry justice
Sent quick and howling to the center headlong.
I, fed with judgement, in a fleshly tomb, am
        Buried above ground.

Cowper described this verse—written during one of his periodic fits of religious terror—as Sapphic. A Sapphic line is supposed to have eleven syllables and a dactyl in the third foot. The last line in each stanza, the adonic, consists of five syllables, two feet, the first a dactyl, the second a spondee or a trochee. It is a question whether Cowper conceived this poem as written in quantitative verse—that is, one based on vowel length—or in accentual-syllabic verse employing the pattern of the classical form but using stressed and unstressed syllables rather than long and short vowels as the measure. This is made more difficult to resolve on inspection because of the fact that in most English words, the syllables containing long vowels (the ones that take longer to breathe out) also tend—usually, not always—to be the ones that are stressed. (Consider how the vowel in the first syllable is lengthened in the noun "convict" and shortened in the verb "convict.")

If one even begins to try to scan it, one takes Robert Wallace's second point. You would need some kind of machine, such as speech therapists use, to measure the duration of the vowels if you were going to approach it that way. There are simply no fixed rules in English. And so, one sees immediately, there cannot in this sense be a quantitative meter in our language.

As for the other locution, in which the *i* in "bid" is short and the *i* in "bide" is long—what would one do with the first line of Cowper's last stanza: "*Him* the vindictive rod of angry justice"? According to this terminology, the *i* in *"Him"* and the two *i*'s in "vindictive" are all short. Clearly, what Cowper was writing was an accentual-syllabic meter based on the pattern of the classical poets. *"Him"* is stressed, the "dic" in "vindictive" is stressed and these account for the rhythm we hear in the line. There is a wonderful assonance in the line in short *i* sounds—him, vin, dict, tice—but it has nothing to do with meter.

This settled, there is the problem of scansion. If we begin with the line above, the pattern seems clear:

/ ∪ ∪ / ∪ / ∪ / ∪ / ∪
Him the vin | dictive | rod of | angry | justice

A dactyl followed by four insistent trochees. A poem in trochaic pentameter, one might say, according to the old prosodic conventions, with a dactylic substitution in the first foot. If we try to go back to the beginning of the poem and see if this pattern fits, it's clear that it does:

/ ∪ ∪ / ∪ / ∪ / ∪ / ∪
Hatred and | vengeance, | my e | ternal | portion,

/ ∪ ∪ / ∪ / ∪ / ∪ / ∪
Scarce can en | dure de | lay of | exe | cution,

/ ◡ ◡   / ◡   / ◡ / ◡   /   ◡

Wait, with im | patient | readi|ness to | seize my

and the last line is a perfectly correct adonic:

/   ◡ ◡   / ◡

Soul in a | moment.

(How wonderful, or terrible, that this eighteenth-century English priest's dark night echoes Sappho's cry to the god—we don't know whether of anguish or awe or ecstasy; it survives as a fragment— *O Ton Adonin.*)

Readers will see, if they apply this scansion to the rest of the poem, that Cowper has made strategic substitutions or variations in the basic meter, and it's not always clear how to describe them. In lines 7, 11, 13, 14, 15, 18, and 19, it's stretching things a bit to call the first foot a dactyl. There are variations for emphasis. But if you allow each of the opening three-syllable phrases as some kind of dactylic substitution, the rest of the verse is perfectly regular. It would be hard to argue that this is not a poem written in trochaic pentameter on the model of quantitative Sapphics, which seems to put Mr. Wallace's argument that the only meter in English is iambic in doubt—though not his banishing of quantity.

Wallace's argument on this subject is that if it looks like a trochaic meter, it's headless iambic. Hence, I think, he would scan the line we began with as iambic, in this way:

/ ◡   ◡   /   ◡   /   ◡ /   ◡ /   ◡

Him the | vin dic | tive rod | of ang | ry just | tice

and the next line like this:

/   /   ◡   /   ◡   / ◡ /   ◡ /   ◡

Sent quick | and how | ling to | the cen | ter head | long

It certainly sounds like an iambic line. The next one is more problematic. It can be scanned a couple of ways. The first honors what must have been Cowper's intention:

/   ◡   /   ◡   / ◡   / ◡ /   ◡

Fed with | judgement, | in a | fleshly | tomb, am

It consists of five trochees—a trochaic pentameter—which, I assume, Wallace would allow as an extreme instance of substitution. He might be more inclined to scan it this way:

/　　∪　 /　　　∪　 /　∪　 /　　∪　 /　　　∪
Fed | with judge | ment, in | a flesh | ly tomb, | am

The test of Wallace's hypothesis is in these details. And what one can grant him in this case is that, even when a poet sets out to write a trochaic or quantitative verse, we do hear underlying it and giving it aural structure the persistence of the iambic measure. So, it makes entire sense to grant him his main point—there are no quantitative meters in English—and turn to the next proposition.

(2) "THE ONLY ACCENTUAL-SYLLABIC METER IN ENGLISH IS IAMBIC."

George Saintsbury, 1910: "The iamb, the trochee and the anapest are by far the commonest English feet; in fact, the great bulk of English poetry is composed of them. . . . The dactyl, on the other hand, though observable in separate English words, does not seem to compound happily in English, its use being almost limited to that of a substitute for the trochee."

Here is how Wallace frames his argument: "Poems in accentual-syllabic meter are overwhelmingly iambic, so it makes sense to see iambic as the metrical base; and, given substitution, the other so-called sub-meters . . . all lie along a *continuous* spectrum of variations." In other words, the basis of metrical poetry in English is the iambic measure. Period. Most prosodists would differ. They say there are four measures in English and the one most commonly and widely used is the iambic measure. Simply as a pedagogical matter, this means that students of the subject are likely to approach each poem they read asking themselves which of four meters it's written in. Wallace tells them to figure out if a poem is metrical, then to assume it's iambic and begin to look to the details of the meter. As a tactic for teaching, this makes perfect sense to me.

It also makes a deeper conceptual sense. I think he's right as a matter of fact—the basis of meter in English is the iamb, and there is a reason why this is so. Saintsbury, when he takes up the question of whether the basis of meter in English is iambic or trochaic in an appendix to his study of prosody, remarks that there was a time when "the metrical basis of English poetry, so far as it had any, was trochaic. The trochaic cadence sounds—if any foot-cadence does—in the whole body of Anglo-Saxon verse." And he observes that the slow development of iambic meters parallels in time the passing of Old and the coming of Middle English and that the iambic measure is firmly established with the arrival of modern English.

I don't know enough about the history of language to know for sure why this should be so, but it seems clear that the language itself, in its Germanic roots, is heavily trochaic; it employs stress very often, almost always in disyllabic and polysyllabic words, in ways that invite us to hear a falling cadence. Almost every two-syllable English name I can think of, for example, is a trochee. Consider the list of English poets: Wyatt, Sidney, Spenser, Shakespeare, Herrick, Marvell, Milton, Cowper, Wordsworth, Hopkins, Hardy, Auden, Larkin—a procession of trochees. The only English poet I can think of whose name is an iamb has a French name: Gascoigne. Two-syllable words with Germanic roots, especially verbs, have a rising sound mostly when they have been formed by a Latin prefix: *invent, recant, dethrone.* And almost all the nouns one thinks of with a rising beat are also formed from prefixes and are Latin or Norman French in origin: *descent, garrotte, sabot, lament.* These di-syllabic words and the great number of monosyllables in the language make possible the play between rising sounds and falling sounds in English speech—make possible, in Saintsbury's pleasant phrase, "the peculiar fashion in which iambic and trochaic measures intermix, set to each other, and carry out a complicated country dance." My guess about this is that, at a certain point in the history of the language, the combination of the long use of Latin by the learned classes as a basis for word formation, continental borrowings, and the incursion of Norman French provided speakers with enough rising sounds to make possible a principle of contrast as the basis of expressive play in speech. It made possible a way of speaking which played a rising sound in the sentence against the predominantly falling sound in the stress pattern of the language's

Germanic word-horde. And it is this play that got inscribed in the emergence of accentual-syllabic meter.

It's interesting to look at a typical passage of Renaissance verse with this phenomenon in mind. Here's a stanza from Spenser's "Epithalamion":

> Ye gentle Birdes! the world's fair ornament,
> And Heaven's glorie, whom this happy hower
> Doth leade unto your lovers' blisful bower,
> Joy may you have, and gentle heart's content
> Of your love's couplement;

Among the Anglo-Saxon falling sounds, "happy," "lover," "blisful," and the borrowed words that came to have a falling sound when they migrated into English, "gentle," "glorie," are three French borrowings, all accented, in Spenser's pronunciation, on the final syllable to make a rising sound: "ornament," "content," "couplement." Two Old French loan words—"hower" and "bower"—are reduced to a single syllable by English pronunciation—

> And let faire Venus, that is Queene of Love,
> With her heart-quelling sonne upon you smile,
> Whose smile, they say, hath virtue to remove
> All love's dislike and friendship's faultie guile
> Forever to assoile.

"Venus," "quelling," "virtue," "friendship," "faultie," in descent, are lifted by the prefixed disyllables of "dislike" and "remove" and the French loan word "assoile."

> Let endlesse Peace your steadfast hearts accord,
> And blessed plenty wait upon your bord;
> And let your bed with pleasures chaste abound,
> That fruitful issue may to you afford,
> Which may your foes confound,
> And make your joyes redound
> Upon your Brydale day, which is not long:
> Sweet Thames! run softly, till I end my song.

Again, it is "accord," "abound," "afford," "confound," and "redound," a mix of iambs made from Old French and Old English prefixed disyllables, playing off of "endlesse," "steadfast," "blessed," "plenty," "pleasures," "fruitful," "issue," "brydale," and "softly," that give variety from the English trochees and also from the monosyllabic rhyme words and that are strategically placed to lift the poem into its rising rhythm.

The principle of iambic meter seems to be that the ear will hear it if the line ends on a stressed syllable, or if the line establishes the iambic cadence so clearly that it invites us to hear an iamb in the last position—and hear the last syllable therefore as unstressed—even when the final word is a trochee.

An example of this can be found in two lines of Ezra Pound:

> ˘　/ ˘ /　˘ ˘　/　˘
> The petals fall to the fountain,

> ˘ / ˘　/ ˘　/　˘
> The orange-colored rose-leaves.

The last line of this little poem returns to the iambic base:

> ˘ / ˘ /　˘ ˘　/
> Their ochre clings to the stone.

This is the principle, I think, that leads Wallace to argue that there is no trochaic meter in English poetry. One could scan the strongly trochaic cadence of much folk poetry in English to reflect that sound—like this, for example:

> / ˘　/ ˘　/ ˘ /
> Bobbie | Shaftoe's | gone to | sea,
> / ˘　/ ˘　/ ˘　　/
> Silver | buckles | on his | knee.
> /　/　/ ˘　/ ˘　/
> He'll come | back and | marry | me.
> / ˘　/ ˘　/ ˘
> Bonnie | Bobbie | Shaftoe!

But Wallace notices, in fact insists on, the poem's impulse to end on a strong rising beat and therefore scans it this way:

<pre>
 /   ◡   /   ◡   /   ◡ /
Bob | bie Shaf | toe's gone | to sea,
  /   ◡   /   ◡ /   ◡   /
Sil | ver buck | les on | his knee.
   /   /   /   ◡   /   ◡   /
He'll | come back | and mar | ry me.
    / ◡   / ◡   / ◡
Bonnie | Bobbie | Shaftoe!
</pre>

His scansion emphasizes the predominance of the iamb in the iamb-trochee country dance of English syllables and lets an echo of the elder trochaic cadence have its say in the last line.

This is the historical basis for his argument against a supposed trochaic meter in modern English. Another argument for it, we have already seen, is Cowper's "Lines," a poem that seems to me to have been, quite self-consciously, composed in a trochaic meter, and, as we've seen, it too can be easily construed in such a way that the iambic base seems to predominate.

His argument about anapestic meters is slightly different. They are, for one thing, much less rare—they enjoyed a boomlet in the popular verse of the nineteenth century. Indeed every American has heard their existence thumped out on a high school band's bass drum:

Oh-oh SAY can you SEE by the DAWN'S early LIGHT
What so PROUDly we HAILED in the TWIlight's last GLEAMing

There are many Americans who can recite—so I read recently—a continuous sequence of lines from only one English language poem, which is also in anapests:

T'was the night before Christmas, and all through the house,
Not a creature was stirring, not even a mouse.

I take his argument to be that these anapestic rhythms are simply a derivation from metrical poetry's iambic base. They are, if one stops thinking about Greek categories, skipping iambs to which an extra unaccented syllable per foot has been added, or, if one wants to say it another way, they are a sub-meter of the iambic base. Again, this way of thinking about the matter seems to me both useful and persuasive. It observes the trajectory in the history of the language that gave us a trochaic cadence in the very beginnings of the language, impossible to say now for how many years, but for at least two hundred in which manuscripts survive, followed by a period of four centuries from about the twelfth to the fifteenth when the language changed and an experimental play of iamb and trochee was the main feature of verse, followed by the modern period of accentual-syllabic meter based on the iamb which was the unchallenged source of the rhythm of English poetry for another three hundred years. That there were, here and there, anapestic expansions and counter-iambic experiments during the high tide of accentual-syllabic verse, in this sense of things, only reinforces the fact of the long reign of the iamb in the ears of poets.

(3) "ACCENTUAL VERSE AND SYLLABICS ARE SPECIES OF FREE VERSE."

Syllabics: if some device to measure the line,
    however arbitrary it seems,
is a meter, then syllabics is a meter.
    If all meters involve what's hearable
in stress, syllabics may very well be a me-
    ter, since lines contain a finite number,
upwardly fixed, of stresses. And if the notion
    of meter is conceptual

purely, if it simply involves cognitive
    recognition of some play between fixed
and variable elements, some palpable
    shudder in the mathematics of chance,
a grid for chaos theory, a violent silence
    to supercede the music of the spheres,
then syllabics, pure will and freed from bodily
    urgency, is meter purely.

Syllabics and accentual verse are (Coleridge notwithstanding) twentieth-century inventions. They were experiments in finding alternative measures, ways of getting rid of or at least turning down the volume on accentual-syllabic verse without losing the idea of measure altogether. Wallace is proposing that we admit—for different reasons in the two cases—that these experiments have failed to produce an intelligible measure and stop classifying them as meters. This is, of course, partly a question of definition, and Wallace's comes to this: *meter is a system of measurement based on stressed and unstressed syllables that produces in the listener the perception of a pattern which organizes the syllables within the line in a more or less predictable way.*

One could remark that this definition of meter so closely resembles a description of accentual-syllabic meter that his conclusion—that the only meter is accentual-syllabic—should come as no surprise. A way to test it is to ask if there are alternative definitions. For example, a definition that included syllabics might be "a system of measurement that tells readers and writers when the line comes to an end." This leaves out the idea that an auditory pattern has to be established and the idea that the system has to organize the relation of syllables within the line. Another definition might be "a system of measurement based on stressed and unstressed syllables that produces in the listener, line by line, the perception of a more or less predictable pattern." This leaves out only the notion that the pattern must make the position of stressed and unstressed syllables within individual lines predictable.

The first definition is the one we would need to claim a meter based on syllable count. The second would accommodate accentual verse, if it can be demonstrated that accentual verse can produce the perception of a pattern that auditors can anticipate and hear changes rung on. And one can imagine a third alternative definition designed to accommodate various post-modern practices: "Meter is a system that puts the line of verse, or some other unit of composition, under the pressure, by rules previous to composition, of containing at least one fixed and one variable formal element."

It's worth emphasizing that—the last, perhaps, only conceptually or intellectually—all of these definitions depend upon the creation of the perception of pattern. This ability to hear and anticipate an auditory pattern is a basic human capacity, variable in different individuals, and it can be made much more acute by training. Its fundamental formal principle is repetition. People have to hear a thing more than once to recognize a pattern.

In poetry this is true both at the level of the syllable and at the level of the line. It would be easy, in fact, to construct an argument that accentual-syllabic meters are a trick played on the autonomic nervous system, that they take a quite arbitrary and unnatural speech pattern that requires alternating stressed and unstressed syllables, and use it to establish a physiological habit, and therefore give it the authority of bodily need. This is the principal way in which the educated classes in Europe mystified their utterance and gave it repressive authority, which they called poetry. The pattern makes the fall of syllables seem inevitable. Makes any kind of nonsense seem inevitable and therefore natural—because the poor body is subject to all sorts of addiction and because the soul craves the sensation of safety and order endlessly. Hence the repeated assurance of prosodists—those low proppers-up of state ideology—that accentual-syllabic meters are "natural" and the still more absurd assertion that humans, whenever they are seized by strong emotion, tend "naturally" to speak in iambic pentameter, or perhaps tetrameter, or perhaps a mix of the two.

Syllabics, it could be argued, deconstruct this habit by imposing what is clearly a pattern, but one that's not addictive, on speech and give it order without some Pavlovian salivating-at-the-sound-of-a-bell undergirding. Give it, in fact, an intelligent sense of shape while leaving the reader's mind free from compulsion. In this view of things, Wallace's complaint that "we do not hear the count of syllables" in syllabics would be tantamount to a slave's complaint that he doesn't feel right without his chains. Surely, this sense of freedom and willful patterning is the expressive effect of Marianne Moore's syllabic practice:

> I, too, dislike it: there are things that are important beyond all
> this fiddle.
> Reading it, however, with a perfect contempt for it, one
> discovers in
> it after all, a place for the genuine.
> Hands that can grasp, eyes

> that can dilate, hair that can rise
> if it must, these things are important not because a

And, when she wants to induce the physiological response, she can do so in controlled doses through rhyme, as she does in "The Fish":

> wade
> through black jade.
>> Of the crow-blue mussel shells, one keeps
>> adjusting the ash heaps;
>>> opening and shutting itself like

> an
> injured fan.

This same sensibility would account for some of the poetic practice of Louis Zukovsky and for, if one is going to use the term in this way, the meter of Lynn Hejinian's *My Life,* which is composed in forty-five prose sections of forty-five sentences each. And it would account, in an allied art, for what is metrical in the compositional practices of John Cage. And it could be justified, or privileged, as professors of literature like to say, by appealing to the recently fashionable terms of post-structuralist discourse. It is a prosody that foregrounds the materiality of language, a revolt of the signifier against the mimetic tyranny of the signified.

All of this said, I am inclined to grant Wallace his definition. In the first place, not all syllabic verse has this effect. In the seven-syllable line of Kenneth Rexroth's "The Signature of All Things," for example, the intent seems to be to loosen the headless tetrameter line it begins with, not to produce a sense of willful pattern. On the contrary, the expressive effect is naturalness, relaxation:

> Deer are stamping in the glades,
> Under the full July moon.
> There is a smell of dry grass
> In the air, and more faintly,
> The scent of a far off skunk.
> As I stand at the wood's edge,
> Watching the darkness, listening
> To the stillness, a small owl

Comes to the branch above me,
On wings more still than my breath.
When I turn my light on him,
His eyes glow like drops of iron,
And he perks his head at me,
Like a curious kitten.
The meadow is bright as snow.

And John Logan's nine-syllable line in "On Reading Camus in Early Spring" seems similarly a loosening somewhere between tetrameter and pentameter. It sits in some mid-place between Moore's willed artifice and Rexroth's naturalness and adds to them Logan's own subtle play with rhyme:

That boy in the red coat packing snow
mixes in my mind with the obscure
taste for beauty Camus' writing stirs.
I don't say the beauty of the boy—
open only through his naked face,
only his eyes drawing the full stores
of his emerging life, that seems to
root back deeply toward the dead. (See
how the boy stands footless in the snow,
like some smashed piece of Italian stone.)
Not that, but what he does to the cold,
pure seed or sand through his muffled hand:
how he brings the Midas touch of art—
I don't care how crude he seems to mold.
Not sad or old, not adult, the boy
has no more need of art than a saint;
and as he throws against the wall, shat-
tering what his hand could form, I feel
the older, more yearning child's alarm.

It would be possible to argue that both these poems, or rather the passage from Rexroth and the complete Logan poem, are in fact metrical; and, of course, their rhythms have to be construed accentually, syllabics or not. But I will come back to that. The compositional principle in both is clearly syllable count. And the point I am making here is only that not all syllabic verse does what Moore's verse does, so that the argument for syllabics as a conceptual meter would have the problem that in syllabics that sense of willed artifice is only one possible expressive effect.

The question remains whether meter is to be defined in terms of its ability to elicit this pattern-anticipating response. Another tack to take, of course, before we are through with the argument for a purely conceptual meter, is that syllabic verse does, in fact, elicit that response. I think it is true that we do not hear syllable count. It would be interesting to ask poets who wrote in it regularly if they did, through practice, hear syllable count, or more to the point write verse that regularly, without counting, produced the requisite number of syllables. It's feasible that one could train oneself to hear it, though I am inclined to doubt that, and for the purposes of this discussion set the possibility aside.

Still, one could argue that one was, through repetition, being asked in Rexroth's and Logan's poems to anticipate lines of a certain length—"more or less," as Robert Wallace says. And that Moore's practice—which seems to be based on an imitation of the knotty and willful stanzaic patterns of seventeenth-century English poetry—does in fact establish an expectation of lines of a certain length in a certain order. It could seem to be a difficulty of Wallace's argument in this matter that he thinks he has cinched his case by saying that in corresponding lines in Moore's "Critics and Connoisseurs" the syllable count can't be intuited. But clearly in that poem, it is the regularly varying line lengths that do the patterning, as well as the syllable count within the lines. The lines

    proclivity to more fully appraise such bits

and

    itself, struck out from the flower-bed into the lawn

do not intuitively seem to me equivalent, but in one view of the matter, that's not the point. The point would rather be that the pair of lines

    /   / /   / / /
    proclivity to more fully appraise such bits

$$\overset{\text{/}}{\text{of food}} \text{ as the } \overset{\text{/}}{\text{stream}}$$

and

$$\overset{\text{/}}{\text{itself,}} \overset{\text{/}}{\text{struck}} \overset{\text{/}}{\text{out}} \text{ from the } \overset{\text{/}}{\text{flower-bed}} \overset{\text{/}}{\text{into}} \overset{\text{/}}{\text{the}} \text{ lawn}$$

$$\text{and } \overset{\text{/}}{\text{returned}} \text{ to the } \overset{\text{/}}{\text{point}}$$

do seem intuitively equivalent; that is, one is more or less long and one is more or less short, and when this pattern is repeated, we might come to expect it. Moreover, to my ear, the pattern of strong stresses, six and two, and then seven and two, are close enough to make for accentual patterning.

The answer to this problem is, I think, that Moore's main effect is created by stanza pattern, not syllable count. Stanza pattern is also based, after all, on our tendency to take pleasure in the patterns we perceive. The stanza is a proposition of order. Some of them are so conventional that they have come to seem natural, especially accentual-syllabic stanzas with familiar rhyme schemes. Some, like Moore's and her models in Donne and Herbert are extraordinarily strenuous. And some of them—the Spenserian stanza of *The Faerie Queen* and Chaucer's stanza in *Troilus and Cresside*—are hallowed by a particular use. They set up and fulfill patterns of expectation, and they parallel the activity we associate with meter, but nothing is gained by calling them meters. They are an aspect of poetics, they are not prosody. In this sense blank verse is not a meter, either. It's a poetic form, composed in iambic pentameter, which is a meter. As a form, what distinguishes it from other iambic pentameter verse is the absence of rhyme. It's in this sense that I would argue that syllabic verse is not a meter but a form, more specifically an accentual form.

(4) ACCENTUAL VERSE AND FREE VERSE

There is no accentual meter, in Wallace's terms, because meter organizes unaccented syllables and accentual verse, explicitly, does not. Is there any reason to reject this proposition? I don't see one. And here it would seem we have come to the end of the argument.

But there are reasons to pause over his discussion of accentual verse. Here is what he says about it: "Whereas accentual-syllabic meter has evolved a roughly workable way of bringing the wide variety of stress-levels in speech into its binary counting, accentual meter offers no way at all. Anything that might be a stress in speech might equally be a stress in accentual meter—*or not.*" And this: "counting only stresses offers no meaningful predictability and is, ultimately, hopelessly subjective." This is almost always what prosodists say when they are, implicitly, advocates of metrical poetry, rather than students of the language. And I think it can be demonstrated that they are wrong.

So we need to look at speech stress. Wallace assumes that there is "in speech . . . any number of levels of stress." While this is true of the play of language when we talk, and true of the voice we intuit making its rhythmic sense over and around the foot pattern in metrical verse, it is also true that, so far as intelligibility is concerned, speech stress is binary, rule-governed, and not at all arbitrary, though, as Wallace points out, the so-called scansion of accentual verse often is. Therefore, it will be useful to remember what those rules are.

Three rules govern stress in spoken English. The first kind of stress is *semantic,* and it governs all words of more than one syllable. That this is rule-governed behavior should be clear from the fact that these stresses are always marked in the dictionary.

inhi*bi*tion con*cede* re*sent*ment *ar*bitrary

This is based, of course, on the fact that in English, we pronounce one and sometimes more syllables in a word more emphatically than others. It is a binary system, made slightly more complicated by the fact that in polysyllabic words there are sometimes—*arbitrary* is an example—a primary and a secondary stress. Though, if one pronounced it neutrally, both *ar* and *trar* would receive equal stress, in a sentence *ar* receives the primary stress, so that one might very well hear a protest—

That is com*ple*tely *ar*bitrary!

—as three strong beats.

This is because a second rule has come into play, the one that governs *grammatical stress*. In English, stress is also used to underline the key elements of grammatical structure in a sentence, which means that, normally, the main syllables in the key words in a sentence, the ones that convey primary meaning, receive more emphasis than the ones that indicate relation like articles, prepositions, and pronouns. Thus, in the sentence "He went to the store," the key words—"went" and "store"—receive more emphasis than "he" and "to" and "the." The pronoun isn't emphasized—I suppose—because it is the marker for a previous emphasis. If one said, "Sheila went to the store," the syllable "Shei-" would receive stress. This principle of pronunciation is not codified in the same way that semantic stress is, but one has only to pronounce the sentence placing the stress on "he," "to" and "the" to see that it no longer sounds like English—indeed, that it sounds like a nonnative speaker attempting English. Of course there are circumstances in which the "he" in "he went to the store" would receive stress. For example, "She did the cooking. He went to the store." Which means that, in this case, context plays a role in determining grammatical stress.

The third kind of stress is *rhetorical*. This is another of the places where Wallace's notion of different levels of stress comes into play. One might want to emphasize that he went to the store when he was supposed to go the bank. In which case "store" might receive more emphasis than "went," though both would be more emphatic than the article and preposition. Thus, for different reasons, in different situations, one might say, "Are you *totally* out of your mind?" or "Are *you* totally out of your mind?" or "Are you totally *out* of your mind?" or "Are you totally out of your *mind?*" Rhetorical stress is often hard to determine on the printed page because it has to be inferred from the context. "Who wants to be a millionaire?" the song goes. "*I* do." "Do you take this woman? . . ." "I *do.*" But it is not arbitrary. Rules that speakers understand govern it, and intelligibility depends on it.

The rhythms of speech, the play of accented and unaccented syllables, are based on these rules. According to them, the rhythm of the sentence we've been looking at is what a prosodist would call three anapests:

> Are you *tot* (semantic stress)

> al ly *out* (grammatical stress: "out" is a subject-complement)

> of your *mind*? (grammatical stress)

What happens to these nine syllables when we add a fourth kind of stress, *metrical stress,* an artifice that got invented sometime between the Norman conquest and the reign of Henry Tudor, is not governed by the rules of English pronunciation:

> *Are* | you *tot* | al *ly* | *out* of | your *mind*?

All the syllables have been organized into alternating stressed and unstressed syllables to make a line of headless iambic pentameter. "Are" and "ly," which do not receive stress in speech, have been organized into a pattern which requires us to hear them as stressed. The demands of grammatical stress have interceded to insist on "out," and metrical stress has accommodated itself to this necessity by developing the concept of substitution.

With these rules in mind, let's go back and look at Rexroth's syllabics. The first line, as we have seen, is headless tetrameter:

> /   ∪   /   ∪ /   ∪   /
> Deer | are stamp | ing in | the glades,

Seven syllables, three stresses—*deer, stamp, glades*—provided by grammatical stress and one by metrical stress. A determined champion of meter would be hard-pressed to accommodate the next two lines to this pattern:

> /   ∪   /   ∪   / ∪   /
> Un | der the | full Ju | ly moon

doesn't work because the article "the" cannot, in any natural hearing of the line as speech, be made to yield a stress. Perhaps this:

> / ∪   ∪   /   ∪ /   /
> Under | the full | July | moon.

Though it introduces the monosyllabic foot that Robert Wallace has abolished, it gives us the four feet, it marks the four strong stresses that semantic and grammatical stress give us, and it notices

the pleasure of the relation of the two lines—the second reverses
the pattern of the first.

The next line is a harder case:

```
  /    / ∪    / ∪    /  /
There | is a | smell of | dry grass
```

Not an iamb anywhere, and it produces a much stronger stress on
the first syllable, *there*, than one hears. What one hears, in fact, is
an easy three syllables leading up to the speech stress of *smell*. The
speech rhythm expresses lull, hiatus, and it is hard to see the point
of doing violence to the feel of the line for the sake of the imposition of a pattern. And the alternative seems even farther from the
line's actual rhythm:

```
   /  ∪ ∪   /  ∪   /   /
There is | a smell | of dry | grass
```

Either you call the first foot a trochee or promote *is* to a stressed syllable, which changes the meaning and the feeling of the line. So you
stay with the first alternative, and you have Wallace's forbidden
monosyllabic foot again and a marking of the strong spondee *dry
grass* that has nothing to do with the rhythm of the line. Rhythm and
metrical pattern, of course, don't have to correspond point by point,
but they have to correspond enough to justify the imposition of the
pattern, and here, for two lines in a row, we seem to be pushing it.

The line after that is a little easier:

```
 /   ∪ /   ∪   /   /  ∪
In | the air, | and more | faintly
```

However, it once again gives a light stress to an initial syllable that
one wonders about. But if one concedes that, the line can be scanned.
And so can the line after that, allowing for the double iamb:

```
 /  ∪ /   ∪ ∪   /    /
As | I stand | at the wood's edge,
```

But the next one is trouble again:

```
 /    ∪ ∪ /   ∪  /  ∪
Watch | ing the dark | ness, lis | tening
```

It has three feet, and scanning it to enforce the pattern requires a dubious stress on the article:

/ ⌣ / / ⌣ / ⌣
Watch | ing the | darkness | listening

The next line is also a problem:

To | the still | ness, a | small owl

It might make more sense just to contend that it is a three foot line:

⌣ ⌣ / ⌣ ⌣ / /
To the still | ness, a small | owl

or

⌣ ⌣ / ⌣ / / /
To the still | ness, a | small owl

The objection to the first is the admission of a monosyllabic foot, to the second that it hasn't solved the problem of promoting the article to a stressed syllable.

There are fairly regularly lines ahead:

/ ⌣ / ⌣ / ⌣ /
When | I turn | my light | on him

and

/ ⌣ / ⌣ / ⌣ /
And | he perks | his head | at me.

These lines are almost enough to make one want to persist. But there is another way to describe the rhythm of the poem, which is to treat it as accentual verse, noticing the pattern of stresses that the speech rhythm creates. And there is a compelling reason to do so, because it's evident that the poet took care to write in syllabics, a method that has been used for the most part to circumvent accentual-syllabic meter. Here is how it looks:

/ / /
Deer are stamping in the glades,   3

   /   /   / /
Under the full July moon.   4

         /   / /
There is a smell of dry grass   3

     /   /   /
In the air, and more faintly,   3

     /   / /   /
The scent of a far off skunk.   4

    /   /   /
As I stand at the wood's edge,   3

  /   /   /
Watching the darkness, listening   3 (2/1)

      /   / /
To the stillness, a small owl   3 (1/2)

   /   /   /
Comes to the branch above me   3

  / / /   /
On wings more still than my breath. 4

    /   /   /
When I turn my light on him,   3

  / /   /   /
His eyes glow like drops of iron, 4

    /   /   /
And he perks his head at me,   3

 /   /   /
Like a curious kitten.   3

    /   /   /
The meadow is bright as snow.   3

I think my marking of the stresses is uncontroversial. It is based on the rules that govern speech. In the third line someone might want to mark *there*. It is a pronominal, however, and usually receives rhetorical stress only when there is some reason to emphasize it, as there is not here. I have stressed the pronouns in *on him* and *at me* because, while pronouns in the subject position are usually not stressed, pronouns in the object position often are—but not always. I did not mark a stress on *me* in *above me* because, unless for reasons of special emphasis, pronouns following a two-syllable preposition—hence one that contains a stressed syllable—aren't stressed. I know I am belaboring this issue, but it is so often asserted by apologists for accentual-syllabics that speech stress is arbitrary or subjective—as if children imitating the speech patterns of their parents were not learning rules—that it seems necessary to get this (side) issue straight. The point is that the passage is based rhythmically on a relaxed pattern of three and four accentual stresses.

This is not, by Wallace's definition, a meter, but it is certainly recurrent enough so that reader and writer would notice a variation, a sudden piling up of five or six stresses in the line. In this way, it can serve as a principle of composition for writers and as an aural patterning for readers. For this possibility it seems useful to reserve the term "measure." It is how accentual verse works. It does not manage unstressed syllables, and it does not add metrical stress to syllables which would not be heard as stressed in ordinary speech as accentual-syllabic meter does, but it makes an underthrumming and clear pattern that comes to govern the music of the poem. Rexroth, of course, was attending to syllable count, but there are a great number of poems in which the syllable count is not fixed which deploy this measure, or one based on a steady pattern of two and three or four and five stresses. It is one of the types of free verse.

Measure, naturally, leaves many aspects of the music of the lines unaccounted for, but so does a marking of the accentual-syllabic pattern. I think Wallace has asserted, on behalf of metrical prosody, that a meter accounts for *more* than an accentual pattern does, and I think he is right. Meter governs and determines rhythm in a line more completely than an accentual measure. That's why some writers have preferred accentual rhythms and why some haven't. To account for the rhythms of Rexroth's lines, one would have to examine the pacing of the stresses and notice what we have been noticing, the way it hovers about and sometimes coincides with a metrical stress. There is no problem in doing this. And there's nothing subjective about it. To notice, for example, that the first three sentences in the passage, which consists mostly of three-beat lines, are brought to conclusion with four-beat lines. To notice that after initial stresses in the first two lines, there is a perceptible easing of tension in the skipping unaccented entry into the next two. To notice that the last line is a firm, slightly skipping iambic trimeter. What this would do is bring us closer to the music of the poem—and therefore, moment by moment, to its meaning—which is presumably the point of prosodic study. What it would not do is give us the satisfaction of accommodating the speech rhythms to a predetermined pattern which, like working out crossword puzzles, is one of the incidental pleasures of the scansion of accentual-syllabic verse, but not its reason for being.

There are a variety of measures in accentual verse. Some of them are quite regularly fixed: two, three, four, five beats to the line or more. More often, they are variable, but within limits, establishing a base measure of two to three, three to four, or four to five stresses per line. In this way they correspond to the trimeters, tetrameters, and pentameters of metrical verse, and indeed they often flirt with these meters in something like the way jazz flirts with familiar melodies. Others use a quite variable mix of stresses in each line as the ode form often does in metrical verse. Some of them—the Pound tradition, for example, as it passes into the hands of writers like Gary Snyder—are very strongly accentual. Others—in the traditions of Stevens's and of Eliot's free verse—tend to subdue the urgency of accentual stress, to subordinate it to sentence rhythm, as John Ashbery usually does. Others have continued the tradition of Marianne Moore, a willful patterning that is not just immune but averse to the lure of the iambic base. One could go on. There is by now a large body of work that deploys accentual measures in a rich variety of ways. It seems to me that it would be actively stupid of prosodists to spend all their time arguing about the scansion of some line in Hardy—as if they were anthropologists after the last preliterate societies had disappeared endlessly reinterpreting the same data—when there is so much new work to attend to.

WORDS MOVING

METRICAL PLEASURES
OF OUR TIME

Margaret Holley

Ever creative, the present spins the future out of the past. In one of his colloquies Goethe spoke of "the abyss of the seed," its endless depths of history and futurity. At this moment in the late twentieth century, we are already at work on our new poetry. Its seeds are long sown. The flood of flaccid free verse has truly come to bore and irritate us, just as the mountains of metrical sentiments irritated our forebears when the century turned. We cannot yet consciously hear the new music, the great poetry of the twenty-first century. We can say that we are postmodern, but we can't say precisely what we are pre-, on the verge of. What is clear, I believe, is that we need all of the poetic resources of the past and the present in order to imagine, listen for, and delight in the poetry of coming generations. What we need is not to limit but rather to welcome and legitimize these various resources.

In a time of relative metrical ignorance on the part of most younger readers and writers, the project of paying close attention to the resource of meter is even more important than a similar attention to the full spectrum of rhyme. What the layperson often asks about a poem is "Does it rhyme?" But what he also means to ask about—what engages his visceral response in the first line and a half, before the rhyme appears, or doesn't—is rhythm, the music that the language plays on the instrument of his body even before the sentence is complete and his mind has made full sense of the words. However, he has still asked the right question, for rhyme and meter are both recurring patterns, and what he wants to know is "What kind of universe we are inhabiting in this poem?" Is it a universe that the Newtonian mind identifies as orderly, or is it some newfangled quantum chaos spawned in a primal soup prior to narrative, tonality, and recognizable objects?

One of the possible universes a poem might offer us is suggested in an early and fundamental contention in Bob Wallace's essay that is not by itself singled out for discussion. In the penultimate paragraph of part 1 of "Meter in English," Wallace says, "This meter, accentual-syllabic, as described, *is* [his emphasis] English meter. There is no other" (10). He reiterates this position in the closing of part 2: "There is one meter in English: accentual-syllabic, and its base is always iambic" (22). With so much else in our minds and libraries, we have to think hard what he means by these statements. A good half of the propositions Wallace offers are based on his premise that iambic accentual-syllabic meter is all there is and ever will be in English meter. Certainly a vast majority of English-language poems, and surely many of the best of them, have been accentual-syllabic, and these have been predominantly iambic. But to claim that this is the *only* meter that exists in English, and that its base is *always* iambic, seems to me both untrue and unnecessarily limiting. This is not economy for the sake of clarity; this is a defense of canonical meter to the exclusion of all else. One might wish for tolerance, at least, of marginal meters as quarters of possible surprise. We should not be narrowing the word "meter" to make it a synonym for "iambics" but rather broadening our understanding of meter's exciting developments in this century.

We should be urging recognition of how splendidly diverse, instead of how "splendidly unitary" English meter is (30). Why should we welcome anything less than *all* available possibilities as the raw material of something new? And to begin answering with another question, we might ask what this century has already offered our minds and our libraries that speaks to our longing for rhythmic delight.

The difference between rhythm and meter, as John Frederick Nims reminds us in *Western Wind*, is the difference between flow (from the Greek *rhythmos*, from *rhein*, to flow) and measure (from the Greek *metron*, measure) (268). Current and counting in counterpoint. Now there is nothing in the term itself that requires meter to be invariably audible; measurable is the key. To certain traditional English-language metrists, "inaudible meter" may seem like a contradiction in terms. Wallace's objection to the notion of syllabic meter is that "we do not *hear* the count of syllables" (12). But it was this very inaudibility of the meter that recommended syllabics to Marianne Moore and, along with unaccented rhyme, released her very distinctive voice on the modernist scene, just as it released the sonorous rhythms of some of Dylan Thomas's most wonderful poems. We experience poems with many more faculties than just the ears, and elegant measure is not limited to just one of the senses. The intertwining of natural speech rhythms with awareness of a strict but silent pattern provides a different kind of counterpoint from the counterpoint of speech rhythms with the echo or anticipation of a regular pattern of accents.

Accent is one of the more obvious elements of the English language; syllables are one of its more fundamental and universal elements. A poem composed entirely of three-, four-, or five-syllable lines might sound for all intents and purposes like prose or free verse, but visually and intellectually it would quickly become obvious and monotonous; it would require virtuoso gymnastics to bring up its virtues. However, a different effect occurs when lines of three and five are interwoven with lines of twelve and nine syllables: the stanza pattern of "Poem in October" creates and repeats a silent cognitive music, an unheard melody.

> It was my thirtieth year to heaven
> Woke to my hearing from harbour and neighbor wood
> And the mussel pooled and the heron
> Priested shore
> The morning beckon
> With water praying and call of seagull and rook
> And the knock of sailing boats on the net webbed wall
> Myself to set foot
> That second
> In the still sleeping town and set forth.

(Thomas 113)

One needn't be an expert in early Welsh prosody to delight in Thomas's interweaving of accented language with the inaudible line measure. Likewise, the 6-5-4-6-7-9-syllable pattern of lines in Moore's "The Mind Is an Enchanting Thing" is an enactment of the poem's subject, the mind that "can hear without having to hear."

The Mind Is an Enchanting Thing

> is an enchanted thing
> like the glaze on a
> katydid-wing
> subdivided by sun
> till the nettings are legion.
> Like Gieseking playing Scarlatti;

(Moore 134)

Along with inaudible rhymes (interwoven with audible ones), the silent pattern of Moore's syllabic verse is an art that calls no attention to itself whatever.

The writing of syllabic verse is a very different kettle of fish from the writing of free verse. The effect of a line break on rhythm and meaning is always at issue in all kinds of poetry. However, to the subtle and sense-oriented elements of the overall syntax and pacing in free verse lineation, syllabic verse adds the challenge of a repeated pattern derived from a very elementary and abstract source—word structure itself. I'm not sure it was any easier for the French to count the twelve syllables of their classic alexandrine—to distinguish between eleven, twelve, and thirteen syllables—than it is for us. In composing syllabically, and especially when working without haste, one comes to recognize the smaller units of two-, three-, and four-syllable words and phrases. Just as in music we tend to grasp a measure of seven-four time as a combination of three and four beats, and just as we tend to divide alexandrines into two groups of three, and fourteeners into four and three, so one tends, after paying attention for a while, to recognize syllables in small clusters of two, three, and four, to see and hear them without counting these smaller clusters on one's fingers. In Thomas's "Fern Hill" the fourteen syllable line moves syntactically as three groups of four plus a two—"All the sun long - it was running - it was lovely - the hay / (fields high as the house)" (Thomas 178). It is not difficult to sense when such words and phrases in simple combinations make up a line of five to seven or eight syllables. Even rather long lines, like the eighteen-syllable opening line of each stanza of Moore's "Those Various Scalpels," fall fairly naturally into four ("various sounds"), four ("consistently"), three syllables ("indistinct") making eleven, and then one ("like"), four ("intermingled"), and two syllables ("echoes"), making seven more. Granted I had to count my insensitive, thumping way on the fingers of both hands about halfway through Moore's complete collected and uncollected *oeuvre* before such clusterings began to rise to the surface of my awareness. But we have largely forgotten how much trotting and galloping of nursery rhymes and other thumping of heavily accented verses echoed in our minds before we arrived at the meter of our own first ballads and sonnets. The syllabic method is no more artificial than the dash-and-slash method of scanning is for the accentual-syllabic method, and in syllabically-measured verse there is no temptation to disturb the natural speech rhythms in reading aloud. Accentual-syllabic meter becomes a predictor of sound patterns only when we have heard and remembered the stanza form and seen that it is going to be repeated. Repeated syllabic stanzas have the same predictive effect, but it is accomplished cognitively rather than aurally.

James Tate's poem "Miss Cho Composes in the Cafeteria"

(included in Nims, 302–3), pictures the peculiar challenge of learning to write syllabically in English. In China, Miss Cho's "home," the lines of classical verse were measured by characters, each character being uttered as one syllable. A native reader would have not the slightest need to count such a line on her fingers, since the pattern of five characters or syllables is so easy to recognize, even through all its many other required embellishments of sound. And yet here sits Miss Cho in an American cafeteria counting up to five on her "tiny bamboo fingers" in the effort to produce a poem of five-syllable lines in English (we assume). Does she have some difficulty with English as a language, or is this the poet's way of commenting on her tragic distance from her own classical heritage? Let's say it's both. Our varied and polysyllabic language moves in a different way than does her mother tongue over the grid of repeated fives. The accents of English rise and fall rather freely within the precise numerical grid, although they move much more simply than do the multiple tonalities of Chinese. Much more is contained in five Chinese characters than in five English syllables. The autonomy of the character and the partiality of most English syllables makes a very great difference to the pace, makes it speed along, and to the relation of the unit of measure to the unit of sense.

In his section of *Western Wind* titled "Syllabic Meter," Nims points to other examples of syllabic form—Plath's "Mushrooms" and "Metaphor," Auden's "Moon Landing," and Richard Howard's "Private Drive: Memorial for a Childhood Playmate" (305). But aside from the timeless and wonderful work of Moore and Thomas, syllabic measure remains an occasional choice, albeit one with some unexplored possibilities for poets in English. It may well be that verse that is syllabically measured but without any other significant audible graces—such as the rich and alliterative patterns of "Poem in October" or the syncopated audible and half-audible rhymes of "The Mind Is an Enchanting Thing"—will never be as pleasing to many ears as a poem *with* such graces of sound. Some of Moore's most popular poems are just such blends of syllabic precision, prose rhythms, and unaccented but palpable rhymes. The 1-3-9-6-8-syllable pattern of "The Fish" gracefully supports its pattern of rhymes:

The Fish

wade
through black jade.
     Of the crow-blue mussel-shells, one keeps
     adjusting the ash-heaps;
         opening and shutting itself like

an
injured fan.
     The barnacles which encrust the side
     of the wave cannot hide
         there for the submerged shafts of the

sun,
split like spun
     glass. . . .

In "A Carriage from Sweden," too, with its 8-8-8-9-8-syllable pattern, Moore creates music through an end rhyme enclosed by internal rhymes in the first and last line of each stanza:

They say there is a sweeter air
     where it was made, than we have here;
     a Hamlet's castle atmosphere.
At all events there is in Brooklyn
something that makes me feel at home.

The relative quietness of the syllabic mode and the predominance of other music does not mean that such a poem is not metered, that it has not been written in the discipline of a pattern of measure. It does not *sound* like a majority of the great poetry written in English during the fifteenth through the nineteenth centuries, since it is not accentually driven, but to the iambically jaded ear this departure can bring relief.

The case of accentual meter in English is more complex and less clear than that of syllabic measure. Accentual meter—as a form of measure apart from the further embellished form of the Old English strong-stress verse—is a meter without feet, a paradox as unnerving to some as the inaudible meter of syllabic verse. Accentual verse moves always in between the Scylla of accentual-syllabic meter, into which, with too little variation, it will tend to fall, and the Charybdis of free verse, into which, with too much variation, it will tend to blend. Wallace rejects the notion of accentual meter on the one hand because in many examples "there is scarcely any irregularity" (17) and on the other hand because in other examples it "offers no predictability at all" (15). Accentual meter moves precariously between our long tradition of accentual-syllabic verse and our century's by now also canonical form of free, meaning unmetered, verse. It offers some of the satisfactions of each type, a form for the "informalist." Its line is not intended to be measured in feet but can slip in and out of foot-patterns at will. We do not usually speak or write prose in accentual-syllabic meters: we do it occasionally and for effect. But stress itself is ever present: all of our polysyllabic words contain two or more levels of accent. *Webster's Ninth New Collegiate Dictionary* and *Webster's New World Dictionary* indicate both primary and secondary accented syllables. It is unusual in ordinary English for more than four or five unaccented syllables to pile up between two accented ones. Then the natural human propensity to perceive pattern enters the picture, with culture and schooling not far behind.

The first significant modern poet of accentual meter, Gerard Manley Hopkins, recognized its dual nature. "Why do I employ sprung rhythm at all?" he asked in a letter to his friend and fellow poet Robert Bridges.

> Because it is the nearest to the rhythm of prose, that is the native and natural rhythm of speech, the least forced, the most rhetorical and emphatic of all possible rhythms, combining, as it seems to me, opposite and, one wd. have thought, incompatible excellences, markedness of rhythm—that is rhythm's self—and naturalness of expression. . . . (Hopkins 249n)

In stating that "strict Sprung Rhythm cannot be counterpointed" (Hopkins 10), Hopkins was guarding against the reading of his lines against a mental backdrop of accentual-syllabic meter. He provides for "one, two, or three slack syllables" in each foot but does not intend the pattern of stresses and slack syllables to be intertwined in a reader's mind with any set pattern. It is not always possible to avoid at least some such counterpointing, especially when a poem that is clearly a sonnet opens with a pentameter line in duple rhythm. "Nothing is so beautiful as Spring—" leads into the metrically rather regular sonnet "Spring," while a line with exactly the same pattern, "Glory be to God for dappled things—" introduces the more varied pentameter of "Pied Beauty." Hopkins teaches the reader more immediately how to read "Hurrahing in Harvest" by springing the meter in the very first line: "Summer ends now; now, barbarous in beauty, the stooks rise. . . ." Spoken naturally, the line does not yield any iambic echo until "the stooks," by which time we are fully "sprung" loose from traditional scansion and well into a new accentual music.

> Around; up above, what wind-walks! what lovely behaviour
> Of silk-sack clouds! has wilder, wilful-wavier
> Meal-drift moulded ever and melted across skies?
>
> (Hopkins 31)

Surely it is no coincidence that the overriding music of Hopkins's verse, like the music of Moore's and Thomas's, lies in its very rich alliterative patterns. It is possible that all three poets were responding to traditional Celtic prosodies, particularly to the intricate and sonorous patterns of alliteration and rhyme known as *cynghanedd* (pronounced approximately king-hah-*neth*). We know that Hopkins was interested in these patterns of what he called "chimes" and that he learned Welsh, wrote some verse in that language, and translated the varieties of *cynghanedd* as musically as he could into English. We know that Moore was reading Hopkins during the 1930s and felt that her own work was "influenced somewhat, I think" by his (Holley 163). And Thomas's sense of his own Welsh heritage was the most natural of all. It may be that syllabic and accentual meters, while releasing prose rhythms rather freely into verse, can benefit from the enrichments of rhyme patterns that bring the lyric into a new sense of "the poetic." Far from impoverishment, these less usual meters are opportunities for a more fundamentally new sound than could be achieved by variations on the canonical iambic meters.

It is exciting, if occasionally confusing, to be living in a time when new poetries are being created by departure from the iambic measure that has virtually defined the great works of the last five centuries. As Annie Finch has detailed in her excellent book *The Ghost of Meter*, the so-called "revolution" of free verse at the beginning of this century has lasted much longer than its first advocates suspected it would. The view of free verse as a sudden break with the past, she suggests, "rests on the work of traditional theorists of accentual-syllabic prosody, such as T. S. Omond and George Saintsbury, who did not anticipate the free-verse movement" (84). Various ways of swerving from the regnant iambic pentameter were at the heart of the prosodies of Dickinson, Whitman, and Crane. And yet, as Finch shows, the poetic ear of, say, 1912 was amusingly described by Harriet Monroe in an editorial in the inaugural issue of *Poetry*:

> After forming—generally in preparation for entering one of our great universities—the habit of blinding the inner eye, deafening the inner ear, and dropping into a species of mental coma before a page of short lines, it is difficult for educated persons to read poetry with what is known as "ordinary human intelligence."
>
> (Finch 88)

It is little wonder, as Finch and others have suggested, that T. S. Eliot had to immerse himself deeply in the non-accentual poetry of France and its rage for *vers libre,* in order to emerge with his hearing restored and with a larger-than-English world view of things poetic. Eliot did not reject traditional meter—he rescued it from itself. He did not in any way underestimate what Paul Fussell has termed the "vatic role of the poet," the need for a prophetic voice in a cultural waste land (13–14). He was able to combine iambic pentameter with accentual and free verse in one poem. He was able to move from one metrical basis to another and in and out of meter itself from one line, stanza, or section poem to the next and to turn their various echoes and reverberations loose in the poem like a cultural accompaniment. Harvey Gross highlights this movement in "The Waste Land," verse which sometimes "seems to fall between two metrical types" (37) and which at other times clearly "alternates between two metrical modes. . . . Prosody shifts with the changing voices" (187). The principle of one meter per poem, like one point of view per narrative and per painting, has been replaced by movement among multiple possibilities. The poet's access to a world wider than one specific culture has allowed flexibility to take precedence over predictability, and this trend in our century shows no sign of abating.

It is not always easy to know which metrical universe one is passing through as "The Waste Land" shifts rapidly from voice to voice and as the "Quartets" pass through their stately movements. One might hear "Prufrock" as iambic pentameter antiphonal with free verse. One can read "The Waste Land" as free verse filled with metrical echoes. One can see the "Quartets" as free verse with accentual verse that modulates among three-, four-, and five-stress passages. In the final section of "Burnt Norton," for example, each significant syntactic unit seems to call up its own pattern. The strong, broad four-beat opening line, "Words move, music moves," gives way to three pentameter lines that resist both iambic music and end-stopping, "Only in time; but that which is only living / Can only die. Words, after speech, reach. . . ." In the same stanza, however, a particularly moving shift from a four-beat to a five-beat line calls up definite and resonant echoes of the heroic line. Here are the three lines before and after the modulation as Eliot reads them on the Caedmon recording of the "Quartets":

4 beats	∪/∪∪/∪/∪∪/∪	Or *say* that the *end* pre*cedes* the be*gin*ning,
	∪∪/∪∪∪/∪∪/∪/	And the *end* and the be*gin*ning were *al*ways there
	∪/∪∪/∪∪/∪∪/	Be*fore* the be*gin*ning and *af*ter the *end.*
5 beats	∪/∪/∪///	And *all* is *al*ways *now. Words strain,*
	/∪/∪//∪∪/∪	*Crack* and *some*times *break, un*der the *bur*den,
	/∪∪/∪///∪	*un*der the *tension, slip, slide, per*ish. . . .

(Eliot, *Complete Poems and Plays* 121)

The stanza soon shifts back into four-beat lines, and then the quartet ends with a stanza that, as Eliot reads it, returns repeatedly to three-beat lines. The stanza leaves iambic rhythm almost entirely behind, especially where the last three lines quicken to five beats and slow through four to a final three.

3 beats	∪/∪∪/∪∪/∪	The *de*tail of the *pat*tern is *move*ment,
3	∪∪∪/∪∪∪//	As in the *fig*ure of the *ten stairs.*
3	∪/∪/∪/∪	De*sire* it*self* is *move*ment
3	/∪∪/∪/∪∪	*Not* in it*self* de*sir*able;
3	/∪∪/∪/∪	*Love* is it*self* un*mov*ing,
4	/∪∪/∪/∪/∪	*On*ly the *cause* and *end* of *move*ment,
3	/∪∪/∪/∪	*Time*less and *un*de*sir*ing
3	∪/∪∪/∪∪/	Ex*cept* in the *as*pect of *time*
3	/∪∪/∪∪∪/∪	*Caught* in the *form* of limi*ta*tion
3	∪/∪/∪∪/∪	Be*tween* un-*be*ing and *be*ing.
3	/∪∪∪/∪/∪	*Sud*den in a *shaft* of *sun*light
3	/∪∪∪//	*Ev*en while the *dust moves*
3	∪/∪∪/∪/∪	There *ris*es the *hid*den *laugh*ter
2	∪/∪∪∪/∪	Of *chil*dren in the *fol*iage
5	/////∪	*Quick now, here, now, al*ways—
4	∪/∪∪∪///	Ri*dic*ulous the *waste sad time*
3	/∪∪/∪/∪	*Stretch*ing be*fore* and *af*ter.

Eliot's poetry, early and late, moves through these eloquent shifts of rhythm. There are no announcements about what comes next: unpredictability and echo intertwine, giving us the sense of repeatedly entering new lands and reentering old lands, whole metrically suggested worlds, each one of them partial yet meaningful, each one existing beside something different from itself, a new sound, a new dimension and possibility. To resist this shifting and try to pin down whole poems with one meter is to miss the symphonic breadth and depth of Eliot's vision.

It would be hard to improve on Helen Gardner's analysis of Eliot's metrical development from the "duple rising rhythm" characteristic of *Prufrock and Other Observations,* "the staple rhythm of English verse, the basis of our heroic line" (17), to the four-beat lines of "Sweeney Agonistes" and the recurrent accentual passages of "Four Quartets," both meters intermingled with passages of free verse. "The norm to which the verse constantly returns," Gardner notes of the "Quartets," "is the four-stress line, with strong medial pause, with which 'Burnt Norton' opens" (29). To this picture Annie Finch adds an astute reading of Eliot's major poems in terms of the "metrical codes" which they use and elude in the movement from the predominantly iambic earlier work to the predominantly dactylic later poems. She asserts that as early as "The Waste Land" of 1922, "[that] poem's prosody was an attempt to establish a new metrical idiom for a generation jaded and disillusioned with free verse, and exhausted by the apparent lack of any viable prosodic alternative to it" (128). In spite of Eliot's brilliant synthesis, which we scarcely even know how to describe, the predicament remains with us today. Free verse is clearly such a powerful element that it has taken over much of this century's work. It has made meter share the stage with absence of meter and made it—as other arts have been made to—question its own fundamental ground, its place within an enlarged universe of possibilities.

The argument between meter and free verse has been going on throughout this century. Auden was a "new formalist" par excellence; Lowell began in formalism and then, in frustration with his own forms, plunged into free verse. And much of the best free verse of recent decades has been written by poets who have also written elegantly in meter—Elizabeth Bishop, Richard Wilbur, Seamus Heaney, and one could name many others. Formalism of many kinds will always be with us; it is literally in our bones. It is limiting, in a way, to think of the verse of our time in terms of the dichotomy of metered versus unmetered, even if many individual poems fall into one of the two camps. Free verse is now the new canonical mode, and meter is somewhat ghostly in most of our classrooms, since historical studies of literature have had to make plenty of room for theory and multicultural studies. The good writers in meter are searching for rhythms and verbal music that are not just replays of past glories, and the good free verse poets are searching the chaotic current scene for signs of intelligibility. We have not yet seen any lasting synthesis of this tension in our poetic scene, in spite of the laurels we have heaped on Eliot, Thomas, Moore, and their fellow modernist pioneers. But surely one of the grounds of their greatness is that they searched in what might have seemed to others unlikely places. They gathered strength both within and beyond the bounds of the traditional "top hits" of English pentameter. They learned Welsh and imitated its forms; they emigrated poetically to France or the Middle Ages or into small-town American life; they persisted in what nobody wanted to publish. They did their heritage the honor of extending its boundaries and broadening our sense of the possibilities of this wonderful language.

❧

[Discussion of Wallace's proposals not
covered in the preceding essay]

(1) "Instead of the term 'feminine ending,' we should say simply extra-syllable ending."

The New Princeton Encyclopedia of Poetry and Poetics notes that the terms "masculine" and "feminine" for stressed and unstressed final syllables, line endings, and rhyme words were originally derived from the grammatical genders, which have played a leading role in the prosodies of inflected languages like French and Russian (737). There does not seem to me to be anything inherently "sexist"—that is, negatively discriminatory—about the carry-over of the terms into English. It would be a shame to lose some evidence of the organic growth of our language and terminology from its earliest sources. A simple statement of the origin of these two terms can forge the link in a student's or reader's mind between modern English and one of the languages from which it arose. For this reason, I think it would be unwise to spend energy trying to eradicate the use of "masculine" and "feminine" from our discussions of meter and rhyme.

At the same time, the phrase "extra-syllable ending" may be a useful additional term to have available for some discussions of lines in the rising meters. If the phrase is used, it should be used in its entirety and not abbreviated: it is a self-explanatory term, and its clarity should not be lost in shorthand. Difference of opinion is not always tantamount to confusion, and there is nothing wrong with having synonyms to choose from here as elsewhere.

(2) "For an omitted first syllable of a line, we should use the term anacrusis."

Regarding proposition 2, the reference to Saintsbury appears to generate some confusion about the use of the term "anacrusis." Should it be used to denote something added or something omitted? In the passages that Wallace cites from volume 1 of *A History of English Prosody*, Saintsbury does indeed use that term to suggest an omission, the abbreviation of an initial foot. However, in his "Glossariolum Technicum" at the opening of that volume, he offers the traditional definition of the term as an addition or expansion, and then he adds a note which accounts for his use of it for an omission. "Anacrusis: A half-foot or syllable prefixed to the regular metrical scheme. In English," he continues, "though there are examples of pure anacrusis, it generally takes the form of a monosyllabic foot which *may* be included in the scheme. Some have preferred to call it 'catch'" (xvii). Thus he merges the original sense of the term (an added extra-metrical syllable) into its seeming opposite (an omission resulting in an opening monosyllabic foot).

The word's original Greek meaning—"the striking up of a tune," the *Auftakt* or upbeat—is the sense that appears to have come into most common twentieth century usage. *The New Princeton Encyclopedia of Poetry and Poetics* defines anacrusis as "one or more extrametrical syllables at the beginning of a line, normally unstressed. 'Procephalous' would be a more accurate and better attested descriptor" (68). The *OED* defines "procephalic" as "having a syllable too many at the beginning." Harvey Gross concurs in the glossary in *The Structure of Verse*, defining anacrusis as "an extra syllable, occurring in a metrical pattern. It is like the upbeat preceding the main accent in a musical bar" (279). Shapiro and Beum also treat it as an addition rather than an omission, calling it "the result of prefixing with one or two unstressed syllables a line that theoretically should begin with a stressed syllable" (183). *The Oxford Companion to English Literature*, too, considers anacrusis "an additional syllable at the beginning of a line before the normal rhythm" (26).

There are simple enough alternatives to the mutilative terms "acephalous" and "decapitated." In the case of an omitted first syllable of a line, we may easily speak of an omission or an abbreviated foot. In prosody in our time, plain English may be our best ally.

(3) "Quantities are not a basis for meter in English."

The Greeks appear to have based their quantities at least in part on pitch, while Latin verse makes duration primary, and we have no firsthand experience of how either pitch or duration sounded in those spoken languages in relation to our own sense of stress. Thus quantitative verse in English remains necessarily a speculative, imitative exercise—one that could possibly be of some value to students and scholars but that is bound to remain somewhat academic. Since quantitative verse has clearly been written in English, I don't see the value of arguing that it does not exist. However, I am not enough of a classical scholar to mount a technical defense of it, and so my acceptance of quantity as a basis for meter in English is based simply on my inclination to honor the undertakings of others, however few, who have found it interesting.

(7) "We should drop the pyrrhic foot (◡◡) and accept in its place the double-iamb (◡◡//), as one of the six foot-terms necessary: iamb, trochee, anapest, dactyl, spondee, double-iamb."

The case of the pyrrhic foot is similar to that of the spondee (see proposition 10), which is, indeed, "a good and fairly frequent foot in English." If pressed, we can often scan the pyrrhic, as we can the spondee, as an iamb or trochee, but when the passage in question reads rhythmically as a clear variation or a deliberate lightness, it would be misleading to scan it iambically. Use of the pyrrhic foot allows us to preserve the distinct qualities of such a passage.

To call the juxtaposition of a pyrrhic and a spondee by a special name could be useful, if we find it turning up frequently, but to choose the term "double-iamb" for it seems misleading about what the two feet together actually sound like. The Greek term for the pyrrhic-spondee combination is *ionic minor*; its reverse, the spondee-pyrrhic, is the *ionic major* (Williams 17, Fussell 22). Call them both ionic feet, or call them a pyrrhic-spondee, anything that will respect what comes across—especially in an otherwise iambic passage—as a strong rhythmic change.

(8) "Anapestic, trochaic, and dactylic meters do not exist in English."

I categorically disagree with this statement. Iambic, anapestic, trochaic, and dactylic meters are the four types of accentual-syllabic meter commonly found in English-language verse. In anapestic verse, "Twas the night before Christmas when all through the house," the iamb appears occasionally as a substitution. In dactylic verse, "This is the forest primeval. The murmuring pines and the hemlocks," the iamb occurs as a substitution within the dactylic norm. And in trochaic verse, "Once upon a midnight dreary, while I pondered, weak and weary," the iambic foot is a substitution. We may discuss the relative merits and effects of such poems and many others written in these meters, but nothing is gained by claiming that they don't exist.

(9) "We should *never* use four degrees of speech stress for scanning."

We should not. But never say never. Say, "Well, hardly ever."

(10) "The spondee is a good, and fairly frequent, foot in English."

Yes, it is. We should continue to try to understand poems at least partly on the terms on which they were written, to the extent that we know what those terms were. The spondee is one of the Greek feet which have found new life in English verse. It is one of the most striking and powerful devices of accentual-syllabic meter.

WORKS CITED

Drabble, Margaret, ed. *The Oxford Companion to English Literature*. 5th ed. Oxford: Oxford University Press, 1985.

Eliot, T. S. *The Complete Poems and Plays 1909–1950*. New York: Harcourt, Brace & World, 1962.

———. *"Four Quartets" Read by T. S. Eliot*. Caedmon Recording, TC 1403, issued 1972.

Fussell, Paul. *Poetic Meter and Poetic Form*. Rev. ed. New York: Random House, 1979.

Finch, Annie. *The Ghost of Meter: Culture and Prosody in American Free Verse*. Ann Arbor: University of Michigan Press, 1993.

Gardner, Helen. *The Art of T. S. Eliot*. London: The Cresset Press, 1949.

Gross, Harvey. *Sound and Form in Modern Poetry, A Study of Prosody from Thomas Hardy to Robert Lowell*. Ann Arbor: University of Michigan Press, 1965.

———, ed. *The Structure of Verse, Modern Essays on Prosody*. Rev. ed. New York: The Ecco Press, 1979.

Holley, Margaret. *The Poetry of Marianne Moore, A Study in Voice and Value*. New York: Cambridge University Press, 1987.

Hopkins, Gerard Manley. *Poems and Prose of Gerard Manley Hopkins*. Ed. W. H. Gardner. Middlesex, England: Penguin Books, 1978.

Moore, Marianne. *The Complete Poems of Marianne Moore*. New York: Macmillan/Viking, 1981.

Nims, John Frederick. *Western Wind, An Introduction to Poetry*. New York: Random House, 1974.

Preminger, Alex and T. V. F. Brogan, eds. *The New Princeton Encyclopedia of Poetry and Poetics*. Princeton: Princeton University Press, 1993.

Saintsbury, George. *A History of English Prosody from the Twelfth Century to the Present Day*. Vol. I. London: Macmillan, 1906.

Shapiro, Karl and Robert Beum. *A Prosody Handbook*. New York: Harper & Row, Publishers, 1965.

Thomas, Dylan. *The Collected Poems of Dylan Thomas*. New York: New Directions, 1953.

Williams, Miller. *Patterns of Poetry, An Encyclopedia of Forms*. Baton Rouge: Louisiana State University Press, 1986.

OUR MANY METERS

STRENGTH IN DIVERSITY

John Frederick Nims

quem criminosis cumque voles modum
pones iambis . . .

—HORACE,
Odes, I, xvi

Probably never in the history of poetry have poets had so little interest in or knowledge of the arterial systems through which the lifeblood of poetry flows. One can read through whole issues of "poetry magazines" and find not a glimmer of concern with prosody; even to know the word, some writers seem to feel, puts a sort of stigma upon them. As Anthony Hecht has said in his recent Mellon Lecture on poetry and music: "the rich and versatile instruments of prosody . . . in these latter days, have been rather too hastily consigned to the dustbin under the impression, on the part of some poets, that if they are strident, or shocking, or emphatic enough, all the artifices will be superfluous. Such poets incline to argue, and to believe, that anything in the least contrived, and as seemingly artificial as metrical regularity, would compromise and incriminate their passionate integrity."[1]

Our congratulations and thanks therefore to Mr. Wallace for having disinterred prosody. About his courage and confidence there is no doubt; with his energy, his zeal, and his boundless enthusiasm he might even convince diehard geographers that the world is flat. These are no mere windmills he is tilting at: Chaucer, Langland, Coleridge, Hopkins, Hardy, Ransom, Eliot, Auden, Marianne Moore, and others equally illustrious bite the dust before his spear. Or so he thinks.

But for some reason the very heart of his message is not among the ten propositions he nails to the door of his cathedral of prosody. Instead it sidles in, unnumbered, in his discussion of the second of the propositions, and is repeated after the sixth: "There is one meter in English: accentual-syllabic, and its base is always iambic." He means *only* one meter, as the other propositions show.

The basic meter? Probably so. But the *only* meter? Tell that to the Assyrian who came down like the wolf on the fold. Tell it to Joris and Dirck, who brought the good news from Ghent to Aix. Tell it to Poe, whose trochees show us a raven that speaks only in amphimacers. Tell it to Hopkins, who saw the evening as straining to be tíme's vást, womb-of-all, home-of-all, hearse-of-all night. Tell it to Whitman, whose song comes out of the cradle endlessly rocking. Tell it to Gary Snyder, who says

> I slept under   rhododendron
> All night   blossoms fell
> Shivering on   a sheet of cardboard
> Feet stuck   in my pack
> Hands deep   in my pocket . . .

or to Dudley Randall with his

> Black girl black girl
> lips as curved as cherries
> full as grape bunches
> sweet as blackberries . . .

Most poetry in English is iambic, like our language itself and like the heartbeat which, months before we are born, first tells us we exist. But it is far from being the *only* rhythm. Aristotle called it the most conversational *of the meters* (τῶν μέτρων), more like speech than "the others"(τῶν ἄλλων). There were many others then as now; paging through a book on Greek metrics we come across glyconics, dochmiacs, dactylo-epitrites, choriambi, choliambi, asclepiads, and many more.

As for "Meter in English," I wish the author had provided us with references more impressive than those he uses. Often he refers to the work of George Saintsbury with apparent deference, the same Saintsbury that T. S. Eliot said had "an insatiable appetite for the second-rate. . . . Who but Saintsbury, in writing a book on the French novel, would give far more pages to Paul de Kock than to Flaubert?"[2] As Austin Warren and René Wellek appraise Saintsbury's work on prosody: it "rests on completely undefined and vague theoretical foundations. In his strange empiricism, Saintsbury is even proud of his refusal to define or even describe his terms. . . ."[3] Derek Attridge, who calls Saintsbury's work "a late bloom of the Victorian tradition," goes on to say that "Saintsbury resolutely, almost gleefully, refuses to give a theoretical account of this distinction" between long and short vowels, which Attridge considers the starting point of Saintsbury's approach to meter.[4] Saintsbury does not seem to offer solid ground for building on, and yet he is the authority from whose work Wallace takes the very epigraph that heads his own study, and from whom he derives the "great touchstone" he invokes more than once.

But let's cut to the propositions themselves. The first is **"Instead of the term 'feminine ending' we should say simply extra syllable ending."**

On the chance there are some who don't know this, I'd remind them that the terms *masculine* and *feminine* endings originated in Provence many centuries ago. They were in no way sexist; their origin was grammatical. In Provençal, as in French today, many words referring to what is grammatically feminine tend to add an unaccented syllable to the masculine form of the word. In Provençal the masculine words for *beautiful, white,* and *fresh* are *bel, blanc,* and *fresc;* the feminine forms are *bela, blancha,* and *frescha,* accented on the first syllable. If a masculine rhyming word ended a line of poetry, that line would end with an accent (masculine rhyme); if a feminine word ended it, it would end with an unaccented syllable (feminine rhyme). Wallace's first proposition has nothing to do with his basic contention that iambic is the only meter. The unaccented eleventh syllable in regular pentameter lines has been so common as to be taken for granted ever since Chaucer, who has more eleven-syllable lines than ten-syllable ones. Though Wallace doesn't mention it, occasionally we find two extra syllables, as in *Richard III,* 1. 1. 16:

I that am rudely stamped, and want love's maj | esty . . .

Wallace next wonders about the unstressed syllable sometimes omitted from the beginning of a line, as when Chaucer begins his "Prologue" with

Whan that Aprill with his shoures soote . . .

instead of "And whan. . ." or "So whan. . ." or any unstressed syllable that would complete the iambic foot. Poets have taken this liberty ever since, though it has never become a common variation. Attridge (213n) refers to a 1979 Cambridge dissertation that cites eighty such lines from the sixty-eight thousand lines of Shakespeare's plays: about one-tenth of one percent. Is this worth bothering about in determining whether or not the iambic meter is the only English meter? Whether it is or not, Wallace is concerned again with the question of nomenclature: what to call this irrel-evant variation. It has always been called a headless line, and that has satisfied most of us. But Wallace is squeamish about that and other "current" terms for the missing syllable: "acephalous line, decapitation, and initial truncation." To him they smell of the guillotine. To gentrify the vocabulary Wallace has a suggestion in his second proposition: **"For an omitted first syllable of a line, we should use the term anacrusis. . . ."** Here Wallace adds to what he considers the confusion in prosody by giving the word *anacrusis* a totally different meaning than it has had for at least two thousand years.

It is more aptly used of music; if a tune begins with a rousing

RUM-*di-dum*, RUM-*di-dum*, the band can add a tootle or two before the first beat: *di di RUM-di-dum, RUM-di-dum.* . . . That is anacrusis in the true sense, a meaning that has carried over into prosody. From the time of the ancient Greeks up to today it meant an additional syllable or two *prefixed* to the regular meter of a line; it did not mean, as Wallace would have it, that something had been subtracted from the first foot. The *OED* defines it as "a syllable at the beginning of a line of verse, *before the just rhythm*" [my italics]. The *New Princeton Encyclopedia of Poetry and Poetics* says it is "one or more *extrametrical* syllables at the beginning of a line. . . ." The half-dozen or more reference books I have checked all emphasize that it refers to an additional syllable or two *before* the regular rhythm gets under way; none calls it a subtraction from the regular first foot. So where did he get the idea that it was a subtraction? Probably from Saintsbury, who grudgingly admits it as a possibility. In the "Glossariolum Technicum," at the beginning of volume I, Saintsbury defines it correctly as "a half-foot or syllable prefixed to the regular metrical scheme." But he adds, "in English, though there are examples of pure anacrusis, it generally takes the form of a monosyllabic foot which *may be* included in the scheme." The italics are his, and would seem to express hesitation or dubiety. Where he got the notion that anacrusis could be an intrusion *into* the regular meter of the line I have no idea. Saintsbury published volume I of his *A History of English Prosody* in 1906; when four years later he published his *Historical Manual of English Prosody,* he corrects his definition in the new Glossary: "Anacrusis.—A syllable or half-foot *prefixed* [my italics] to a verse, and serving as a sort of 'take-off' or 'push-off' for it. . . ." No nonsense this time about a monosyllabic foot that "may be" included in the metrical scheme. If Wallace had used the term at all for a curtailed line, he might have called it "false anacrusis." It is regrettable that he has muddled prosodic terminology by sponsoring this term, especially in that anacrusis is rare in English poetry and has little to do with his main concern, the pan-iambic hegemony of English verse.

Having considered the terminal extra syllable and false anacrusis, Wallace goes on to a "third convention," the substitution of other feet for the iamb: trochee, pyrrhic, spondee, anapest, and dactyl.

"There has been," he says, "and remains now, some prejudice against the legitimacy of trisyllabic substitutions. . . ." This is not true; the anapest has always been snugly at home in iambic verse, from the time of Chaucer right down to the present: "Like most English poets, he not infrequently has . . . a trisyllabic foot in place of the regular iambus. . . ."[5] As for the dactyl, to say there is prejudice against it as a substitute for iambic is like saying there is prejudice against pounding nails with a screwdriver. Dactyls do not jibe with iambic lines, which can absorb the reversal of a trochee, but with difficulty absorb the longer reverse drag of the dactyl. We *can* put a dactyl in place of an iamb, but it's likely to rest uneasily there:

> True ease in writing comes from art, not chance,
> As those move easiest who have learned to dance.

Substitute a dactyl for the fourth iamb in the second line, and the reader who has been dancing along with Pope's rhythm will feel something is wrong:

> True ease in writing comes from art, not chance,
> As those move easiest who dexterously dance.

Wallace next runs into trouble with elision, which he considers "another convention." Elision (the omission or slurring of a syllable) is anything but a convention; even unliterary people elide all the time:

> "Yuh willin' t'exchange th'extra ticket?"

I don't understand his saying that *"th'ex"* and *"y a"* are "barbarous, artificial syllables" that "one is required to mouth." *"Th'ex"*—we have the same sound in "wi*th ex*cuses," which is not hard to say. *"Y a"*—we have the same sound in "Oh *yeah?*" which I say frequently, and without mouthing, in reading the sentences of "Meter in English."

A few pages later Wallace introduces what ought to be stated as his main proposition: "This meter, accentual-syllabic . . . *is* English meter. There is no other." It evolved, he says, from the accentual-alliterative meter of Old English. But it did not "evolve," unless by "evolve" we mean "appear later." There is general agreement that Chaucer's innovation marks a clean break with the older system, for which Chaucer had little use and even seems to burlesque. As Attridge says, Chaucer is "the founder of the strict pentameter in English."[6] Wallace objects that, "if it was Chaucer's meter," it is puzzling that there were uncertainties about it for a century and a half after him. But the reason is obvious: In that century and a half the language was changing rapidly. Final *e*'s that would have counted in his meter were no longer pronounced, leaving many of his lines in what seemed to be metrical disarray. As F. N. Robinson, Chaucer's modern editor, puts it, "It is because this knowledge [of his older pronunciation] was lost from the fifteenth century down to the middle of the nineteenth that many of Chaucer's most enthusiastic admirers . . . have regarded his meter as irregular and rough."[7] Chaucer himself puts his finger on the reason in *Troilus and Criseyde* (II, stanza 4):

> Ye know ek, that in forme of speche is chaunge
> Withinne a thousand yeer . . .

He was more specific toward the end of that poem (V, stanza 257):

> And for ther is so gret diversite
> In Englissh, and in writyng of oure tonge,
> So prey I god that non myswrite the,
> Ne the mysmetre for defaute of tonge,
> And red whereso thow be, or elles songe,
> That thow be understonde, god I biseche. . . .

But he was in effect "miswritten," "mismetered," and therefore misunderstood.

II. ONE METER

The "one meter" of the section numbered II is the iambic meter. Wallace begins by mentioning what have been thought to be the four meters in English: syllabic, accentual, accentual-syllabic, and quantitative. He then dismisses three of them. The first to go is quantitative meter—meter, that is, by length of syllable, as in Greek and Latin poetry, rather than by accent.

In the 1580s a few poets and scholars had tried to reform English metrics along classical lines, but their quantitative experiments were soon dropped, because, as Samuel Daniel said in *A Defense of Ryme* (1603), "though it [English verse] doth not strictly observe long and short syllables, yet it most religiously respects the accent. . . ." Except for an occasional eccentric, English poets gave up composition by quantity, according to Tennyson "a barbarous experiment," within a generation after it was first promoted. The only objection we might have to Wallace's third proposition, that **"Quantities are not a basis for meter in English,"** is that it has not been necessary to make this point since about 1590.

Wallace, however, has overlooked one inheritance from the world of classical metrics. Many poets, English and American, have taken over the ancient prosodic patterns, transposing their longs and shorts into our accented and unaccented syllables, and so adding a richly non-iambic trove of poems to our native inheritance.

Among these forms are the classic hexameter, the elegiac couplet, hendecasyllabics, Sapphics, Alcaics, Pindar's combination of pherecratic and glyconic, and the galliambics made famous by Catullus. Among the poets who have used them: Isaac Watts, Cowper, Longfellow, Tennyson, Clough, Kipling, Swinburne, George Meredith, Robinson, Pound, Auden, William Meredith, James Wright, and Marilyn Hacker. Of special interest to us now is Frost's use of hendecasyllabics in "For Once, Then, Something." Frost was well aware that these were not the iambic meter he favored. Mischievous as always, he gloated over the fact that "none of my Latin people recognized it." Let's remember Frost's hendecasyllabics when we are tempted to take too seriously his pronouncements about strict and loose iambics. The hendecasyllabic line, in English, is made up of four trochees and a dactyl.

Having dismissed as "imitations" the classical meters used by such poets as Tennyson and Auden, Wallace arrives at his fourth proposition: **"Syllabics is not a meter in English."** Again we confront a question not of substance but of nomenclature. Syllabic poems do exist, are among the most distinguished of our time, but can we call their patterns a *meter?* In the root meaning of the word, of course we can. The Greek *metron* means "that by which anything is measured"—anything: content, space, weight, distance, duration, whatever. A yardstick is a *metron;* numbers are *metra.* Marianne Moore, W. H. Auden, Dylan Thomas, and many such younger poets as Philip Levine and Robert Morgan have measured their lines by syllable count. For them it is a *metron.*

But in prosody "meter" has come to have a more restricted sense—not any measurement, but only a measurement of binary relationships: of long and short syllables, or of accented and unaccented ones. If we limit ourselves to this meaning, we exclude syllabic systems, in which all syllables have the same value. But isn't there reason to be leery of any prosodic theory which would exclude many of the best poems in the language?

Wallace objects that "We do not hear the count of syllables." Often enough we do. We hear them easily in haiku and in short syllabic lines, like those in James Tate's charming five-syllable lines about Miss Cho, sighing as she does her assignment for the poetry workshop:

> . . . You
> count on your tiny
>
> bamboo fingers; one,
> two, three—up to five,
> and, oh, you have one
>
> syllable too much

We hear the fives in Sylvia Plath's "Mushrooms":

> Overnight, very
> Whitely, discreetly,
> Very quietly
>
> Our toes, our noses
> Take hold on the loam . . .

And I suspect we even hear the nines in "Metaphors," her poem about pregnancy. But only an idiot savant would hear the fourteen syllables in a line of Dylan Thomas or the twenty-two in a line of Marianne Moore. No matter: the poets themselves clearly had their numerical meters in mind.

In attempting to rule out syllabics as a meter, Wallace concentrates his fire on two poems only, both by Marianne Moore. Why does he ignore W. H. Auden, surely one of the great names of contemporary poetry, whose many syllabic poems include "In Memory of Sigmund Freud," "Ode to Terminus," "Prologue" to "Thanksgiving for a Habitat," and, appropriately, "A Mosaic for Marianne Moore"? In speaking of his poems "based on syllable count alone and ignoring stresses," Auden could insist, "I am a fanatical formalist." Why does Wallace ignore Dylan Thomas, whose syllabic "Fern Hill," "Poem in October," and others are among the glories of poetry in our time?

Only Miss Moore's "Poetry" and "Critics and Connoisseurs" are considered. The first is utterly exceptional in her career: a thirty-line poem reduced to its first three lines, with a clause removed even from these. It seems that she regarded this as an alternative version; the notes in her definitive edition also include what she calls the "Longer version." Wallace says the poem "has claim to be the most famous poem in syllabics in English—*if* it is in syllabics at all, which is a question open to a good deal of doubt."

There is no doubt whatsoever. As published in *Poems* (Egoist Press, London, 1921) it is rigorously and impeccably in syllabic lines, whose count, in each of the five six-line stanzas, is 19, 22, 11, 5, 8, 13. The one apparent deviation (21 syllables instead of 22 in the second line of the last stanza) is a typo corrected in later editions; "the" is omitted from "on the one hand." Some of the lines in her stanzas are so long that the concluding words have to be printed below their lines as a run-on fragment. This confuses some readers, who do not recognize a run-on line when they see it, and think it an additional line in the stanza.

The two tests he proposes to discredit her syllabics are not convincing. In the first, he offers four corresponding syllabic lines and asks us to count the syllables to see if their number is really identical. His first line, syllabified, is

sim i lar de ter mi na tion   to   make a pup

Anyone who knows what a syllable is, can, with the help of his fingers and two big toes, instantly arrive at the right answer: twelve.

The three matching lines are equally easy: twelve also. The only possible ambiguity is the word "flower," which some of us pronounce as two syllables and some, like Miss Moore, as one.

His second test, for "any reader still unconvinced" (that syllable count is a snare and a delusion), invites us to spend an hour studying the texts of the two Moore poems as printed in different versions. But has he taken his own test? If he has compared the 1921 version of "Poetry" with the longer version in her "Definitive Edition" of 1967, he knows that only five of her thirty lines have been changed by the removal of three short passages (of three, five, and ten words) and of two single words. Two other words are changed; "the" is transferred from one line to the next. A typo is corrected. There are a few punctuation changes. No other material is reorganized or added. Though it had fluctuated through several revisions, most of the poem is exactly as forty-six years before: unmistakably syllabic. In "Critics and Connoisseurs" there is one difference between the 1935 and the 1951 editions: "which" is changed to "what." Between the 1951 and the 1967 editions there are two changes: two words are omitted and a comma is changed to a dash. Neither change has the devastating effect on the meter that Wallace seems to predict. In her syllabic poems, Miss Moore is amazingly faithful in her calculations. The metrical pattern of "A Carriage from Sweden" should have resulted in a poem of 492 syllables. And it does: 492. In "The Fish" all 216 syllables are correctly aligned, if twice we allow her to pronounce "iron" as "ir'n," as many of us would pronounce it. I mention these details because Miss Moore's sinewy and elegant structures have been unfairly handled by Wallace, who seems embarrassed enough to have to admit that the two poems he has roughed up are "good, if not exactly fair, examples."

He concludes, however, with the claim that syllabics as an English meter "rests in quicksand." I would say it's set in concrete. What is simpler and surer than finger count, with toes to call on if we have to? Are there disadvantages to a meter set in concrete? There may be. But that is not the question we are investigating.

We leave his "quicksand" for something "even more problematic," accentual meter; that is, meter determined by accent alone, with no regard for number of syllables. Wallace claims that no such meter exists. But again, do we have a problem that is only verbal? Wallace concludes part 2 with "Let's put 'accentual meter' into the dustbin. . . . The more common terms 'alliterative meter' or 'Old English meter' will do." Wait—accentual meter does not exist? But if we call it "alliterative meter" it does exist? Whatever he means, Wallace contends in the fifth and most insensitive of his propositions that **"In modern English, accentual meter does not exist."**

It has always been acknowledged that there are two kinds of accentual meter in English: one in which only the accents are counted and unaccented syllables left to fall where they may, and one in which stressed and unstressed syllables alternate in a regular pattern. The first is the accentual verse—more often called strong-stress—which proposition 5 denies the existence of. The second is a syllable-stress system like the iambics Wallace is stumping for. As long ago as 1575 George Gascoigne could write, "We have used in the past other kinds of meters [besides the iambic], as for example this following:

/   /   /   /
No wight in this world that wealth can attain
/   /   /   /
Unless he believe that all is but vain. . . ."

He is referring to, and marking the accents in, the accentual alliterative verse of earlier centuries, the kind that Chaucer abruptly broke with in his admiration for the more disciplined poetry of France and Italy. Attridge, as I have mentioned, calls Chaucer the founder of the strict pentameter in English. Paull Baum is equally insistent: modern English versification starts with Chaucer, almost a *de novo* creation. There are no native models.[8] The two systems are distinct.

Everybody knows the first two lines of *The Canterbury Tales*. With Chaucer's smooth andante rhythms in mind, now listen to the more *marcato,* more *staccato* opening of *Piers Plowman* (the "B" text) with its strong-stress rhythm:

In a somer seson · whan soft was the sonne,
I shope me in shroudes · as I a shepe werre. . . .

Hear the difference? The jazzier, more syncopated, more percussive rhythm of Langland, with the strong midline pause, marked by a raised period? Most of us can tell the rugged strong-stress from the more regular syllable-stress of Chaucer—though, just as there are people who will cheerfully admit they are tone-deaf, so there are others who are deaf to the nuances of accent. To the few who cannot feel the beat, there is not much use trying to explain. As Louis Armstrong said when asked what jazz was, "Man, if you gotta ask, you'll never know."

Most speakers find the accents in strong-stress strong indeed, though Wallace thinks that "what we may count as stress seems extremely subjective." Children have no trouble with strong-stress, probably the first rhythm they hear:

/   /   /   /
One, two, | buckle my shoe . . .

/   /   /   /
Hey diddle diddle, | the cat and the fiddle . . .

The basic iambic meter, according to Wallace the only meter in English, might be schematized as

de DUM de DUM de DUM de DUM . . . .

There is no such regularity in the strong-stress line. It has a midline pause with two beats (accents, stresses) in each half. It might be represented in many ways, perhaps

DUM DUM | de de DUM DUM

or

DUM de de de de DUM | DUM de de DUM de

Though always surviving in popular poetry, strong stress has attracted renewed attention in the last century or so. Gerard Manley Hopkins explains in his "Author's Preface" that "common English rhythm" is measured by feet of two or three syllables, but since verse measured that way (as Wallace would have it measured) becomes "same and tame," poets have brought in various "irregularities" to enliven it. He then describes his "sprung rhythm," which is "measured by feet of from one to four syllables, regularly, and for particular effects any number of weak or slack syllables may be used." "Any number"—but, even more shocking to scanners of the "same and tame," he would also allow "hangers" or "outrides"; that is, "one, two, or three slack syllables added to a foot and not counting in the nominal scanning. . . ." Hopkins has much more to say about meter in that "Preface" and in his *Journals and Papers.* Wallace quite ignores Hopkins, whose apparently revolutionary theories take us back to a livelier kind of pre-Chaucerian strong-stress.

Brooks and Warren, in their celebrated *Understanding Poetry,* describe what they call the "Old Native Meter" as "still characterized by the presence of four heavily accented syllables and a varying number of unaccented syllables."[9] W. K. Wimsatt holds that "there are in fact two main kinds of stress meter in English; the very old (and recently revived) meter of strong stress with indeterminate or relatively indeterminate number of syllables between stresses, and the other . . . of counted syllables. . . ."[10]

John Crowe Ransom, in his theory and his practice, is another exponent of strong-stress. "It goes back to the Anglo-Saxon meters; it persists against the romanic or syllabic meters which followed the Normans into England. It lingers in the rhythm of the oral ballads . . . in the eighteenth century it comes back into print in the recovered ballad, in Mother Goose. . . ."[11] More informally, he remarked, "I would call it, perhaps, accentual meter . . . we just count the number of accented or stressed syllables in a line and let the unstressed take care of themselves." Ransom gives Thomas Hardy's "Neutral Tones" as an example of this "folk rhythm": stanzas of three four-beat lines with a caesura in the middle, and a final three-beat line. He illustrates with the first stanza; I have marked the stresses:

　　　/　　　　/　　　/　　/
We stood by a pond | that winter day,

　　　　/　　　/　　　　　　/　　　　/
And the sun was white, | as though chidden of God,

　　　　/　　　/　　　　/　　/
And a few leaves lay | on the starving sod;

      /   /   /

—They had fallen | from an ash, | and were gray.

Ransom had a long time to think about that meter. Thirty years before, he had published in *The Fugitive* his "Bells for John Whiteside's Daughter," which has the same stress pattern as the Hardy poem, three four-beat strong-stress lines and one three-beat:

      /   /   /   /

There was such speed | in her little body,

   /   /   /   /

And such lightness | in her footfall,

  / /   /   /

It is no wonder | her brown study

   /   / /

Astonishes | us | all.

In denying that strong-stress exists as a meter, Wallace says it is nothing but "accentual syllabic meter allowing trisyllabic substitutions. . . ." That is, it is nothing but the *de DUM de DUM de DUM* meter which allows a *de de DUM* to be substituted now and then for a *de DUM*. "The student will search in vain," he says, "for the strings or three or four unstressed syllables . . . or, for that matter, for stressed syllables clumped or otherwise not regularly spaced. . . ."

    I can't imagine where Wallace thinks the student will be searching, but if it occurs to that student to look at poetry in English, an endless supply of clumped syllables and strings of three or four unstressed syllables is available. Clumped syllables were so common that there was even a name for them: "clashing stress."

    One does not have to read far into *Piers Plowman* to come across accents clumped together:

      /   /

Vnder a brod banke · by a bourne syde . . .

      /   /

Ac on a May mornynge · on Maluerne hulles . . .

From popular verse Hopkins quotes:

   /   /

March dust, | April showers

      /   /   /   /

Bring forth | May flowers.

"Strings of three or four unstressed syllables" are also not hard to find. Early in *Piers Plowman* we have

              ᵕ   ᵕ   ᵕ ᵕ   ᵕ   ᵕ   ᵕ

Summe putten hem to the plough · and pleiden hem ful seldene . . .

    ᵕ ᵕ   ᵕ   ᵕ   ᵕ   ᵕ ᵕᵕ

Feyneden hem for heore foode · foughten atte alle . . . .

Five hundred years later Auden wrote his book-length *The Age of Anxiety* (1947) in pure strong-stress, with the familiar two accents on each side of its mid-line caesura. In some lines we find the clumped accents, in others the strings of unstressed syllables, and often enough combinations of both:

              /   /

Many have perished; more will . . .

             /   /

Now the news. Night raids on

 /   /   /   /

Five cities. Fires started. . . .

    ᵕ ᵕ   ᵕ   /   /

Untalkative and tense, we took off . . .

       ᵕ ᵕ ᵕ   ᵕ   ᵕᵕ

As absurd as they are savage; science or no science . . .

    ᵕᵕ ᵕ ᵕ   /   /

Security at all costs; the calm plant. . . .

About a decade earlier, T. S. Eliot had frequent recourse to strong-stress in *Murder in the Cathedral* (1935). Among more relaxed lines like

Seven years | and the summer is over

Seven years | since the Archbishop left us . . .

are others drawn tight into clumped stresses:

     /   /

King rules | or barons rule . . .

/   /   / /

Shall these things | not end . . .

/   /   /   /

Your Lordship | is too proud. . . .

He makes even more frequent use of lines with runs of three unaccented syllables or more:

                ∪   ∪   ∪

You are right to express | a certain incredulity . . .

         ∪ ∪   ∪ / ∪ ∪ ∪

Assured, beyond doubt, | of the devotion of his people . . .

          ∪   ∪   ∪

Lining the road | and throwing down their capes,

   ∪   ∪   ∪   ∪

Strewing the way with leaves | and late flowers of the season.

              ∪   ∪   ∪

He is at one with the Pope, | and with the King of France,

                ∪   ∪   ∪

Who indeed would have liked to | detain him in his kingdom. . . .

In his later plays Eliot treated strong-stress more freely, lengthening even more the runs of unaccented stresses. In *Poetry and Drama* he describes his efforts to find a satisfactory rhythm for the drama. The essential, he thought, was to "avoid any echo of Shakespeare,"[12] to get away, that is, from the syllable-stress iambic that Wallace fancies is our only rhythm. He tells how, in preparation for writing *The Family Reunion* (1939), his "first concern was the problem of versification, to find a rhythm close to contemporary speech. . . . What I worked out is substantially what I have continued to employ: a line of varying length and varying number of syllables, with a caesura and three stresses. The caesura and the stresses may come at different places, almost anywhere in the line; *the stresses may be close together or well separated by light syllables* [my italics], the only rule being that there must be one stress on one side of the caesura and two on the other."[13] This is a description of strong-stress meter, with three stresses instead of four, as in the last line of the stanzas by Hardy and Ransom. Or did Eliot slip into the familiar four-stress line? Northrop Frye thinks he did: "I usually hear four beats, and so apparently do most of the actors."[14] On the stage, it might sound like this:

        /   /   /   /
You may think it laughable, | what I'm going to say—
          /   /   /   /
But it's not really strange, Miss, | when you come to look at it:
   /   /   /   /
After all these years | that I've been with him
    /   /   /   /
I think I understand his Lordship | better than anybody;
     /   /   /   /
And I have a kind of feeling | that his Lordship won't need me
 / /   /   /
Very long now. | I can't give you any reasons.

Whether three- or four-beat, what Eliot describes is a strong-stress meter, totally unlike the regularity of iambic with its "echo of Shakespeare." It would take a good deal of aplomb to tell a metrist experienced as Eliot that he doesn't know what he is doing, and that there is no such meter as the one he thinks he is writing in.

Lines of the chorus may be even longer, with longer runs of syllables felt as unstressed in this meter. Some actors might choose to dwell on the syllables marked below; others might interpret the lines differently. However they are read, they could never be dragooned into an iambic lockstep.

        /   /
Why should we stand here like guilty conspirators, | waiting for some
       /
revelation . . .

      /   /
In a horrid amity of misfortune? | why should we be implicated,
             /
brought in and brought together?

My incommunicative Peruvians would be perfectly at home in their company.

Here, then, are examples of the strings of three or four unstressed syllables, and of the clumped stresses that Wallace says "the student will search in vain for." Thousands more are available in English and American poetry.

In Wallace's view, "the source of all the confusion about 'accentual meter' is of course Coleridge's brief, grossly inaccurate note about the meter of 'Christabel.'" There is no confusion about accentual meter; its nature has been perfectly clear for at least ten centuries. "Christabel" itself is hardly an example of healthy strong-stress, although Coleridge's note, off the mark but by no means "grossly" so, sounds as if it were. As we have seen, true strong-stress is interestingly irregular; it has intervals between stresses that go well beyond the two unaccented syllables of anapests; its own unstressed syllables are placed irregularly and unpredictably around its four strong pylons, so that it has the air of ruggedness and informality, almost of improvisation, quite missing from Coleridge's conventional lines.

His much maligned note is by no means "the seed" from which "notions of accentual meter have grown." That seed had been planted centuries before Coleridge. Nor is it the source of the idea that "trisyllabic substitution somehow means a separate meter." The autonomy of trisyllabics was well established at least a century and a half before, when Thomas Jordan, laureate to the city of London, wrote his jolly "The Careless Gallant," which begins

Let us drink and be merry, dance, joke, and rejoice,
With claret and sherry, theorbo and voice;
The changeable world to our joy is unjust,
All treasure uncertain, then down with your dust;
 In frolics dispose your pounds, shillings, and pence,
 For we shall be nothing a hundred years hence . . .

This must be the "A Hundred Years Hence" that Saintsbury praised for its "triumphant sweep" (appendix 2, volume 3). Dryden, Charles Cotton, Charles Sackville, Prior and many others had been fluent in trisyllabics; it had long been recognized as a meter in its own right. In an appendix following the one mentioned above, "Tri-Syllabic Meters Since 1600," Saintsbury simply took it for granted that they existed.

Wallace concludes his part 2 with a sixth proposition: **"Anapests and dactyls are legitimate substitutions in the iambic norm of**

English meter." Anapests, yes. This had been obvious ever since Chaucer, and need not be stated as if it were "a new principle." I have already explained why the iambic meter is resistant to dactylic substitution.

III. COMING TO TERMS

Near the beginning of this section, Wallace takes up the question of whether Auden's "O where are you going . . ." should be scanned with amphibrachs or "in the traditional way with anapests, iambs, trochees, and extra-syllable endings." Since he believes in only an iambic meter, this question would seem either to contradict his central thesis or to be irrelevant to it. Hopkins makes the most sense about such questions: " . . . it is very hard to tell whether to scan by dactyls, anapests, or amphibrachs. . . ." And probably not worth the trouble, since the meter will sound the same no matter what we call it. The marked caesura, sometimes emphasized by off-rhymes *(midden-madden; looking-lacking, swiftly-softly),* suggests that Auden feels his poem is in strong-stress.

One difficulty with anapests and amphibrachs, says Wallace, is that they cannot really carry stress on more than one of the three syllables. I think they can. Listen to how the anapests turn amphimacers (–‿–) in Blake's "Ah, Sun-flower":

$$/ \quad ‿ \quad / \quad ‿ \quad ‿ \quad / \quad \quad / \quad ‿ \quad /$$
Seeking af | ter that sweet | golden clime . . .

$$‿ \quad ‿ \quad / \quad \quad / \quad ‿ \quad / \quad \quad ‿ \quad ‿ \quad /$$
Where the Youth | pined away | with desire,

$$‿ \quad ‿ \quad / \quad \quad / \quad ‿ \quad \quad / \quad \quad ‿ \quad ‿ \quad /$$
And the pale | Virgin shroud | ed in snow . . .

We come next to the seventh proposition: **"We should drop the pyrrhic foot (‿‿) and accept in its place the double-iamb (‿‿//), as one of the six foot-terms necessary."** But what he calls the "double-iamb" can never take the place of the pyrrhic alone; it would have to substitute for *two* feet, the pyrrhic foot *and* whatever foot follows it. Even so it would not fit in for just any pyrrhic; it could not be used with these lines or many such in Shakespeare:

<pre>
        ∪ ∪ / /   ∪ ∪ / /
Advant | age on the king | dom of the shore . . .
                    /   ∪   ∪ / /
A horse! A horse! My king | dom for a horse!
</pre>

Scan those lines with "double-iambs" as marked above and you make "the" a stressed syllable twice in the first and "a," the least accented of all syllables, a stressed syllable in the second. This proposition can be dropped like a hot potato. Wallace says "this change was suggested by John Crowe Ransom" in his *Kenyon Review* essay of 1956. He means "was suggested to me"; it was not "suggested by" Ransom. In mentioning exceptions to regularity in iambic pentameter that Bridges had codified, Ransom had said, "I wish Bridges had added: Any two successive iambic feet might be replaced by a double or ionic foot." He did not say that the ionic foot (∪∪//) could replace *one* pyrrhic foot, or that the pyrrhic foot should be dropped. Nor did he ever call the replacement a "double-iamb"; he called it a "double-foot" or an "ionic." The conclusive argument against Wallace's "double-iamb" is that the term already has a different meaning: two iambs together, as in dipodic iambic rhythms. Saintsbury's later Glossary covers it under "Di-iamb.—A double iamb—short, long, short, long (∪/∪/). Not wanted in English. . . ."

And so we come to a more serious and more preposterous proposition, number 8: **"Anapestic, trochaic, and dactylic meters do not exist in English."** Saintsbury of course thought they did; the appendix 3 in volume 3 has the title "Trisyllabic Meters Since 1600."

"I hope we can agree," says Wallace, "that, properly, meter refers to *poems,* not lines *per se.*" No, we cannot agree to that. Meter refers even to feet, and certainly to lines. A spondaic line like "And with old woes new wail my dear time's waste" remains a spondaic line even in Shakespeare's iambic context. It does not become iambic, any more than a cow among sheep becomes a sheep and should be called one. True, the spondaic line accommodates itself to the iambic meter, just as the cow may get along with the sheep. But it does not become one of them.

Another dubious assertion in this section is that "poems do not change meter from line to line." Yes they do; maybe not often, but often enough so that the assertion is untrue. A spectacular example is William Browne's "On the Countess Dowager of Pembroke," fortunately short enough to quote:

Underneath this sable hearse
Lies the subject of all verse:
Sidney's sister, Pembroke's mother.
Death, ere thou hast slain another
Fair, and learn'd, and good as she,
Time shall throw a dart at thee.

Winifred Nowottny, in *The Language Poets Use,* thinks that the poem's brief magnificence comes in part from a change in rhythm.[15] The first three lines are trochaic (catalectic), except for one reversed foot. But with the word "Death," a reversal of attitude, from mourning to triumph, is accompanied by a reversal to rising iambs.

Other examples are not hard to find. In Thomas Nashe's "Adieu, Farewell Earth's Bliss," written during a time of plague in Elizabethan London, the lines seem to waver between iambic and dactylic, a shiver appropriate to the apprehension felt at the time. The earlier "As You Came from the Holy Land," probably by Sir Walter Raleigh, has a similar metrical wavering. Ben Jonson's fourth poem in "A Celebration of Charis" has stanzas that begin by alternating lines of anapestic trimeter with lines of hypermetric iambic trimeter. Blake's "Night," in the "Songs of Innocence," is more daring: the first half of each eight-line stanza is in iambic tetrameter, the second half in rough anapestic dimeters. He actually combines syllable-stress and strong-stress in the same stanza. Thomas Hardy's "The Voice" has a final stanza in a meter so unlike that of the first three that Attridge can say, "We are in a different rhythmic world."[16] There is also de la Mare's "The Listeners," in which odd- and even-numbered lines have a different rhythm (notice the runs of unstressed syllables in the odd-numbered lines).

Wallace rules anapestic, trochaic, and dactylic meters out of existence by testing with what he has called "Saintsbury's great touchstone," which he quotes as "The only safe and philosophical rule in prosody, as in other things, is not to multiply your entities."

But that is not what Saintsbury wrote. His words are: "The only safe and philosophical rule in prosody, as in other things, is not to multiply your entities beyond necessity." (volume 1, 403) Rather different? The key words, as Wallace probably knows, and as Saintsbury certainly did, are translations of those of William of Occam, the fourteenth-century Franciscan philosopher. They have long been known as "Occam's razor": "Entia non sunt multiplicanda praeter necessitatem." *Praeter necessitatem*—Occam did not say that things are to be needlessly expunged, ruled out of existence; he said they are not to be proliferated *unnecessarily*. He certainly did not mean that what is vital and integral, what is alive, should be cut off and thrown away. If he had meant that, we should all aspire to be quadriplegic.

The kinds of meter that Wallace would deny existence to have long been integral and organic parts of the body of English prosody; they are not to be amputated. It would no doubt be "simple, elegant, and comprehensive" to have all of our English meters in one iambic basket—but who wants to make a basket case of our poetry? Wallace might as well declare that what we call the different keys in music do not exist, since all are played on the same one keyboard. All that "guff" about A-major and D-minor, he might say, is nothing more than "snobbish purism." Abolish the keys and we have a theory of music that is "splendidly unitary."

For poets, the anapestic, trochaic, and dactylic meters are at least as different, and as real, as the keys are for composers. They are not different because of the scansion marks one makes on a blackboard for students; they're different because of their different effect on the ear and mind and soul of listeners. Nobody, swinging into Byron's lusty

> Oh, talk not to me of a name great in story;
> The days of our youth are the days of our glory . . .

is going to think, "Ah, trisyllabic substitutions for the basic iambs!" No, one is carried away happily on the anapestic surge. When Wallace protests that "it makes sense to see iambic as the metrical base," because poems in general "are overwhelmingly iambic," all one has to reply is, "But *this* poem is not." The number of Russians in the world is overwhelmingly greater than that of Madagascans, but a crowd of nine Russians and eighty-seven Madagascans is not a Russian crowd.

In Byron's "The Destruction of Sennacherib," there are nine iambic feet and eighty-seven anapestic ones. Yet Wallace claims that it is an iambic crowd because elsewhere in poetry there are far more iambs than anapests. Confronting a poem that is undeniably nine-tenths anapestic, he can insist that "Anapestic . . . meters do not exist in English." His admired Saintsbury thought they did; about Poe's "Annabel Lee" Saintsbury wrote: "the miraculous power of the anapest, which we have traced and studied so long, seems to have gathered itself into something superhuman here." (volume 3, appendix 2, 485.) But an anapest, Wallace believes, is no more than a substitute for an iambic foot. Sometimes it is, as in Frost's "A Leaf-Treader":

ᵕ   ᵕ   /

All summer long | they were o | verhead, more lifted up than I . . .

But what if there are four, and they outnumber the iambic feet?

ᵕ ᵕ /   ᵕ ᵕ /   ᵕ ᵕ

They tapped | at my eye | lids and touched | my lips | with an

/   ᵕ ᵕ /

in | vita | tion to grief . . .

I doubt that the line can properly be called "iambic" any more. It might be called logaoedic, if one wanted a fancy but useful word of honest lineage for a meter of mixed feet. Frost, who said there are "virtually" two meters in English, strict iambic and loose iambic, knew his iambics in that line were so loose they had lost their virginity. And if he had been questioned he would have been forced to admit that his "Blueberries" was not iambic but anapestic. It begins

> You ought to have seen what I saw on my way
> To the village, through Patterson's pasture today:
> Blueberries as big as the end of your thumb. . . .

The lines may begin with an iamb or trochee, but each immediately yields to the anapestic cadence, which continues for 105 lines. Frost's "Good-by and Keep Cold" has the same anapestic swing.

Wallace: ". . . Trochaic . . . meters do not exist in English." The "so-called trochaic meter" (So-called indeed! Like saying, "Fido, the so-called dog.") is dismissed by Wallace as "merely a mirror image of iambic." Is a left-handed pitcher merely a mirror image of a right-hander? Tell that to a left-handed batter! Say "mirror image" to a molecular biologist and he/she will tell you that while certain molecules support life, their mirror image can kill you.

Trochaic meters have long been recognized as a staple of English prosody. Saintsbury never questioned their existence; he may even have wondered at times whether they or iambs were the more important; certainly the trochee was a strong second. His appendix 2 in volume 3 asks "Is the Base Foot of English Iamb or Trochee?" He concludes, "Of the iamb and trochee it were superfluous to speak at length, for everybody . . . admits the former as the ruling constituent of English verse, and the latter as an important and most valuable alternative. . . ." No nonsense here about its not existing. Though he finds the trochees in "Hiawatha" monotonous, he has high praise for the "rolling, racing trochaics" of "The Raven," and praise too for those of "The Haunted Palace."

The credit for their establishment goes to Sir Philip Sidney. "His greatest triumph," says W. A. Ringler, his modern editor, "was naturalizing an entirely new rhythm, the accentual trochaic," which he "brought to perfection in the songs of 'Astrophil and Stella.'" Because of his influence, Ringler says, accentual trochaic rhythms "became exceedingly popular and were used by many poets of the 1590's."[17] It would be news to them and to poets ever since that the rhythm they excelled in did not exist.

Probably our best known trochaic poem is Poe's "The Raven": "Once upon a midnight dreary, while I pondered, weak and weary. . . ." It continues with these trochees, relentlessly, for eighteen stanzas. Wallace, concerned for "the students," is less attentive to what the poets themselves say, and would perhaps shrug off Poe's remarks on his meter: "I pretend to no originality in either the rhythm or meter of the 'Raven.' The former is trochaic, the latter is octameter acatalectic . . . terminating with tetrameter catalectic."[18] According to my count, each stanza has 44 feet, some catalectic, so the whole eighteen-stanza poem has 792 feet. And how many are survivors of Wallace's iambic base? Four or five, like "and each," "of each," "my sad," and "that lies," all easily overridden by the meter. There are pyrrhics and spondees, regular variations in trochaic meter. Can anyone believe that five iambic feet, as against nearly 800 trochaic feet, can be said to give this poem an iambic base, just because there are lots of iambs elsewhere in the language?

Trochees are still alive in our time. Among scores of other trochaic poems, there is Philip Larkin's "The Explosion," with its breath-taking change of meter in one middle stanza.

Wallace: ". . . Dactylic meters do not exist in English . . ." In his "The Poetic Principle," Poe quotes Thomas Hood's "universally appreciated 'The Bridge of Sighs,'" a poem we used to read in high school. About a poor girl who throws herself into the river in despair, the poem is in dactylics, the meter least likely to have an iambic base, since it differs from iambic both in number of syllables and position of accent. It begins

> One more unfortunate,
> Weary of breath,
> Rashly importunate,
> Gone to her death!
>
> Take her up tenderly,
> Lift her with care;
> Fashioned so slenderly,
> Young, and so fair. . . .

There are two dactylic feet in each line, the even-numbered lines catalectic. In its eighteen stanzas the dactylic onrush is nowhere balked by a single iambic foot. For a recent poem equally resistant to iambic reduction, there is George Starbuck's "A Tapestry for Bayeux," each of its 156 lines a dactylic foot. It begins

> Over the
> seaworthy

cavalry
    arches a
rocketry
    wickerwork . . .

And what about the double-dactyls that Wallace used to publish in his charming *Light Year* anthologies? We little suspected at the time that their meter didn't exist.

Prosody-shmosody,
Our meterologist
Doesn't believe that a
Dactyl's a fact.
"Dactylophobiac!
Iambomania's
Boggled your noggin," I
Yackety-yacked.

IV. TWO LEVELS OF STRESS

Section 4 offers a ninth proposition: **"We should *never* use four degrees of speech stress for scanning."** A reminder again that poems exist to be scanned. As for the four degrees of speech, this point had been made on Wallace's second page: "Despite the wide range of levels of stress occurring in speech, syllables are counted as either stressed or unstressed. . . ." Section 4 is a long appendix giving us statistics, et cetera, about the Jespersen and Trager-Smith theories, which I thought had been laid to rest on that second page. There is an oddly worded tenth proposition: **"The spondee is a good, and fairly frequent, foot in English."** A foot, yes. But there is no such thing as spondaic meter.

NOTES

1. Anthony Hecht, *On the Laws of the Poetic Art* (Princeton: Princeton University Press, 1995), p. 58.

2. T. S. Eliot, *To Criticize the Critic* (New York: Farrar, Straus & Giroux, 1965), p. 12.

3. René Wellek and Austin Warren, *Theory of Literature* (New York: Jonathan Cape, 1949), pp. 167–68.

4. Derek Attridge, *The Rhythms of English Poetry* (London: Longman, 1982), p. 19.

5. F. N. Robinson, *The Works of Chaucer,* 2nd ed. (New York: Houghton Mifflin, 1957), p. xxxv.

6. Attridge, p. 180.

7. Robinson, p. xxx.

8. Paull F. Baum, *Chaucer's Verse* (Durham: Duke University Press, 1961), p. 11.

9. Cleanth Brooks and Robert Penn Warren, *Understanding Poetry,* rev. ed. (New York: Henry Holt, 1953), p. 702.

10. W. K. Wimsatt, "The Concept of Meter," *Hateful Contraries* (Lexington: University of Kentucky Press, 1966), p. 127.

11. John Crowe Ransom, "The Old Age of an Eagle," *Poems and Essays,* (New York: Vintage Books, 1955), p. 80–81.

12. T. S. Eliot, *Poetry and Drama* (Cambridge: Harvard University Press, 1951), p. 27.

13. Eliot, p. 32, 33.

14. Northrop Frye, "Lexis and Melos," *Sound and Poetry: English Institute Essays, 1956* (New York: Columbia University Press, 1957), p.xx.

15. Winifred Nowottny, *The Language Poets Use* (Oxford: Oxford University Press, 1962), pp. 108–11.

16. Attridge, p. 332.

17. W. A. Ringler, *The Poems of Sir Philip Sidney,* (Oxford: Oxford University Press, 1962), pp. lv; xliii, footnote.

18. Edgar Allan Poe, "The Philosophy of Composition," *The Portable Poe,* Ed. Philip Van Doren Stern (New York: Penguin Books, 1973), p. 559.

METER AND THE FORTUNES OF THE NUMERICAL IMAGINATION

David J. Rothman

As Harvey Gross points out at the opening of *Sound and Form in Modern Poetry*, all prosodists face a terminological menace, and much of what I disagree with in Wallace's essay can be traced to this problem. I will try to indicate this where I can, for it is important to acknowledge that within each prosodical system there are consistencies that give merit to many of its practical observations because (to offer a first principle of my own)

> (1) All systems of versification are abstractions, and therefore theoretical, because they bear a systematic but also provisional relation to the artifacts they describe.

The highly speculative nature of prosody explains why, as many before me have pointed out (including Wallace, and Omond, whom Wallace quotes in this context), poets and scholars have utterly disagreed, for centuries, over terms, issues, and even questions, in "the science of verse."

What I admire in Wallace's essay is his clear, even polemical commitment to a standard accentual-syllabic model for English verse. It is useful to have such a direct restatement of this position, even though I think it is reductive and anachronistic. The general problems I see are (1) oversimplification of the basic metrical concept; (2) internal confusion—or at least inconsistency—on fundamental questions like the distinction between rhythm and meter in English verse; and (3) a poorly orchestrated response to the linguistic models (which, although I too dislike them, must be engaged at greater length and brought up to date).

Much of the problem can be traced to Wallace's zeal for the standard terms we have derived from Greek for our literary prosody. I support the use of these terms as heuristic tools and as shorthand for further discussion, but they are problematic if taken as the foundation of all prosodical description, and should be treated—even centuries after their adaptation—as always provisional and theoretical, not factual.

My reasoning will become more clear in my responses to Wallace's ten specific points, to which at once.

(1) "Instead of the term 'feminine ending,' we should say simply extra-syllable ending."

It is odd that this should be the first highlighted principle in a major re-evaluation of current verse theory, although to his credit, Wallace does later refer to this principle and his second (with which I have no quibbles),

(2) "For an omitted first syllable of a line, we should use the term anacrusis."

as "minor propositions about terminology."

Still, there are some important questions here. As Wallace does not give us an argument for his renaming ("We need a fresh term for this . . . ") we must speculate upon his motive. The only one that makes sense is current political sensitivities. Presumably the notion that a feminine ending is a "weak" one is a patriarchal notion which relies on the representation of one gender as more powerful than the other. Therefore the term "feminine ending" must be changed to eliminate a sexist bias in prosodical terminology (although Wallace is adamant about retaining most other traditional terms).

If this is the case, then this is the first place where we encounter a major confusion of the kind I indicated above. First of all, linguists long ago dispensed with this term in favor of others that are more descriptive (for with the appropriate terminology we can account for one, two, or three unaccented syllables at the end of an accentual-syllabic line). But more importantly, as I indicated above, a term like "feminine ending" can still serve as an appropriate heuristic device (like the other terms Wallace employs). After all, the word is not tied to any depiction of physical femininity, nor have I seen any serious argument that it should be understood as such. Indeed, words like "manhood," "rapist," and even "penis," if they happened to fall with their first syllables in the accented position at the end of an iambic line, would scan as "feminine endings," whereas a word like "girl" would not. The term "feminine" in this case is a prosodical marker, nothing more.

The comments leading up to Wallace's first principle are actually more important than the numbered sentence. While his scansion of the various lines he cites makes sense within a descriptive system based on Greek-derived terms, there is a much more important confusion at work than the one I just described, a confusion which runs through the entire essay. Wallace is quite right to point out that in the line

> Nor services to do till you require

the fourth syllable stands in a stressed position, and "That determination is made *relative* to the stress of neighboring syllables, that is, by comparison, and not absolutely . . ." But when he says that it "counts fully," he avoids a fundamental question, which is "why?"

It is impossible even to describe this problem without a dual, or palimpsest system of scansion, in which variations are understood and demarcated against an underlying norm, what John Hollander has called (in *Vision and Resonance)* "the metrical frame."

This notion must be in place before an advanced concept like relative stress even makes sense. Despite Wallace's critique of structural linguistics, this is a concept that has been quite well articulated in that field (despite other problems with the approach), and it is something that Wallace assumes (and scans quite accurately) without fully articulating.[1] Hence he starts talking about "the pyrrhic foot" as "puzzling," presumably because it does not appear to be a possible basis for a metric. Well, of course not, as it only makes sense as one way of describing modulation over the abstraction of an iambic metrical grid (assuming we stick with the Greek terms).

Further, the ways in which this modulation can succeed or fail have still been best described by Jespersen's model of relative stress within feet and across foot boundaries in the article of 1900 (reprinted in Gross's *The Structure of Verse*), which Wallace criticizes so aggressively later in his essay. Jespersen argues that consideration of the foot as an ontological fact, the inevitable building block of English verse, has made it impossible to understand the regular patterns of stress that also pertain *between* feet, and that are an integral part of any metrical line. This observation has become one of the fundamental principles of linguistic inquiries into verse structure (which are summarized in the first chapter of Attridge's *The Rhythms of English Poetry).*[2] In fact, for his own scansion of the lines in question, Wallace is relying on the same principle that Jespersen articulates, and this is one of the strange critical inconsistencies that I find in his argument.

In sum—it is much more important, at the opening of a prosodical manifesto, to articulate basic issues more clearly. And the second such concept I present as a corollary to my first has to do with the nature of the metrical abstraction. If metrical composition is an abstraction enacted upon language, then we should articulate this abstraction in a clear and precise way, and we should do so at the beginning:

(2) The metrical abstraction is number.

Or, as William Carlos Williams wrote in his oft-cited entry on "free verse" in *The Princeton Encyclopedia of Poetry and Poetics,* "The crux of the question is measure" (289). He was not the first to say it, and it seems ancient and obvious, but this idea has radical and far-reaching implications.

First among these implications is the recognition that there can be more than "one meter" in English. Wallace writes that

> Meter is . . . a system of measurement, conventional but natural to the language, which makes the rhythmic units of line more or less predictable to a reader or hearer of verse.
>
> What meter measures is speech . . .

And I agree with much of this, and find it well put. Further, I wholeheartedly agree with Wallace that accentual-syllabic verse along "iambic" principles is the root and trunk of meter in English. Where we differ is that I am convinced that there are many other meters (and kinds of meters, including highly sophisticated reactions *against* meter) that have undergirded great poetry in our language.

The reason for this multiplicity is that it is not the function of meter merely to follow particular patterns that already exist in language. Meter does not function as an ideal scoring of language, merely a measure of preexisting speech, but is a kind of magic enacted upon it. Prosodists and poets are very good at realizing the heightening effects that measure has on language, for our sense of *words* is acute. But we tend to be less aware of exactly what is doing the heightening, which is *counting,* a very different human artifact that we rarely associate with language. This amazing technology—which prosodists more or less take for granted as a given of verse craft, without paying sufficient attention to it on its own—is the ground of the mysterious power of meter *and* free verse. Meter is so powerful because it is radically *different* from ordinary language, not because it imitates it. Meter is a mixing of heterogeneous elements. Verse, both free and metrical, achieves its effects by synthesizing language with the magic of number, without which none of its patterns and modulations would be possible. And there are many imaginatively generative ways to count language in English other than iambic meters.

Before I turn to some of them, in response to Wallace's other points, I need to suggest a further complication:

(3) Writing is the technology which fuses language and the abstraction of number together to create verse.

This requires some explanation. Most critical models of versification emphasize aural patterns as the ground of verse making, assuming that the function of writing in verse is only to imitate an orchestration of speech. In contrast, my hypothesis is that the synthesis of language with number, no matter what form it takes in verse, is only conceivable as writing, as inscription, a graphic technology. To put it another way: the counting that we rely on to describe versification is only possible because of writing. Verse—a word which derives from the Latin term that originally meant the turn a plow makes at the end of a furrow (Beare 20)—is inherently a graphic, and therefore literate phenomenon, not an aural one.

The background to this argument lies in recent speculation that writing may have evolved out of counting in the first place. Roy Harris argues in *The Origin of Writing* that the earliest writing did not grow out of attempts to represent speech, or draw pictures, but to record number. According to Harris, the oldest "writing" that we have, like that on the eleven thousand-year-old Ishango bone, is in "lines"; the surface is scored with rows of short, parallel strokes, which probably served a numerical function (we still use such scoring systems today on occasion, when we count on our fingers, or draw slashes). As Harris points out: "It makes no difference whether we 'read' the sign pictorially as standing for so many fingers held up, or scriptorially as standing for a certain numeral" (137). Along with other evidence, this leads him to argue that the invention of writing—or the division of writing and drawing into separate functions—occurred when the graphic representation of number shifted from the token-iterative system that appears on the Ishango bone, to type-slotting. Harris gives the following example of what he means:

The progression from recording sixty sheep by means of one "sheep" sign followed by sixty strokes to recording the same information by means of one "sheep" sign followed by a second sign indicating "sixty" is a progression which has already crossed the boundary between pictorial and scriptorial signs. A token-iterative sign-system is in effect equivalent to a verbal sublanguage which is restricted to messages of the form "sheep, sheep, sheep, sheep . . .", or "sheep, another, another, another . . ."; whereas an emblem-slotting system is equivalent to a sublanguage which can handle messages of the form "sheep, sixty." Token-iterative lists are, in principle, lists as long as the number of individual items recorded. With a slot list, on the other hand, we get no information simply by counting the number of marks it contains. (145)

When this change occurred it opened "a gap between the pictorial and the scriptorial function of the emblematic sign" (133), which had been previously inseparable in the counting represented by rows of slashes. This semiological gap made writing possible because it meant that signs could be manipulated to "slot," or identify, anything what-soever (155). The open-ended quality of the scriptorial sign was a nec-essary precondition for the development of writing systems.

The implications of such an argument for versification are pro-found, for it suggests that the catalyst of language and number in verse—an obsession of most strong poets—is writing. Indeed, verses are no more or less than written language intentionally broken up into numerable segments, and this is why even metrical verse loses its magical quality when rewritten as prose. The point is that such "rewriting" is in effect the creation of a radically different artifact. The fact that verse can be "rewritten" at all—one cannot perform a comparable function on "oral" poetry—indicates that the art of verse has always been ineluctably tied up with literacy. Indeed, the very idea of "oral" poetry cannot be conceived except by literate people.

The idea that writing grew out of counting can shed bright light on a wide range of questions in versification. It is uncanny that lines of verse look exactly like the most primitive ways of counting—parallel scorings that can be numbered—and that verses are there-fore countable in exactly the way that token-iterative digits are countable, from either end of the sequence. Each one indicates only its singularity, not a particular number. Every poem in lines effaces, or predates, the distinction between writing and drawing in the same way as the lines on the Ishango Bone; lines of verse combine functions of writing, drawing, and counting.

Among other things, the graphic quality of verse helps to explain the ghostly quality of meter. Because it relies on counting, meter is an abstraction that can never be fully embodied in any given performance, as Wimsatt and Beardsley realized in "The Concept of Meter: an Exercise in Abstraction" (Gross, *Structure of Verse* 147–72). The fact that a metrical poem can be performed orally in no way weakens this argument. Such a performance is simply one enactment of the underlying abstraction out of which the verse was forged. One can never, after all, simply perform *meter;* even nonsense syllables are actual verses designed to clothe an abstract figure. One can only perform particulars, not abstractions, yet it is these abstractions that guide the making of the verse. This is the case even if they are absent, as in free verse, which retains countable lines, but intentionally frustrates the numerability of their parts. And these metrical abstractions, which are ways of counting, find their origin in the writing system.

Verse is not an orchestration of preexisting speech, but rather a fusion of speech with number by means of lineation, which casts writing in numerable segments at the same time as it embodies words. There are basically two ways to do this: metrical verse, in which lines are graphically and aurally equivalent to each other (and the parts within them, feet, are equivalent); and free verse, in which lines are graphically equivalent, but cannot be construed as aurally equivalent, either with each other or in their own parts.[3]

A persistent question is why we are attracted to counting as a way of organizing art. The answer is surprisingly simple. Counting language is attractive not because it recapitulates breath, or the heartbeat, or the sound of beating on an anvil, or the movement of oars in oarlocks, or the cadences of music, or the meaning of the poem's words (all arguments that have been invoked to explain its force). Counting is not an ornament of the poem, but part of its ground, and it is attractive because, as Coleridge realized, it is exciting. Number in its simplest form, counting, is an abstraction so powerful that it verges on the supernatural:

> Counting is in its very essence magical, if any human practice at all is. For numbers are things no one has ever seen or heard or touched. Yet somehow they exist, and their existence can be confirmed in quite everyday terms by all kinds of humdrum procedures which allow mere mortals to agree beyond any shadow of

doubt as to "how many" eggs there are in a basket or "how many" loaves of bread on the table. (Harris 135)

Or, one might add, for how many stanzas there are in a poem, or lines in a stanza, or stresses, feet, or syllables in a line, or occurrences of particular syntactical or grammatical patterns, and so on.

Poets write in verse because it excites not only the verbal imagination, but also the numerical imagination, which is both rational and superstitious, quotidian and magical. Versification is a way of asserting the relatedness of things to one another, and it makes sense that poets, even if they define what they are doing exclusively in terms of "voice," or in resistance to "meter," also organize their writing to take advantage of the numerical possibilities of writing, the ways that counting interacts with language. They play with writing as they do with speech in order to garner and concentrate as much energy for their work as possible. This is why meter, or measure, is at the heart (although often only implicitly) of debates over all verse forms, including free verse—it is also why Wallace's notion that there can only be one meaningful "meter" in English, which follows particular oral patterns, is misguided. There is a primary tradition—the accentual-syllabic, which has its various roots and branches—but there are alternatives, and they are powerful.

Wallace distantly realizes the significance of graphic organization to versification as early as his second paragraph, where he writes

It is the unit of line that distinguished verse from prose or speech. Lines introduce into the sentences of a verse a further set of breaks or pauses complementary to those already present in syntactical organization.

True—but, more importantly, those breaks are not just pauses in language. They are a function of *counting*, which is what writing in lines engenders (not introduces, for writing is not merely a transcription of speech, but a different technology altogether).

Thus the fundamental question is what kinds of rules can we derive for counting language, given that verse is a written phenomenon as much as a representation of speech. Obviously, if the rules are utterly arbitrary, they are unlikely to excite us, either as poets or readers. We could write lines based on how many times we use the letter *o,* and it might work as a compositional device, but holds little inherent interest beyond nonce cases. There must be enough material in the language, or the underlying concept must be simple and yet profound enough to pique our interest, to require ingenuity and yet produce meaningful patterns.

As a result, when Wallace writes

(3) "Quantities are not a basis for meter in English."

I agree, although I would add the adjective "compelling" before "basis." Obviously, syllables take time to pronounce, and different syllables take different amounts of time, but lineation seems to have little interaction with this quality in a perceptibly metrical way. Writing verse does not cue regularly measurable syllable length (as opposed to tonic stress) in English. It is not that the phenomenon does not exist or cannot be measured (many fine poets have believed deeply in its possibility); the problem is that there is too much variation and the rules (if there are any) are too complicated. The reason, as Derek Attridge has discussed in *Well-Weighed Syllables,* is that these rules derive from Latin and Greek, where orthography did cue a systematic length of pronunciation, which therefore could be understood as a criterion for measurement.[4]

On the other hand, when Wallace writes

(4) "Syllabics is not a meter in English."

I disagree. It certainly is not anywhere near as powerful a meter as the accentual-syllabic patterns, but it is a meaningful measure, and emphatically not a form of free verse, in which there is no predictable measure of speech within lines. Wallace is right to point out that syllabics in no way modulate stress and are therefore not a measure in that sense. But they do perform another function of stichic organization that accentual-syllabic meters also perform, which John Lotz and others have described as "the word boundary rule."[5] After all, one of the (usually unspoken) criteria of accentual-syllabic lines is that the line-end must correspond with a word end (statistically, very few accentual-syllabic lines are hyphenated, although it is theoretically possible in all cases). Syllabic lines retain this rule—in fact, they heighten it if they are rigorous, as there is no room for hypersyllabic lines because of unstressed syllables at line-endings (as in accentual-syllabic meters).

Syllabic meter in English is a compelling measure because it is clear, simple, consistent, and regulates phonemic flow, albeit minimally. In contrast, quantitative meter only satisfies the last of these four criteria. While syllabics may not be aurally perceptible to listeners or readers, there is a pleasing and challenging strain between numbers of syllables and numbers of words to a line; at the end of each line, word choice becomes highly constrained by syllable count. In this sense syllabic meters differ from Wallace's example of counting letters as the basis of lines, for numbers of letters do not systematically correspond to sounds or words in our language (it meets the first three criteria, but not the fourth). This is not to say that one could not create a nonce-meter on this principle (in fact, I rather like the idea, and E. E. Cummings did do things like this); but it does give us a sense of why syllabic meters do have a tradition in English, although it is a relatively minor one. But the point matters: syllabics create meaningful numerical boundaries for stichic organization in English, even if they may not be apparent to the ear.

For that matter, it is important to point out that highly regular accentual-syllabic meters can be just as difficult to discern aurally. This is prosodical heresy to most—but perform an experiment: compose a number of passages (or pick sufficiently obscure ones) of heavily enjambed, unrhymed lines of iambic tetrameter, pentameter, and hexameter, along with iambic-like free verse, then read them aloud without making any prefatory comments about meter to a listener, and without rhetorically indicating line endings in your performance. Then ask if the listener can, in retrospect, correctly identify the meters involved. It is quite difficult, and often impossible, even for highly trained ears. This is why, despite its intense regularity (as Bridges showed long ago), there was such extensive debate over whether *Paradise Lost* was, as Johnson put it, "verse only to the eye."[6]

Indeed, the way words appear on the page is just as crucial for metrical poetry as it is for free verse and concrete forms. Among other things, relineation of metrical poetry into either irregular lines or prose inevitably changes relative stress values. Consider this passage, the opening to book 9 of *Paradise Lost*:

> No more of talk where God or Angel Guest with Man, as with his Friend, familiar us'd to sit indulgent, and with him partake rural repast . . .

If we recast these lines into blank verse, we can measure the transformation of the sensual impact of the language by looking at the varying stresses of a word that occurs three times in this short passage, "with":

> No more of talk where God or Angel Guest
> With Man, as with his Friend, familiar us'd
> To sit indulgent, and with him partake
> Rural repast . . .

In the verse passage, the second line places "with" in the first unstressed position of an iambic pentameter line, then in the second stressed position. In the prose passage, this tension—or, at the very least, this description of a hypothetical tension—cannot exist, as there is no metrical frame. Removed from the artifice of lines, Milton's highly calibrated metric collapses; it loses the force of measure and modulation. Without the ground of counting syllables and stresses by line, the delicate relations among syllables vanish (and note that this rewriting experiment to test measure is possible only as writing).

On accentual meter, Wallace is even further off the beam:

(5) "In modern English, accentual meter does not exist."

More specifically, he argues that

> Far from aiding in understanding, the attribution of accentual meter to a poem appears likely to plunge us into confusion . . . from which we can rescue ourselves only by returning to accentual-syllabic scansion, recognizing trisyllabic feet.

We can begin by dispensing with the objection that "counting only stresses offers no meaningful predictability and is, ultimately, hopelessly subjective." Measuring stress in accentual-syllabic meters is also subjective. Accusations of subjectivity hardly disprove the existence of that which is perceived.

More importantly, Wallace casts aside a great deal of poetry—and research into its metric—that deserves attention if he is to make his argument convincing. Quoting "The Waste Land" as an example won't do, even if it has been asserted that the opening of the poem is accentual, for it is a weak example, obviously more a parody than anything else; and the notorious "Christabel" example is easy to overturn (and has been by many). What about Longfellow's narratives? What about Bridges's *Testament of Beauty?*

And what about Robinson Jeffers? Wallace devotes only one part of a brief paragraph to Bridges's seminal discussion of accentual meter in *Milton's Prosody,* but he does not follow that lead into Jeffers's work. Yet as early as 1925 James Daly sensed the stress-based origins of Jeffers's metric, and argued that it had evolved from blank verse (*Critical Essays,* ed. Karman, 47). Harold Klein's unpublished master's thesis at Occidental College, the first long critical work on the poet (1930), is *The Prosody of Robinson Jeffers.* It was never published, but Lawrence Clark Powell's *Robinson Jeffers: The Man and his Work,* the first book-length study (1934), quotes Klein at length and explicitly discusses the same issues (the two men were friends). These two critics laid the groundwork for all further study of Jeffers's versification, emphasizing a stress-count model, ramified through (published) correspondence and discussion between Klein and Jeffers.[7]

The key theoretical passage that Klein excerpted from Bridges and sent to Jeffers describes pure accentual verse exactly as Jeffers used it. In the crux of that lengthy passage, Bridges writes (as Wallace quotes)

> Now the primary law of pure stressed verse is, that there shall never be a conventional or imaginary stress: that is, *the verse cannot make the stress, because it is the stress that makes the verse* [emphasis in original] . . . If the number of stresses in each line be fixed, (and such a fixation would be the metre,) and if the stresses be determined only by the language and its sense, and if the syllables which they have to carry do not overburden them, then every line may have a different rhythm; though so much variety is not of necessity.

Jeffers responded to Klein:

> People talked about my "free verse" and I never protested, but now I am quite touched to hear that someone at last has discovered the metrical intention in it. Thank you.
> ("Klein-Jeffers Correspondence" 15) [hereafter "KJC"]

He then discusses Coleridge's meter in *Christabel* (which Bridges, long before Wallace, had shown is more syllabic than either Coleridge or Jeffers thought), questions of syllabic quantity (which Jeffers raises but does not claim to have solved), and several other points. Later, after reading Klein's study, Jeffers comments

> Of course you have noticed that (chiefly in my narrative poems) many lines are of irregular length—"free" no doubt—as are many lines in Elizabethan dramatic verse—but it seems to me there is a metrical pattern—if only, at most irregular, as a background from which to measure departures from the pattern. ("KJC" 20)

The key word here is "measure," not "free." Klein responds by sending Jeffers a summary of Bridges's seven rules of accentual verse from the revised 1921 volume of *Milton's Prosody* ("KJC" 22), for which Jeffers again thanks him.

Thus, despite some indication that Jeffers was also playing with classical scansion as he thought about his new metric, the underlying principle of his verse is stress unmodified by regular syllabic counts, exactly as Jeffers, Klein, Powell, Ghiselin, Nickerson, and several others have described it, and as Hymes has set about analyzing it in the shorter poems. As Hymes and others have shown, and any reader who bothers to start counting can soon realize, Jeffers was extremely inventive with his stress-count verse, endlessly spinning out new patterns.

Recently recovered evidence further indicates Jeffers's intentions, and shows him clearly echoing Bridges's formulation that in stress-based verse, "the verse cannot make the stress because it is the stress that makes the verse," more than a decade after his initial exchange with Klein. This is the entire text of "Rhythm and Rhyme," an unpublished poem Jeffers drafted during the late 1940s:

The tide-flow of passionate speech, breath, blood-pulse, the sea's
    waves and time's return,
They make the metre; but rhyme seems a child's game.
Let the low-Latin languages, the lines lacking strong accents,
    lean on it;
Our north-sea English needs no such ornament.
Born free, and searaid-fed from far shores, why should it taggle
    its head
With tinkling sheep bells, like Rome's slaves' daughters?[8]

Jeffers makes his original technical sources in Old English meter clear, alliterating frequently (as in line 3, on *l*), and yet also displays his original technique, as he forges the lines in alternating lengths of nine and five strong stresses.

A naive reader might at first think that this poem justifies an organicist program, because of the sources for craft that Jeffers cites in the first line; but Jeffers ultimately cites "strong accents," a purely linguistic feature, as necessary to all these other phenomena. Jeffers fully understood that only languages which have such accents to begin with can make "metre" from passionate speech, breath, blood-flow, and so on. This poem not only exhibits the craft it describes, both innovatively and deeply informed by tradition, it shows in what way Jeffers saw that craft as an essential ground of his poetics. For ultimately, this poem says that the embodiment of "The tide-flow of passionate speech, breath, blood-pulse, the sea's waves and time's return" in poetry lies in "strong accents."

There is no question that stress-based meters are messy, complex, subjective, and spectral, and that Jeffers's work can be notoriously difficult to scan along its principles. But is Wallace willing to throw the entire notion out as a principle simply because it does not conform to Procrustean accentual-syllabic norms? That makes little sense. These poems (like other accentual poems in the language) were written under a metrical principle, but because it is such a loose one—governed only by the most relaxed kind of pattern counts for each written line—Wallace wants either to rename or jettison it, even though there is a substantial body of work that it has inspired. Indeed, as Bridges argued, this tradition goes back not only to the strong-stress meter of England, but to Milton, as Jeffers well understood in his remarks about rhyme in the poem quoted above (just as in "Mal Paso Bridge" he vows "to shear the rhyme-tassels from verse").

The reason that stress-based meters are hard for Wallace and others to accept is that they are highly abstract, appearing to look only like prose cut into lengths (which, in some sense, they are). After all, the only principle of counting at work is lineation, as there is no syllable limitation, no word-boundary rule, no rhyme or other alliterative rules, and therefore no structural resistance to placing any word at any point in any line. And yet, there is a powerful underlying abstraction in these meters if one realizes the importance of writing and counting in forging verse.

I have no problem with Wallace's sixth principle:

(6) "Anapests and dactyls are legitimate substitutions in the iambic norm of English meter,"

assuming his terminology. Of course, I would divorce this principle from a notion of how to straightjacket accentual experiments. Also, I would point out that there is some debate about how these substitutions came into being, as many prosodists have disallowed them, and debate continues on how many there can be before the underlying abstraction of an iambic meter breaks down.[9]

Wallace's seventh principle,

(7) "We should drop the pyrrhic foot ($\cup\cup$) and accept in its place the double-iamb ($\cup\cup//$), as one of the six foot terms necessary: iamb, trochee, anapest, dactyl, spondee, double-iamb"

is simply a renaming that grows from a confusion of terms. The essential concept was long ago articulated by Ransom ("The Strange Music of English Verse" 471), as Wallace acknowledges. It doesn't matter what we call these "feet," as long as we understand that this modulation works in iambic meters.

It is at this point that my marginalia on Wallace's essay begin to read "no" in more and more insistent letters. In his disagreement with Donald Hall about the distinction between rhythm and meter, he seems not to understand a principle that he has been using himself at other points in the essay, and to good effect (at one point he writes that "Poems do not change meter from line to line"). This is in large part because his scansion system cannot accommodate it. When Wallace writes

> . . . if I understand Hall's view . . . the *meter* of "To a green thought" is / ∪ | ∪ /, but the *rhythm* could be ∪ ∪ | / /,

he reveals this problem. For Wallace's first notation, of the supposed meter of Marvell's line, could never be a "meter," which is a regular abstraction and does not vary from foot to foot in English. All that Wallace has done is oppose two rhythms against each other, not a rhythm against a meter. It is a case of terminology hampering scansion, for in this case I think that Wallace's actual scansion of the line is better than Hall's—but his explanatory system is weaker.

Wallace's eighth principle makes little sense to me:

(8) "Anapestic, trochaic, and dactylic meters do not exist in English."

He elaborates on this to say

> At some point iambic meter with anapestic substitutions turns into anapestic meter with iambic substitutions—and the distinction is, thus, needless.

His scansion to prove the point is deeply flawed:

> I count the first stanza of "How They Brought the Good News from Ghent to Aix" as comprising 18 anapests, 4 iambs, 2 spondees. So, "heavily anapestic."

But no doubt Wallace realizes that all his iambs and spondees *occur at the beginning of the line* (Wallace's "spondees" lie at the beginnings of lines 3 and 4). There are no other stress groups of fewer than three syllables in the entire stanza! The stronger explanation by far is that this is an anapestic poem with many lines that begin with an anacrusis. The "spondees" are thus acceptable variations of rhythm over this pattern, analogous to rhythmic variation in iambic meters. There are many other kinds of variation in the poem as well, but that's another story, as is the interesting question of dipodic meter, which this poem (like most anapestic and dactylic forms) suggests.

Again, I think that the Greek terms are not the best way to approach scansion, unless it is always understood that they are provisional borrowings that make teaching and discussion easier. That is the way I am using them here, but I do insist that "anapests" are a perfectly good way to organize lines of English meter, and in this case there is a truly great tradition in this form, including what may still be the most popular American poem ever written, Clement Clark Moore's "A Visit from St. Nicholas," which begins—well, you know how it begins.

I would like to address Wallace's two final points in reverse order.

The tenth,

(10) "The spondee is a good, and fairly frequent, foot in English"

is just another terminological note. Yes, things that we can call "spondees" appear regularly in iambic verse in English, none better as an example than Milton's famous "Rocks, Caves, Lakes, Fens, Bogs, Dens, and shades of death" (*Paradise Lost* 2.621). What we call them does little to help us understand the underlying metrical principles at work.

That understanding is all the more likely to proceed if we take what linguists do seriously, as Wallace does not. For example, Wallace is right to disagree with Chatman's characterization of the spondee as impossible—from his perspective, Chatman is making minute differentiations between prosodical levels—but the fact is that *both* Wallace and Chatman can be right because they are looking for different things. The purpose of linguistic prosody is to investigate, as accurately and closely as possible, how language actually works. Wallace is interested in describing patterns; Chatman in describing minute actualities—both models feed into any full understanding of prosody.

Hence, Wallace's ninth principle,

(9) "We should *never* use four degrees of speech stress for scanning"

is far too absolute. I too do not care for the theories of the structural linguists, for a number of reasons too detailed to go into here. Most importantly, they cannot account for meter as an abstraction that is performed on language in written verse, but treat poems as merely scores for performance (others have pointed this out). But I know I have learned a good deal from this work, and find it fascinating. Indeed, I think students *must* study it, and at least learn how to read its scansion, to be familiar with the theory, whatever approach they ultimately settle upon. Otherwise, they simply cannot join the conversation.

To get a sense of just how much work has been done in this area, I urge Wallace and anyone else who is serious about prosody to go to Brogan, the recent MLA bibliography in linguistics, and Derek Attridge's *The Rhythms of English Poetry,* where they will discover that there is a tremendous amount of prosodical scholarship in linguistics (that often deals with literary questions) that Wallace does not even begin to touch. Especially glaring is Wallace's lack of discussion of generative metrics, a major field; he dismisses Halle-Keyser with a comment, and does not even mention subsequent work.

I hope I am being clear: the point is not to agree with the linguists, who often disagree violently with each other, but to foster exchange with them, to create dialogue. We are unlikely, for example, to gain a clear understanding of how meter works unless, as I suggested at the beginning of this essay, we articulate basic principles about its purpose. If you are a linguist, and believe that literary meters follow patterns of preexistent language use, your assumptions will be quite different than if you think of meter as an exercise in abstraction performed upon language. But this crucial issue cannot even be brought to the surface without a lot of work.

Indeed, my own ideas about the importance of writing in metrical systems (which most linguists would hotly oppose) draw directly on debates within linguistics.

My view is that in general the structural and generative linguists' readings of actual poems, as Wallace rightly points out, are weak, and their systems cumbersome; but literary prosody tends to be correspondingly sloppy and ill-informed about how language actually works. Jespersen, Jakobson, Tynianov, Trager-Smith, Halle-Keyser, Kiparsky, and others have, *pace* Wallace, influenced poets who work in this area, among them John Crowe Ransom, John Hollander, and Tim Steele. They have also had a substantial impact on literary scholars who approach the subject, including the very best in the field, such as those poets, along with Brogan, Attridge, and John Thompson. We need more discussion in this area, more dialogue and exchange, not less.

Unlike so much of what passes for theory in the contemporary academy, and is actually politics or empty professional fashion, prosody is truly and inevitably a realm of *theoria*, astonishingly diverse, abstract, slippery, technical, profound, and complex. There is and has been so much disagreement about it because it is, along with semantics, morality, psychology, and a very few other subjects, one of the oldest and most enduring fields of inquiry into literature, beginning quite explicitly with Plato and Aristotle. But what we need is more confusion, not less, in the sense that people on the literary side simply need to read more, discover the real problems and wrestle with them, and to teach the subject in a historically and theoretically rigorous way. We need more books like this one, in which those differing views are brought clanging together. Only then, by reimagining ancient and difficult questions, will we improve the general understanding—and practice—of meter in English.

NOTES

1. I am surprised, for example, at the omission of John Thompson's *The Founding of English Metre* and John Hollander's *Vision and Resonance* from Wallace's discussion. He also omits Terry Brogan's *Versification, 1570–1980: A Critical Bibliography with a Global Appendix*. This book made it possible for students of the subject to gain a well-organized overview of the whole field. Modern prosodical study is inconceivable without it. If Wallace turned to this book, he would quickly be able to place his own theory—a traditional accentual-syllabic system—in its appropriate context.

2. For a recent discussion of the problem see Timothy Steele's "On Meter."

3. There is a lengthy bibliography in this general area, but much of it goes astray. The groundwork for the growing interest in what has (unfortunately) come to be known as "visual prosody" was laid by Wimsatt's "In Search of Verbal Mimesis" in *Day of the Leopards* (1976), and Hollander's *Vision and Resonance* (1975): "[h]ow various modes of free verse take shape on the page, what occasional sound patterns they may or may not embrace . . . are all matters for a theory of graphic prosody" (*Vision and Resonance* 277).

For close studies of the graphic in individual modern poets, see Cureton's essay on Cummings; Sayre's and Cushman's books on Williams; Perloff's essays on Williams and Oppen in *The Dance of the Intellect*, and her more general essay "The Linear Fallacy." Brogan indexes many of these works, and others on specific poets, in his bibliography. A number of period studies have taken up the problem of the graphic, including Attridge's *Well-Weighed Syllables: Elizabethan Verse in Classical Metres* (1974); Griffiths's *The Printed Voice of Victorian Poetry* (1989); and Bradford's work on Milton. Important general works include articles by Derek Attridge, Eleanor Berry, and E. A. Levenston's *The Stuff of Literature*.

4. There is another quantitative tradition which Wallace does not consider which grew out of attempts to score lines of verse like music. The best known treatises in this area are by Joshua Steele and Sidney Lanier, although it has roots in Rousseau's treatise on language, and ultimately classical sources such as Augustine's *De Musica*.

5. See Lotz's article in *Versification: Major Language Types* (ed. Wimsatt).

6. Richard Bradford shows that Johnson was far from the first to make this observation, in a lengthy debate over Milton's prosody. See Bradford's essay "'Verse only to the eye'?: Line Endings in *Paradise Lost.*"

7. Other significant essays on Jeffers's versecraft include Cornelius Cunningham's "The Rhythm of Robinson Jeffers' Poetry as Revealed by Oral Reading" (1946) in which he wrongly concludes that "The beat to which Jeffers' verse tends is iambic-anapestic duple meter" (356); two essays by Edward Nickerson, one on Jeffers's use of rhyme in later poems (1974), and another that speculates on Jeffers's use of the paeon as a technique for controlling his "pace" (1975); an earlier essay by Brewster Ghiselin on the paeon in modern poetry, which briefly discusses Jeffers (1942); and Dell Hymes's recent "Jeffers' Artistry of Line," in Zaller, ed., *Centennial Essays* (226–47), which relies on Klein and Powell.

8. I am grateful to Professor Tim Hunt, editor of *The Collected Poetry of Robinson Jeffers*, for providing me with this quotation from the forthcoming volume 4, which will include Jeffers's early and unpublished work.

9. See, for example, Bastiaan A. P. Van Dam and Cornelis Stoffel's *Chapters on English Printing, Prosody, and Pronunciation (1550–1700)*, first published in 1902. The authors argue that the major German and English nineteenth century prosodists who codified the rule of trisyllabic substitution in English iambic meters (particularly as they came into being in the sixteenth and seventeenth centuries) were duped by printer's corruptions of the poets' manuscripts. The errors were compounded by the later critics' inability to determine accurately when syncope and synizesis would have produced bisyllabic pronunciations in earlier times, thus rendering the rule (which itself came to justify later practice) superfluous.

WORKS CITED

Attridge, Derek. "Poetry Unbound? Observations on Free Verse." *Proceedings of the British Academy* 73 (1987): 353-74.

———. *The Rhythms of English Poetry*. London: Longman, 1982.

———. *Well-Weighed Syllables: Elizabethan Verse in Classical Metres*. Cambridge: Cambridge University Press, 1974.

Augustine, St. *On Music*. Books 1–6. Trans. R. Catesby Taliaferro. Annapolis: The St. John's Bookstore, 1939.

Beare, William. *Latin Verse and European Song: A Study in Accent and Rhythm*. London: Methuen, 1957.

Berry, Eleanor. "Visual Form in Free Verse." *Visible Language* 23 (1989): 89–111.

Bradford, Richard. "'Verse only to the Eye'? Line Endings in *Paradise Lost*." *Essays in Criticism* 33 (1983): 187–204.

Bridges, Robert. *Milton's Prosody & Classical Metres in English Verse (by William Johnson Stone)*. Oxford: n.p., 1901.

———. *Milton's Prosody, with a Chapter on Accentual Verse, & Notes*. Revised Final Edition. Oxford: Oxford University Press, 1921.

Brogan, T. V. F. *English Versification, 1570–1980: A Reference Guide with a Global Appendix*. Baltimore: Johns Hopkins University Press, 1981.

Cunningham, Cornelius Carman. "The Rhythm of Robinson Jeffers' Poetry as Revealed by Oral Reading." *Quarterly Journal of Speech* 32 (1946): 351–57.

Cureton, Richard D. "Visual form in e. e. cummings' *No Thanks.*" *Word & Image* 2 (1986): 245–77.

Cushman, Stephen. *Williams Carlos Williams and the Meaning of Measure*. New Haven: Yale University Press, 1985.

Ghiselin, Brewster. "Paeonic Measures in English Verse." *Modern Language Notes* 57 (1942): 336–41.

Griffiths, Eric. *The Printed Voice of Victorian Poetry*. Oxford: Clarendon Press, 1989.

Gross, Harvey. *Sound and Form in Modern Poetry: A Study of Prosody from Thomas Hardy to Robert Lowell*. Ann Arbor: The University of Michigan Press, 1964.

———, ed. *The Structure of Verse: Modern Essays on Prosody*. Rev. ed. New York: The Ecco Press, 1979.

Harris, Roy. *The Origin of Writing*. La Salle, Ill.: Open Court Press, 1986.

Hollander, John. *Vision and Resonance: Two Senses of Poetic Form*. New York: Oxford University Press, 1975.

Jeffers, Robinson. *The Collected Poetry of Robinson Jeffers*. Ed. Tim Hunt. 4 vols. Stanford: Stanford University Press, 1988–91, and forthcoming.

Karman, James, ed. *Critical Essays on Robinson Jeffers*. Boston: G. K. Hall & Co., 1990.

Klein, Harold. "The Prosody of Robinson Jeffers." MA Thesis, Occidental College, 1930.

"Klein-Jeffers Correspondence: 1930 & 1935." *Robinson Jeffers Newsletter* 67 (July 1986): 11–27.

Lanier, Sidney. *The Science of English Verse and Essays on Music*. Ed. Paull Franklin Baum. Vol 2 of *The Centennial Edition of the Works of Sidney Lanier*. Gen. ed. Charles R. Anderson. Baltimore: The Johns Hopkins Press, 1945. 10 vols.

Levenston, E. A. *The Stuff of Literature: Physical Aspects of Texts and Their Relation to Literary Meaning*. Albany: State University of New York Press, 1992.

Nickerson, Edward. "The Return to Rhyme." *Robinson Jeffers Newsletter* 39 (1974): 12–21.

———. "Robinson Jeffers and the Paeon." *Western American Literature* 10 (1975): 189–93.

Perloff, Marjorie. *The Dance of the Intellect: Studies in the Poetry of the Pound Tradition*. Cambridge: Cambridge University Press, 1985.

———. "The Linear Fallacy." *The Georgia Review* 35 (1981): 855–69.

Powell, Laurence Clark. *Robinson Jeffers: The Man & His Work*. Foreword by Robinson Jeffers. Los Angeles: The Primavera Press, 1934.

Ransom, John Crowe. "The Strange Music of English Verse." *The Kenyon Review* 18 (1956): 460–77.

Sayre, Henry M. *The Visual Text of William Carlos Williams*. Urbana: University of Illinois Press, 1983.

Steele, Joshua. *Prosodia Rationalis*. London: 1779.

Steele, Timothy. "On Meter." *Hellas* 1.2 (1990): 289–310.

Thompson, John. *The Founding of English Metre*. New York: Columbia University Press, 1961; reprint, with an introduction by John Hollander, 1989.

Van Dam, Bastiaan A. P. and Cornelis Stoffel. *Chapters on English Printing, Prosody, and Pronunciation (1550–1700)*. Heidelberg: Carl Winter's Universitatsbuchhandlung, 1902. Reprinted New York: AMS Press Inc., 1973.

Williams, William, Carlos. "Free Verse." *Princeton Encyclopedia of Poetry and Poetics*. Ed. Alex Preminger. Enlarged ed. Princeton: Princeton University Press, 1974: 288–90.

Wimsatt, W. K. *Day of the Leopards: Essays in Defense of Poems*. New Haven: Yale University Press, 1976.

———, ed. *Versification: Major Language Types*. New York: Modern Language Association, New York University Press, 1972.

Zaller, Robert, ed. *Centennial Essays for Robinson Jeffers*. Newark: University of Delaware Press, 1991.

STAUNCH METER,
GREAT SONG

Timothy Steele

Prefacing a discussion of Milton's versification, Samuel Johnson remarks in *Rambler* number 88:

> However minute the employment may appear, of analysing lines into syllables, and whatever ridicule may be incurred by a solemn deliberation upon accents and pauses, it is certain, that without this petty knowledge no man can be a poet; and that from the proper disposition of single sounds results that harmony that adds force to reason, and gives grace to sublimity; that shackles attention, and governs passion.

Johnson makes here a perennially relevant point. Though we probably prize poems most for their capacity to illuminate the world and reconcile us to our experience, nothing in a poem makes a stronger or more immediate appeal than its rhythmical element. Even if we are greatly interested in a poem's theme, it alone is rarely sufficient to hold our attention or move our heart. The poem must also please aesthetically, and this requirement can be met only if the versification is lively, skillful, and faithful to its conventions. And however trivial may appear diagrams of scansion and divisions of feet, metrical questions are crucial to anyone who cares for poetry as an art with its own special beauty and integrity—as an art, that is, distinguishable from other arts and other forms of human expression.

With this point in mind, I welcome the opportunity to participate in this forum on meter, and I thank Professor Wallace for providing a basis for discussion. Professor Wallace's essay offers provocative observations about English verse. Particularly valuable is his insistence that metrical theory should not prescriptively lay down laws, but should rather adopt the more modest aim of trying to describe and to account for accurately the practice of our finest poets. If I take exception to some of Professor Wallace's remarks, I do so only with respect and in hopes of contributing to that increased appreciation of metrics that he eloquently advocates.

Because Professor Wallace criticizes my views on spondees and on the Jespersen-Trager-Smith concept of four levels of stress, I should like at the outset to address these points (9 and 10 in his essay: **"We should *never* use four degrees of speech stress for scanning"** and **"The spondee is a good, and fairly frequent, foot in English."**). In fact, I shall devote much of my essay to them, since the issues they involve seem critical. However, it will first be necessary to explain briefly my understanding of English versification. A more detailed explanation appears in the earlier article of mine ("On Meter," *Hellas* 1 [Fall 1990], 289–310) that Professor Wallace cites. Readers interested in a fuller examination of matters summarized below can consult that article.

Versification involves the concurrent but distinguishable phenomena of meter and rhythm. Meter is the basic norm or paradigm of the line. It is an analytical abstraction. In the case of the iambic pentameter, for example, the norm is:

one **two**, one **two**, one **two**, one **two**, one **two**

Rhythm, on the other hand, is the variable realization in speech of this fixed pattern. On rare occasions, poets will write pentameters in which the realization virtually coincides with the paradigm. They will write lines consisting of five successive two-syllable, rear-stressed phrasal or verbal units:

But we, alas! are chased; and you, my friends
　　(Christopher Marlowe, *Edward II*, 4.6.22)
One soul, one flesh, one love, one heart, one all
　　(John Ford, *'Tis a Pity She's a Whore*, 1.1.34)
Above, below, without, within, around
　　(Alexander Pope, "The Temple of Fame," 458)

More frequently, the rhythm may involve an alternation that approximates the norm fairly closely:

I **think** of thee!—my **thoughts** do **twine** and **bud**
　　(Elizabeth Barrett Browning, *Sonnets from the Portuguese*, 29.1)
Per**haps,** if **sum**mer **ever came** to **rest**
　　(Wallace Stevens, "The Man Whose Pharynx Was Bad," 10)

However, most pentameters do not feature such uniform fluctuations. Though the type with five obvious off-beats and beats is the most common, it can claim only a smallish plurality in our verse. In his entry for "Meter" in *The New Princeton Encyclopedia of Poetry and Poetics,* T. V. F. Brogan plausibly suggests the figure of 25 percent. Poets write not only in feet, but also in phrases, clauses, and sentences, and these have all sorts of different lengths and shapes and stress-shadings. As a result, most iambic lines exhibit a fluctuation between lighter and heavier that is not absolutely regular, but is instead sometimes more emphatic, sometimes less. Many pentameters have fewer than five strong beats:

The **right** pre**cau**tions to a**void** a **fall**
　　(W.H. Auden, *The Quest,* 10.8)
The **ar**my of un**al**terable **law**
　　(George Meredith, "Lucifer in Starlight," 14)
A deso**la**tion, a sim**pli**city
　　(William Wordsworth, *The Prelude,* 4.402)

Many have more than five:

No **self**ish **wish** the **moon's bright glance** con**fines**
　　(Jones Very, "The Absent," 7)
Full season's **come,** yet **filled trees keep** the **sky**
　　(Louise Bogan, "Simple Autumnal," 13)

True thoughts, good thoughts, thoughts fit to treasure **up**

(Robert Browning, "Transcendentalism," 5)

Yet, however different their rhythms, all these verses realize the same metrical paradigm. Even Browning's line, which reiterates a word consecutively in the fourth and fifth positions, maintains the basic iambic fluctuation.

In my earlier essay, I suggested that we might think of iambic lines as mountain ranges. Peaks and valleys alternate. But not every peak is an Everest, nor is every valley a Grand Canyon. Sometimes one of the peaks is lower than the other peaks:

The right precautions to avoid a fall

Sometimes, one of the valleys is more elevated than the other valleys:

No selfish wish the moon's bright glance confines

In addition, iambic verse allows for a number of conventional variations. These include substitutions of inverted (i.e., trochaic) feet for iambic feet, especially at line-beginnings or after midline pauses. Another common variant is the feminine ending. Moreover, from time to time, we will find two adjacent feet whose four syllables represent four rising degrees of stress; and this sequence may appear in any portion of the line—beginning, middle, or end:

    1   2   3   4

With what | sharp checks | I in | myself | am shent

(Philip Sidney, *Astrophel and Stella,* 18.1)

          1 2   3   4

How myght | y and | how greet | a lord | is he!

(Geoffrey Chaucer, *Canterbury Tales,* "The Knight's Tale," 1786)

            1 2   3   4

I sought | it dai | ly for | six weeks | or so

(William Butler Yeats, "The Circus Animals' Desertion," 2)

                      1   2   3   4

One's glance | could cross | the bor | ders of | three states

(Hart Crane, "Quaker Hill," 26)

But the key thing in English iambic verse is the fluctuation. And, generally, the practice of traditional iambic meter involves the poet's taking this basic alternating norm and modulating it internally. The poet works within and conforms to the one pattern, but does so in many and continually different ways.

As for scansion, it treats the verse-line merely as a row of syllables, and the sole requirement for an iambic foot is that its second syllable be heavier than its first. Furthermore, it is with reference to the prevailing metrical pattern of a poem that we divide lines down into their constituent feet. We don't examine words or phrases in isolation, and scan them individually. We perceive the whole and then construe the parts. If prosodists from Pluto, on an expedition to Earth, found a scrap of paper with Shakespeare's line (*Romeo and Juliet*, 3.3.2)

Affliction is enamoured of thy parts

they might, having no frame of reference, misinterpret its versification. Scrutinizing the line's first and third words, for instance, they might speculate that, because these are middle-stressed trisyllables, the earthling was working at least partly in amphibrachs. And seeing the prepositional phrase that concludes the line, they might further hypothesize that here he intended an anapest, and that the line overall was some kind of tetrameter comprised of trisyllabic feet, with, however, a headless iamb substituted in the second foot:

∪ / ∪   / ∪ / ∪   ∪ ∪   /
Affliction | is | enamoured | of thy parts

Yet for those of us familiar with English verse, no such difficulties exist. The line occurs in a long dramatic poem composed largely in iambic pentameter. And hearing the line in this context, we can divide its feet accordingly:

Afflic | tion is | enam | oured of | thy parts

Professor Wallace perhaps confuses this issue when he states, "The naturalness of the anapest derives, if for no other reason, from the structure of simple prepositional phrases." Though the anapest is certainly natural in English, foot division is an analytic exercise. It has nothing to do with phrasal shape or word morphology, as important as these matters are to the overall rhythms of lines. It is the general texture of a language that determines its characteristic rhythms, not this or that particular element of it. (There is nothing especially iambic about English words or phrases, yet the language readily tends to this pattern.) If we deduced a metric from Professor Wallace's observation about the anapest, we could demonstrate the naturalness to English of any conceivable foot of almost any conceivable length. We could point to the presence in our language of such fore-and-rear-stressed trisyllabic words as "gasoline" and "synchronize," and announce that the cretic (/˘/) is therefore fundamental to our prosody. For that matter, since prepositional phrases take different forms, we could point to those whose objects are rear-stressed disyllables—for instance, "in the caboose," "to the hotel," and "on the lagoon"—and urge that the paean (˘˘˘/) is essential. An anapest can occur, to cite Professor Wallace's example from Frost's "The Road Not Taken," in consequence of a prepositional phrase:

        ˘   /   ˘ /   ˘ ˘ /   ˘   /
    Two roads | diverged | in a yel | low wood

But anapests can also result from any number of other constructions, as these two lines from later in the poem illustrate:

        ˘   /   ˘ ˘ /   ˘   /   ˘   /
    And hav | ing perhaps | the bet | ter claim
        ˘ /   ˘ ˘   /   ˘ ˘   /   ˘   /
    Because | it was gras | sy and want | ed wear

By the same token, prepositional phrases commonly figure, as Professor Wallace himself notes, in other metrical schemes, including iambic.

A similar concern might be felt about comments that Professor Wallace makes regarding Andrew Marvell's line:

    To a green thought, in a green shade.

Criticizing Donald Hall for treating this line as having four disyllabic feet—trochee, iamb, trochee, iamb—Professor Wallace suggests that we entertain the possibility that "To a green" is an anapest. (It is not pertinent to the matter in question that his ultimate interpretation of the line does not involve reading its first three words as an anapest.) "It is dubious," Professor Wallace writes, "to assume that, since the meter is iambic, relative stress is to be weighed exclusively as to 'each group of *two* syllables.'" Yet this is precisely how we weigh stress when we scan a meter whose basic organization entails, as iambic's does, two-syllable units. If in scanning iambic verse, we cease to measure the feet in such units, we will cease to record the meter and will find ourselves instead engaged in a sort of grammatical parsing that has no connection to the metrical pattern. If Marvell's line had extra syllables, or was utterly inexplicable in light of the conventions of its meter, we might look for trisyllabic feet. But this isn't the case. The line is one of seventy-two verses of a poem in regular and beautifully modulated iambic tetrameters. However unusual the rhythm of the line, it makes sense metrically. And we can assume that the poet intended it to match—to have the same number of feet as—the other verses in the poem.

An additional point might be made with respect to scansion. If it is important to distinguish between a line's meter and its rhythm, it may also be helpful to distinguish, in terms of its individual syllables, between "metrical stress" and "speech stress." By "metrical stress," I refer to the character of a syllable when it is considered simply according to the weak-strong system of scansion. If it receives more emphasis than the other syllable or syllables of the foot in which it appears, it has metrical stress (i.e., is "stressed"). If it receives less emphasis, it does not have metrical stress (i.e., is "unstressed"). By "speech stress," I refer to the character of the syllable when it is actually spoken. Speech stress involves the emphasis that a syllable carries not merely in the foot in which it figures, but also in the larger phrasal or clausal environment of which it may be part. Metrical stress and speech stress are related, just as the weak-strong pattern and the internal modulations of it in actual lines of verse are related. But the two are not inevitably or exactly the same.

In connection with this point, we might note that often in poetry in English, a metrically unstressed syllable at one point in the line actually carries more speech emphasis than a metrically stressed syllable at another point. Consider, for example, these verses:

Close bosom-friend of the maturing sun
    (John Keats, "To Autumn," 2)
And makes my thought take cover in the facts
    (Richard Wilbur, "On the Marginal Way," 34)

Even as they embody interesting and pleasing modulations, these lines remain conventional iambic pentameters. All the feet are iambic: all exhibit a weaker-to-stronger relationship, and the line itself follows the lighter-to-heavier fluctuation. To return once more to our figure of the mountain range, the peaks are still peaks and the valleys are still valleys:

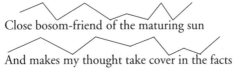

Close bosom-friend of the maturing sun

And makes my thought take cover in the facts

But the metrically unstressed syllable of the first foot of the first line ("Close") has more speech stress than the metrically stressed syllable of the third foot ("the"). And in the second line the metrically unstressed syllable of the third foot ("take") has more speech stress than the metrically stressed syllable of the fourth foot ("in").

    This brings us to pyrrhics and spondees and to why, in my view, it is misleading to use them regularly in scanning English verse. These feet are natural in Greek and Latin prosody, which measures the length of syllables and in which length itself can be determined solely by phonemics and phonetics. If the vowel in a syllable is long or a diphthong, the syllable is long; if the vowel in the syllable is short, but is "closed" by a consonant, the syllable is also long. Otherwise, the syllable is short. And in ancient poetry short syllables appear at short positions in the line and long syllables at long positions. (There are in some meters "anceps" positions, positions that admit either a long or a short syllable. There are also certain anceps syllables, but these mostly occur in words which admit of alternative syllabifications— *ă-gris* or *āg-ris,* for example—and the metrical nature of such syllables can thus be recognized phonetically.)

    English meter, however, measures dynamic stress, and this depends not only on phonemics and phonetics, but also on grammatical and rhetorical context. To determine metrical values, we have to look at more than the intrinsic nature of the syllable. Admittedly, heavy monosyllabic verbs, for instance, tend to appear in stressed positions; but frequently they turn up in unstressed positions, as "fetch" does in the first foot of the following verse:

Fetch wa | ter, dripping, over desert miles
    (James David Corrothers, "The Negro Singer," 10)

And though light monosyllabic articles, prepositions, and conjunctions are most often metrically unstressed, it is not uncommon for them to appear in stressed positions, as "and" does in the fourth foot of this line:

Prepared to scrub the en | try and | the stairs
    (Jonathan Swift, "A Description of the Morning," 8)

Further, frequently in English verse a monosyllabic word will appear in both unstressed and stressed positions in the same line. In fact, this may occur when the monosyllables involved are in adjacent feet or are even, as was the case in Robert Browning's line, side by side. A verse may even feature two monosyllabic words which appear twice and the metrical values of both of which shift in the course of the line:

Up roos | the sonne | and *up* | roos Em | elyë
    (Chaucer, *Canterbury Tales,* "The Knight's Tale," 2273)
All men | think *all* | *men* mor | tal, but | themselves
    (Edward Young, *Night Thoughts,* 1.423)

For that matter, a monosyllabic word may begin with one metrical identity, switch to the other, and then return to its original form:

She was | *so* han | dy, *so* | discreet, | *so* nice
    (George Crabbe, "The Wife and the Widow," 102)

And, to cite another interesting wrinkle, a word may appear as the stressed syllable in a trochaic first foot and reappear as the unstressed, hyper-metrical syllable of a feminine ending—this transformation seeming to occur when, in Edward Thomas's "Up in the Wind," the wild girl says (101) of the desolate rural inn that she runs:

        / ∪ ∪ / ∪ / ∪ / ∪ / (∪)
    Here I | shall die. | Perhaps | I want | to die here

Two factors chiefly cause such shifts. The first is phrasal context. As linguists and prosodists alike have observed, light syllables tend to be "promoted"—tend to receive slightly greater emphasis—when flanked, fore and aft, by other light syllables. When we have to speak a run of three light syllables, their intelligibility increases if we raise the middle one a little. In the following line, for instance, "a" would seem to be promoted the second time that it appears:

    Our birth | is but | *a* sleep | and *a* | forgetting
        (Wordsworth, "Ode: Intimations of Immortality from
        Recollections of Early Childhood," 58)

That is, the first time "a" occurs it is unstressed not only because it is unemphatic to begin with, but also because it stands between two comparatively heavy syllables. When it next turns up, however, it stands between a light conjunction and the unaccented first syllable of "forgetting," and receives in consequence a little more speech stress than it would normally and is metrically stressed.

Conversely, heavy syllables tend to be "demoted" if flanked by other heavy syllables, a circumstance that explains the metrical properties of this line:

    And des | tined *Man* | himself | to judge | *Man* fall'n
        (John Milton, *Paradise Lost,* 10.62)

The first time "Man" appears it is metrically stressed not only because it is a fairly heavy and significant word to begin with, but also because it falls between two light syllables. The second time it appears it is still fairly weighty, but is less emphatic because sandwiched between two other weighty and significant words.

Rhetorical context is the second major factor that produces metrical shifts. Indeed, poets can focus meaning by shuttling words between metrically stressed and unstressed positions. This procedure can be seen in a couplet from William Cartwright's tetrametric "To Chloe Who Wished Herself Young Enough for Me," a poem which celebrates love and in which the poet asserts that love restores youth to those who are aging and maintains youth in those who are young. In the first line of the couplet, Cartwright indicates love's restorative power by setting "young" in a metrically stressed position; in the second line, he highlights the element of maintenance by metrically subordinating the adjective to verbs and an adverb.

⏑ / ⏑ / ⏑ / ⏑ /
Love makes those young whom age doth chill

⏑ / ⏑ / ⏑ / ⏑ /
And whom he finds young, keeps young still.

(The metrical and rhythmical nature of "whom" also shifts, as the focus switches from the activity of Love, in the first line, to, in the second line, the person *whom* this activity affects.)

So, too, when in *Paradise Lost* (10.832) Adam laments that the blame for the corruption of humankind falls

⏑ / ⏑ /
On me, | me on | ly, as | the source | and spring

it is natural as well as metrical that "me" should be stressed in foot one and subordinated in foot two. In the first case, Adam terribly perceives that he bears (on **me**) responsibility for the catastrophe. In the second he realizes—what is yet more terrible—that he alone (me **on**ly) is responsible.

These expressive variabilities comprise a beauty peculiar to modern English versification, as opposed to ancient versification, in which metrical identities are less susceptible to manipulation. However, the variability also indicates the danger of imagining that syllabic stress is as inherently determinable in modern prosody as syllabic length was in ancient metrics.

To approach this issue from another angle, we might say the following. The principle of less and greater—the principle of iambics, trochees, dactyls, amphibrachs, anapests—was readily adaptable to English from Greek and Latin, since the principle is as characteristic of our stress-based metrical feet as it was of the corresponding length-based ancient feet. However, equivalence—the principle of the pyrrhic and spondee—is not for the most part characteristic of English meter or speech. In fact, true spondees perhaps appear in only two cases: first, when the rhythm of a poem or passage is so emphatic and close to the metrical norm that a foot with two relatively weighty syllables really does stand out as unusual; or second, when the syllables are said with the same degree of emphasis, as in the first feet of the impatient exclamations in the bitter exchange in the closet scene from *Hamlet* (3.4.12–13)

Queen.
    Come, come, you answer with an idle tongue.
Hamlet.
    Go, go, you question with a wicked tongue.

There is, moreover, a practical difficulty with regularly scanning spondees and pyrrhics into English iambic verse. If we start marking as pyrrhics and spondees all feet whose syllables are relatively close in their stress properties, we risk confusing our readers, since such feet occur so often. Readers who are young and unfamiliar with verse may be especially puzzled and may well wonder why iambic pentameters, for instance, are so named, since so few of them will appear to conform to the pattern they ostensibly embody.

One sees this problem in the odd scansion—it's from the glossary of the third edition of *The Norton Anthology*—of the fourteenth line of Frost's "The Gift Outright." Though the line is tricky, it can be read as a conventional iambic pentameter with an inverted first foot and feminine ending. This is how the poet himself reads it, if I am hearing accurately, on the Library of Congress recording of his work. The anthology, however, instructs students to read it as an anapest, two trochees, a pyrrhic and a spondee:

$$\cup \ \cup \ / \qquad / \quad \cup \quad / \cup \ \cup \ \cup \qquad / \quad /$$
To the land | vaguely | real | izing | westward

(The anthology also imposes strange scansions on other lines in the poem and draws from the whole the grossly misleading moral that the essence of skillful versification is an adventurous disregard of meter.)

One sees the same problem to a lesser extent in Professor Wallace's more sensitive, but still possibly puzzling, treatment of the opening line of "Desert Places":

/   /   ᴗ   ᴗ   /   /   ᴗ   /   (/)   /
Snow fall | ing and night fall | ing fast, | oh, fast

Professor Wallace calls this "a commonsense scansion." But it gives us an iambic pentameter with only four feet and with only one of those feet being an iamb. Even if one resolves the double-iamb into two feet, so as to allow the pentameter five feet, one is still left with a spondee, a pyrrhic, a spondee, an iamb, and (so far as I can tell) a quasi spondee. The line is unusual rhythmically. Yet there are many other lines of comparative complexity in English verse; and however distinctive the movement, all the feet bear the lighter-to-heavier relationship.

A more specific difficulty seems exhibited by Professor Wallace's scansions of Pope's pentameter and Marvell's tetrameter:

ᴗ   /   ᴗ   /   (/)   /   /   /   ᴗ   /
When A | jax strives | some rock's | vast weight | to throw
ᴗ   ᴗ   /   /   ᴗ   ᴗ   /   /
To a green thought, | in a green shade

It is not just that, to take Marvell's case, there is something disconcerting about scanning a tetrameter as having only two feet. It is also that Professor Wallace renders phrases involving monosyllabic adjectives and monosyllabic nouns ("green thought," "green shade," "vast weight") as spondaic, whereas in speech we usually subordinate the modifier to the substantive. Customarily, we stress the adjective only if we wish to use it contrastively, as in

Strive Ajax! Hurl those *vast* weights, leave the *small*
For Nestor, who can't lift a tennis ball.

or

The punch was spiked with LSD,
And *green* shade now looks *pink* to me.

Professor Wallace does at one juncture offer a reading of Marvell's line in which the adjective takes precedence over the nouns:

To a green thought, in a green shade

But this seems not only to violate normal speech habits; it also spoils the rhyme with the previous verse: "Annihilating all that's made."

The foregoing considerations raise an important point about scansion, so far as it is conceived of as involving two values, off-beat and beat. *With the two-value system of notation, we can scan only the meter of a line; we cannot scan its rhythm.* We can refer the line to its general type. We can, in addition, note clear divergences from it, such as substitutions of trochees for iambs and such as the anapestic substitutions that we noted in Frost's "The Road Not Taken." But scansion involves a certain comprehensiveness and abstraction from the endless variabilities of living language. It is this very comprehensiveness that enables us to use scansion to demonstrate metrical patterns and to relate individual lines of verse to them. If we attempt to force scansion to record rhythmical subtleties, we are likely to muddle matters and even to lose hold of the distinction between meter and rhythm.

I believe that Professor Wallace confuses meter with rhythm when, citing my earlier essay, he reproaches me for "insisting on the absolute iambic regularity" of Donne's line:

Kind pity chokes my spleen; brave scorn forbids

The phrase "absolute iambic regularity" suggests to me verses such as those cited from Marlowe, Ford, and Pope, verses composed of two-syllable units, with stress on the second syllable; I would not use the phrase in connection with Donne's line. What I said of it, and of several other pentameters that had fewer or more than five speech stresses, was that they exhibited "rhythmical differences" while being "metrically identical." They all possessed, I argued, their own distinctive rhythmical contours while adhering to the same underlying metrical pattern. Donne's pentameter is unusual in that both syllables of the first and fourth feet are relatively weighty—the effect of which, one might add, is nicely indicative of the congested emotion of the speaker. Yet this effect is rhythmical, not metrical. When we read "Kind pity," we give greater stress to "pit-" than "kind"; when we say "brave scorn," we give greater stress to "scorn." The syllables in the feet still bear the lighter-to-heavier relationship. The line still fluctuates iambically.

I don't wish to seem spondicidal. However, if we want to distinguish an iamb involving something like "brave scorn" from an iamb involving something like "a scratch," perhaps it would be preferable to speak of a "heavy foot" or "heavy iamb." Likewise, we might use, for a foot in which both syllables are comparatively unemphatic, the term "light foot" or "light iamb." But as for our scansions involving breve and ictus, it seems wisest to treat as iambs all feet whose syllables bear the lighter-to-heavier relationship.

Concerning Jespersen's four-stress register, I suggested, in my earlier essay, that we employ it only as a supplement to conventional scansion. Further, I stressed that the four-level numerical register is, no less than the two-level system, a simplification of the endlessly variable movements of actual speech. What the numerical register can do is express rhythmical fluctuation in a way that the breve-ictus scheme cannot. As such, the register may help some readers to recognize that, for the practicing poet, the iambic pentameter is not so much a single rhythm, consisting of five minimally stressed syllables and five maximally stressed ones, as it is a general model which can be realized in many ways by many different syntactical arrangements. To return to Donne's line, the numerical register allows us to suggest its rhythm without obscuring its meter:

3 4 1 4   1 4   3 4   1 4
⌣ / ⌣ /   ⌣ /   ⌣ /   ⌣ /
Kind pit | y chokes | my spleen; | brave scorn | forbids

Using this or the mountain-range method seems, in any case, preferable pedagogically and linguistically to Professor Wallace's insistence that the heavy feet be scanned as spondees:

/ / ⌣ /   ⌣ /   / /   ⌣ /
Kind pit | y chokes | my spleen; | brave scorn | forbids

This rendering not only arguably traduces the meter, but also falsifies the rhythm, which involves, regardless of the heavy feet, continuous fluctuation—not level stress, then some fluctuation, then another stretch of level stress, and finally a concluding fluctuating unit.

It also might be pointed out that Professor Wallace, in using a scansion mark like (/), is doing what he objects to in the linguistic Jespersen-Trager-Smith analysis. He is attempting to record intermediate stress. My concern with his approach is, again, that he is trying to do this at the level of basic scansion, and in consequence risks imposing unnecessary complexity on a procedure whose instructive capacity depends on its simplicity.

It might be said as well, in defense of the linguists, that given certain syntactical patterns, we do hear the four degrees of stress—weak, tertiary, secondary, and strong—of which they speak. We hear these when stress rises continuously over two feet, especially when the feet are at the beginnings or ends of lines. That is, regardless of how we scan according to breve and ictus, most of us probably hear the first four syllables of "With how sad steps, O moon, thou climb'st the sky" as 1-2-3-4 in stress-level. And most readers probably hear the four degrees, in 2-1-3-4 pattern, in prepositional phrases with a monosyllabic object and a monosyllabic adjective modifying it: "In a cool night," "On a wet lawn," "Up the steep slope." This is the pattern that Donald Hall perceives—in my opinion correctly—in Marvell's line:

> 2 1   3   4   2 1 3   4
> To a green thought, in a green shade

On a smaller point, Professor Wallace characterizes as "astonishing" my hearing Keats's line as having four degrees rising over two feet:

> 1   2   3   4
> The hare limped trembling through the frozen grass

It seems that if one says the line naturally—without pausing between the subject and predicate, between "hare" and "limped"—one hears rising stress. The line's syntax is fairly common; citing another instance of it may clarify its rhythm:

> Her mind kept fading in the growing mist
> (Vladimir Nabokov, *Pale Fire*, 202)

This rhythm appears in these lines as well, which, however, differ in their syntax:

A young man married is a man that's marred
(Shakespeare, *All's Well that Ends Well*, 2.3.301)
A long day's dying to augment our pain
(Milton, *Paradise Lost*, 10.964)

(The light third foot and the rhythmical regularity of the final two feet also contribute to giving the verses their distinctive ring.)

Since Professor Wallace faults me, in connection with Keats's line, for "an attempt (albeit mistaken) to follow a doctrine [of Jespersen]," I should say that I was only trying to follow my ear, however fallible it may be. As for Jespersen specifically, though I admire and have learned from his work, I strongly disagree with his opinion that we should jettison traditional scansion. On the contrary, I concur with C. S. Lewis's view ("Metre," *Selected Literary Essays by C. S. Lewis* [Cambridge, Cambridge Univ. Press, 1969], 280–85) that scansion by foot division is—whatever its flaws and whatever our disagreements concerning it—the best system we have and are ever likely to have.

To summarize, then, I have misgivings with Professor Wallace's point 9, **"We should never use four degrees of stress for scanning,"** to the extent that I believe the four-level register can usefully *supplement* the conventional system and can suggest the rhythmical properties of a line in a way that the two-level register cannot. At the same time, however, I have had success, in teaching literature, with the mountain range procedure. This accomplishes the same end as the numerical register and may seem preferable for those who feel that the register suggests a false precision. Regarding Professor Wallace's point 10, **"The spondee is a good, and fairly frequent, foot in English,"** I disagree, insofar as I do not believe that spondees appear frequently in iambic verse and insofar as I think that scanning them into iambic verse tends to obscure metrical pattern and misconstrue speech rhythm.

With respect to Professor Wallace's point 7 (**"We should drop the pyrrhic foot ($\smile\smile$) and accept in its place the double-iamb ($\smile\smile$//), as one of the six foot-terms necessary: iamb, trochee, anapest, dactyl, spondee, double-iamb."**) and his suggestion that we incorporate the double-iamb into our metrical terminology, I see a couple of problems. First, the foot seems ill defined, as presented by Professor Wallace. In fact, it is not a foot at all, if we think of a foot as reflecting a single contrastive or proportional relationship (e.g., the unstressed-stressed pattern of the modern iamb or the long-short-short pattern of the ancient dactyl). In his essay, Professor Wallace offers at least two different rhythmical types as double-iambs:

> ⏑ ⏑ / /
> Snow fall | ing and night fall | ing fast, oh, fast

> ⏑⏑ / /
> Speech | after long si | lence; it is right

In the first example, we have four degrees of rising stress. In the second, there is a drop from the first to the second syllable and then (if I understand Professor Wallace correctly) a rise through the third and fourth. And if Professor Wallace hears and scans Marvell's line as

> ⏑ ⏑ / /   ⏑⏑ / /
> To a *green* thought, | in a *green* shade

we have another type of double-iamb, this one peaking at syllable three. As much as one might admire its versatility, such a foot is descriptively useless.

Possibly problematical as well is the fact that the combination of a heavy iamb followed by a light one is as common in English verse as the combination of a light followed by a heavy. This other combination occurs in the earlier-cited Richard Wilbur line, which may be reprinted here with two more instances:

>   3   4   1 2
>   ⏑ / ⏑ /
> And makes | my thought | take cov | er in | the facts

>   3   4   1 2
>   ⏑ / ⏑ /
> Expect | things great | er than | thy larg | est hopes
> (Ben Jonson, *Sejanus*, 1.1.362)

>   3 4   1 2
>   ⏑ / ⏑ /
> The day | becomes | more sol | emn and | serene
> (Percy Bysshe Shelley, "Hymn to Intellectual Beauty," 73)

Might Professor Wallace render this configuration as (//××) and call it a reversed double-iamb? (One hesitates to call it a double trochee, since there is no continuous descent over the four syllables, though, to be sure, there is no level ascent in such double-iambs as "after long si-" or "in a *green* shade.")

In any case, not only does this heavy-plus-light-foot combo appear often. It frequently overlaps with the light-plus-heavy combo, as in this pentameter:

> Slow anger to hard answers in a glance
> (Helen Pinkerton, "Elegy at Beaverhead County, Montana," 14)

If we're scanning with double feet, do we have here a double-iamb running from the third to sixth positions,

◡ ◡ / /

Slow an | ger to hard an | swers in a glance

or two reversed double-iambs?

/ / ◡ ◡ / / ◡ ◡

Slow anger to | hard answers in | a glance

And what are we to make of the following verse in the penta-metric "What thou lov'st well" passage of Ezra Pound's eighty-first *Canto,* a verse exhibiting an alternation of heavy and light feet across the entire line:

> Made courage, or made order, or made grace

Would this be a spondee, plus two double-iambs?

/ / ◡ ◡ / / ◡ ◡ / /

Made cour | age, or made or | der, or made grace

Or two reversed double-iambs, plus a spondee?

/ / ◡ ◡ / / ◡ ◡ / /

Made courage, or | made order, or | made grace

These examples may remind us that metrical practice is far more complex than metrical description and that it is probably misguided to ask the latter, which must perforce deal in simplifications, to record all of the subtleties of the former. It may at first blush appear sensible to introduce double-iambs into prosodic discussion. But these may in the long run confuse rather than clarify our understanding of meter.

Also regarding point 7, our terminology will be incomplete if we neglect the amphibrach, since poems have been written using amphibrachic measures.

As might be inferred from that last remark, I disagree with Professor Wallace's assertion, "There is one meter in English: accentual-syllabic, and its base is always iambic," and with his related point 8, **"Anapestic, trochaic, and dactylic meters do not exist in English."** These assertions, while reflecting reasonably the mainly iambic character of English verse practice, seem wrong in a historical sense. When Frost observed, "[I]n our language . . . there are virtually but two [meters], strict iambic and loose iambic," he introduced the adverb "virtually" for a reason. Though iambic meters are the most prevalent in our poetry, other measures have been used, and have in particular periods assumed considerable importance.

Trisyllabic meters, for example, played a key role in the eighteenth century, when the practice of iambic verse became largely restricted to the closed heroic couplet. During this time, the rhythmically and grammatically balanced pentameter so dominated iambic verse, that poets were driven to experiment with a variety of non-iambic lines. An especially interesting practice was that of writing couplets whose first line was in one trisyllabic rhythm and whose answering line was in another. For instance, in one of the "Airs" from John Gay's *Polly,* an air written in tetrameter couplets, the first line is amphibrachic and the answering line is anapestic. (The amphibrachic lines are "catalectic," meaning that they lack their final unaccented syllable—this practice of dropping final light syllables being common in meters that do not conclude with a beat.)

    ˘   /   ˘   ˘   /   ˘   ˘   / ˘ ˘   /
The sportsmen | keep hawks, and | their quarry | they gain;
    ˘   ˘   /   ˘   ˘   /   ˘   ˘   /   ˘ ˘ /
Thus the wood | cock, the part | ridge, the pheas | ant is slain.
    ˘   /   ˘   ˘ /   ˘   ˘   /   ˘ ˘ /
What care and | expense for | their hounds are | employed!

‿   ‿   /   ‿   ‿   /   ‿   ‿   /   ‿   ‿   /
Thus the fox | and the hare | and the stag | are destroyed.
‿   /   ‿   ‿   /   ‿   ‿   /   ‿   ‿   /
The spaniel | they cherish, | whose flatter | ing way
‿   ‿   /   ‿   ‿   /   ‿   ‿   /   ‿   ‿   /
Can as well | as their mas | ters cringe, fawn | and betray.
‿   /   ‿   ‿   /   ‿   ‿   /   ‿   ‿   /
Thus staunch pol | iticians, | look all the | world round,
‿   ‿   /   ‿   ‿   /   ‿   ‿   /   ‿   ‿   /
Love the men | who can serve | as hawk, span | iel or hound.

In the nineteenth century, Christina Rossetti employs the same
technique in her satirical comment on David Garrick's martial and
jingoistic "Heart of Oak." Here Rossetti quotes one of Garrick's
amphibrachic tetrameters, and then answers it with her own anapestic tetrameter:

‿   /   ‿   ‿   /   ‿   ‿   /‿   ‿   /
"Come cheer up, | my lads, 'tis | to glory | we steer"—
‿   ‿   /   ‿   ‿   /   ‿   ‿   /   ‿   ‿   /
As the sol | dier remarked | whose post lay | in the rear.

By the same token, English-language poets have at different
times employed dactylic measures, usually tetrametric (e.g., Byron's
"Saul") or hexametric (e.g., Longfellow's *Evangeline*), and one of the
best loved poems of American literature is in trochaic tetrameters:

/   ‿   /   ‿   /   ‿   /   ‿
By the shores of Gitchee Gumee
/   ‿   /   ‿   /   ‿   /‿
By the shining Big-Sea-Water,
/   ‿   /   ‿   /   ‿   /   ‿
Stood the wigwam of Nokomis,
/   ‿   /   ‿   /   ‿   /   ‿
Daughter of the Moon, Nokomis. . . .

Professor Wallace evidently feels that these lines can be considered as headless iambic tetrameters with feminine endings. But
the verse does not sound iambic. Indeed, readers and parodists have
for generations noted how distinctive—perhaps overly distinctive—
its rhythms are.

The difficulty with trochaics and triple meters is that they seem incapable of the flexible and continual reconciliation of natural speech and meter characteristic of iambic verse. They haven't the suppleness and the capacity for fluid modulation that iambic measures have, nor do they tolerate the sorts of variations (e.g., inverted feet at line-beginnings or after midline pauses) that the texture of iambic verse readily absorbs. The poet working in trochaics or trisyllabics will often find himself or herself asking the meter to override normal rhetorical stress. In the final line of Gay's "Air," for instance, we need to allow the meter to subordinate "Love" and perhaps "hawk":

> ⌣ ⌣ /   ⌣ ⌣ /   ⌣ ⌣   / ⌣ ⌣ /
> Love the men | who can serve | as hawk, span | iel or hound.

And were we to meet this line anywhere but in *The Song of Hiawatha,*

> The blue heron, the Shuh-shuh-gah

it is unlikely that we would emphasize the two definite articles at the expense of "blue" and the first syllable of "Shuh-shuh-gah." But that is what Longfellow wishes us to do, since he is writing in trochaic tetrameter:

> / ⌣   / ⌣   / ⌣   / ⌣
> The blue | heron, | the Shuh | -Shuh-gah

If the genius of our versification has been its fluid harmonization of meter and natural speech, trisyllabics and trochaics are not central to its achievements.

Still, poets have at times done extraordinary work in these measures, and it seems misguided to banish them or to deny the real potentials and benefits that they offer to writers of verse.

I am similarly uneasy with Professor Wallace's points 4 and 5, **"Syllabics is not a meter in English"** and **"In modern English, accentual meter does not exist."** Though I have difficulties, as most readers seem to, with such theories of syllabics as those enunciated by Robert Bridges and such theories of accentuals as those propounded by Gerard Manley Hopkins, both poets have contributed interesting tonalities to our verse. Furthermore, it appears to me that Hopkins's "Inversnaid"—to cite one of his more straightforward experiments—is not only an outstanding poem, but a poem whose four-stress measure is explicable only in accentual terms. It is, admittedly, hard to hear syllabics. Yet Marianne Moore's stanzaic syllabic verse is remarkable, especially in such poems as "No Swan so Fine" and "What Are Years." (In these poems, she sticks to the form she sets herself, though it is true, as Professor Wallace notes, that in other poems she violates her patterns.) And contemporary poetry would be much the poorer without such a poem in the accentual-alliterative tradition as Richard Wilbur's "Junk" or such a syllabic poem as Thom Gunn's "Vox Humana."

I am reluctant to follow Professor Wallace's point 1, **"Instead of the term 'feminine ending,' we should say simply extra-syllable ending, which may be abbreviate as e-s ending.** (Equally, we may speak as extra-syllable or e-s rhymes.)" Admittedly, the conventional terms are not native. They derive from French prosody and refer to the common feminine suffix in French, the mute "e," which is in fact for metrical purposes not mute (unless elidable) and which is allowed as an extra syllable at the end of the verse line. Distinctions involving the gender and inflection of nouns and related words are not as extensive in English as they are in French; and "feminine," regardless of its usefulness as a metrical term in English, cannot claim the grammatical relevance in our language that it can in French. Nevertheless, not only have we adopted the term to describe verses with a hyper-metrical syllable, but also we have employed the term in ways that allude to gender. A well-known instance is Shakespeare's twentieth sonnet. This praises a man for being graceful and appealing in a manner credited customarily only to women; and suiting his technique to his subject, Shakespeare writes the sonnet with exclusively feminine rhymes. Another memorable short poem that uses feminine rhyme for expressive effect is Mary Wortley Montagu's epigram in response to Lord Lyttelton's "Advice to a Lady," an effort notorious for such gems as (51–52):

Seek to be good, but aim not to be great;
A woman's noblest station is retreat.

It seems no accident, that is, that Montagu's neatly caustic rejoinder, "Summary of Lord Lyttelton's *Advice to a Lady*"

> Be plain in dress and sober in your diet;
> In short, my deary, kiss me, and be quiet.

features feminine rhymes. They give, in any event, an added fillip to her irritation with Lyttelton's patronizing poem. So, too, it may be significant that Dorothy Parker delivers her rueful comment ("Sonnet for the End of a Sequence," 4),

> Ever she longed for peace, but was a woman

in a pentameter in which the very word "woman" produces a feminine ending.

In short, if we remove "feminine ending" and "feminine rhyme" from our metrical vocabulary, we will lose a contextual resource on which many poets have drawn.

As for Professor Wallace's point 2, **"For an omitted first syllable of a line, we should use the term 'anacrusis,'"** I have no objection, especially if the alternative is "decapitation."

I agree with Professor Wallace's point 3, **"Quantities are not a basis for a meter in English."** One stumbling block for quantitative measures in modern English is that we do not have long and short vowel pairs in the sense that Greek and Latin and even Old English did. Though we speak of our vowels as being "long" and "short," we are referring mainly to vowel quality (tense vs. lax), not duration. Length in modern English is phonetic rather than phonemic: the environment in which the vowel occurs is more critical to syllabic duration than the vowel itself. For instance, though "bit" and "beat" feature, respectively, short "i" and long "e" sounds, both syllables are short, on account of being stopped by the voiceless "t." And though "beat" and "bead" both feature a long "e," the first is short, whereas the second is long because of its voiced "d." By the same token, while "beat" with its long "e" is short, "jazz" with its short "a" is long. What is more pertinent to versification, even after we ascertain that a certain syllable is short and others are long, when we encounter them in verse, as in these made-up ballad-stanza lines,

They drew a bead on victory
And beat the Utah Jazz

their differences or similarities of length are metrically irrelevant.

What we hear and instinctively grasp is stress. We can recognize duration, particularly when it is pointed out to us, and the lengths of syllables contribute in a general manner to the aural effects of our verse lines. But quantity is not central to our experience of our language. And as A. E. Housman remarked in his review of William Johnson Stone's *On the Use of Classical Measures in English,* to ask English-speaking poets to elevate quantity over stress is like asking athletes to run on their hands and to catch and throw balls with their feet.

This is not, of course, to disparage the many fine poems in English that approximate, in stress-measures, the forms of classical stanzas and lines, poems such as Cowper's sapphic "Lines Written During a Period of Insanity" or Frost's hendecasyllabic "For Once, Then, Something."

I also concur with Professor Wallace's point 6, **"Anapests and dactyls are legitimate substitutions in the iambic norm of English verse."** I agree, too, that dactylic substitutions seem rarer than anapestic ones, a circumstance which exists probably for the following reason. Though we can hear dactylic variations when they occur at the beginnings of iambic lines, or when they occur after midline pauses, we otherwise tend to hear extra syllables in iambic verse as part of the flow of the rising rhythm and thus tend to interpret them as producing anapests.

A cautionary note might be sounded concerning Professor Wallace's remarks about the frequency of trisyllabic substitution in English verse. Professor Wallace appeals to and follows in this regard George Saintsbury's *History of English Prosody* (3 vols. 1906–10; 2nd. ed. 1923). And one should perhaps remember how much Saintsbury's prosodic theory was shaped by his disagreement with Bridges's *Milton's Prosody* (first ed., 1893, rev. final ed., Oxford, 1921). Saintsbury particularly objected to Bridges's contention that most English pentametric verse strictly observed syllable count and that apparently extra syllables could be phonologically or prosodically resolved according to rules of elision. Saintsbury believed that elision was essentially an unnatural convention adopted from ancient prosody and that even when English poets had clearly intended contractions in their iambic verse, these did not necessarily reflect actual speech, and could more properly be regarded in the context of trisyllabic substitutions. Indeed, so vehemently and repeatedly did he hammer away at this point that George A. Kellog once cruelly but not inaccurately suggested ("Bridges' *Milton's Prosody* and Renaissance Metrical Theory," *PMLA* 68 [March, 1953], 270) that Saintsbury's monumental study be re-titled, "The History of the Trisyllabic Foot in English Verse."

Though as sympathetic to Saintsbury as I am to Bridges, I thought, on reading Professor Wallace's article, that Bridges's side of the argument received short shrift. Whatever one thinks of elision *per se,* English is notoriously given to clipping, and syllabic ambiguities are a natural part of the language. Our poets have always used, according to their metrical convenience, contracted or non-contracted forms of such words as "flower," "memory," "hastening," and "notorious." Paul Ramsey, in his *The Fickle Glass,* and George T. Wright, in *Shakespeare's Metrical Art,* have written well about this topic in connection with Shakespeare; and Paul Fussell, in his *Theory of Prosody in Eighteenth-Century England,* has done the same with eighteenth-century verse. And while we no longer in our verse employ trans-verbal elisions like "th'expense" and "th'arch," there are still synalephic tendencies in our speech. I well recall how carefully, in elementary-school phonics classes, my friends and I were instructed to lengthen the quality of the "e" of "the," when it was followed by a word beginning with a vowel. And the reason for this is that if we do not lengthen the "e" in constructions like "the expense" or "the arch," it almost disappears.

To put the matter in more general terms, English verse derives both from the old Germanic tradition, which is more iso-accentual than iso-syllabic, and from the ancient and modern Romance-language tradition, which carefully regulates syllable counts or proportions. Bridges may have over-emphasized the classical and Romanic strains and tidied up English prosody too much. But

Saintsbury may have over-emphasized the Germanic tradition and discerned trisyllabic variabilities where they did not always exist.

I should like to thank Professor Wallace again for his stimulating essay and to express the hope that this forum will interest others in metrics. The masterpieces of our poetry are an enduring resource. They have a singular power to instruct, elevate, console, move, and civilize, particularly if we experience them in the spirit in which they were written and hear and internalize their rhythms of thought and sensibility. Whether we write or read them, verse-measures can help us to a vision of experience more coherent and comprehensive than our own lives generally provide, and can encourage us to fuller and truer ways of acting and being. And it is perhaps appropriate to close with Louise Bogan's words ("Single Sonnet," 13–14) on this subject:

> Staunch meter, great song, it is yours, at length,
> To prove how stronger you are than my strength.

Author's note: For this essay I have used standard editions of the poets cited, in some cases modernizing the spelling of earlier writers, so long as doing so did not obscure their metrical structures and intentions. For background material on classical prosody, I am indebted to M. L. West's *Greek Metre* (Oxford: Oxford University Press, 1982) and Roger A. Hornsby's *Reading Latin Poetry* (Norman: University of Oklahoma Press, 1967). Special thanks are owed to Tom Peterson, my colleague at Cal State, Los Angeles, for his help on phonetics and quantity in modern English.

VERSE VS. PROSE/ PROSODY VS. METER

Lewis Putnam Turco

I. DEFINING "FREE VERSE"

Robert Wallace begins the first paragraph of his essay, "Meter in English," with an assertion that our fellow contributor Charles O. Hartman and others have made before him: "The difference that distinguishes verse from prose or speech is the unit of line." Not so. Much more than merely the existence of "lines" in the genre of "poetry" distinguishes verse from prose, which are the only *modes* of language in which any *genre* (fiction, drama, poetry) may be written.

Wallace begins his second paragraph with another disputable sentence: "In free verse, the units of line are or appear arbitrary, that is, relatively unpredictable." What I object to here is the use of the undefined term "free verse," as though such a term makes sense, for, to reiterate, there are only two modes in which any genre can be written, prose and verse. **Prose** is *unmetered* language; **verse** is *metered* language. If Wallace wishes to take exception to this definition, he should direct his remarks to the editors of the *Oxford English Dictionary* which notes as the first definition of prose, "The ordinary form of written or spoken language, *without metrical structure*" [emphasis added]. Similarly, the first definition of verse in the *OED* is, "A succession of words arranged according to natural or recognized rules of prosody and forming a complete *metrical* line" [emphasis added]." The first definition of metre, "To compose or put into metre," according to the *Oxford*, is obsolete; the second is, "To compose verses; to versify." Wallace, like many traditional prosodists, seems to have forgotten that the term "free verse" came to us in the twentieth century from the nineteenth-century French *vers libre*, but adopting a foreign term does not rewrite history, nor change the definitions in our dictionaries. As to the concept of "line" rather than "meter" being primary in the recognition of "verse," nowhere in the *OED* can one find that *verse* means "a line of language," only that a verse may mean "one of the lines of a poem or piece of versification."

Wallace didn't even bother to try to define the term upon which his essay is built, nor has anyone had success in conventionally defining the term "free verse." The point I make in *The New Book of Forms* is that "poetry" is a *genre*, with fiction, drama, and the various nonfiction genres (autobiography, travelogue, epistles, journalism, and so forth), whereas "verse" is a *mode*, like prose, and, again, *any of the genres may be written in either of the modes.* We are victims of the Anglo-American cultural bias that poetry must be written in verse or it isn't poetry, and that bias clouds our judgment just as it clouded that of the French, forcing them to come up with definitions that transform prose modes into verse modes—hence *vers libre* / "free verse," which is clearly a contradiction in terms: how can "verse" be "free" if it *must* (according to dictionary denotations) be "metrical"?

Anyone who reads the Bible can tell that prose poems have existed from the beginnings of history. Anyone can prove by scanning (if one knows how to scan) nearly any piece of English prose that it consists primarily of iambic and anapestic *rhythms*, not meters, for Whitman was not counting syllables in his prose poems, though the parallel grammatical structures of his prosody certainly did provide repeating rhythms, as *The New Book* discusses also (8–10). We know when Whitman was writing metrical poems, which he did early in his career and when he wrote "O Captain, My Captain," because the *verse lines* are apparent on the page, and one can count the strict lengths of the accentual-syllabic verses. This brings up another point: *the mere act of scanning prose does not turn that prose into verse.* Verse is verse only by virtue of the fact that the maker of the verses counted the syllables, stresses, and/or verse feet in discrete lines.

Why do people insist that poetry in English must be written in some sort of "verse" or it isn't poetry? And why do they have to justify line-phrased prose as verse? The answer is simple: given the former bias, the latter is a requirement if prose works are to be allowed into the poetic canon. Perhaps if we plow a few rows with everyone's exemplar, Walt Whitman, we can illuminate this discussion of "lineation" and "verses." As I type I have beside me several editions of Whitman's *Leaves of Grass.* Let's here set down the first few "lines" of that "poem," together with the poet's own line counts, first from the edition of 1855:

[1]

I celebrate myself,
And what I assume you shall assume,
For every atom belonging to me as good belongs to you.

I loafe and invite my soul,
I lean and loafe at my ease. . . . observing a spear of summer grass.   5

[2]

Houses and rooms are full of perfumes. . . . the shelves are crowded
    with perfumes,

I breathe the fragrance myself, and know it and like it,
the distillation would intoxicate me also, but I shall not let it.

The atmosphere is not a perfume. . . . it has no taste of the
    distillation. . . . it is odorless,

It is for my mouth forever. . . . I am in love with it,   10

I will go to the bank by the wood and become undisguised and naked,
I am mad for it to be in contact with me.

Now, what are the "lines" of this passage? Where, for instance, does line 6 end, with the word "crowded" or with "perfumes"? If with the former, then Whitman's "line 10" is really line 12. What caused Whitman (who was his own printer) to curl line six over? Why, right-hand justification, of course, just as though it were prose. The page wasn't wide enough to print the clause all in one line. Can this be proven? Certainly. Here is line six of the same poem (only now titled "Walt Whitman") from the third edition (1860–61):

Houses and rooms are full of perfumes—the shelves
    are crowded with perfumes, . . .

Why does the "line" now break after "shelves" rather than after "crowded"? Because the pages are narrower in this edition, therefore the right-hand justification required that this prose sentence break elsewhere. Here is the same passage from the edition of 1900:

Houses and rooms are full of perfumes—the shelves are
    crowded with perfumes, . . .

Francis Murphy's edition of *The Complete Poems* breaks this passage of the protean poem in the same place, but now it is line 14, as it is in some of the other editions published during Whitman's life.

What constitutes the Whitmanian "line," then, at least in the poet's own view? *Clauses*, generally independent clauses. Meter has nothing to do with it, nor has "versification" of any known kind. Line one is an independent clause; so are lines two and three and all the rest of the lines of this passage. *They are linked independent clauses in parallel constructions.* One can see the parallelism by running one's eye down the left-hand margin of the poem.

Now, if we scan the "Song of Myself," what will we find? We will find iambs and anapests randomly, except where the parallels require that the same rhythms appear in approximately the same order. This is *not* versifying; these are *not* meters. Although "lineation" is taking place, it is not typographical "lineation" but grammatical lineation. If we want Whitman's prose poem to look even more like a "traditional" verse-mode poem, we may line-phrase it further, in the manner of William Carlos Williams, by breaking the clauses into phrases:

> I celebrate myself,
> and what I assume
> you shall assume,
> for every atom
> belonging to me
> as good belongs to you.

Have we made this poem any more of a "poem" by doing this? Is it any more "verse" than it was before? Have we hurt the poem or helped it? We have done no more to it than draw attention to it for a specific purpose. By the way, did Whitman use the term "free verse"? Certainly not, as it didn't exist in English at the time. He knew he was writing prose poems.

Wallace nevertheless elsewhere in the opening section of his essay continues to treat the term "free verse" as though such a convention actually exists. He writes, "Reading or hearing unmetered verse . . . we are not aware of any fixed or predictable pattern." Does the term **unmetered verse** make sense in terms of the *OED* definition? "In free verse, there will of course be natural patterns and probably significant repetitions of them, but we have no particular sense of predictability or expectation." What does Wallace mean by *natural patterns?* Is this term the same as his other neologism, "speech-run"?

Wallace also refers to "free verse" as "the predominant verse form in the twentieth century." Is prose a *verse form?* One had thought that the term referred to such things as sonnets, sestinas, or villanelles. Does he mean that *prose has become the predominant mode for writing poetry in the twentieth century?* I can agree with that statement, but the "forms" of *prose* used in modern poetry are the forms of grammatical parallelism (synonymous, synthetic, antithetic, and climactic parallels) to be found in Whitman and the Bible.

In the early chapters of his book *Free Verse* Charles O. Hartman talks about the necessity for "conventions" in poetics and prosodics. He reviews the various prosodies and the inappropriate application of the concept of "isochrony," or musical time, to English poetry. Hartman spends all of chapter three telling the reader that no one agrees on a definition of "free verse"; then, in chapter four, ignoring what he has just written, Hartman talks about English poetry primarily in terms of isochrony and begins to come up with yet another definition of "free verse" that I, for one, cannot even understand.

Let me be specific. Hartman writes, *"A meter is a prosody whose mode of organization is numerical"* (17). Certainly not. A meter is a meter; a prosody is a prosody; to wit: a prosody is any system for writing the genre of poetry *(OED);* there are verse systems and prose systems: verse and prose are modes. Some examples of verse systems are accentual verse, syllabic verse, and accentual-syllabic verse (although, as we shall see, Wallace does not believe that the first two of these exist).

Within these prosodies there are various specific meters; for instance, within accentual prosody there can be a meter called dipodics; in syllabics, decasyllabics; in accentual-syllabics, anapestic trimeter (Wallace will deny that any of these things exist). An example of a prose prosody is grammatic parallelism, as in the Bible.

But Hartman is nowhere near establishing a "convention" regarding "free verse," nor even a reasonable definition of it. Until someone else can establish such a "convention"—that is to say, a definition that most poets can agree with, "free verse" will not, in fact, exist except as a confusing term. Despite the fact that we have been using it for most of this century, there is no reason for anyone, at this juncture, to jump on the free-verse bandwagon and define it as anything but prose, whether "lineated" or not. Wallace in his essay attempts a finesse by not trying to establish a definition but simply acting as though one exists. My own definition has the advantage of simplicity and is easily defended: verse is metered language, and prose is unmetered language. The *OED* definition of these terms is the same.

II. THE TEN PROPOSALS
OF ROBERT WALLACE

(1) "Instead of the term 'feminine ending,' we should say simply extra-syllable ending. . . ."

I agree absolutely that not all of the terms for Greek verse feet apply to English prosody (if any of them do), but what is the difference between saying "iamb and extra-syllable ending" and "amphibrach"? The term exists, and it's seven syllables shorter than the awkward phrase. If Wallace is going to toss out this particular term, let's toss them all out and go to a system like that of J. R. R. Tolkien who described a large number of "feet" such as the "rise and ascend," the "double fall," et cetera. For instance, the line "to a green thought in a green shade," scans this way: ∪∪//|∪∪//. It might be considered a "long rise."

In terms of accentual-syllabic prosody, this is a foot that I fought acknowledging for a long time: the "double-iamb"; however, I began finding it in the work of Robert Frost and elsewhere. The double-iamb (∪∪//) takes the place of two iambs (∪/∪/):

/ /| ∪ ∪ / /| ∪ / |. /
Snow falling and night falling fast, oh, fast

There is a spondee substitution in foot one; a double-iamb in feet two and three, and a demotion in the first syllable of foot five: //|∪∪//|∪/|·/—why do I say there is a "demotion"? Because Frost *overstresses* through alliteration and repetition: **fall**ing, **fall**ing, **fast**, **fast**; "oh," though an interjection and overstressed through rhyme (with *snow*), is not as heavy to my ear as all the "eff-words." So, if one acknowledges the double-iamb, as I do, there are the equivalent of four iambs in the line, the only exception being the spondee, but there is a lot of rhythmic variation.

(2) "For an omitted first syllable of a line, we should use the term anacrusis."

Again, why? Because Wallace says so? What's wrong with good old English "headless"? It's two syllables shorter. This is Wallace's scansion of

/ ∪ ∪ / ∪ ∪ / / ∪ /
When to the sessions of sweet silent thought

of which he writes, "Despite substitutions of trochee, pyrrhic, and spondee in the first, third, and fourth places, the line remains iambic pentameter." But this is not iambic if the trochee, pyrrhic, and spondee are viewed as substitutions, because there are only two iambs in the line:

/ ∪ | ∪ / | ∪ ∪ | / / | ∪ /
1   2   3   4   5

However, if the concept of the "double-iamb" is accepted, then it remains "iambic," even though there are only two actual iambs in the line.

In this section of his essay Wallace also questions elision, as in the line,

∪   / | ∪ / |∪ / | ∪ /|∪   /
And moan th'expense of many a vanished sight

"where one is required, in order to keep the regularity of syllables, to mouth such barbarous, artificial syllables as 'th'ex' and 'y a'. . . ." He prefers to sound the syllables and say that there are anapest substitutions. I have no problem with this idea, except that, to my ear, "the expense" and "many a" are obviously y-glide elisions and are not barbarous at all, but merely how we pronounce the phrases, as diphthongs. Few people say, "the / expense," and no one, I think, says, "many / a."

Wallace also talks about something he calls "speech-run" as distinguished from "meter." The Australian poet A. D. Hope has described the same phenomenon, for it is the poet's traditional job to "harmonize" prose rhythms (Wallace's "speech-run") and verse meters. In an essay, "Free Verse: A Post Mortem," Hope wrote that many of us confuse the terms "rhythm" and "metre," as Wallace seems to do. Hope points out that "verse employs another set of rhythmic devices in addition to . . . *natural* [my emphasis—is this what Wallace was talking about in the second paragraph of his essay?] rhythms. . . . We call this metre, or measure."

Thus, once again to emphasize, the essential difference between prose and verse is that prose is unmeasured language, and verse is measured language. If one is counting syllables or stresses, or both—Wallace to the contrary notwithstanding—*by conventional definition* one is writing in verse; if one is not, one is writing in prose. If one breaks prose into lines according to phrasing or punctuation or one of the other "natural" kinds of rhythm, then one is writing in prose still, even if one wishes to justify such writing according to the tradition in English culture that poetry (a genre) is written in verse (one of the two modes) by calling it "free verse." If language is "measured" in verse, it is not "free" as prose is (though it may be "variable"). "The essence of metre," Hope says, "is that it is an organization of rhythm on a basis of recurrence of expectation."

(3) "Quantities are not a basis for meter in English."

He does not elaborate, but he seems to be talking about syllabic prosody rather than, as in Hartman's case, isochronous prosody. If Wallace means the latter, I will agree, but only because no English-language poet has come up with a convention of prosody designating "lengths" of syllables with which most poets can agree, although Robert Bridges and Sidney Lanier were two who tried. If, however, he merely means syllabic prosody, I disagree.

(4) "Syllabics is not a meter in English"

is redundant, and it is wrong in two ways. First, "syllabics" is a prosody, not a meter; a syllabic meter would be, for example, hendecasyllabics, or eleven-syllable lines.

"We do not *hear* the count of syllables," Wallace avers, but Marianne Moore, whom Wallace discusses, evidently did not count syllables, she heard them. She would write the first stanza and then try to make corresponding lines in succeeding stanzas come out the same just by ear, according to Grace Schulman.

"By itself," Wallace says, "and taking no account of where accents occur, a line's number of syllables in no significant way determines its rhythm." Here again Wallace is taking something for granted: he assumes that "rhythm" and not "meter" is a requirement of the syllabic line. But the French, who believe that their language does not have syllable-stress patterns, have for centuries used syllabic prosody as the basis for writing their poetry. It was, in fact, this throwing-over of syllabic prosody that gave rise to *vers libre*, which is what Wallace and Hartman assume contemporary

American poets use in their poems. "Syllabics is a kind of free verse," Wallace says. Not only the French, but the Italians, the Welsh, the Irish and all the other Celtic tribes use syllabic prosody and have done so for centuries. Does an Italian or a Frenchman "hear" syllables any better than an Englishman or an American? "Rhythm" has nothing overtly to do with the system, though such poets as Dylan Thomas (the Welshman) overlaid rhythms upon his syllabic prosody—as many English-language poets do.

Where does one find a dictionary definition that says *rhythm* equals *meter*? No, rhythm is rhythm, meter is meter, and the term "free verse" is merely a synonym for prose. Does Wallace mean that "Syllabics is a kind of prose"? He could argue, it seems to me, that in accentual or accentual-syllabic prosody "meter equals a particular regular rhythm," but "the rhythms of syllabics are the rhythms of prose." I think that's rather accurate in the case of Marianne Moore, but if the poet is *measuring* his or her lines by syllabic lengths, he or she is *by definition* writing in meter, whether or not rhythm is present. Wallace may not like the definition, but it's in the dictionary.

(5) "In modern English, accentual meter does not exist."

Wallace argues that, "In the obvious [?] sense, like syllabics, it does not exist, that is, is not a meter." That is true; like syllabic prosody, accentual prosody does not exist as a meter, because it is a *prosody*, a system for writing poetry. If what one is doing is *counting* stresses, then one is measuring the line, and, by standard definition, one is writing in meters also.

Wallace cites none of the ancient English poems obviously written in the alliterative-accentual system called Anglo-Saxon prosody, but rather "The Waste Land" by T. S. Eliot and Ezra Pound. Wallace cites Harvey Gross's scansion of the line:

    /   /   /   /
"I read, much of the night, and go south in the winter"

This is the correct scansion:

ᵕ / | / ˘ᵕ|ᵕ / | ᵕ /| / ᵕ|ᵕ / ᵕ
"I read, much of the night, and go south in the winter"

This line must be scanned as I have given it, with **much** and **go** taking stresses; **go** is a verb, more important than its adverb modifier **south**. This line splits in half at the caesura: ∪/|/∪|∪/•∪/|/∪|∪/∪, and the halves are nearly identical rhythmically. One can argue (as I would do) that it is actually a prose line, but heavily *rhythmic* (not metrical) because the rhythm is repeated. It's no different from what Whitman did, or the Bible. It is *not*, I agree, a *meter*, but Wallace says, "The second problem is that what we may count as a stress seems extremely subjective—nothing, in theory, makes it other than arbitrary." However, his stance is the thing that is arbitrary. The rules-of-thumb regarding stressing are simple and few:

(1) In every word of the English language of two or more syllables, at least one syllable will take a stress. If one cannot at first hear the stressing, then one may consult a pronouncing dictionary.

(2) Important single-syllable words, particularly *verbs* and *nouns*, generally take strong stresses.

(3) Unimportant single-syllable words in the sentence, such as *articles*, *prepositions*, and *pronouns* (except *demonstrative pronouns*) do not take strong stresses, though they may take *secondary stresses* through *promotion* or *demotion*, depending on their position in the sentence or the line of verse.

(4) In any series of three unstressed syllables in a line of verse, one of them, generally the middle syllable, will take a *secondary stress* through *promotion* and will be counted as a *stressed* syllable.

(5) In any series of three stressed syllables in a line of verse, one of them, generally the middle syllable, will take a *secondary stress* through *demotion* and will be counted as an *unstressed* syllable.

(6) *Any* syllable may be <u>rhetorically stressed</u> by means of italics or some other typographical play.

That's it. What is "subjective" or "arbitrary" about that? I will not waste the readers' time by giving examples; they may look back at the scansions I have given for the Eliot line or at any other poem in the English language.

"Like syllabics, accentuals . . . is not a meter but a form of free verse," Wallace says. One must belabor the obvious: by accepting the undefined term "free verse" Wallace is making things very hard for himself in this argument, because there is certainly something called *accentual prosody*, and there are *accentual rhythms*, whether he thinks there are "accentual *meters*" or not. Like Samuel Johnson kicking a rock to disprove the proposition that there is no such thing as reality, all I need to do is listen to Anglo-Saxon prosody to know it exists. "Let's put 'accentual meter' into the dustbin," Wallace says. "The term has no real legitimacy *even in regard to Old English verse* [emphasis added] (or to contemporary imitations such as Pound's 'The Seafarer' and Wilbur's 'Junk'), as stress is only one of its essential characteristics."

Wallace obviously does not understand the distinction between "accentual meter" and "accentual prosody." More important, if stress is an *essential characteristic* of accentual prosody, no matter how many other things may be required by it, *stress is still essential* to it.

(6) "Anapests and dactyls are legitimate substitutions in the iambic norm of English meter."

I am delighted to be able to agree with this proposition. I confess to having been ignorant that anyone disagreed with it.

III. PUTTING THE METRICAL CART BEFORE THE PROSODIC HORSE

What good does it do to try to cram everything into "accentual-syllabic meter" when, in fact, it can't be done? The ear is the final arbiter. All Wallace and I and Hartman *et alii* can do is create definitions and use terms that will (imperfectly, perhaps) describe what the poet does. But for those definitions to work, we must agree on them. I cannot agree with any definition of "free verse" because it is a contradiction in terms. Free verse is, was, and always will be *prose*. I recall my teachers in high school trying to define it and having no success, and I had as little until finally I gave up and accepted reality. In college and graduate school one kept hearing the assertion, "Free verse is not just chopped up prose," but that's exactly what it is if it is "lineated" or, as I call it, "line-phrased."

Wallace's assertion that "There is one [prosody] in English: accentual-syllabic, and its base is always iambic" cannot be applied retroactively to the English language before Chaucer. The prosody used by the early English was clearly alliterative accentuals, for they knew nothing of accentual-syllabic prosody, nor of such terms as anapestic, trisyllabic, iambic, et cetera, et cetera.

When William the Conqueror invaded England in 1066 he brought with him French syllabic prosody, and that was what the court poets used until the fourteenth century. Then, when Old English and French merged to become Middle English, Chaucer, Gower, Henryson, Dunbar, and all the other "Scottish Chaucerians" transformed French syllabic prosody into one that could accommodate the old strong-stress system as well, and accentual-syllabic prosody was born.

Accentual-syllabic prosody was not well understood in England until the Renaissance poets rediscovered it and applied the Greek terms we use today. But even as poets began writing accentual-syllabics, it was still possible to write in the old strong-stress prosody, as the Pearl Poet, and subsequently John Skelton, the balladeers, Hopkins, and even Wilbur proved. But I have skipped several of Wallace's propositions:

(7) **"We should drop the pyrrhic foot (⌣⌣) and accept in its place the double-iamb (⌣⌣//), as one of the six foot-terms necessary. . . ."**

I am delighted to agree with this remark, though in *The New Book of Forms* I cited Harvey Gross as the originator of the double-iamb, not John Crowe Ransom, who uses the term "ionic foot" in Wallace's citation (23). Although Wallace will admit into English prosody the idea of the double-iamb, he says,

(8) **"Anapestic, trochaic, and dactylic meters do not exist in English."**

Nor, as we have seen, does the amphibrach. I say, "Bah, humbug, Bob! Go read *'The Song of Hiawatha'* again." And while you're at it, tell me what the meter of Longfellow's "The Ropewalk" is. It's even possible to claim that the meters of the limerick are amphibrachic:

```
⏑ / ⏑ | ⏑ / ⏑ / ⏑ | ⏑ /
⏑ / ⏑ | ⏑ / ⏑ / ⏑ | ⏑ /
⏑ / ⏑ | ⏑ /
⏑ / ⏑ | ⏑ /
⏑ / ⏑ | ⏑ / ⏑ / ⏑ | ⏑ /
```

(9) "We should avoid the use of Jespersen's four degrees of speech stress for scanning."

That's all right with me. I use the traditional strong-stress, secondary stress, and nonstress system myself, although it seems to me that a fourth degree of stress—the "sprung" syllable, is used in some kinds of verse (which Wallace says don't exist), such as Anglo-Saxon prosody and Hopkins's system of "sprung rhythm." I agree with the tenth proposition:

(10) "The spondee is a good, and fairly frequent, foot in English."

Indeed it is.

In conclusion, let me say that the greatest flaw in Wallace's essay is that he is never at pains to make distinctions between the terms "prose," "verse," and "free verse" on the one hand, and "prosody," "rhythm" and "meter," on the other. The arguments he bases on this quagmire I find to be a good deal less than convincing.

WORKS CITED

Gross, Harvey. *Sound and Form in Modern Poetry*. Ann Arbor: University of Michigan, 1965.

Hartman, Charles O. *Free Verse*. Princeton, N.J.: Princeton University Press, 1980.

Hope, A. D. *The Cave and the Spring*. Chicago: University of Chicago Press, 1970.

Turco, Lewis. *The Book of Forms: A Handbook of Poetics*. New York: E. P. Dutton, 1968.

———. *The New Book of Forms*. Hanover: University Press of New England, 1986.

———. *The Public Poet*. Ashland: Ashland Poetry Press, 1991.

Whitman, Walt. *The Complete Poems*. Ed. Francis Murphy. New York: Penguin, 1975.

———. *Leaves of Grass*. Boston: Thayer and Eldridge, 1860–61.

———. *Leaves of Grass*. Philadelphia: David McKay, 1900.

———. *Leaves of Grass: The First (1855) Edition*. Ed. Malcolm Cowley. London: Secker and Warburg, 1959.

WALLACE'S RAZOR

METRICS AND PEDAGOGICAL ECONOMY

Barry Weller

I approach Robert Wallace's essay primarily from a pedagogical point of view (but also—to the extent that it is a separable perspective—from the viewpoint of someone who takes pleasure in reading poetry). As a teacher, I can feel only grateful to someone who slashes so many Gordian knots at once and therefore clarifies the central question of what students must learn in order to have access to the metrical rhythms of English and American poetry: namely, the accommodation of semantic stress ("speech-run") to some more formal principle of regularity, and the interplay of repetition and variation (emphases which the first half of Paul Fussell's elegant monograph, *Poetic Meter and Poetic Form*, also keeps clearly in view). As Wallace's essay suggests, there is little need to venture beyond the iambic norm of English poetry to discover the surprisingly varied transformations of the poetic line.

I have a suspicion that much of the historical elaboration of meters, and flirtation with alien principles of scansion, stems from the feeling that, whatever limited variety substitutions may produce, it's rather boring to be tied to a normative alternation of stressed and unstressed syllables; the appetite to discover the equivalent of Greek and Roman feet (including the amphibrach) embedded in more recognizable English meter seems particularly symptomatic in this regard. Even Wallace's handful of examples demonstrates how misleading any supposition that the expressive palette of iambic meter is limited would be. It's finally the interaction of meaning with rhythm—the infinite permutations which the semantic introduces into the metrical medium—which insures the inexhaustibility of English poetic means. To be sure, much of what initially seems sidelined in Wallace's approach gradually reenters: if there is no reason to talk about anapestic or trochaic meters, trochees and anapests are still indispensable to the analysis of iambic meter. Indeed, many of the poetic practices or metrical speculations which Wallace exiles, in his admirable drive towards simplicity, hover about the perimeter of his authentic English metrics, and Robert Penn Warren's strictures against the dangers of "purity" in poetry apply to theoretical enterprises as well. In general, Wallace is careful to leave room for anomalies: "Odd cases can be valued as odd cases" (12). One wants to be able to banish the pedants without scaring off the innovative practitioners (of poetry or of metrical analysis) who are restlessly and ingeniously trying to find new forms of rhythmic interest in English verse, because even the delusions of the latter can be productive.

(1) **"Instead of the term 'feminine ending,' we should say simply extra-syllable ending, which may be abbreviated as e-s ending."**

(2) **"For an omitted first syllable of a line, we should use the term anacrusis."**

I can see little reason to object to either of these terminological suggestions, though I'm skeptical whether the learned-sounding "anacrusis," however apt its etymology, will quickly take root in the average classroom. Before such terms as "masculine" and "feminine" endings or rhymes disappear altogether from currency, someone should probably excavate the gender ideology which underlies them (and related notions—for example, the femininity of the Italian language): the "masculine" rhyme presumably bespeaks tense, efficient muscularity, while the "feminine" rhyme entails the purely ornamental flourish of a superfluous syllable, or perhaps a slyly hidden intent—the rhyme camouflaged, as it were, in the penultimate position. In contemporary usage these labels are simply anachronistic, and Wallace is right to discard them.

(3) "Quantities are not a basis for meter in English."

Wallace's point is carefully stated: "Quantities are not a *basis for meter* in English" (italics mine). Implicitly he is retaining the possibility that quantities might nevertheless importantly influence the shape and feeling of a line, particularly in the case of a classically trained poet—that is to say, virtually all male poets and some female poets writing in English before the twentieth century. (Tennyson is the conspicuous example of someone whose poems—e.g., "Tithonus"—occasionally exhibit this kind of double patterning: metrical but also consciously formed according to classical quantities.) In any case, a heightened attention to the succession of long and short vowel lengths within a line (or poem) would surely be one indication of a reader attuned to the arrangement of sounds distinctive to poetic language. Perhaps it's a desire to keep this dimension of sound-consciousness to the fore that gives a half-life to this specific classical ghost and prompts teachers or metrical critics to remind us of experiments such as Sidney's and Bridges's.

Quantity or length—though not necessarily reckoned by classical rules—also has some effect on how readily a semantically insignificant syllable receives a positional accent. If Wallace is right that the fourth syllable of the line "Nor services to do till I require" receives an accent—one of my colleagues steadfastly maintains the second foot is a true pyrrhic—it's surely helped by the fact that "es" (or "ces"?) takes longer to say than "vi" or "to." As I say, my measurement of "length" is not especially classical, although in Greek or Latin the clustering of consonants will lengthen the value of the preceding vowel. In English or American terms the rule of thumb is that sounds which are difficult to articulate will slow down the poem—as Wallace shows in discussing "When Ajax strives . . ." (8)—and any poet (or reader) who disregards this phenomenon and relies solely on stress to determine or describe a poem's movement will ignore something almost as fundamental as meter.

(4) "Syllabics is not a meter in English."

If "[s]yllabics is not a meter in English," it is also not simply "a kind of free verse." Wallace concedes the point that syllabics might be functional for the writer who is constructing the poem, though "only [as] a trellis" (12), and it seems hasty to conclude that the poem's self-imposed rule will have no effect on the experience of the completed work. When all the lines of a poem or stanza have the same number of syllables, even an approximate sense of the lines' roughly comparable weight would suffice to distinguish the poem from verse in which the line breaks are more intuitively determined. (I am assuming, perhaps optimistically, the performance of the poem would convey some sense of the individual lines' integrity.) Even where the lines vary within the stanza but match up with the lineation in subsequent stanzas, it's not impossible that a listener could still register some sense of recurrent ebb and flow, contraction and expansion, as she took in successive versions of the pattern.

Since Wallace is explicitly concerned with meter as an *auditory* measurement, I have spoken—with some strain—in terms of the poem's *audi*ence, although many poems will be encountered, or ideally encountered, only on the page. It is hard to contest Wallace's assertion that "[w]e do not *hear* the count of syllables," but this proposition is not a sufficient basis for inferring that syllabics is not a meter in English, and I resist Wallace's inclination to restrict the "meter" to purely auditory features of a poem. In the first instance "meter" means simply "measure," and it isn't self-evident this measure needs to be aural rather than visual. Obviously such a doubt challenges not only the focus of Wallace's project but the main tradition of English verse, but the proliferation of shaped poems in the seventeenth century indicates that even before the advent of free-verse writers were looking for non-aural ways of construing a poem's boundaries.

Wallace's arguments are less rigorous than usual in this section of his essay: the typographical vagaries poems may suffer in reprinting seem as irrelevant to the issue of their first design as any other errata they may acquire in the course of their textual histories, and that Marianne Moore's "Poetry" loses its initial contours in revision indicates only that later versions changed it to free verse, and not that the first lacked some form of measure.

(5) "In modern English, accentual meter does not exist."

In general, the critics Wallace cites fail to make a strong case for the presence of accentual meter in the poems that supposedly exemplify its workings. In the case of Yeats, for example, there seems little reason to read "Easter 1916" as anything other than iambic trimeter, with a liberal share of substitutions. Even less convincingly, Fussell cites Yeats's "Why Should Not Old Men Be Mad?" as an instance of accentual meter because "we find four stresses per line, although the number of syllables varies from seven to nine." That a critic whose most extended analysis of metrics centers on substitutions should find this variation evidence that Yeats employs accentual meter for this poem is remarkable and may, unusually, betray the eighteenth century as the home base of Fussell's critical allegiances. It is presumably such Augustan fastidiousness about maintaining a uniform number of syllables per line that prompted "Coleridge's brief, grossly inaccurate note about the meter of 'Christabel'" (Wallace 20); though Coleridge seizes the offensive by announcing "a new principle" of meter, his probable intent was to avert a neoclassical assault on the barbarous and wanton irregularity of his fragmentary narrative.

On the other hand, Wallace sometimes seems to focus a bit myopically on the individual line. The case for scanning according to an accentual measure depends not so much on whether or not a single line can be reconciled to iambic meter as on the number of adjustments, substitutions, anomalies, et cetera which the attempt to maintain traditional scansion throughout the poem as a whole requires. The question is not whether a poem is "scannable" in relation to an iambic norm, but whether that scansion most significantly reveals the essential pulse which directs the poem's negotiations of formal and colloquial cadences. Gerard Manley Hopkins might offer the best example here: most of his experiments with so-called "sprung rhythm" can certainly be scanned iambically (with lots of spondaic substitutions), but such a description of the metrics might well be simultaneously accurate and beside the point. Hopkins *wants* the collision of sense-stress with normative rhythm, wants the line to implode from the superabundance of accents, wants it to "buckle"—both join and collapse—under stress, so that new poetic and spiritual "fire" will "break from [it] then." One can challenge the success of Hopkins's project or even its originality—Father Ong and others have pointed out its continuity with the poetic practice of Shakespeare, Donne, and other pre-Augustan poets—but to point out the persistence in his poetry of iambic meter is merely to point out the intransigent condition (like the pressure of history upon spiritual freedom) with which Hopkins was wrestling.

I agree that it's hard to see "how a student might be expected to recognize a poem in accentual meter" (20), but when a poet deliberately solicits memories of an older metrical norm—as in the "contemporary imitations" Wallace cites, there are usually other clues than the meter itself—it's also unnecessary to resist the prompting to give special attention to the placement of stress. Perhaps any notion that we are recovering some approximation of pre-iambic, proto-English verse is purely nostalgic and impressionistic, but imagining that stress supplies the defining character of certain lines requires less effort than perceiving the effects of quantity in an English poem. (One specifically political dimension of nostalgia for a stress-based metrics is suggested by Anthony Easthope's *Poetry as Discourse*, which one of my colleagues flippantly summarizes as arguing that "iambic pentameter is a bourgeois plot." According to Easthope, in accentual meter the coincidence of intonation and abstract metrical pattern produces "an emphatic, heavily stressed performance," and "this is the metrical 'space' for a collective voice" (Easthope, 73), whereas iambic pentameter "gives space to the 'natural' intonation and so to a single voice in the closure of its own coherence" (73–74), that is, to the bourgeois illusion of individuality. Easthope's analysis is Marxist, but Ezra Pound's interest in a stress-based meter might be taken as an indication that such nostalgia for collectivities could as easily be Fascist as progressive, and a kind of nationalistic romanticism—a wishful evocation of Celtic or Saxon "magic"—underlies the attempt to uncover accentual meter in such poets as Yeats and Hardy.)

Still, I regard most Anglo-American experimentation with an older meter as affecting the texture rather than the structure of the poem, and as Wallace firmly states, such reminiscences of Old English or ballad-style meter are not the basis for an alternative metrics. When Timothy Steele observes that Hardy's "Neutral Tones" "approaches the condition of a sort of rhymed accentual verse," he is making *at most* a critical, rather than a metrical, observation, though I'm inclined to think that Hardy's simplicity of form and (arguably indigenous) fatalism have led the critic to project something onto the verse. Gerard Manley Hopkins's more drastic and self-conscious experimentation warrants further examination as a more challenging test case for Wallace's claim that accentual-syllabic scansion is wholly adequate to the varieties of English metrical verse.

(6) "Anapests and dactyls are legitimate substitutions in the iambic norm of English meter."

The sixth proposition should be noncontroversial.

(7) "We should drop the pyrrhic foot (⌣⌣) and accept in its place the double-iamb (⌣⌣//), as one of the six foot-terms necessary: iamb, trochee, anapest, dactyl, spondee, double-iamb."

I like the term "double-iambic" insofar as it emphasizes the predominant effect of a pyrrhic foot on the movement of a line, but I see no compelling reason to discard the notion of a pyrrhic foot as such, however unusual its occurrence may be. As Wallace's discussion acknowledges, scansion serves the performance (whether internal or uttered aloud) of a poem and, in the case of alternative scansions, rehearses the different semantic and rhythmic possibilities a line may encompass. Marking a foot as pyrrhic—as relatively devoid of stress—may be at least as helpful a cue to performance as marking the positional stress of its second syllable, since according to Wallace's own argument this positional accent will take care of itself. If anything, by marking this stress one runs the danger of overemphasizing—or prompting someone else to overemphasize—both the prominence of the accent and the regularity of the verse. For example, in the final line to Keats's "Ode to Autumn"

$$\breve{} \quad / \quad \breve{}\breve{} \quad / \quad \breve{} \quad / \quad \breve{}\breve{}\breve{} \quad /$$

And gath | ering swal | lows twit | ter in | the sky

an audible stress on "in," in the penultimate foot, would give a spurious importance to the location "in." (Are there preferable ways to scan this line? To give "-ering" a foot of its own and thus turn "swallows" and "twitter" into trochees before a final anapest, would give excessive, countersemantic weight to the third and fourth syllables of the line. If anything, I suspect that in idiomatic delivery "er" would be slightly abridged—"And gath'ring swallows . . ."—and the second foot is not even an anapest but a regular iamb.)

The principle of binary alternation, or positional stress, will also, unless there is a strong semantic motive to the contrary, tend to throw greater weight on the second syllable of a spondee ("brave scorn," "vast weight"), yet later on in the essay Wallace rightly resists the purist notion that because the levels of stress on two successive syllables are inherently unequal, no "true spondees" exist: "Meter cannot depend on discriminations too fine for ordinary mortals, poets or readers, to make out pretty easily" (39). The case for the existence of pyrrhics is not quite symmetrical with that for the existence of spondees, since it's easier to load additional (and at least approximately equal) stresses onto a line of English poetry than to avoid them altogether. Nevertheless, the possibility of marking a foot as pyrrhic may well in certain situations contribute to a "more finely responsive" scansion (40). There's no pressing motive to eliminate the pyrrhic from English metrics (especially since, even in Wallace's scheme, it persists as the "first half" of a double-iamb). Here, for once, Wallace may get carried away with the project of throwing as much as possible overboard.

Wallace's discussion of the first line of Yeats's "After Long Silence" provokes the suggestion of one supplement to his account of metrics. It seems to me possible for an internal pause, like a musical rest, to carry the weight of a syllable in scansion. In this particular case, the semicolon marks a beat:

$$/ \quad \cup \quad \cup \quad / \quad\quad / \cup \quad\quad \cup / \quad \cup \quad /$$
Speech af | ter long | silence; | ^{x} it | is right

The pause marks the effortfulness of resuming speech after its interruption, maybe even the threat that it will relapse into silence again. (A similar difficulty in recovering the thread of a disrupted reality seems registered in Sir Thomas Wyatt's "They Flee from Me": "It was no dream, I lay broad waking," where the medial caesura may even the carry the value of a full foot, with "-ing" as an extra-syllabic ending. Different scansions of the second half of the line seem possible— for example, allowing "broad" to occupy a monosyllabic foot or somehow sharing the extra metrical weight between the stressed syllables of "broad" and "wak-"—but in one way or another the missing "time" has to be distributed throughout the line. The clumsy emendation in *Tottel's Miscellany*, "It was no dream, for I lay broad awaking," indicates the sense of metrical expectation which the pentameter norm of the lyric created among Wyatt's near-contemporary readers.) The uses of silence in English poetry lie beyond the scope of this discussion, but gaps and breaks in the line, more jagged than the domesticated caesura of traditional scansion, deserve some place in any full-scale reconsideration of accentual-syllabic metrics.

(8) "Anapestic, trochaic, and dactylic meters do not exist in English."

As long as we continue to talk of anapests, trochees, and dactyls, how much is gained by declaring that "[a]napestic, trochaic, and dactylic meters do not exist in English"? There are few instances to the contrary, but were dactylic and anapestic meters, in English, ever considered as something more than the Platonic ideas of themselves, a kind of thought-experiment proposing "What if a poem were made up of nothing but? . . ." What's useful about those few putative, schoolbook examples of anapestic meter (most frequently, "How They Brought the Good News from Ghent to Aix ") is that they more vividly illustrate the characteristic tendency of anapests than the slight quickening of isolated anapestic feet within an iambic poem.

As another instance of a poem which seems markedly anapestic, consider D. H. Lawrence's "Piano":

> Softly, in the dusk, a woman is singing to me;
> Taking me back down the vista of years, till I see
> A child sitting under the piano, in the boom of the tingling strings
> And pressing the small, poised feet of a mother who smiles as she
>> sings.
>
> In spite of myself, the insidious mastery of song
> Betrays me back, till the heart of me weeps to belong
> To the old Sunday evenings at home, with winter outside
> And hymns in the cozy parlor, the tinkling piano our guide.
>
> So now it is vain for the singer to burst into clamor
> With the great black piano appassionato. The glamour
> Of childish days is upon me, my manhood is cast
> Down in the flood of remembrance, I weep like a child for the past.

Most of the lines contain at least three anapests. (If the first stanza establishes a pattern for the rest of the poem—that is, that the first and second lines of each stanza have five feet while the third and fourth have six—then the third lines of the second and third stanzas would be exceptions to the three-anapest norm. However, unless one deliberately sets out to find six feet in these lines, they are more readily scanned as pentameter with three anapests.) Whether or not the anapests are the foundation of the meter, they are crucial to the poem's effect, suggesting not only the naive da-da-dah of the piano rhythms that the speaker recalls from childhood but the emotional impetus that his memories receive from "the insidious mastery of song"—a phrase in itself composed of three anapests. Does the prevalence of anapests make the meter anapestic? Such a conclusion would at any rate be the best operating assumption for the practical scansion of "Piano." The third line of the first stanza is tough enough to scan according to any metrical scheme, but if one approaches it with the notion that the meter is basically iambic, she is likely to come up with an eight-foot line.

The jokey double-dactyl joins the limerick in the limbo of doggerel. Otherwise, as the basis for a meter, rather than a substitutive resource, the dactyl, so essential to classical poetics, is almost as out-of-place in Anglo-American poetry as quantitative metrics.

The effect of a trochee is probably more evident when it functions as a substitution for an iamb than where trochees abound. (In the chapter of *Poetic Meter and Poetic Form* on "Metrical Variation" Fussell provides a fine initial survey of how such substitutions function expressively.) Since, as Wallace says, "trochaic meter is merely a mirror image of iambic," and the trochee is such a common substitute for an iamb, the rhythm of even a heavily trochaic poem will seem, in rendition, little different from that of an iambic one. Still, when Wallace asserts that "even . . . a poem entirely of [lines such as Milton's 'Then to come in spite of sorrow']—that is, with no lines ending in a stressed syllable—would remain iambic, scannable with anacrusis and extra-syllable ending," I can't see what has been gained by substituting this cumbersome description ("iambic . . . with anacrusis and extra-syllable ending") for the economical, if rarely applicable, label "trochaic meter."

Pedagogically, it seems sufficient to alert students to the rarity and largely notional character of anapestic, dactylic, and trochaic meters (at least as providing the metrical structure for an entire poem) and to make it clear that nearly all the metered poems in English they will encounter have an iambic base.

In my experience, undergraduates will not find it self-evident that "meter refers to *poems,* not lines *per se*" and that "[p]oems do not change meter from line to line" (29), and, with certain qualifications, these points should indeed be inculcated. It seems likely, however, that Wallace is thinking primarily in terms of a poem in which the lines are of uniform length. A poem which alternates lines of iambic pentameter and tetrameter doesn't necessarily contradict his propositions, since one would describe the poem as a whole in terms of these *regular* alternations (even if, for example, the tetrameter lines more frequently use trochaic substitutions than the pentameter lines). On the other hand, a poem like Donne's "A Valediction: Of Weeping" moves more jaggedly, and the pattern of feet for each of its stanzas is 2-5-5-5-2-2-5-5-7:

> Let me pour forth
> My tears before thy face whilst I stay here,
> For thy face coins them, and thy stamp they bear,
> And by this mintage they are something worth,
> For thus they be
> Pregnant of thee;
> Fruits of much grief they are, emblems of more;
> When a tear falls, that Thou falls which it bore,
> So thou and I are nothing then, when on a diverse shore.

Despite the consistently iambic composition of the individual lines, their varied lengths will produce the *effect* of shifting meters. In George Herbert's "Discipline," a more modest variation of the metrical pattern produces an equally dramatic effect:

> Throw away thy rod,
> Throw away thy wrath:
> O my God,
> Take the gentle path.
>
> For my heart's desire
> Unto thine is bent:
> I aspire
> To a full consent.
>
> Not a word or look
> I affect to own,
> But by book,
> And thy book alone.

On one level, the difference of the third line from the first, second, and fourth lines seems slight. While the latter consist of three iambic feet, with the first marked by anacrusis, the third line merely shortens the pattern to two iambic feet, the first again displaying anacrusis. Nevertheless, this third line appears to function as an autonomous metrical unit and not as a mere extension of the iambic meter. The evidence is to be found in its effect: these feet slow down the poem, reflecting the speaker's effortful steps towards salvation. The Donne and Herbert poems are borderline cases, but I suspect that a full census of sixteenth- and seventeenth-century lyrics would reveal more decisive instances of hybrid meters within a single poem, and if it's reasonable to analyze the form of lyrical stanzas in terms of their individual structural components, there may after all be a place for anapestic, dactylic and trochaic meters in the discussion of English metrics.

(9) "We should *never* use four degrees of speech stress for scanning."

"We should *never* use four degrees of speech stress for scanning," because the degrees of speech stress are effectively illimitable. Here, in discussing the limitations of a linguistically oriented, more "scientific" metrics, and in his succeeding discussion of the spondee, Wallace beats a welcome retreat from the austere reductions (not to say, reductiveness) of his immediately preceding points. Wallace convincingly devastates the mechanical, tone-deaf, thesis-driven scansions produced by efforts to equilibrate levels of speech stress more precisely. Indeed, his emphasis on the relational, "binary nature of English meter," seems much more faithful to the Saussurean principle of linguistic difference than the schemata which Jespersen, Chatman et al. attempt to impose on the complex phenomena which the inflection of a metrical utterance entails. Saussurean linguistics helps to demonstrate why a binary system—that is, the underlying principle of iambic meter—represents not a poverty of two choices, stressed or unstressed, but the gateway to an infinity of alternatives.

(10) "The spondee is a good, and fairly frequent, foot in English."

I agree with Wallace on the issue of spondees; my relevant comments are incorporated in the responses to number 7 and number 9.

Author's note: I want to thank Jacqueline Osherow for her suggestions and advice on earlier drafts of these comments.

TWO LETTERS

Richard Wilbur

[Although Mr. Wilbur declined an invitation to participate in this symposium, he commented on the project in letters to Robert Wallace and permitted these excerpts to appear.]

25 October 1993

Your essay seems to me a clarifying reduction of the number of entities in most prosodic discussions; I am all for saying that we work in strict or loose iambic, and that the full description of what we hear in a line would require a language too complex to be useful.

I am not sure that the bang, bang of English makes it impossible for us to hear syllabics if the lines are short enough and the forms familiar, as in haiku. I *think* that I do, after long exposure to that form, hear the five or seven syllables, enjoying the different rhythms with which they may be filled, or fulfilled. I agree entirely with what you say about long syllabic lines: a discipline for the poet, perhaps, but not audible for the reader.

It seems to me that you make a good case against "accentual meter." Here is how I would scan the Eliot line, using a caret to represent a pause:

⏑ / ∧ / ⏑ ⏑ /   ⏑ ⏑ /   ⏑ ⏑ / ⏑

I read, | much | of the night, | and go south | in the win | ter.

That's unsatisfactory, of course, and if I am going to put a pause in the second foot why don't I do something about the pause between "night" and "and"? Well, since in any case I am sure of hearing the line as a pentameter, perhaps I should correct my scansion by making the fourth foot a bit hyper-metrical. My certainty of the pentameter is based on two things: (1) one's tendency to see any line, if possible, as the fundamental English measure, and (2) the way those words would normally be spoken.

Of course, "Spoken by whom?" is a big question. I once asked Auden to look at Bill Williams's springtime poem and say if he felt confident about the stresses:

Love Song

Sweep the house clean,
hang fresh curtains
in the windows
put on a new dress
and come with me!
The elm is scattering
its little loaves
of sweet smells
from a white sky!

Who shall hear of us
in the time to come?
Let him say there was
a burst of fragrance
from black branches.

He said he did not, whereas I, having been brought up not far from Rutherford, can often find a largely observed stress-norm in Williams. For me, in short, Williams can write successful accentual verse, sometimes.

I like your double-iamb, for it really does help one describe what in some cases is being heard. The lameness of the lame foot (in the scansion of "Speech after long silence; it is right" on page 26) might be bettered if my opprobrious caret were allowed into it. It is heresy, I suppose, to put duration into English scansion, yet a non-bang or delay-of-bang is heard as part of the rhythm of any line, as decidedly as in the opening of Vaughan Williams's "For All the Saints." Do we not need little carets to describe "Hark, hark / The dogs do bark"?

19 December 1993

Yes, I would scan the second line of my poem "The Writer" as you suggest, with a caret and strong stress as the second foot:

$$\overset{\wedge}{} \quad \overset{/}{}$$

Where light | breaks, | and the win | dows are tossed | with linden.

I see each stanza of that poem as consisting of trimeter, pentameter, trimeter. I recall John Ciardi saying that he worked mostly with "a reminiscence of the pentameter" rather than a strictly scannable line, and maybe some of my poems have come to be that way here or there. I wouldn't do it deliberately.

REAL METER IN IMAGINARY ENGLISH

A RESPONSE TO ROBERT WALLACE

Susanne Woods

I might have called this response to Robert Wallace's "Meter in English," "Imaginary Meter in Real English," since meter is generally conceded to be a construct for and by poets, while language is part of the fabric of even non-poetic lives. Instead, I want to begin by borrowing a premise from the title of my book, *Natural Emphasis,* which is in turn a quote from that great pioneer of English metrical theory, George Gascoigne: meter depends on, is derived from, the natural emphasis of the language.[1] By "natural" I simply mean the ordinary patterns of stress-accent that most native-born speakers of the language use to communicate with one another.

To be sure, "native-born speakers" are a more various and complicated lot now than they were in 1575 when Gascoigne published his "Certain Notes of Instruction on the Making of Verse or Rime in English" and coined the term "natural emphasis." The Elizabethan poet and tutor, Samuel Daniel, would marvel at the answer to the prophetic question he posed in 1599 in "Musophilus":

> And who, in time, knows whither we may vent
> The treasure of our tongue, to what strange shores
> This gain of our best glory shall be sent,
> T'enrich unknowing nations with our stores?
> What worlds in th'yet unformed Occident
> May come refin'd with th'accents that are ours?[2]

Yet with all the varieties of English that now sound around the world, patterns of emphasis, what we usually call "stress-accent," remain remarkably consistent and, as best as I can determine, consistent as well with the tradition of stress-accent patterns in English from at least Early Modern English (c. 1500) forward.[3]

My focus in this essay is on some claims Wallace makes about accent and stress patterns in meter, which I have tested against what I have observed to be the history of "natural emphasis" in English versifying. In this sense, I will be pursuing meter derivable from the real patterns of the language—real meter—as it is (in my judgment) most effectively used in the imagining language of poets writing in English. I mostly agree with Wallace but will take up one small but crucial matter on which we disagree most emphatically: the spondee.

Wallace's essay sets up certain assumptions about meter with which I profoundly agree: that the formal genre of poetry depends on the line, that metrical poetry derives from a conventional counting of derivable stress patterns, that we perceive syllables as stressed relative to neighboring syllables, and that we have established a set of conventional terms to describe the formalizing patterns that poets use. I certainly have no quarrel with Wallace's efforts to change some of the terminology we generally employ (e.g., in his points 1 and 2: **"Instead of the term 'feminine ending,' we should say simply extra-syllable ending, which may be abbreviated as e-s ending"** and **"For an omitted first syllable of a line, we should use the** term anacrusis."), and agree with his rejection of the idea of classical quantity for English verse (point 3: **"Quantities are not a basis for meter in English."**), and his suspicion of both syllable and accent (i.e., stress-accent) as independently sufficient for meter, at least since the later seventeenth century (points 4 and 5: **"Syllabics is not a meter in English"** and **"In modern English, accentual meter does not exist."**).[4] I accept heartily the general doctrine of "substitution" (point 6: **"Anapests and dactyls are legitimate substitutions in the iambic norm of English meter."**), and concur that "elision" (actually, synalepha) was a recognized device in English verse before metrical substitution gained general acceptance in the early nineteenth century.

In other words, Wallace expresses what I hope is a general agreement that English verse is based on the relation of relatively stressed and unstressed syllables and not on conventions of quantity or duration, that meter, or measure, is derived by abstracting patterns of stressed and unstressed syllables and counting them in a line of verse, according to more-or-less objectifiable conventions, and that our poets have developed acceptable ways of adding emphasis or relieving monotony (through such things as substitution) without destroying the meter that underlies the poem. I believe this view is consistent with the observable history of English verse as it developed from Early Modern to Modern English between the fifteenth and eighteenth centuries and can be found evolving theoretically from Gascoigne to Edward Bysshe's *The Art of English Poetry* (1702) through the idiosyncrasies of Edwin Guest's *History of English Rhythms* (1838) to J. B. Mayor's excellent *Chapters on English Metre* (1901).

This agreement is very probably enough for most of us to discuss and teach a fairly consistent and sophisticated analysis of English versification. But, as Wallace points out, we metrists just can't help ourselves. We simply must disagree. And the smaller the issue, the more heated the disagreement is likely to be. So I would like to inflame the dialogue over my own pet peeve—the persistent, irrational, superstitious belief in the spondee (point 10: **"The spondee is a good, and fairly frequent, foot in English."**). What, sir, have you no shame?

Real meter is based on real language. In English, patterns of language rhythm depend most fundamentally on stress-accent. Stress-accent is relative. So far Wallace would, I think, agree. I take this one step further, however: given any two syllables, one will be relatively more accented than the other. It is therefore possible, and desirable, to abstract from the normal patterns of English speech a binary pattern of stress from any two syllables.

When I first proposed this notion to the late William Nelson, the great Spenserian (and my dissertation adviser a century ago at Columbia), he put one query in the margin: "tom-tom?" Because versification was not his field, and I had the greatest respect for Professor Nelson, I did not point out that Longfellow had written a whole poem based on the assumption that "tom-tom" was a trochee, as indeed it is. The difference between Nelson's view and mine can be traced to whether one thinks of stress-accent as absolute or relative; Wallace at least agrees that it is relative. Where Wallace and I apparently disagree is in whether metrical pattern is derived foot-by-foot or in relation to the whole line. I want to use one of his own examples to make the distinction I make elsewhere, between meter and rhythm, and to argue for the utility of denying the spondee.[5]

Wallace rightly challenges Otto Jespersen and others when they try to derive metrical patterns across a whole series of syllables, although we can see some clear progressions in levels of stress across more than two syllables. As Wallace notes, Sidney's *Astrophil and Stella* Sonnet 31 provides a good example of the 1-2-3-4 progression in its first four syllables:

>   1   2   3   4
> With how sad steps o Moon thou climbst the skies

Wallace nonetheless rejects Jespersen's and Steele's efforts to create artificial patterns from schemes across four syllables, or to make those schemes into English meter. So far we are in accord. In rejecting some of the implications of Jespersen's scheme, however, Wallace concludes: "in speech, two equal or nearly equal stresses may occur together; so a spondee is plainly possible in meter. The refusal to accept it is mere dogma, borrowed from the failed theory of Jespersen's meter."

What chasm falls between "equal or nearly equal"! What dogma is in fact buried in this assertion of spondee! I, no friend of Jespersen's (he was a notorious linguistic sexist, among other things), reject outright Wallace's claim that to reject the spondee is to embrace Jespersen! Indeed, I would assert that belief in the spondee is nothing more than a secret belief that stress is absolute, not relative; this is clearly inconsistent with Wallace's other (correct) beliefs.

Of course we are not really talking about religion, although some metrical discussions tend to take on that fervor, but really about a difference in terminology. I want to argue for my terms, for the utility of my view of what "meter" means and of its distinction from "rhythm": Meter, I claim, is derived from pairs (occasionally triads) of syllables, and depends on one syllable being relatively more stressed than the other (or others). Meter is therefore an abstraction from the spoken properties of language and, as with any abstraction, exercises some power of idea over the physical enactment from which it is derived (in this case, spoken language). Rhythm, on the other hand, is the movement of a whole line of actual language which embodies the abstract scheme we call meter. The tension between the derivable binary abstraction of meter on the one hand, and the patterns of speech in a normal enaction of utterance on the other, is the rhythmic movement of a line of verse. Rhythm is the performance of the metrical line.

The distinction between meter and rhythm may be difficult to grasp at first, and I think that difficulty is largely responsible for disputes over such issues as the presence of the English metrical spondee. Such disputes are often between practicing poets, for whom the movement of the living line is paramount, and theoreticians of prosody, for whom the interactions between speech stress and its artistic mimesis are important and fascinating in their own right. For the theoretician, the distinction between meter and rhythm provides a useful analytical tool for understanding something of the artistry of our most powerful poets. Consider, for example, how the meter/rhythm distinction can be used to analyze overall pacing in the Sidney line noted earlier.

In meter/rhythm scansion we determine meter by measuring the relative stress within each foot (usually a syllabic pair), and then we count the number of feet. So the meter of Sidney's Sonnet 31 is iambic pentameter with no substitutions (not even the ubiquitous initial trochee):

```
     ×    /    ×    /    ×   /     ×    /      ×    /
With how | sad steps | o moon | thou climbst | the skies.⁶
```

With how | sad steps | o moon | thou climbst | the skies.[6]

The meter depends on which syllable is relatively more stressed *in the context of the foot only*: "With" or "how"; "sad" or "steps"; "o" or "moon," and so forth. (In order to avoid premature assumptions based on individual performance of the whole line, some metrists advise doing this sort of relative scanning from right to left—starting, that is, with "the skies" and moving backward.)

The rhythm, on the other hand, must take into account the variation among stress levels within and *across the foot-boundaries of the line.* If we accept, for the moment, that Jespersen, and Trager and Smith, and Steele are onto something when they all assume that we can hear roughly four levels of stress, then we can superimpose those four levels across the whole line:

```
    1    2    3    4    2    4    3    4    1    4
With how sad steps o moon thou climbst the skies
```

The beauty of the mimetic rhythm is evident here: the stress level climbs as does the moon, and the line is rather heavily stressed overall, reinforcing the ponderous, contemplative tone. By contrast, consider the movement of the first line of Sonnet 28, "You, that with allegory's curious frame," which is less heavily stressed and speeds the more conversational tone:

```
   4    2     1   4   1 2   1    3    2    4
   /    ×     ×   /   × /   ×    /    ×    /
You that | with al | legor | y's cur | ious frame
```

A phrasal or linear reading is clearly more subjective than a metrical reading, but so is any actual performance of a poem more subjective than the abstraction of a meter. Nonetheless, a reading sensitive to the meter is not completely subjective, because the direction of the reading is pulled by the presence of an underlying binary pattern.

An example from yet another Sidney poem will illustrate how important the pull of the metrical foot can be to the meaning of a poem, and, in addition, how inappropriate a belief in a metrical spondee can be. In the poem beginning "Leave me O Love, which reachest but to dust," a conventional renunciation sonnet, Sidney distinguishes passionately between human and divine love. The Petrarchan power of the beams of the beloved's eyes and the fire of sexual passion are to be subdued to a divine light "That doth both shine and give us light to see." This line, which concludes the octave, is followed by the interesting first line of the sestet "O take fast hold; let that light be thy guide." If we define stress-accent in relation to the whole line rather than to pairs of syllables, we can allow for spondees and anapestic substitutions (although it is early for the latter in English metrical history), and, in its otherwise iambic pentameter context, we have an unmetrical line that (by plurality of anapests) should probably be called anapestic tetrameter:

$$\times \ / \quad / \quad / \quad \times \ \times \ / \quad \times \ \times \quad /$$

O take | fast hold | let that light | be thy guide

Historically, however, those anapestic substitutions are unlikely, and if we trust the basic iambic pattern of the poem and derive stress-accent foot by foot rather than in relation to the whole line, we get something very different:

$$2 \quad 4 \quad 3 \quad 4 \quad 1 \quad 3 \quad 4 \quad 1 \quad 2 \quad 4$$
$$\times \ / \quad \times \ / \quad \times \ / \quad / \quad \times \quad \times \quad /$$

O take | fast hold | let that | light be | thy guide

There is a trochaic substitution in the fourth foot—unusual, but not unheard of—and it has the expected effect of forcing attention on how the line is to be performed. I have indicated, above the scansion, one possible phrasal performance, using the conventional four levels of stress. I freely admit that there are other reasonable performances of this line. But the meter forces us to pay attention to the contrastive stress on "that," and the trochaic substitution that follows throws central emphasis on "that light," God's light, the true light, the light the speaker is so powerfully trying to invoke in the face of a much more earthly and demanding Petrarchan passion. Tone and even denotation are artfully enforced by this interaction of meter and the expected patterns of normal speech. The result is the rhythm of the line. The spondaic rhythm—the place where the stress accents are most importantly nearly equal—actually moves across metrical feet: "that | light." The metrical spondee, if we had metrical spondees, would occur with "fast hold"—important and emphatic, to be sure, but nothing like the importance of "that light." Assuming a metrical spondee in this line would weaken the emphatic tension of the line's rhythm as a whole.

Meter is derived and measured foot by foot. Since all stress-accent is relative, there is no metrical spondee. Since, in relation to a whole line, accents may in fact be *nearly equal* (though never precisely equal in relation to each other), lines may be rhythmically loaded unequally; there may be variations in stress-levels across the line, which create the art of linear movement that depends on variation across an underlying pattern, and which direct performance and shade emphasis. I argue, in short, that the very artistry of conventional metrical verse depends on the absence of the spondee. To believe in the spondee is to deny subtlety, to deny the care and control the poet brings to the embodying of a metrical abstraction, and to see meter as a sledgehammer that destroys rather than a blueprint that directs a unique creation.

On the other hand, so that we few who toil in the unappreciated vineyards of versification may remain appreciative at least of each other, let me affirm that Wallace's essay is a fine exposition of a traditional view of English meter, as advocated (for example) by Wimsatt and Beardsley in 1959 and (despite Wallace's own hesitations) essentially confirmed by linguistic investigation into English stress patterns and their relation to verse.[7] I was pleased and delighted to read it. It is churlish to disagree so heartily where one otherwise agrees so much. So I'll grant him one small point, suggested above: there are what we might call *rhythmic* spondees, syllables so close in emphasis when we perform them that we might as well call them spondees. As long as we understand that we are not referring to metrical abstraction, why not?

NOTES

1. Susanne Woods, *Natural Emphasis: English Versification from Chaucer to Dryden* (San Marino, Calif.: Huntington Library Press, 1985); George Gascoigne, "Certain Notes of Instruction Concerning the Making of Verse or Rime in English," in *The Posies of George Gascoigne* (London, 1575): "4. And in your verses remember to place every word in his natural emphasis or sound; that is to say, in such wise and with such length or shortness, elevation or depression of syllables, as is commonly pronounced or used." I have modernized the spelling.

2. *The Poeticall Essayes of Sam. Danyel. Newly Corrected and Augmented* (London, 1599), vol. 2. 701–6. I continue to modernize the spelling except where clues to syllabification or a pronunciation different from our own would be erased.

3. There are unquestionably exceptions: American "garAGE" vs. British "GARage," or "TheAtre" vs. "THEatre," but these are rare enough to be noticeable and the subject of occasional mirth. There are interesting historic and class reasons for some of these differences, but they are beyond the scope of this paper.

4. Although I believe stress-accent persists as a measure of English verse well into the sixteenth century. See, for example, Gascoigne's description of "ryding rime" in the *Certain Notes*, and some of Spenser's four-stress experiments in *The Shepheardes Calendar* (1579). For a discussion of the transition from accentual to accentual-syllabic meters, see John Thompson, *The Founding of English Meter* (New York: Columbia University Press) 1954, and Woods, *Natural Emphasis*, chapters 2 ("Chaucer and the Fifteenth Century") and 3 ("Wyatt and Surrey"), pages 21–103. I am inclined to believe that much late-twentieth-century poetry is actually more accentual than accentual-syllabic, but whether such poetry should be considered "metrical" is probably a matter for debate.

5. For a more extensive discussion and analysis of the relation between meter and rhythm, see Woods, *Natural Emphasis*, 4–10.

6. From *Astrophil and Stella*, 1591 and 1598 ("Leave me o love which reachest but to dust," quoted below, is from the 1598 edition only, among "Certain Sonnets"). I use "x" to mean "relatively unstressed" and "/" to mean "relatively stressed" within a metrical foot. The use of the classical symbol for a short syllable ("⌣") to mean relatively unstressed tends unnecessarily to confuse the quantitative and accentual-syallabic systems.

7. W. K. Wimsatt and Monroe Beardsley, "The Concept of Meter: An Exercise in Abstraction," *PMLA* 74 (1959): 585–98. The basis for much later linguistic work is Morris Halle and S. J. Keyser's *English Stress: Its Form, Its Growth, and Its Role in Verse* (New York: Harper and Row, 1971). See also Paul Kiparsky, "The Rhythmic Structure of English Verse," *Poetics I*, ns 6 (1977): 111–53.

PART THREE

COMPLETING
THE CIRCLE

Robert Wallace

I am grateful to the contributors here for responding generously to "Meter in English." In one particular, I would amend the essay. In ending the second section—"There is one meter in English: accentual-syllabic"—I regret adding "and its base is always iambic." As to fact, this is accurate; but the tone seems misleading. The point, made more carefully at pages 28–29, may be restated: In the continuum of *equally valid* feet that make our meter, the iamb will continue to be accounted the norm. The most frequent foot, it is also the most rhythmically neutral. As long as we use the metaphor of substitution to describe how one kind of foot (rather than another) appears at some point in a line, the paradigmatic foot will remain the iamb. Nothing in that is intended to newly privilege the iamb.

Every poem establishes its own norm. A poem beginning generously with anapests, like "How They Brought the Good News from Ghent to Aix," creates an anapestic expectation for what follows. (The expectation does not depend on determining what the poem's meter is.) A poem steadily using anacrusis, like Larkin's "First

Sight," makes its occasional lines beginning with iambs seem divergences. And so on. It will ordinarily be enough to say "pentameter" and take account of whatever feet fill the lines, and so describe the particular rhythm we find. If the rhythm is anapestic, we will find that. No metrical rigidity is involved. Modulation and diversity will be seen easily. Finch provides an opportunity to test that claim with a passage by Robert Louis Stevenson, and I will do that below.

Gladdened as I am by the many points of accord or consent here, what my essay did not do clearly enough is sound the alarm. Particulars aside, the contributors' agreements with my propositions (by rough count, seventy-three) and disagreements (fifty-four) demonstrate the lack of consensus which was the starting point of my inquiry. Moreover, those who disagree often do not agree with one another. Hartman's accentual meter is not Holley's accentual meter is not Gioia's accentual meter, and so on. Nims faults me for raising the question of quantitative meter ("it has not been necessary to make this point since about 1590") (176), although he himself makes the point in *Western Wind* (266) and knows that Fussell and others standardly list quantitative as a meter in English.

My purpose in this afterword, completing the circle, is to assess my ten propositions in light of the arguments made against them. This must be both detailed and, given the overlapping of objections, somewhat circuitous. It must also be rigorous. Toleration of confusion is hard to tell from indifference and would leave us no good answer to the dean and with-it professor of English who remarked, of rhyme and meter, "Should we even be teaching that?"

It seems to me hard to doubt that there is a crisis. *The New Princeton Handbook of Poetic Terms*, edited by T. V. F. Brogan, has no entry at all for meter.

Nor am I reassured by *The New Princeton Encyclopedia of Poetry and Poetics*, from which *The Handbook* is lifted. There, Brogan remarks

> Some central concepts of meter are now clear, but there is as yet no general theory in place and shockingly little available data. . . . In general, modern work has dissolved the old notions of meter without yet having anything solid to put in their place. The old

age has passed away, but the new age has not begun. . . . At the turn of the 21st century, pretty much everything still remains to be done. (781)

I confess to being unable to follow with clarity much that Brogan says in some fifty double-column pages, spread among entries on *meter, rhythm, prosody, foot, scansion, iambic,* and so on. But I seem to gather, for instance, that the trochee in "Haply I think on thee, and then my state" is not a trochee, is not a foot, and (substitution being an unsatisfactory doctrine) is not even a substitution, but is (the preferred terms) a "variation," "variance," "irregularity," or "complication" (esp. 419, 549, 773, 1233). Brogan's position, thus, leaves 75 percent of the lines of English poetry moth-eaten with "irregularities" for which he allows no systematic accounting.

Things are a mess, and I see no reason for the rest of us to wait around till the linguists do "the pretty much everything [that] still remains to be done" before the new age begins—if it ever does. As Brogan himself notes, "Modern metrists have embraced every new theory in linguistics and thereby suffered their fate, as theories were proposed then discarded in the 1970s and '80s with increasing rapidity" (778).

I can't resist adding that Brogan also ends up at a wonderful pass about syllabics:

> Further, absent the whole notion of meter as *pattern,* one may question whether syllabic verse is "metrical" at all. And, if not metrical, and not free, one may question whether "verse" at all.

He is quite serious, and he goes where we guess he's headed:

> Fuller suggests that Moore has brought into poetry the resources of prose; this suggests that the form of syllabic verse should be conceived more properly alongside those of the verset and the prose poem. (1249)

Brogan steps off the cliff into thin air, like Matthew Arnold deciding that "Dryden and Pope are not classics of our poetry, they are classics of our prose."

We should stick with making cucumbers from sunlight.

II.

Mirror-image, alternative scansions bedevil our prosody by allowing us to call the same thing by different names. For example, a line of John Gay cited by Steele (240–241) as being in amphibrachic meter (with catalexis in the last foot) might equally be construed as being in anapestic meter (with anacrusis); or as being in dactylic meter (with a hypermetrical initial syllable and with double catalexis in the last foot):

$$\cup \quad / \quad \cup \quad \cup \quad / \quad \cup \quad \cup \quad / \quad \cup \quad \cup \quad / \quad x$$
What care and | expense for | their hounds are | employed

$$x \quad \cup \quad / \quad \cup \quad \cup \quad / \quad \cup \quad \cup \quad / \quad \cup \quad \cup \quad /$$
What care | and expense | for their hounds | are employed

$$\cup \quad / \quad \cup \quad \cup \quad / \quad \cup \quad \cup \quad / \quad \cup \quad \cup \quad / \quad x \quad x$$
What | care and ex | pense for their | hounds are em | ployed

Nims makes excellent sense about the problem. He quotes Hopkins: "it is very hard to tell whether to scan by dactyls, anapests, or amphibrachs," and himself adds, "And probably not worth the trouble, since the meter will sound the same no matter what we call it" (188). Exactly!

Our prosody is also bedeviled by the notion that we may or must ascribe meter by *line*. One *can* assess the meter of a line. But properly meter refers to poems, as we say the meter of the sonnet beginning "Let me not to the marriage of true minds" is iambic pentameter, though there is only one iamb in that line. Classifying the *line's* meter as trochaic, based on a plurality of trochees, seems unuseful. A poem's foot-type either goes virtually without saying or, as in the Stevenson passage below (eleven iambs and nine anapests), is meaninglessly ambiguous.

Moreover, we risk confusion. Consider this paragraph (189) in which Nims rejects the point I am now trying to restate:

"I hope we can agree," says Wallace, "that, properly, meter refers to *poems*, not lines *per se*." No, we cannot agree to that. Meter refers even to feet, and certainly to lines. A spondaic line like "And with old woes new wail my dear time's waste" remains a spondaic line even in Shakespeare's iambic context. It does not become iambic, any more than a cow among sheep becomes a sheep and should be called one. True, the spondaic line accommodates itself to the iambic meter, just as the cow may get along with the sheep. But it does not become one of them.

The line's three substituted spondees do largely determine its *rhythm*, but it is *meter* Nims insists he is talking about when he calls it a "spondaic line," so his contention seems—needlessly—confusing. In my view, it doesn't matter a whit whether the line's meter is iambic or spondaic. That just isn't helpful information.

Thinking about the dangers of line-meter and mirror-image scansion, we may advantageously look at the lines Finch cites from Robert Louis Stevenson's "From a Railway Carriage" (in *A Child's Garden of Verses*). Readers can compare my account, based on the simple metrical continuum I propose, with Finch's account. Let's take it very slowly and carefully, as issues raised along the way are important. My scansion:

```
    ˘    /    ˘  ˘ /    ˘    /    ˘  ˘ /   ˘
And charg | ing along | like troops | in a bat | tle,
  /    ˘     ˘    /   ˘    ˘   /   ˘   ˘   /   ˘
All through | the mea | dows the hor | ses and cat | tle:
  /  ˘   ˘  /     ˘  ˘   /    ˘   ˘    /
All of | the sights | of the hill | and the plain
 X   /   ˘   /   ˘   /   ˘   /
Fly | as thick | as driv | ing rain;
   ˘   /   ˘ ˘ /    ˘  ˘    /    ˘ ˘ /
And ev | er again, | in the wink | of an eye,
 X   /    ˘   /   ˘     /   ˘   /
Paint | ed sta | tions whis | tle by.
```

The passage is tetrameter, primarily mixing iambs (11) and anapests (9). Lines 1 and 2 are lengthened a little by e-s endings; lines 2 and 3 begin with trochaic inversions; and lines 4 and 6 are shortened a little by anacrusis. The motion of the speeding train-window, transferred in effect to the generic scenes passing in the middle distance, registers in the loping but easy rhythm produced by the eleven extra syllables of lines 1, 2, 3, and 5. The decisive effect, though, is that of still greater speed—due to nearness—suggested by the rhythmically clipped, succinct lines 4 and 6. Also the only lines without anapests, they register first the laterally driving rain (only metaphoric? also literal?) and then, close up, the painted stations. Unanticipated, the stations seem to whip by—so quickly that the imagery, hitherto visual, shifts to the auditory "whistle by."

Compare that account with Finch's (67–68). She only reports the meter of each line, as shown at right, but here is what appears to be her scansion:

> ‿ / ‿ ‿ / ‿ / ‿ ‿ / ‿
> And charg | ing along | like troops | in a bat | tle,   *anapestic*
>
> / ‿ ‿ / ‿ ‿ / ‿ ‿ / ‿ x
> All through the | meadows the | horses and | cattle: *dactylic*
>
> / ‿ ‿ / ‿ ‿ / ‿ ‿ / x x
> All of the | sights of the | hill and the | plain   *dactylic*
>
> / ‿ / ‿ / ‿ / x
> Fly as | thick as | driving | rain;   *trochaic*
>
> ‿ / ‿ ‿ / ‿ ‿ / ‿ ‿ /
> And ev | er again, | in the wink | of an eye,   *anapestic*
>
> / ‿ / ‿ / ‿ / x
> Painted | stations | whistle | by.   *trochaic*

As to five of the lines, Finch's determination is equivocal. Line 1 (two iambs, two anapests, e-s ending) can't be described accurately as either iambic or anapestic. The other pairs, lines 2 and 3, 4 and 6, are mirror-image, alternate scansions and might with equal accuracy be described as anapestic (rather than dactylic) and iambic (rather than trochaic). Indeed, avoiding the need for catalexis, my scansion of lines 2 and 3 seems preferable to her dactyls.

Such alternative scansions may occasionally be unavoidable. As shorthand for talking about rhythm, they aren't very useful. Harmless when nothing depends on them, they nonetheless risk confusion. And they make it easy to manipulate the system, as Turco tries to do by describing an iamb and e-s ending as an amphibrach, or as Finch does in *The Ghost of Meter* when she interprets the meter of Dickinson's "After great pain, a formal feeling comes—." "This is the Hour of Lead," Finch tells us, "scans most readily as a dactylic line" and

has the immediacy of self-realization, conveying the assertive quality of Dickinson's dactyls . . . [which] seem to be associated with
a relatively powerful feminine principle contrasted with a masculine force. (29–30)

I have difficulty finding one dactyl in the line, which seems a simple
instance of trochaic inversion followed by two iambs. Finch apparently reads not only "Thís ĭs thĕ" but also "Hóur ŏf Leăd" for her
count is plural—"the sudden dactyls"—and "the dactylic movement
seems to counteract the lethargy into which the previous stanza's
iambs had fallen. . . ."

   No less arbitrary is her preference for a dactylic reading of lines
2 and 3 of the Stevenson and, in lines 4 and 6, for a trochaic (with
catalexis) as opposed to an iambic (with anacrusis) reading. This is
the old mirror-image problem of "L'Allegro." She holds a strong
view about "lines like 'Come, and trip it as ye go'—particularly when
they are the norm of the poem and not a variation in an iambic
context" (66). As to norms, however, "L'Allegro" has ninety-six
iambic lines to fifty-six "trochaic," only *five* of which don't require
catalexis (lines 19, 20, 45, 69, and 70); so I am unsure how she determines a norm. Nonetheless, Finch and her students *hear* "a distinct
trochaic rhythm." This claim for a line such as "Painted stations
whistle . . . ," where the wordshapes themselves are "trochaic,"
appears plausible; but it seems implausible for Milton's line, where
the caesura after the monosyllable "Come," effectively sets the
rhythm going again with a distinctly iambic "ănd tríp. . . ." I have
trouble trying to "hear," without forcing, the trochees of lines like
these that Finch quotes McAuley quoting as examples:

/ ᵕ / ᵕ / ᵕ /
In the | last knot | love could | ty

or

/ ᵕ / ᵕ / ᵕ /
Pillow | hard, and | sheetes not | warm

"Pillow" is OK, but "hard, and" or "sheetes not"?
   All this *should* be moot, of course. Meter is essentially notional,
an abstract pattern. Feet cross word boundaries, phrase boundaries,

and even full-stop caesuras. The metrical pattern is an essential part of what we interpret when we discuss rhythm, and will often be decisive, but it is always only a part. No pattern itself, certainly no symmetrical pattern like /∪/∪/∪/, can be either "rising" or "falling."

Although Finch's determinations are questionable, let us suppose that the Stevenson passage shows two lines of anapestic meter, two of dactylic, and two of trochaic. The passage, thus, she says, unites "lines in conflicting accentual-syllabic meters."

What *are* "conflicting meters"?

Finch first uses the term at page 65 when "Shakespeare follows two lines with trochaic-spondaic substitution with a strictly iambic one, in the very nick of time," rescuing Sonnet 116 "from the dangerously close presence of a conflicting meter which would, if indulged too excessively, undermine the poem's actual meter." The dangerously close, conflicting meter apparently is trochaic, since three of the five substitutions in lines 1 and 2 are trochees. The point seems to be that substitution, as long as it doesn't actually break the metrical thread, is a "tension between conflicting meters, a source of beauty and excitement." If so, the term is empty.

As applied to the Stevenson passage, however, the term refers to *lines,* not merely substituted feet, of another meter. But some lines of different meter may be peacefully combined—that is, are not conflicting meters:

> A poem combining two duple feet could be scanned as "mixed duple meter," one with two triple feet as "mixed triple meter," one with two rising feet as "mixed rising meter," and so on; but this passage combines three different meters that could not *by definition* coexist in any one accentual-syllabic meter. (68)

Iambic and trochaic meter can coexist ("mixed duple meter"), as in "L'Allegro," though for some reason not in Sonnet 116. Anapestic and dactylic meter can coexist ("mixed triple meter"). Iambic and anapestic meter can coexist ("mixed rising meter"). And presumably trochaic and dactylic meter can coexist (mixed falling meter). So, apparently, only iambic and dactylic are "conflicting meters," and anapestic and trochaic. *Lines* of anapestic and trochaic meter can't "*by definition* coexist."

Where, one wonders, is this defined and by whom? Yet of course the Stevenson passage is there to prove that they *do* coexist. The whole idea of "conflicting meters" seems unnecessary. It is a knot of prosodic jargon. If line 1 of the Stevenson had been declared, with equal plausibility, iambic and line 5 tightened by a syllable; or if lines 2 and 3 had been declared, with in fact greater plausibility, anapestic, there'd have been no problem at all.

And it turns out there *is* no problem. Conflicting meters can be made justified by *saying* the passage is in "accentual meter." Like Jason back for another movie—"I am still not convinced that there is not some genuinely accentual poetry according to that definition" (67)—accentual meter rises from the dead. The new accentual meter will reconcile lines "which can be predicted to carry metrically contradictory audible stresses" (68)—whatever those are, and putting aside curiosity about inaudible stresses. Moreover, it will be as arbitrary as ever. Finch remarks:

> It is sometimes difficult to determine the number of accents in isolated lines of accentual poetry, because their number of accents depends in part on the context of other lines in the poem. This fact in no way undermines the integrity of accentual scansion. (68)

Fussy readers will notice that Finch tells us nothing about what goes on in the rhythm and sense of the Stevenson passage.

III.

The tune is not that meter, not that rhythm,
But a resultant that arises from them.
Tell them Iamb, Jehovah said, and meant it.
                                        —ROBERT FROST

An occasional sticking point in the symposium is the proper understanding of the relationship between meter and rhythm. I can expand a little on what I said in the first section of my essay and will consider several issues raised by that relationship in the essays of Hartman, Rothman, and Steele.

Verse differs from speech or prose in that it *turns* (from the Latin verb, *versare*). Lines of verse, thus, cut across the on-going sentences as a set of units *in addition to* the sentences' built-in units of morphology and syntax. If we take measuring to mean that something (cloth) is counted *in terms of something else* (yards), we can say: speech is counted or measured by line.

$$\frac{\text{speech-run}}{\text{measure (line)}} = \text{poetic rhythm}$$

The figure, put this way, will serve for free verse. However arbitrarily the lines may be determined, free verse has *measure*: the flow of speech is divided by the measure of its line units. That is the irreducible meaning of the term "verse."

Perhaps we therefore need in English, as separate but parallel terms, both *meter* and *measure*. Measure will serve for free verse, being general and accounting for all verse. Meter will serve for metrical— that is, accentual-syllabic—verse, which is a specialized case of measure. The figure I used at page 7:

$$\frac{\text{speech-run}}{\text{meter}} = \text{rhythm}$$

As feet or inches are to yards in measuring cloth, so metrical feet are to lines of meter. When the speech-rhythm or -run is heard in interaction with the pattern of meter, a *second* sort of rhythm—now, technically, "poetic rhythm"—is generated. In addition to the line-breaks' regulation of flow, at least three things make the poetic rhythm different from the speech-rhythm. In general, listening for or paying attention to the *binary* values of meter gives a more formal, even, measured feeling to the speech-rhythm. Specifically, moreover, where a light syllable counts as a metrical accent, as in

  ᵕ / ᵕ / ᵕ / ᵕ / ᵕ /
And held in ice as dancers *in* a spell,

we either ideally perceive or in some measure actually say or hear a stress where there would have been little or none in speech. The process is genuinely interactive, for—the third thing—patterns in the speech-rhythm may trigger automatic, conventional adjustments in the metrical pattern, loosening it with substitutions or e-s endings. The poetic rhythm of a passage is, thus, neither the speech-run nor the paradigmatic meter, but a confluence of the two—"the tune," as Frost calls it, "a resultant that arises from them."

Nothing similar, beyond the line breaks' end-stop or enjambment, occurs in free verse. There is no metrical interaction; except for the line-breaks, the speech-rhythm passes along into the poetic rhythm. In Whitman, where there is no enjambment, the effect is limited to subordination (caesura) or promotion (end-stop) of normal syntactical pauses. In free verse using enjambment (even between article or adjective and noun), the effect may be quite pronounced, as in Pound's

> See, they return; ah, see the tentative
> Movements, and the slow feet,
> The trouble in the pace and the uncertain
> Wavering!

Such enjambment, far stronger than any usual in metered verse (like Milton's lines about Mulciber, *Paradise Lost.* 1. 739–46), is certainly the main characteristic of one sort of free verse. Free verse, properly understood as having measure, is not just a featureless limbo.

Hartman—to return to my thread—is decisive in discussing meter and rhythm:

> The role of scansion is to diagram the interaction between the two. The influence of rhythm on meter emerges as substituted feet. The influence of meter on rhythm emerges as "promoted stress"—most commonly, turning what might be a pyrrhic into an iamb. I have sometimes used parenthesis around a virgule to indicate a promotion, and so to underscore the interplay with rhythm that is central to the *functioning* of meter. (119)

That is worth quoting in itself. I do so also, though, to point out that when he says "meter" he means only accentual-syllabic meter, *not* also accentual and syllabic meters. My dumb point is that the common usage, when we generalize about "meter," has long since anticipated my view that there is one meter in English. It isn't dumb, however, to point out as well that "the interplay with rhythm *that is central to the functioning of meter*" (my italics now) is exactly what is missing with syllabics or accentuals. That is why, as I say, we can't *hear* them. When Hartman notes (117–19) that I confuse meter and rhythm, the trouble comes in the fact that he is applying two accounts of that relationship, one to accentual-syllabics, a different and simpler one to syllabics and accentuals. The problem with the latter is that scansion of syllabics or accentuals can't diagram any interaction between meter and rhythm, there being none.

Hartman is usually a notable exception to the generalization that nobody bothers to actually count syllabics or accentuals, or cares whether the count is kept. But he seems to be struggling here:

> If a poet subjects syllable counts to a rule, *and* the reader has some reason to know this (if, for instance, the poet's practice becomes famous), then a syllabic meter is possible. (my italics)

Or, we can

> recognize, either in detail (by counting on our fingers) or in general (by recognizing visually the regularities of length in the corresponding lines in different stanzas), the metrical basis of the poem. (117)

Just glance at it and determine the meter. So much for "the strictness made necessary by the system's [syllabics'] unfamiliarity."

Rothman finds it a general problem with my essay that I mix up "the distinction between meter and rhythm" (198), and his exasperation comes out on page 213. He quotes me speculating about whether Hall might mean that the meter of "To a green thought" is /∪|∪/ but the rhythm could be ∪∪|// (28). Then he comments

> Wallace's first notation, of the supposed meter of Marvell's line, could never be a "meter," which is a regular abstraction and does not vary from foot to foot in English. All that Wallace has done is oppose two rhythms against each other, not a rhythm against a meter.

Since Rothman allows substitution, his concern about my confusing meter and rhythm is a metaphysical issue. When we scan a substitution, does the substituted foot *actually* enter the line's meter or not? The metrical norm doesn't change, to be sure, but does the *meter*? Or are we scanning only rhythm? The question might be fun around a campfire with a liter of bourbon, Rothman arguing that we can scan only rhythm and Steele arguing that we can scan only meter (234); but here we will do best to prefer Hartman's elegant threading of the needle: "The role of scansion is to diagram the interaction between the two."

IV.

Meter and rhythm are, Steele rightly says (222), "concurrent but distinguishable phenomena."

> Meter is the basic norm or paradigm of the line. It is an analytical abstraction. . . . Rhythm, on the other hand, is the variable realization in speech of this fixed pattern.

The relationship appears to be interactive.

But, for Steele, except for the single clear case of trochaic substitution, all of the interaction favors meter. Scansion serves "to record the meter" (227) or, again, "to demonstrate metrical patterns and to relate individual lines of verse to them" (234). With the one exception of trochaic substitution, the original rhythmic qualities of a line—what I call the speech-run—are systematically made to conform to the meter.

> *With the two-value system of notation, we can scan only the meter of a line; we cannot scan its rhythm.* . . . If we attempt to force scansion to record rhythmical subtleties, we are likely to muddle matters and even to lose hold of the distinction between meter and rhythm.

Scansion, thus, requires two steps. First, things a good deal more obvious than rhythmical subtleties must be pressed down into metrical regularity, in support of an alternation theory of meter that seems adapted from Jespersen's footless model—"the key thing in English iambic verse is the fluctuation" (225). Then, the suppressed rhythmical qualities may be unpacked again, not entirely uncrumpled, by a rhythmic analysis using Jespersen's four levels of stress. Thus, Steele is able to find "that rhythmical variety in traditional verse chiefly involves not 'departures' from metrical pattern"—that is, substitutions—"but rather internal modulations of it"—that is, modulations *within* the iambs ("On Meter," 289).

Let's follow Steele's procedures as to three lines by Donne, Frost, and Marvell that remain under discussion. For each, we have, first, Steele's notation of speech stresses in boldface; then, his metrical scansion; then, his analysis by four levels of stress, for rhythm. (Asterisks indicate my extrapolations where Steele's formulation isn't in the record.)

Kind pity **chokes** my **spleen; brave scorn** for**bids**

∪ / ∪ / ∪ / ∪ / ∪ /
<u>Kind pit</u> | y chokes | my spleen; | <u>brave scorn</u> | forbids

3 4 1 4 1 4 3 4 1 4
Kind pity chokes my spleen; brave scorn forbids

* **Snow fall**ing and **night fall**ing **fast, oh fast**

∪ / ∪ / ∪ / ∪ / ∪ /
<u>Snow fall</u> | <u>ing and</u> | <u>night fall</u> | ing fast, | oh fast

3 4 1 2 3 4 1 4 2 4
Snow falling and night falling fast, oh fast

* To a **green thought** in a **green shade**

/ ∪ ∪ / / ∪ ∪ /
* <u>To a</u> | <u>green thought</u> | <u>in a</u> | <u>green shade</u>

2 1 3 4 2 1 3 4
To a green thought in a green shade

Objections must be raised:

(1) In two of five feet in Donne's line, in three of five feet in Frost's line, and in all four feet in Marvell's line—shown by my underlining—the speech rhythm is misrepresented by the metrical scansion. On the face of it, Steele's transactions don't indicate the speech stresses we actually hear. Strong beats are translated into unstressed syllables: "**Kind**" becomes "kĭnd"; "**Snow**," "snŏw"; and so on.

The demotions are unnecessary. Speech stresses already occupy the metrical-stress positions in these feet, in "brave scorn," say, so there is no difficulty in hearing the main beats that keep the meter going. Steele is, in effect, scanning the positions. To record speech stress in scansion—"bráve scórn"—is not to "confuse meter with rhythm," as Steele says (234). It is the only accurate way to study their intersection.

(2) Insofar as scansion serves to aid the analysis of poetic rhythm, Steele's regularizing of the Donne and Frost lines provides little information. We needn't scan a Shakespearean sonnet to demonstrate or determine its meter, except as a student exercise; or Frost's "Desert Places" to conclude, having over-ridden its variations, the meter is iambic pentameter.

Steele's scansion, therefore, without a further analysis by Jespersen four-stress, would be empty. Hence, his claim (235) that "we employ [four-stress] only as a supplement to conventional scansion" is disingenuous. It would work better for Steele to scan metrically *by speech stress* and then record any relevant four-stress modifications *after* that, to make whatever fine distinctions or show "internal modulations"; as in

```
2  1   3      4     2  1   3      4
ᴜ  ᴜ   /      /     ᴜ  ᴜ   /      /
```
To a **green thought** in a **green shade**

Such use of four-stress would be in fact supplementary.

(3) Steele's system, therefore, is essentially circular. Four-stress is the implicit rationale for not carrying the strong beats and light syllables of speech into scansion. The exclusion of pyrrhics or spondees is based, *a priori,* on the fine distinctions recordable as 1, 2, or 3, 4. Linguistics apparently tells us that no two adjacent syllables will ever have exactly identical stress. Even so, however, that will be true only given the virtually infinite levels of stress possible. If we use a *forty*-levels scheme, it may well be true that a 39 and 40 aren't identically stressed—though note, they would seem so in a four-stress scheme. So would a 31 and a 40. Steele acknowledges this— "the four-value numerical register is, no less than the two-value

system, a simplification of the endlessly variable movements of live speech" ("On Meter," 300)—and then ignores it. In the Frost line, finding "fall-" to be a 4 (or a metrical stress), he requires that the preceding "Snow" be automatically counted a 3 (and so a metrically unaccented syllable, no matter what we actually hear).

What happens in reading, of course, is that we readily sort the varying levels of stress into two levels of metrical stress, presumably shading 1s and 2s into unstressed, 3s and 4s (or 39s and 40s) into stressed. We respond, almost without thinking, to adjacency. So the middle of three unaccented syllables will seem to carry a metrical stress. So also, often, we will count as metrically unstressed a syllable that could be *argued* to carry speech stress—like "Two" in "Two roads diverged in a yellow wood," or "take" in "And makes my thought take cover in the facts." Context apparently suggests no reason to notice a stress, and we don't. If another reader does, weighing the meaning a little differently and finding something in the context we hadn't noticed, then the disagreement will be fruitful. Such openness seems preferable to the rigidity of four-stress.

(4) A particular problem, following Steele, is that we can never quite unpack what disappeared into his iambs. Saying "Snow fall-" is 3 4 doesn't allow hearing the two words as of equal weight—or of "Snow" as perhaps being the weightier. Suppose we hear, not "snow and night *falling*," but "*snow* and *night* falling"? Or "To a *green* thought"? The adjective can never catch up to—or pass—the noun, though to me "green" is the surprising and instrumental word, not "thought." The full irony of Shakespeare's "Let me not to the marriage of *true minds* / Admit impediments" can't register, because 3 4 makes "minds" the important word, though the weight is arguably on the sardonic "true." Four-stress makes assumptions about meaning which can't be undone. The misrepresented speech stresses *can't* simply be restored.

(5) The ostensible purpose of four-stress is greater precision as to rhythm. What it provides, however, as applied, is greater opportunity for manipulation. For instance, Steele scans

    1   4   1   4   1   4
*The trib*ute of *the curr*ent to *the source*   ("On Meter," 300)

but

$$\overset{1}{\text{The}}\,\overset{2}{\text{hare}}\text{ limped trembling}\dots$$

"The hare," clearly 1 4, seems deliberately misrepresented as 1 2 ("half-weak"!) in order to demonstrate the four degrees of rising stress Steele wants to show.

(6) A further oddity in Steele's system, since he accepts trisyllabic substitution, is this insistence on scanning by *two-syllable* units. "If in scanning iambic verse, we cease to measure feet in such units, we will cease to record the meter . . ." and the roof will fall in (227). In reading, in fact, we quite easily track anapestic feet without losing the metrical thread. Steele's reluctance about anapestic substitution comes from holding on to linguistics-based fluctuation theory, and perhaps from being aware that anapests make four-stress analysis a trip to the funny farm. How rate a foot like "*in a yel*low wood"—2 1 3? Is that an anapest or a cretic?

That is why he just backpedals from scanning the hypothetical line I offered:

$$\overset{}{\smile}\,\overset{}{\smile}\,\overset{}{/}\quad\overset{}{\smile}\quad\overset{}{/}$$
To a green | est thought | in a green shade

Susanne Woods inadvertently allows a glimpse of four-stress at work, too. Using a line of Sidney (here, 289, and in *Natural Emphasis,* 9), she intends to show the advantage of scanning by "pairs of syllables," that is, foot by foot, rather than "by stress-accent in relation to the whole line," which I assume means by the speech-rhythm, without reference to meter. Here is the line as it appears in the poem, with what Woods intends to be the undesirable ("whole line") scansion:

Leave me O Love, which reachest but to dust,
And thou my mind aspire to higher things:
Grow rich in that which never taketh rust:
What ever fades, but fading pleasure brings.

Draw in thy beams, and humble all thy might,
To that sweet yoke, where lasting freedoms be:

Which breaks the clouds and opens forth the light,
That doth both shine and give us light to see.

```
×  /    /   /    ×  ×  /    ×  ×   /
O take | fast hold, | let that light | be thy guide . . .
```

Woods wants this hypothetical speech-rhythm scansion, which doesn't show a contrastive stress on "that," to prove the superiority of scanning "foot by foot," where the contrastive stress appears. But the poem compares an earthly love (imaged as light: "thy beams") to the heavenly; so the hypothetical reader might perfectly well get the emphasis right anyway. Moreover, since Woods allows trisyllabic substitution (287), the poor scansion might equally result from going "foot by foot."

"If," she continues, "we assume that the received meter will help the line resolve into its true rhythm, however, we discover a contrastive stress important to the meaning and tone of the poem." She then scans, in *Natural Emphasis:*

```
            I   4    2    3
×  /   ×  /   ×  /   ×  /   ×  /
O take | fast hold, | let that | light be | thy guide
```

And there she leaves it, without even a comment on the four-stress notation added.

The third foot, "let that," is now correctly seen as an iamb. But the speech stress on "fast" has been eliminated, and the second foot, "fast hold," becomes an iamb, too. And the speech stress on "light" has also been eliminated; and the fourth foot, "light be," becomes an iamb as well, making the line absolutely regular. This is resolving the line, as Woods puts it, "into its true rhythm"?

A straightforward scansion would be something like:

```
ᵕ  /    /   /    ᵕ  /    /   (/)  ᵕ  /
O take | fast hold, | let that | light be | thy guide
```

I wouldn't disagree if someone scanned the fourth foot as a trochee, though if the line ran "let that light *serve* as guide," or some such, the spondee would be clear. In any case, Woods's iamb for "light be" and her attribution in four-stress of 2, 3 are doubtful.

In her essay here (289) she corrects the problem:

```
2  4     3   4     1  3   4    1  2   4
×  /     ×   /     ×  /   /    ×  ×   /
O take | fast hold, | let that | light be | thy guide
```

My purpose in laying this out is to let us inspect first the assignment, then the difficulty, of the four-stress values in Woods's two
scansions. From 2 "light" has been moved up properly to 4. But,
notice, "that" has therefore been *nudged down* from 4 to 3 since
adjacent stresses can never carry the same value. It could presumably have been a 3 in the first place, but "let that" was arbitrarily
marked 1 4, no doubt to show sharply the "contrastive stress." At 1
still, "let"—the verb of command—may be a little low?

Moreover, "be" has now dropped startlingly from 3 to 1. Surely
it is more than flat-out "weak," a 1? But, notice again, "be" can't be
raised to a 2 because "thy" next door is already a 2, and nudging it
up (3) or down (1) would misrepresent that foot. So Woods stays
with misrepresenting "be" as a 1.

Precision is not the main characteristic of four-stress.

N.B. In their essays here, Steele and Woods follow Jespersen in designating *weak* as 1, and so on. But the reverse scheme, designating
weak as 4, and so on, is also in use, in Woods's book, in *The New
Princeton Encyclopedia,* and elsewhere. (So I have transposed the values in the scansion from *Natural Emphasis* above.) The oddity arises
because Trager and Smith, in *An Outline of English Structure* (1951),
refer to what Jespersen called 2 as "tertiary," to what Jespersen called
3 as "secondary," and to what Jespersen called 4 as "primary," Hence,
the Celsius and Fahrenheit of four-stress.

V.

Gioia derives accentual meter in two ways: (1) by examining nursery rhymes and (2) by arguing that "too many anapests . . .
added to an 'iambic' poem" *change the meter* "into something else"
(87)—that is, that verse with *too many* anapests for iambic meter but
too few anapests for anapestic meter should be called accentual meter.

As to nursery rhymes, Gioia comments: "the real system is utterly simple—four beats per line with an audible medial pause, just like Anglo-Saxon, just like rap. Why complicate the obvious?" (81). One answer is that a majority of nursery rhymes don't follow this formula ("Hickere, Dickere Dock" doesn't). Another answer is that, though it's fun thinking about Anglo-Saxon, few of the rhymes were transcribed before the eighteenth century, and so the versions we have are largely accentual-syllabic. Look back at Gioia's scansion of "Tom, Tom, the piper's son" (85). Whether or not the monosyllabic feet in line 1, "Tom, Tom," recall some more rudimentary meter, the poem is iambic tetrameter. The rhythm in each of the four lines is a little different (the trochaic inversions in line 2, for instance); and, as opposed to just marking stresses, accentual-syllabic scansion begins to give us a way to talk about these differences. Gioia complains that accentual meter gets a bad press because "most prosodists habitually try to make sense of it in terms of metrical feet" (81). But no one is putting in feet; the feet are there, as in "Christabel."

As to the too-many-but-too-few-anapests meter, one problem is that Gioia doesn't specify how many are too many, so the concept is arbitrary, a matter of taste. The more serious problem is that treating such poems as accentual significantly reduces the information scansion provides.

Look back at the first two quatrains of "Break, Break, Break" (93). Gioia remarks: "To label this poem iambic or anapestic, therefore, is misleading since almost every line would, then, to some degree, be irregular." The solution? "The only consistent and comprehensive explanation . . . is a three-stress accentual measure. Every line unfailingly fulfils this norm."

But, alas. I'm not thinking primarily of the fact that two lines in stanzas 3 and 4 are unquestionably tetrameters: "But O for the touch of a vanished hand" and "But the tender grace of a day that is dead"— that's a niggling difficulty. The real weakness of seeing the poem as three-beat accentual is that, unless we also scan feet, there is no way to discuss the poem's modulations of rhythm. Even line 1 becomes *just metrically regular*. Distinctions one might hear between lines with three, with two, or with only one anapest are lost. Moreover, scanning accentually, Gioia cannot consider the possibility (as I hear it) of a spondee in line 2, such that its three clumped stresses *answer* the three in line 1—a matching of equivalent forces—and so make the added "O Sea" a rhythmic equivalent for the splashing spray:

```
x    /   x  /   x  /
Break, | break, | break,
 ∪  ∪   /    /   /   ∪  /
On thy cold| gray stones, | O Sea!
```

"The problem"—as Gioia accurately but inadvertently puts it (81)— "is that the concept of a foot is meaningless in accentual verse."

We might follow Gioia's argument in two further cases—"the great accentual trimeter poems of Yeats and Auden" (82). First, Auden's "September 1, 1939," a stanza of which Gioia scans (85–86). "A significant problem" is that, scanned as iambic, he notes, "only one line in eleven is altogether regular! . . . almost every line differs from the one before and after it in its arrangement of stressed and unstressed syllables. Exception, therefore, becomes the main rule." Here comes the reduction of information. "If, however, one scans the passage as accentual meter, every line is absolutely regular."

The stanza is disorderly: thirteen iambs, seventeen anapests, three trochees. But the metrical disorder, *a diagram for rhythm,* is thematically relevant. The stanza is the poem's nadir, the moment before the speaker, isolated and helpless, regains a hopeful determination.

To see the stanza in context, we must scan the whole poem. Here, in tabular form, is what turns up:

	iambs	anapests	trochees	spondees	anacrusis	anomaly
stanza 1 —	19	10	3			1
2 —	24	4	4	1		
3 —	21	10	2			
4 —	23	5	4	1		
5 —	20	8	5			
6 —	24	7	2			
7 —	17	10	5		1	
8 —	13	17	3			
9 —	28	3	1	1		
297 feet	189	74	29	3	1	1

Gioia has chosen the poem's least regular (eighth) stanza for his example—the only one in which anapests outnumber iambs. The poem, as a whole, is a good deal less disorderly. Its 189 iambs are 64 percent of total feet, so the average is almost two iambs per line. Its 74 anapests—25 percent of total feet, spread over 99 lines—average under one per line. The anomalous foot ($\cup\cup\cup/$, in stanza 1: "The unmen*tionable od*our of death") is probably an unimportant elision, but one of the spondees seems noteworthy, in the last stanza: "Yet, dotted everywhere, / Ironic points of light / *Flash out* wherever the Just . . ."

Further, the *ratio* of iambs to anapests, stanza by stanza, provides a useful profile or graph of the poem's changing rhythm:

	iambs		*anapests*
stanza 1 —	2	to	1
2 —	6	to	1
3 —	2	to	1
4 —	4	to	1
5 —	2	to	1
6 —	3	to	1
7 —	2	to	1
8 —	1	to	1
9 —	7	to	1
poem:	2.5	to	1

The contrast between ratios in stanzas 8 and 9 is startling. And, from stanza to stanza, the ratios let us almost take the poem's pulse. Metrical feet, if we listen to their rhythms, are telling us something.

Turning to "Easter 1916," I note a number of pretty clear spondees. How, without loss, can one rationalize, as three-beat, lines like "Until her voice grew shrill," "A horse-hoof slides on the brim," "No, no, not night but death," or "All changed, changed utterly"? Will "Enchanted to a stone" be irregular, a two-beat line? Gioia is firm: "the accentual line will have a constant number of strong stresses" (81). He does not allow a three-beat line to actually have from two to five or six or ten stresses, as others do. But the firmness locks him into logical difficulties, since a spondee can't be permitted, and since a two-beat line subverts the regularity.

To save space I won't give a tabulation of feet for "Easter 1916."
But here are the ratios of iambs to anapests:

	iambs		*anapests*
stanza 1 —	1	to	1
2 —	2.5	to	1
3 —	2	to	1
4 —	4	to	1
poem:	2.5	to	1

They are similarly revealing.

VI.

Counting something, anything—we are told—establishes
a meter. But, with proponents of syllabics and accentuals, *not* counting is more often what we encounter.

Holley, for instance, describes syllabics as "a *strict* but silent pattern" (my italics, 153). However, a syllable-count problem shows up
with every poem she offers to exemplify the form—and though my
essay explicitly raises the question, she does not explain.

The first line she quotes of Thomas's "Poem in October" (154)
supposedly has *nine* syllables, but has *ten:* "It was my thirtieth year
to heaven." An elision no doubt, but is it "thirt-yeth" or "heav'n"?
Nor will we find the predicted *twelve* syllables in "Summertime of
the dead whispered the truth of his joy."

Line 24 (not quoted, 154) of "The Mind Is an Enchanting
Thing" has *ten* syllables instead of the reported *nine:* "it's conscientious inconsistency."

Both Holley (155) and Nims (177) cite James Tate's "Miss Cho
Composes in the Cafeteria" as *five*-syllable. But note the sixth line
here in the poem's climax—line 28 of the poem:

if, perhaps, there might
exist another

word that would describe
the horror of this
towering, tinselled

symbol. And . . . now
you've got it! You jot
it down, jump up, look

at me and giggle.

Surely, a line of *four* syllables must be a significant variation, in a
syllabic poem about Miss Cho writing a syllabic poem about a
Christmas tree.

In Moore's "The Fish," line 6 (quoted, 157) supposedly has *eight*
syllables, but has in fact *nine*: "opening and shutting itself like."
Nims mentions this poem, too, noting that *all* its syllables "are correctly aligned" (179).

Line 40 of "A Carriage from Sweden," not quoted, supposedly
has *eight* syllables, but has nine: "you have a runner called the Deer,
who." Nims cites the poem as an instance of how "amazingly faithful in her calculations" Moore was. Look back at the poem's first
stanza (Holley, 157). It has the announced 8-8-8-9-8 pattern, but it
is also quite readily scanned *iambic tetrameter*—a fact surely relevant
to deciding about the poem's meter? Boland is right about Moore's
syllabics' being often "an aggressive and disruptive dialogue with
historic iambic meter" (50).

It seems fair to say that, if a count of syllables matters, then it
matters when the count is not kept. There are only two possibilities:
the poem or passage ceases to be in syllabics, *or* the variation may be
taken as significant or expressive, like a substitution in metrical verse.
Weller opts for the first as to "Poetry": Moore's revisions, he concludes, "changed [the poem] to free verse" (269). The changes are so
extensive that it is hard to disagree. As to "Bird-Witted," Hartman
opts for the second and his discussion (*Free Verse,* 19–20) is a model
of careful interpretation. It is hard to disagree. In the examples we
have just been looking at, "it's conscientious inconsistency" seems
itself a deliberately conscientious inconsistency.

This is a very tricky problem, whether one considers syllabics as
a meter or as a measure. A variation that turns out to be expressive,
like "it's conscientious inconsistency," is a delightful discovery. One
that doesn't, however, risks wearying the reader who after all has gone

to some trouble to find only that the poet is sloppy. Such a poet might have been better off not to have been seen using syllabics.

At some point, clearly, not keeping the syllable-count violates the form. In "Poetry," as revised, nine of the original thirty lines have changed syllable-counts; and the most substantial of these erases an entire line—stanza 3 is reduced from six to five lines. A total of twenty-six syllables have been removed, and one syllable added, for a net loss of twenty-five syllables in the poem. Four of the poem's ten rhyme pairs are removed or displaced. Here are syllable-counts for the lines that Moore altered:

1921	1951	
line 2 : 22	line 2 : 19	- 3 syllables
line 8 : 22	line 8 : 21	- 1 syllable
line 9 : 11	line 9 : 12	+ 1 syllable
line 15: 11	line 15: 7	- 4 syllables
line 16: 5	0	- 5 syllables
line 17: 8	line 16: 5	- 3 syllables
line 21: 11	line 20: 10	- 1 syllable
line 26: 21	line 25: 13	- 8 syllables
line 30: 14	line 29: 13	- 1 syllable

If a poem, one-third of whose lines do not keep the syllable count, often quite markedly, is "unmistakably syllabic" as Nims says (179), one must wonder where he would draw the line. The form's limit is surely an important question for anyone interested in syllabics.

My purpose in suggesting a study of several versions of "Poetry" and "Critics and Connoisseurs" (14) was, as I said, the *uncertainty*—resulting from printers' handling of run-over or "widowed" lines—of keeping in focus even how many *lines* the stanzas have. If one can't keep track of where the lines are, it is impossible to suppose that one can count and compare their syllables. As to Moore's 1951 and 1967 versions of "Critics and Connoisseurs," I doubt that one *can* make a correct determination. Versions on which Moore was unable to read proof, as in anthologies, may be off the wall.

In the 1967 version, there appear to be only two run-over lines—those ending "but I have seen something" and "in an attitude of self-defense"—where the run-overs are set flush right. But what are the run-overs in the 1951 version? *What are the syllable-counts of matching lines in the four stanzas?*

When I completed my essay in December 1993, I couldn't have given a good answer. Now I believe I can—thanks to the help of John M. Slatin, to whom I was led by his fine book on Moore, *The Savage's Romance,* published by Penn State in 1986. He provided copies of "Critics and Connoisseurs" as it appeared in *Poetry* in July 1916 and in *Observations,* 1st ed., 1924. In these, it is clear that the poem had four stanzas of eight lines each. In 1951, however, stanza 4 became *nine* lines; and in 1967, all four stanzas were made *nine* lines.

Although there were several verbal alterations from 1916 to 1924, Moore maintained the syllable-count exactly, so I will show these versions together and in a simple form in the following tabulation. Two lines in *both* 1916 and 1924 diverge from the line-count norm, *and* continue to do so in 1951 and 1967: "of food as the stream" has *five* rather than the norm's six syllables; "understanding in a variety of forms. Happening to stand" has *seventeen* rather than the norm's sixteen syllables. Noted in parentheses in the tabulation, this suggests the possibility of a still earlier, unpublished version in which syllable counts were exact throughout. Below is the count of syllables per line in this four-stanza poem:

1916/1924	1951				1967			
14	14	14	14	14	14	14	14	14
8	8	8	8	8	8	8	8	8
12	12	12	12	12	12	12	12	12
16 (17)	16	16	17 — 14		16	13	17 — 14	
6	6	6	6	2	6	6	6	2
20	20	20	20	6	13	15	14	6
12	12	12	12	20	7	5	6	20
6 (5)	6	5	6	12	12	12	12	12
				6	6	5	6	6

Moore's revision over fifty years is fascinating. In 1916, line 2 of stanza 4 read: "Useless and overtaxing his," which made a rhyme with "What is" at the end of line 4. In 1924 Moore, presumably aware that referring to the swan with "its" made referring to the ant with "his" silly, changed the line (also dropping its line-capital) to "useless and overtaxing its." In 1951, with the rhyme long gone, she shifted "What is" down to a line of its own, presumably for emphasis—giving the stanza nine lines. In 1967, to regularize all the stanzas to nine lines, Moore in effect made the *run-overs* of the twenty-syllable lines in stanzas 1, 2, and 3 into separate lines, *but* kept the twenty-syllable line in stanza 4 as was. (Perhaps we owe the line-break "bal- / lasted" to a printer's innovation the poet liked.) As Nims alertly notes, in 1967 a small verbal change in stanza 2, line 4—dropping "the staple" (and disconnecting another rhyme)—made that line thirteen rather than the norm's sixteen syllables. Lines 1, 2, and 3 of all stanzas remain faithfully syllabic. But *massive* changes in the other lines' syllable-counts leave little room to believe the poem remains in syllabic verse—changes made as if by "a perhaps hand," as Cummings might have said, "and / without breaking anything."

Syllabics is not a meter, but the mere idea of a meter.

As Yvor Winters points out (*Forms of Discovery,* 1967, 200), "meter is the measure of what we hear in a poem, and if we do not hear it, then it is not there." And we do not hear the count of syllables. As Holley notes (155), "in syllabically-measured verse there is no temptation to disturb the natural speech rhythms in reading aloud." There is no pattern, nothing for the speech rhythms to interact with. Except for the measuring of the lines' turn, the speech-rhythm simply passes through into the poetic rhythm.

Holley's rationale, "inaudible meter" (153), is weak:

> The intertwining of natural speech rhythms with the awareness of a strict but silent pattern provides a different kind of counterpoint from the counterpoint of speech rhythms with the echo or anticipation of a regular pattern of accents.

"Awareness" appears to be just *knowing in general* that there is "a strict but silent pattern." One needn't know or discover the syllable-counts of the lines one is reading, and indeed it wouldn't matter if those syllable-counts *weren't* exact—believing is enough. Hence, no doubt, the indifference to the problem raised by Moore's often syllabically inexact revisions—which give us, then, notice, "an *inexact* but silent pattern." A reader's difficulty in recognizing the syllable-counts, whether by finger-counting or speed-arithmetic, is the obverse of this problem. Counting a pattern that "calls no attention to itself whatever" (Holley, 154) is onerous because it is useless.

Like Hartman with "recognizing visually" (117), Weller speculates that the measure may be "visual" (268) and mentions seventeenth-century shaped poems. Gioia claims that "One can establish *meters* by counting . . . visual line-lengths" (my italics, 79), and affirms that "the formal principle of syllabic verse is visual not auditory. A reader usually recognizes the syllabic pattern of a poem only by seeing it on the page" (80). This is a dead-end. Syllables are an auditory, not a visual property of language ("ricotta" has three times the syllables of "through"); so the link is indirect at best. We don't hear, and we can't see, the count of syllables. Like Williams's indented triads or the couplets of "The Red Wheelbarrow," Moore's stanzas have visual interest, but that is a consideration apart from syllable-count—as, with "Easter Wings," it is a consideration apart from meter.

VII.

With accentual meter of the kind derived from Coleridge's "new principle" (20), *not* counting is virtually a principle of structure. Two stresses is the same as five. Three is the same as ten.

Harvey Gross, recall, referred only to "a *more or less* regular number of stresses per line," allowing "lines of three or five stresses" to count automatically in four-beat accentual meter (cited, 14). To this, he added the arbitrariness of just being untroubled by the presence of more stressed syllables than one officially counts, as in

      /   /   /   /

I read, *much* of the night, and *go* south in the winter

So it is routine for Rothman to describe a line like this, from Jeffers's "Divinely Superfluous Beauty," as having *three* stresses: "And hills tower, waves fall." So, in "Rhythm and Rhyme," he avers, Jeffers "forges the lines in alternating lengths of nine and five strong stresses" (211). But I don't find the forged nine, or the forged five, stresses in any of the lines. I would have said there were eleven stresses in

> / / /   /   /   /   /
> The tide-flow of passionate speech, breath, blood-pulse, the
>
> /   /   /   /
> sea's waves and time's return,

and six stresses in

> /   /   /   /   /   /
> With tinkling sheep bells, like Rome's slaves' daughters?

Rothman sums it up accurately, though: "There is no question that stress-based meters are messy, complex, subjective, and spectral" (211).

Holley, stretching accentual meter, improves on Gross's rule: a poem apparently may *shift its norm* from passage to passage, or even line to line. She notes, in a stanza of "Burnt Norton," "a particularly moving shift from a four-beat to a five-beat line . . ." (161). The quartet then closes with a stanza that "returns repeatedly to three-beat lines" and ends, as she scans it, in two-beat, five-beat, four-beat, and three-beat lines. She comments: "the last three lines quicken to five beats and slow through four to a final three" (161). Thus, in four lines, we have four different stress-counts. If Turco is still looking for a definition of free verse, he might start here—verse in which the norm may shift from line to line. If "the principle of one meter per poem . . . has been replaced by movement among multiple possibilities" (160–61), as Holley says, accentual meter is indeed "a form for the 'informalist'" (158).

But why stop there? Based on Eliot's practice in *The Family Reunion* and account in "Poetry and Drama," as Nims explains (185–86), a range of three to ten (or more) stresses per line is possible. The meter is three-stress accentual (Nims's scansion, though I take the liberty of showing possible speech stresses in boldface):

> /   /
> **Why** should we **stand here** like **guil**ty conspir**a**tors, **wait**ing
>
> /
> for some revel**a**tion . . .
>
> /   /
> In a **hor**rid **am**ity of mis**for**tune? **Why** should **we** be im**pli**cated,
>
> /
> **brought in** and **brought** to**geth**er?

As Nims remarks, his incommunicative Peruvians would be perfectly at home in this company. There might be a snag, since the Peruvians line is in *four*-stress meter. But of course three-stress and four-stress meter are the same, since scansion of accentual meter amounts to just *not counting* stresses you don't want to bother about.

The whole thing is so absurd that Northrop Frye's worrying lest Eliot had accidentally slipped from three-stress into four-stress seems Lagadoan high comedy. Four *is* better than three for

> /   /   /   /
> I think I understand his Lordship better than anybody . . .

but five, or six, or seven would be better still. Indeed, the metrical problem in *The Family Reunion* is that it is difficult to *find* clear instances of the line "with a caesura and three stresses," the supposed norm. Neither three nor four stresses can make any sense at all of lines such as (the second is from *Murder in the Cathedral*):

> Like amateur actors in a dream when the curtain rises,
> > to find themselves dressed for a different play, or
> > having rehearsed the wrong parts . . .

> The living lobster, the crab, the oyster, the whelk and
> > the prawn; and they live and spawn in my bowels,
> > and my bowels dissolve in the light of dawn. I
> > have smelt . . .

I find it impossible to credit that the line

> Dull roots with spring rain

is *metrically identical* to the "living lobster" line, as two lines of iambic pentameter from different poems would be, and is *metrically longer* than the "amateur actors" line.

I was an undergraduate in the mob who heard Eliot read "Poetry and Drama" in Sanders Theater in 1951. Removing rubbers and tucking them beside his chair on the platform, he seemed an earnest person. I would have relished the occasion more had I realized how splendidly he was having everybody on.

In a consideration of accentual meter, Hopkins is a special case. "Sprung rhythm," whatever it is, was written with all of Hopkins's eccentric machinery of paeons and outriding feet in reference to accentual-syllabic meter. Hopkins wrote sonnets. The meter of "The Windhover" is iambic pentameter—*sprung* after line 1:

```
 ◡  /     ◡    /    ◡    /    ◡    /    ◡   /
I caught | this morn | ing morn | ing's min | ion, king-
```

To call Hopkins "the first significant modern poet of accentual meter" (Holley, 158) seems therefore to misread Hopkins's very careful enterprise. And to say that Hopkins "was guarding against the reading of his lines against a mental backdrop of accentual-syllabic meter" (158)—which would make the frequent regular pentameters in these poems colossal blunders—seems less than fully reliable. So does Nims's claim that Hopkins "takes us back to a livelier kind of pre-Chaucerian strong-stress" (182).

Nor does it appear truly accurate to say of "Inversnaid" that its "four-stress measure is explicable only in accentual terms" (Steele, 243). Lines like "His rollrock highroad roaring down" or "A windpuff-bonnet of fawn-froth" don't fit *four*-stress very well, but—with a spondee or so—scan comfortably enough as accentual-syllabic. Anapests and trochees do nicely for

```
 ◡  /     ◡  ◡  /    ◡    /    ◡  ◡  /
In coop | and in comb | the fleece | of his foam
 /   ◡   /    ◡  ◡   /     /    /
Flutes and | low to | the lake | falls home.
```

Hopkins, I conclude, is odd and wonderful. But his poems give little support to adherents of accentual meter.

VIII.

In the sixteenth century, as the new English prosody clarified, two nonnative models remained influential, the Romance syllabic-meter and the classical foot-meters. Both, long familiar, had been compelling. Both were also deeply flawed as they applied to

English. Foot-meter was confused by the issue of quantity and, moreover, by its clutter of feet. Decisively, however, Romance syllabism had no way at all to account for patterns of English stress; so it yielded to foot-meter as the determining theory of English verse.

It is hard to tell, looking back across that divide, how Romance syllabism had influenced metrical practice. In *The Arte of English Poesie* (1589; facsimile edition, Kent State University Press, 1970, 76), George Puttenham describes Chaucer's meter in *Troilus and Criseyde* as "keeping the staffe [stanza] of seven, and the verse of ten." Thomas Cable (*The English Alliterative Tradition*, 117–22) posits a pentameter tradition based on syllabism *and* a regularly alternating pattern of unstress/stress, rather than on feet—in his view, Chaucer's meter. The evidence is stylistic, not historical, however; and Cable suggests no source for the idea of alternating stresses, though surely it didn't just happen. D. W. Harding (*Words into rhythm*, 1976, 63) speculates that, in verse of the earlier sixteenth century, "clumsy rhythms may have resulted from a conception that a verse line consisted essentially in a fixed number of syllables, without regard to patterns of differentiated stress." He cites Wyatt's sonnets, "modelled on Italian poems," for inexplicable lines like

If thou seke honor to kepe thy promes

In any case, by the time of Tottel's *Miscellany* (1557) and *Gorboduc* (1561), a rigid and exclusively iambic verse was the vogue. Wyatt's metrical waywardness had been corrected, much as Shakespeare's would later be corrected by Pope. In 1575, in "Certayne Notes of Instruction," George Gascoigne lamented that "now a days in english rimes (for I dare not cal them English verses) we use none other order but a foote of two sillables." He scans the couplet (cited by Nims)

ᵕ / ᵕ ᵕ / ᵕ / ᵕ ᵕ /
No wight | in this world | that wealth | can attain
ᵕ / ᵕ ᵕ / ᵕ / ᵕ ᵕ /
Unless | he believe | that all | is but vain . . .

to exemplify "other kindes of Meeters" we have used in times past, and goes on to refer to "our father Chaucer [who] hath used the same libertie in feet and measures that the Latinists do use"—by which Saintsbury takes him to mean "equivalent substitution" (*Manual of English Prosody,* 1910, 235). Gascoigne marked the unaccented syllables in his scansion—which Nims neglects to show (180)—so it seems clear that Gascoigne's concern was the loss to English meter of other feet, particularly anapests, not as Nims would have it the accentual alliterative verse of long ago. No question, John Thompson says, Gascoigne meant anapests.

We find Puttenham in 1589 considering the same question (it remains a live issue in 1995): which classical feet do we need to account for English verse? He has pointed out that "our Norman English . . . doth admit any of the auncient feete" (130); but in chapter 16 (140–41), weighing explicitly molossus, anapest, bacchic, amphimacer, amphibrach, and tribrach, he concludes by preferring

> the continuance of our old maner of Poesie, scanning our verse by sillables rather than by feete, and using most commonly the word *Iambique* and sometime the *Trochaike* which ye shall discerne by their accents, and now and then a *dactill* keeping precisely our symphony or rime without any other mincing measures, which an idle inventive head could easily devise, as the former examples teach.

Puttenham's point is simply to limit English verse to disyllabic feet, with "now and then a *dactill*," presumably for an occasional extra syllable. The opposition between scanning by feet or by syllables is, otherwise, now a distinction without a difference. These parallel ways of referring to English meter—feet, syllables—persist well into the eighteenth century. Although Dryden, in the dedication to his *Aeneid* (quoted by Omond, 6), proposes "an English Prosodia" treating "with some exactness of the feet, the quantities and the pauses," Edward Bysshe in *The Art of English Poetry* (1702) states that "The structure of our Verse . . . consists in a certain Number of Syllables, not in Feet compos'd of long and short Syllables." Bysshe's rules, as A. Dwight Culler points out (*PMLA* 63, 1948, 858–85), "are simply a translation and adaptation, . . . with English examples replacing the French," of the French section of Claude Lancelot's *Quatre Traitez de Poësies, Latine, Françoise, Italienne, et Espagnole* (1663).

The rigid founding meter of the mid-sixteenth century may be seen, then, as the Elizabethan *compromise*. Romance syllabism and classical foot-meter in effect coalesce. As long as English verse sticks to disyllabic feet, the two models are reconciled. Untidy evidence is simply swept under the rug, as Puttenham may be observed doing with the e-s ending. It is allowable, he says (85), "for that the sharpe accent falles upon the *penultima* or last save one sillable of the verse, which doth so drowne the last, as he seemeth to passe away in maner unpronounced, and so make the verse seem even." Again (143), it "is in a maner drowned and supprest by the flat accent, and shrinks away as it were inaudible and by that meane the odde verse comes almost to be an even in every man's hearing."

Gascoigne practiced the disyllabic-foot system faithfully, though he found it impoverishing. Soon enough, however, although the compromise held in theory for two hundred years, it collapsed in practice. Within a decade, it had yielded incontrovertibly to the surreptitious and disreputable anapest:

> ⌣ / ⌣⌣ / ⌣ / ⌣⌣ / ⌣ / ⌣
> His acts | being sev | en ag | es. At first | the in | fant
>
> *As You Like It,* 2.7.143

Pretending otherwise has been sometimes a delusion, sometimes an editorial growth industry. All those little surgical apostrophes! To make Donne and Shakespeare talk pidgin!

By syncopation "*Majesty* becomes *Ma'sty,* and so on," the usually sensible George T. Wright tells us (*Shakespeare's Metrical Art,* 1988, 152). But this is nonsense. In the passage Wright is probably thinking of (104) he says "wouldest," "flattery," and "majesty" are syncopated and "hideous" synaeresized, thus getting rid of four of the six anapests:

> ⌣ ⌣ /
> What would*est thou do,* old man?
> Think'st thou that duty shall have dread to speak
>
> ⌣⌣ /
> When power to flat*tery bows*? To plainness honour's bound
>
> ⌣⌣ / ⌣ ⌣ /
> When ma*jesty falls* to folly. *Reserve* thy state;

And in thy best consideration check

     ⏑ ⏑ /   ⏑   ⏑ /

This hid*eous rash*ness. An*swer my life* my judgement,
Thy youngest daughter does not love thee least . . .

                                 King Lear, 1.1.146–52

This is the second great moment in the play, and the most deliberate moment of Kent's life. He does not rush. He does not slur, nor mumble and shuffle. The First Folio says he says "would*est thou do*"; and plaintiveness and pity are in that rhythm. He does not mute the charge against Goneril and Regan to "flatt'ry," nor the valuation he places on his friend and master's role to "ma'sty." He will not hide. However he might say it another time, he gives every syllable of his treason its full measure, and the words hang in the air between Kent and his King: "hideous rashness." "This hideous rashness." And Kent knows the price: "An*swer my life* my judgement."

That anapest, like the similar one two lines above, *"-ly. Reserve,"* Wright tells us, isn't an anapest. There is just "an extra syllable . . . [an] epic or lyric or feminine caesura" (165) and I guess it's not supposed to count. But if *"-ing. Speak"* is an iamb in "Nothing will come of nothing. Speak again"—and it is—these are anapests. (Even in Homer the short syllable at a "feminine" caesura was not extra or uncounted, but was the first short syllable of a line's third dactyl.) There are in the plays, Wright reports, more than sixteen hundred of these "epic caesuras."

Six anapests, then, and line 148 is a hexameter. (The First Folio gives it as two equal lines.) Kent no more says "Ma'sty" than, in the play's first great moment, which this one echoes, in order to avoid a hexameter or double e-s ending, Cordelia says "Ma'sty":

    I cannot heave
My heart into my mouth. I love your Majesty
According to my bond; no more or less.

Wright comes around far enough to speculate:

    Even when we can trust th' apostrophes, it may be that many o'
    th' elisions they request us to make, and the sync'pations required

by the meter, are metrical only, not phonetic, that they signal a direction, not an achieved pronunciation, that we may *pronounce* one way and *measure* another.

(his joke and italics, 158)

—Indeed, just like Puttenham's magically disappearing e-s ending which "*seemeth* to passe away in maner *unpronounced,* and so make the verse *seem* even" (my italics). In the secrecy of the stage the new meter could show its genius: it counts syllables, it counts accents, and yet may vary either with great freedom. Gascoigne needn't have worried.

Some poets kept the decasyllabic line strictly. Some, sometimes at least, did not. One need only read Gascoigne, Marlowe, or for that matter "Venus and Adonis"—in which elision and syncopation are extremely rare—to know that Shakespeare *could* have managed perfectly well without these tricks in metering *King Lear.* Unless we believe that he wanted a deliberately artificial idiom on the stage, Shakespeare substituted anapests, often freely. If Wright is correct that we may pronounce one way and measure (or pretend to measure) another, there is rarely any way of telling in specific cases. In Sonnet 114, is it "flattery" at the end of line 2, but "flatt'ry" in line 9? In Sonnet 124, should we read "flowers" as one syllable or two, or both ways, in line 4? The text shows

Weeds among weeds, or flowers with flowers gather'd.

The syllabism of the Elizabethan compromise served, at the outset, to shield the new meter from the utter confusion that the clutter of classical feet might have entailed. But it was also essentially a fiction, even then, and no barrier to the trisyllabic feet potential in the English language itself.

IX.

It was natural at the outset to assume that English verse would develop a number of separable meters, each with its own qualities and uses, like the meters of Greek and Latin. Thus, Puttenham assumes "Iambique" and "Trochaike"; and since the eighteenth century, when trisyllabic meters found their way from popular into literary poetry, the assumption has hardened around anapestic and dactylic as well.

But languages differ. Quantity and stress don't work the same way. Despite classical models, English verse has remained quite rudimentary. In classical hexameter—five dactyls and a spondee—*only* spondees may be substituted for any of the first four dactyls, on the basis that two short syllables equal one long syllable. But in English, meter is not formulaic and feet may be substituted freely. Trisyllabic feet, for instance, do not break the disyllabic meter. Trochaic lines appear in iambic poems, and vice versa, and we scarcely notice. Indeed, for the great majority of trochaic lines, it seems clear that we can't really be sure that they *are* trochaic lines.

The idea of separable meters in English remains, in my view, an assumption never questioned. When we question it, it vanishes, happily along with untold confusion and nonsense.

There are of course imitations of classical meters, but that does not make them into meters in English. Nims (176), wanting to question Frost's comment about loose and strict iambic, produces Frost's little joke of the hendecasyllabics of "For Once, Then, Something." This is *not* the iambic meter Frost favored, Nims says. Well, yes and no. One *can* scan the poem as hendecasyllabics (trochee-dactyl-trochee-trochee-trochee), but it scans quite naturally as iambic, in either of two ways:

```
 /  ᴗ   /    ᴗ    ᴗ  /   ᴗ  /   ᴗ /    ᴗ
Others I taunt me I with hav I ing knelt I at well- I curbs . . .
X   /  ᴗ /  ᴗ ᴗ  /    ᴗ /    ᴗ   /    ᴗ
Truth? I a peb I ble of quartz? I For once, I then, some I thing.
```

If Nims's story has a moral, it is perhaps how simply the single continuum of our meter makes unnecessary the old assumption of separable meters. Our different rhythms flow into and out of each other without a seam.

Over and over, metrical distinctions turn out to be only mirror-image, alternative scansions. Gioia quotes (92) two pairs of lines from Swinburne's "Hesperia" to illustrate the poem's "constant shifting" of meter from dactylic hexameter to anapestic hexameter. Gioia scans both dactylic lines this way (I take the liberty of marking the double-catalexis):

$$- \; \cup \; \cup \quad - \cup \; \cup \quad - \quad \cup \; \cup \quad - \; \cup \cup \; - \cup \cup$$

Filled as with | shadow of | sound with the | pulse of in | visible

$$- \qquad x \; x$$

| fear

We might *with equal plausibility* call the line anapestic, marking a double-anacrusis at its beginning. A yet more logical scansion, however, needs no variation or exception at all:

$$/ \quad \cup \; \cup \quad / \quad \cup \cup / \qquad \cup \; \cup \; / \quad \cup\cup / \; \cup\cup \quad /$$

Filled as | with shad | ow of sound | with the pulse | of invis | ible fear

So no wonder, as Gioia comments, "Swinburne obviously hears the two metrical schemes as interchangeable." Scanned simply, they are in fact the same meter. There is no presumption even that the poem's meter is trisyllabic, though its rhythm clearly is, since we have (in one of the "dactylic" line positions):

$$/ \quad / \qquad / \qquad / \quad \cup \; / \qquad \cup \; \cup / \quad \cup \cup / \qquad \cup \; \cup \; /$$

One warm | dream clad | about | with a fire | as of life | that endures

Gioia adds, "For reasons not adequately explained in prosodic literature, English triple meters sound fine when they are mixed, which was not the case with Latin." There's the old assumption, unquestioned, causing mischief. The puzzle is now, I trust, sufficiently explained in the prosodic literature.

A trick of those affirming trochaic and dactylic meters is to neglect to mark catalexis. True dactylic meter, that is, *without catalexis,* hardly exists; and true trochaics are extremely rare. Hence, the wish to pass off as trochaic *symmetrical* lines like

$$/ \qquad \cup \quad / \quad \cup \quad / \quad \cup \; /$$

Wouldst thou hear what man can say

If we compare this line with another, also from Jonson's "Epitaph on Elizabeth, L.H."—

Than that | it lived | at all. | Farewell.

—it's clear that the actual difference is the omission of an initial unaccented syllable in line 1: anacrusis, *not* the omission of a final unaccented syllable: catalexis. The poem (printed over-page) has eleven symmetrical lines and one iambic line. There isn't a truly trochaic line in it. Yet the meter is said to be—surprise—trochaic. Nor is there a truly trochaic line in Blake's "The Tiger." Six lines are iambic, and the rest are symmetrical.

The reason that truly trochaic lines are so rare is that they don't work very well; and "trochaics," if not in this line then in the next, tend to turn themselves into "iambics" for resolution, as in Suckling's "Song":

> Why so pale and wan fond Lover?
>   prethee why so pale?
> Will, when looking well can't move her,
>   looking ill prevail?
>   prethee why so pale?
>
> Why so dull and mute young sinner,
>   prethee why so mute?
> Will when speaking well can't win her,
>   saying nothing do 't?
>   prethee why so mute?
>
> Quit, quit for shame, this will not move,
>   this cannot take her;
> If of herself she will not love,
>   nothing can make her:
>   the divel take her.

In stanzas 1 and 2, four lines might count as true trochaics; the rest are symmetrical, and the rhythm regularly resolves itself or finds closure on stressed syllables of the symmetrical lines.

For me, as I don't recognize trochaic meter, this requires a messy scansion. In both stanzas, all five lines show anacrusis, and lines 1 and 3 have e-s endings. It is worth something to be consistent, however; and when we come to stanza 3, everything is on my side. The spondee and the trochaic inversion smooth the change in lines 1 and 3 to eight-syllable iambic. I'm not sure what happens in lines 2 and 4. In line 2, the three-stress pattern may still work:

/ (◡) / (◡)   /
this cannot take her;

but both lines would scan more smoothly as dimeter, as

◡   /   ◡ /   ◡
this can | not take | her . . .

The confusion caused by our expectation is deliberate, reflecting in the ambiguous rhythm the lover's or the speaker's emotional perturbation. For line 5 is unquestionably—dramatically—dimeter:

◡   /   ◡ /   ◡
the div | el take | her.

The cleverness is Suckling's use of the meter against itself. The apparently trochaic lines (lines 1 and 3 of stanzas 1 and 2) and the ambiguously symmetrical lines are all unmasked in stanza 3 by the plain iambic of the speaker's finally asserted good sense.

It is simply not true that "trochaic poems [tend to resolve passages of rhythmic complication] on trochaic lines," as Hartman says (112). Far more often, they resolve on iambic or at most symmetrical (that is, catalectic) lines, as in "L'Allegro" or "The Tiger." The reason is that "trochaic meter" is inherently unstable in English. Repeatedly ending lines with unaccented syllables quickly seems a mannerism, for one thing. Many supposedly trochaic poems, like "Epitaph on Elizabeth, L.H.," are, if trochaic at all, catalectic throughout:

Wouldst thou hear what man can say
    In a little? Reader, stay.
Underneath this stone doth lie
    As much beauty as could die;
Which in life did harbor give
    To more virtue than doth live.
If at all she had a fault,
    Leave it buried in this vault.

One name was Elizabeth,
  Th' other let it sleep with death;
 Fitter, where it died to tell,
  Than that it lived at all. Farewell.

The other, greater problem of "trochaics" is a tendency to cause a false promotion of the first syllables of lines, as happens here in lines 2, 4, and 6 at least. Read naturally, line 2 will scan

  ⏑ ⏑ / ⏑ / ⏑ /
 In a lit | tle? Read | er, stay.

In lines 4 and 6, "much" and "more" would carry stress more naturally than "As" or "To." Promotion will work seamlessly almost anywhere else in a line, even for a final stressed syllable; but *in this position* it is likely to seem artificial. The voice needs to read awkwardly *by the meter* in order to keep trochaics going. Dove-tailing can help, as in

 And at | my win | dow bid | good mor | row
 x
 Through | the sweet- | briar, or | the vine . . .

Occurring occasionally in iambic verse, this sort of promotion slips by smoothly enough. But in trochaic verse, repeated incessantly, punching the initial stress becomes a deadly mannerism. The problem is exacerbated when—that is, most of the time—the lead-in line is catalectic, and so offers no help of dove-tailing.

Jonson is an able metrist and experimenter. If he means us to hear these forced initial stresses in order to keep the meter, as I assume, then he is himself a victim of the assumption of separable meters in English. Perhaps in a very short poem this artificial stress-thumping may be judged bearable. Or perhaps this is another instance of pronouncing one way and measuring another. (Given the unquestionably iambic last line, perhaps the klutzy elision "Th' other" is also merely notional.)

Defending trochaic and triple meters "in a historical sense," Steele has nothing good to say of them. They "seem incapable of the flexible and continual reconciliation of natural speech and meter characteristic of iambic verse" (242). Steele is right. Trochaic verse tends to fall quickly into the mannerisms I mentioned, and unrelenting anapests tend to develop a momentum that can override both sense and idiom—an issue I'll return to in the next section. It seems useful therefore to regard trochaics, dactylics, and anapestics, not as viable, independent *meters*, but as *extremes* of rhythms natural to the continuum of English meter. Like the tour de force of double-dactyls, such verse may have its uses (often comic).

In a historical sense, we may also be able to judge the damage done by the old assumption of separable meters, when poets have tried to work in good faith in these "meters." "The Song of Hiawatha" is a case in point. The poem justly gets a bad press, but Steele seems hard on it, insisting on an utterly rote reading (242):

$$\text{/ } \cup \text{ / } \cup \text{ / } \cup \text{ / } \cup$$
The blue | heron, | the Shuh- | shuh-gah

It is not clear, as Steele assumes, that "that is what Longfellow wishes us to do, since he is writing in trochaic tetrameter."

Longfellow is a good metrist. He isn't writing a comic poem. So we are looking at either a blunder caused by the old assumption or—this is my guess—at another instance of pronouncing one way and measuring another. What happens, if one forgets the meter and doesn't hit the first beats with a pile-driver, is that lines and passages in effect turn into trimeters as we read. This occurs in the opening:

> Should you ask me, whence these stories?
> Whence these legends and traditions,
> With the odors of the forest,
> With the dew and damp of meadows,
> With the curling smoke of wigwams,
> With the rushing of great rivers,
> With their frequent repetitions,
> And their wild reverberations,
> As of thunder in the mountains?

"With the dew," "With the curl-," "With the rush-" become anapests, so that we tend to hear

˘ ˘ / ˘/ ˘/ ˘
And their wild | rever | bera | tions,

˘ ˘ / ˘ / ˘ / ˘
As of thun | der in | the moun | tains

and of course the double-iamb in line 6:

˘ ˘ / ˘ ˘ / / ˘
With the rush | ing of great riv | ers

Heard so, the poem has some "iambic" resolution, despite the wearying e-s endings, and there are lovely bits throughout, as in book 5:

. . . Till the shadows, pointing eastward,
Lengthened over field and forest,
Till the sun dropped from the heaven,
Floating on the waters westward,
As a red leaf in the Autumn
Falls and floats upon the water,
Falls and sinks into its bosom.

Not, surely,

/ ˘ / ˘ / ˘ / ˘
Till the | sun dropped | from the | heaven

but

˘ ˘ / / ˘ ˘ / ˘
Till the sun dropped | from the heav | en

And so perhaps not Steele's

/ ˘ / ˘ / ˘ / ˘
The blue | heron, | the Shuh- | shuh-gah

but

˘ / / ˘ ˘ ˘ / ˘
The blue | heron, | the Shuh-shuh- | gah

There is no doubt that we sometimes enjoy artificial rhythms for incantations and in poems about ghosties like "The Raven," or about General William Booth, jolly St. Nick, or galloping on horse-back. But we may account for these easily as extremes of normal rhythm or, perhaps more accurately, as mannerisms resulting from excessive rigidity of rhythm and performance together, since it occasionally happens even to iambics in fourth-grade recitations. We don't need a Pandora's box of separable and mirror-image meters for the purpose.

X.

Bacchic (∪//), cretic (/∪/).

In considering what classical feet are needed to account for our meter, we have the advantage, over Gascoigne and Puttenham, of four hundred years of English verse. The amphibrach is irrelevant, since in practice it turns out to be simply a mirror image of anapestic. So is the dactyl; and I confess to foolish caution in not excluding dactyls from the necessary feet in proposition 7. I will do so below.

But trisyllabic feet with two stresses—bacchic and cretic—remain a lively question. Considering them lands us in the middle of a dispute in which both sides are right: Does the bounce-along of triple rhythms "override normal rhetorical stress" (Steele, 242), as in Browning's

I turned | in my sad | dle and made | *its girths tight*

or Clement Moore's

The moon | on the breast | of the new- | *fallen snow*

The uneasy answer has to be, yes, often. Plainly the bounce-along itself is part of the pleasure with lighter poems like "'Twas the Night Before Christmas." In a context of *pentameters,* for instance, the problem with Clement Moore's line would disappear, the double-iamb crediting both stresses:

∪　　/　　∪　∪　/　∪　∪　/　/　∪　/
The moon | on the breast | of the new-fal | len snow

So it is the pace itself that largely causes the problem. And that, in the case of cretics at least, may well make it primarily an issue of performance, not of meter.

Although Finch later values poems that "encourage (or allow) the reader or speaker to stress words differently than would be done in normal speech" (69), she sees a loss of "modulation" in not recognizing, say, "fallen snow" as a cretic (64–65). And Hartman is quite right to point out the expressive effect that may be lost in the Browning if we don't read a bacchic—the little "jerking effort with which the rider cinches the girth" (113).

My attempt in offering the term "false anapest" (25), therefore, was to balance these competing demands of pace and expression. But that was temporizing. I agree with Finch, Hartman, and others that *we should accept the bacchic as a normal foot in English.* The bacchic will allow the straightforward scansion of phrases like "its girths tight" or lines like Clement Moore's "As dry leaves | that before | the wild hur | ricane fly," although performance may often override that modulation in strongly anapestic rhythms. In more serious contexts the bacchic will be useful, frequently enough, for lines like Webster's

Cover | her face; | mine eyes daz | zle; she | died young

or Middleton's

As the parch'd earth | of mois | ture, when | the clouds weep.

We may well differ, as we sometimes do about spondees, in scanning particular lines; but that can only encourage helpful discussion in interpreting rhythm—as, say, about these trimeters by Dickey in which I might mark three bacchics:

I heard Dor | is Hol | brook scrape
Like a mouse | in the south | *ern-state sun*
That was eat | ing the paint | in blis | ters
From a hun | *dred car tops* | and hoods.

There is some risk of misuse or confusion, nonetheless, as in Shakespeare's

∪ / / / ∪ ∪ / ∪ / ∪ /
My playfel | low, your hand, | this king | ly seal

but on balance such occasional alternative readings—correct, but inaccurate—seem an acceptable hazard. So long as the rhythm is reflected well, we needn't trouble overmuch about the number of feet in a line—as we don't with Cordelia's "My heart into my mouth. I love your Majesty."

On practical grounds, however, I must continue to hold that the cretic would be a disaster—pedagogically, a bull in a china shop. What about, say,

/ ∪ /
Come, and trip | it as | ye go

or, indeed, Lear's

∪ ∪ / / ∪ / ∪ / ∪ / /
In a wall'd | prison, | packs and sects | of great ones

which, though it has phrase-logic, would be *totally* correct but inaccurate? The point is really that, as is not the case with bacchics, lines for which cretics might be useful can be scanned without them, like the one about "new-fallen snow," if we aren't fussy about the number of feet in a line.

I am not sure I can satisfy Hartman, who cites Blake's "Ah Sun-flower." In line 3, "Seeking after that sweet golden clime," he notes, "the first and third feet are cretics, pure and simple" (113). My suggestion:

x / ∪ (/) ∪ ∪ / / ∪ /
Seek | ing af | ter that sweet gold | en clime

Perhaps it is only that I am unaccustomed to cretics, but this seems more natural than

/ ∪ / ∪ ∪ / / ∪ /
Seeking af | ter that sweet | golden clime

And I much prefer

∪ ∪ / / ∪ / ∪ ∪ /
And the pale Vir | gin shroud | ed in snow,

to the version using a cretic:

⏑ ⏑ /   / ⏑   /   ⏑ ⏑ /
And the pale | Virgin shroud | ed in snow

Since Blake mixes trimeters and tetrameters freely (or carelessly) as in "The Garden of Love," insisting on trimeters in "Ah Sun-flower" isn't a priority to me, so long as we are precise about the rhythm. We don't know how Blake counted, and I am wary of the critical rule that wanted to fix Wyatt's tetrameter in "They Flee from Me" (see below).

Otherwise, the simple if inelegant option is to leave cretics off the list and just call them up from the Greek closet when occasion requires. I suppose that is what we have been doing.

Pause.

However tempting the notion, pauses can't be metrical. A caesura, even the full-stop between sentences, may occur in the *middle* of a foot. Weller's suggestion as to Yeats's line "Speech after long silence; it is right," that "the semicolon marks a beat" (273), therefore risks confusion. The missing syllable in the lame foot—"^{x} it"— perhaps emphasizes the pause, but the pause occurs in the syntax, not in the meter; and in any case the "beat" of the foot surely falls on "it," as it would if the line read "and it." The valid point is that the clause set off by the semicolon remains only a sentence fragment, so the rather formal punctuation emphasizes the oddness of the pause, which therefore seems both longer and more awkward than normal.

Weller goes on to mention Wyatt's line in "They Flee from Me": "It was no dream, I lay broad waking." A tetrameter among pentameters, the line has seemed a problem since the sixteenth century, when the shortage was repaired in Tottel's *Miscellany:* "It was no dream, *for* I lay broad *a*waking." Weller speculates that "the medial caesura may even carry the value of a full foot . . . but in one way or another the missing 'time' has to be distributed throughout the line" (273).

But why?

The line's simplicity (four feet, medial caesura) itself expresses the speaker's blunt clarity about the recollection. And both in the Muses Library edition (Kenneth Muir, ed., 1949) and in Emrys

Jones's *The New Oxford Book of Sixteenth Century Verse* (1991) the mid-line punctuation is—wonderfully—a colon with its two wide open eyes. Perhaps as with Blake's "Ah Sun-flower" the assumption that the poet always intends absolute regularity of line-length isn't reliable. Pope made that mistake in editing Shakespeare.

I must have a similar reservation about Richard Wilbur's perceptive scansion of Eliot's line, using a caret for a pause (279–80):

<pre>
 ˘ /   ˄   /   ˘ ˘ /   ˘ ˘ /   ˘ ˘ / ˘
I read, | much | of the night, | and go south | in the win | ter
</pre>

Gross's four-beat accentual line, heard by Turco as a hexameter (258–59), is also a plausible and limpid pentameter. Expectation and fulfillment obviously play a crucial part in the working of any meter. Wilbur is aware that he is not laying out a complete system of scansion, as his comment about not careting the line's second pause shows. In scanning his own line,

<pre>
               ˄   /
Where light | breaks, | and the win | dows are tossed | with linden
</pre>

the caret marks the slight pause in the juncture of the two stressed words, a small "delay-of-bang," not the caesural pause after "breaks." In effect, both of Wilbur's scansions replace the slight backward tug of trochees by a simplification in which light syllables always move *toward* the beat. Hence, the sense of limpidity—as well as the lack of a need to count the pause in "of the night, and go south. . . ." Like John Ciardi's writing mostly with "a reminiscence of the pentameter" (as Wilbur quotes it), the poet's working awareness is primarily of rhythm. Poets, we know, don't arrive at effects by the kind of analysis metrists use to explain them.

XI.

Hass's heartily welcome "Prosody: A New Footing" helps to mark out the path from here.

I didn't quite say, but happily endorse Hass's summary: "there are two kinds of verse in English: metrical and accentual" (125). Although other factors, like syllable-count or spatial arrangement, may contribute to determining line in nonmetrical verse, speech stresses are the basis of rhythm, and so of analysis: pattern, repetition or variation, balance or imbalance, and so on.

"For this possibility," Hass notes, "it seems useful to reserve the term 'measure'" (148). We now need the terms meter and measure, long only familiar synonyms, for quite precise and separate purposes, as I mention. The historical novelty of nonmetrical verse, which nonetheless has measure, makes this distinction essential. We have seen the confusion created by trying to classify syllabics and accentuals as meters; and prosody has been blind to much other verse that hitherto could only be lumped into the slippery non-class, "free verse." It is a simple point, a secret hidden in the open, but as Hass says "it involves a paradigm shift."

The study of accentual measures must be inductive, taking into account stresses that occur and not generating a fictitious order, like "four-beat accentual," based on some indeterminate range of stresses or on selective counting. It is not Hass's intention to relegitimize "accentual meter" under a new name.

There is reason for caution in this regard if the terms that come to be used are "accentual verse" and "accentual measure/measures." Hass already seems to privilege measures "quite regularly fixed: two, three, four, five beats to the line" and those "establishing a base measure of two to three, or three to four, or four to five stresses per line" (149), though such steady patterns are likely to make up only a minority of accentual verse. These aspire to the dignity of seeming to be "a measure" in a simple, definable way that the great majority of more flexible verse may not; and this emphasis risks blurring the very distinction we need. Lines of quite unequal length are equally accentual measures, like those Hass cites in Moore's "Critics and Connoisseurs" (140–41), or like the lines of "Song of Myself" he scans in "Listening and Making" (126):

> /   /   /
> I loaf and invite my soul,
> /   /   /   /   /   /   /
> I lean and loaf at my ease, observing a spear of summer grass.

The pattern of three to seven stresses is no less an accentual measure than a pattern of three to four stresses, and is no less measured or, we might properly say, is no less measuring.

Accentual measure, as Hass says (148), "does not manage unstressed syllables." But the poet does; and analysis should be able to take account of them in order to consider rhythm and "the pacing of the stresses" (148). (A weakness of Gioia's accentual scanning, recall, is that the line "Break, break, break" becomes merely regular.)

In the passage of Rexroth's "The Signature of All Things" (146–49), clumped stresses occur near line-end in lines 2, 3, 4, 5, 6, 8; and in the first parts of lines 10 and 12. Lines with only separated stresses—lines 1, 7, 9, 11, 13, 14, and 15—become frequent and then regular. I'm not sure why Hass scans "Like a curious kitten" with three stresses rather than two. (Has some expectation been created? Does alliteration let us hear a stress on "Like"?) But the poem has other two-stress lines; and if some rhythmic lightening characterizes the episode, reading a two-stress line here would be confirming.

The poem is interesting not least for its delicate poise *near* meter. The presence of metrical cadences will often be notable in accentual verse—as indeed in prose (the "blank verse" passages in *Moby-Dick*). A clear pentameter ends Whitman's "When I Heard the Learn'd Astronomer," for instance. "Poetry" begins with a firmly iambic cadence:

⏑ / ⏑ / ⏑ / ⏑ / ⏑ / ⏑ /
I, too, dislike it: there are things that are important . . .

How accentual poems use, or evade, or are trapped by metrical cadences will be a useful study. When Moore begins

/ ⏑ ⏑ /
Never | theless

                        / ⏑
you've seen | a straw | berry
    that's had a struggle; yet
    was, where the fragments met,

she hits such a metrically sour-note in line 1, that the poem's trimeters (and its wonderful little dialogue of iambic and trochaic rhythms) never quite seem metrical, certainly never routine.

XII.

A few summary comments, after all:

(1) Instead of the term "feminine ending," we should say simply extra-syllable ending. For those who dislike the stereotype, a neutral alternative should be in use.

(2) For an omitted first syllable of a line, we should use the term anacrusis. "Headless" exaggerates; its overtones (gruesome, out of control) are inaccurate. Borrowing "anacrusis" lets one cheerful term refer to both an omitted or an added syllable—that is, a minor metrical offset in starting a line. If we stop talking about trochaic and dactylic *meters*, as I surmise we must, the second meaning can simply vanish (along with "catalexis").

I am not convinced that anacrusis, in the sense of *added* initial syllables, exists at all in English verse, despite Nims's comment about the band's being able to "add a tootle or two before the first beat" (173). If it does exist, it is rare to the point of extinction. Many of the standard texts—Brooks and Warren, Fussell, Nims, Miller Williams, Kennedy and Gioia—don't even mention it. Myers and Simms give the term (13), but cite no examples—or cite only one, weirdly, of its occurring "at the terminal position of a line, in which case it is called *end anacrusis:* 'Their shoulders held the sky suspended.'" This is Housman of course and the metrical phenomenon is only what some call feminine or e-s ending.

Babette Deutsch (*Poetry Handbook*, 2nd ed., 1962, 23) cites Blake's line in "Song of a Shepherd": "The jewel health adorns her neck." But this is merely one of the poem's three iambic lines, the other five lines being symmetrical. Brogan notes that in Blake's "And watered heaven with their tears," "one might take 'And' to be an anacrusis," but that in fact it isn't, the line being just iambic tetrameter. He concludes that another example isn't anacrusis either, but notes that "indisputable cases do exist, as in Shakespeare" (68). Possibly he is thinking of lines like those George T. Wright cites (170) as "double onset" or "hypermetrical onset" (Wright doesn't bother with the term anacrusis):

*And so riv*eted with faith unto your flesh
   (*The Merchant of Venice,* 5.1.169)

> *Or we'll burst* them open, if that you come not quickly
> (*1 Henry VI,* 1.3.28)

These, I believe, are called anapests in English. Interestingly, the *Henry VI* line has two of them and thirteen syllables in all. The date? 1591. The line agitatedly bursts open with extra syllables.

It already seems safe to borrow the term anacrusis, if we wish.

(3) Quantities are not a basis for meter in English. The point is not to change the history of these interesting but failed experiments, but to leave this "meter" out of our practical concerns—and out of our textbooks.

(4) Syllabics is not a meter in English. Syllabics is a recognizable and unique form of free verse. Like other types of free verse, it has measure, but is not a meter.

Nonetheless, what Holley elegantly and accurately describes as "the syllabic method" (155) may be very useful to the poet. Boland also refers to syllabics as a "method" (50) and Gioia remarks that it is "as much a compositional technique as a meter" (80). Moore's revisions should perhaps be interpreted as making the same point. Gunn's teaching himself to write free verse by working with syllabics, as Hadas helpfully reports (100), suggests the advantage of the method: it is free but exacting. Note that in composing Moore-stanzas nothing at all controls or limits the number of syllables in lines of the *first* stanza, which is utterly free verse. The form comes into existence or operation only in duplicating these syllable-counts in second and subsequent stanzas.

(5) In modern English, accentual meter does not exist. Two quite different things are referred to as "accentual meter." In the sense of Coleridge's practice in "Christabel," it turns out to mean merely accentual-syllabic meter with (or with too much) trisyllabic substitution (Auden's "September 1, 1939") or with a few anomalous monosyllabic feet ("Tom, Tom, the piper's son"). In that sense, it doesn't exist, being a mere statement of taste; and it reduces the information obtainable by scansion.

In the sense of Coleridge's rhetoric, accentual meter is a concept virtually empty of meaning, countable only in ways that are arbitrary, inconsistent, subjective, "spectral." All that can be measured is the determination of the scanner to impose a count.

Moreover, the claim to a tradition or historical analogue going back across a *huge* discontinuity to the medieval alliterative revival, much less to Anglo-Saxon, is spurious. As J. V. Cunningham concluded (*The Collected Essays,* 1976, 260), this supposed meter, without structural alliteration and without two and two phrasing, "remains wavering and ambiguous. It will not do." Needless to say, there aren't any Peruvians or "living lobster" lines in *Everyman, Piers Plowman,* or *Sir Gawayne and the Grene Knight.* What we do find occasionally, for what it's worth, are lines like these:

O Deth! | thou comest | when I had | ye leest | in mynde!

Ich went | forth in | the worlde • wonders | to hure

Bot Arth | ure wolde | not ete • til al | were served

(6) Anapests and dactyls are legitimate substitutions in the iambic norm of English meter. Happily—the only instance in the book—we agree unanimously *about anapests,* although Gioia holds that there is a definite, if unspecified, limit.

Finch, like Halle and Keyser, contends that dactyls may not be substituted in iambic verse.

I now disagree with myself, believing that the dactyl should not be accounted a foot in English at all, so the proposition may be restated: **Anapests are legitimate substitutions in English verse.**

(7) We should drop the pyrrhic foot (⏑⏑) and accept in its place the double-iamb (⏑⏑//) as one of the six foot-terms necessary: iamb, trochee, anapest, dactyl, spondee, double-iamb. In the single continuum of our meter, it seems clear that we do not need the dactyl for scansion, as Weller all but says (275). I mark only two in my essay (18, 40); neither is necessary or even particularly helpful. Since I completed the essay, I have been on the lookout for dactyls—and there aren't any. So let's drop the dactyl from the list.

As I report in section 10 here, I am now persuaded that, rather than trying to make-do with my "false" or "token" anapest, we should add the bacchic (⌣//) to the list. "In English," as Saintsbury says, "the poetry makes the rules."

So the proposition may be amended to end: . . . **the six foot-terms necessary: iamb, trochee, anapest, bacchic, spondee, double-iamb.**

I am not tempted to restore to the list the pyrrhic, despite Finch's argument on behalf of "*It is the star* to ev'ry wandering bark"(72). As I read, I just do not register two unstressed syllables as a *unit*; and except in the double-iamb formation, the pyrrhic may usually be rationalized as /⌣ or ⌣/:

    ⌣   /   (/) ⌣ ⌣ / ⌣ (/) ⌣ /
Or bend | with the | remov | er to | remove

Advantageously, this is the principal way in which we feel the influence of meter on rhythm. Its naturalness is clear from the sort of slurring, or hurrying, necessary to avoid the slight promotions:

    ⌣   /   ⌣   ⌣ ⌣ /⌣ ⌣ ⌣ /
Or bend with the remover to remove

During the two years since my essay was written, however, I have been several times tempted by the possible utility of the fourth paeon: ⌣⌣⌣/. Like the double-iamb, the paeon (we don't need the other three) would count as two feet. And if Finch is right about "It is a star," it might be an instance. I scanned one in Meredith's "An im*age of arti*culateness is what it is" (18) and mentioned one in Auden's "The unmen*tionable od*our of death." There are several in "Musée des Beaux Arts" and (produced by speed that damps promotion) in "The Raven." Hopkins, of course. Are there, conceivably, *two* in the line of Sonnet 116 above?

(8) Anapestic, trochaic, and dactylic meters do not exist in English. This little nest of confusion, note, is the *second* list of meters in English. The only reason I don't include iambic meter in the proposition is that we need something for the paradigm.

Iambic and trochaic, anapestic and dactylic rhythms are mirror-image and, with anacrusis, catalexis, or e-s ending, indistinguishable from one another as meter. Moreover, with substitution, any may ambiguously move toward or become one or more of the others. These rhythms, therefore, form a continuum—the single meter of English.

This understanding avoids a Pandora's box of confusions. It should also encourage a fuller analysis of the rhythm of poems like "September 1, 1939" or "Hiawatha," where now discussion is cut off by the assumption that naming a meter is sufficient.

(9) We should *never* use four degrees of stress for scanning. Stresses occur together in speech, so there is no reason for a system whose main function is to exclude the possibility from meter.

(10) The spondee is a good, and fairly frequent, foot in English. The remark of Paul Kiparsky, quoted by Finch (72), sums up the problem: "The question is purely terminological: do we want spondee to refer to a foot with two stresses? or with two equal stresses?" Since truly equal stresses are extremely rare (Steele, Winters) or utterly impossible (snowflake theory), we'd better make do with two stresses.

If snowflake theory—"given any two syllables, one will be relatively more accented than the other" (Woods, 286)—is true, or true in any way we need to accept, then anapests are quite as impossible as spondees, since they depend on two equally light-stressed syllables—and no such equality is possible. This is why you will never see a four-stresser scanning anapests. They can't. It is an uncomfortable little secret.

"The reading of a spondee is not always easy," as Boland says (56). But discussion will be illuminating when we disagree.

BIBLIOGRAPHY

This is a listing of major works on meter cited in the previous essays, as well as selected general sources for further reading in prosody and metrics. Contributors to this book aided me in compiling this bibliography.

Alden, Raymond MacDonald. *English Verse: Specimens Illustrating Its Principles and History.* New York: Henry Holt, 1903; reprint, New York: AMS, 1970.

Allen, Gay Wilson. *American Prosody.* New York: American Book Company, 1935; reprint, New York: Octagon, 1978.

Attridge, Derek. *Poetic Rhythm: An Introduction.* Cambridge: Cambridge University Press, 1995.

———. *The Rhythms of English Poetry.* London and New York: Longman, 1982.

———. *Well-Weighed Syllables: Elizabethan Verse in Classical Metres.* Cambridge: Cambridge University Press, 1974; reprint, 1979.

Baum, Paull F. *Chaucer's Verse.* Durham: Duke University Press, 1961.

———. *The Principles of English Versification.* Cambridge: Harvard University Press, 1929.

Borroff, Marie. *Sir Gawain and the Green Knight: A Stylistic and Metrical Study.* New Haven: Yale University Press, 1963.

Bridges, Robert. *Milton's Prosody.* London: Oxford University Press, 1901.

Brogan, T. V. F. *English Versification: 1570-1980: A Reference Guide with a Global Appendix.* Baltimore: Johns Hopkins University Press, 1981. A comprehensive listing of studies in English poetry.

———. *Verseform: A Comparative Bibliography.* Baltimore: Johns Hopkins University Press, 1989. An historical bibliography of prosody and poetic forms from around the world.

Cable, Thomas. *The English Alliterative Tradition.* Philadelphia: University of Pennsylvania Press, 1991.

Chatman, Seymour. *A Theory of Meter.* The Hague: Mouton, 1965.

Chomsky, Noam and Morris Halle. *The Sound Pattern of English.* New York: Harper & Row, 1968.

Crombie, Winifred. *Free Verse and Prose Styles.* London: Croom Helm, 1987.

Cunningham, J. V. "How Shall the Poem Be Written?" *The Collected Essays of J. V. Cunningham.* Denver: Alan Swallow, 1976.

Cureton, Richard. *Rhythmic Phrasing in English Verse.* New York: Longman, 1991.

Easthope, Anthony. *Poetry as Discourse.* New York: Metheun, 1983.

Feirstein, Frederick, ed. *Expansive Poetry: Essays on the New Narrative and the New Formalism.* Santa Cruz, Calif.: Story Line Press, 1989.

Finch, Annie, ed. *Beyond New Formalism: Contemporary Essays on Poetic Form and Narrative.* Brownsville, Ore.: Story Line Press, 1996.

————. *The Ghost of Meter: Culture and Prosody in American Free Verse.* Ann Arbor: University of Michigan Press, 1993.

Frank, Robert and Henry Sayre, eds. *The Line in Postmodern Poetry.* Urbana and Chicago: University of Illinois Press, 1988.

Fussell, Edwin S. *Lucifer in Harness: American Meter, Metaphor, and Diction.* Princeton: Princeton University Press, 1973.

Fussell, Paul, Jr. *Poetic Meter and Poetic Form.* New York: Random House, 1965; revised edition, 1979.

————. *Theory of Prosody in Eighteenth-Century England.* Hamden, Conn.: Archon, 1966.

Gascoigne, George. "Certain Notes of Instruction Concerning the Making of Verse or Rime in English." *The Posies of George Gascoigne,* London, 1575; reprinted in *Complete Works.* Ed. John W. Cunliffe. Cambridge: Cambridge University Press, 1910.

Gaylord, Alan T. "Scanning the Prosodists: An Essay in Metacriticism." *Chaucer Review* 11 (1976): 22-82.

Greenblatt, Daniel L. "The Effect of Genre on Metrical Style." *Language and Style* 2 (1978): 18-29.

Gross, Harvey. *Sound and Form in Modern Poetry: A Study of Prosody from Thomas Hardy to Robert Lowell.* Ann Arbor: University of Michigan Press, 1965; revised and expanded edition, Robert McDowell, 1995.

————, ed. *The Structure of Verse: Modern Essays on Prosody.* 2nd ed. New York: The Ecco Press, 1979.

Hall, Donald. *The Pleasures of Poetry.* New York: Harper & Row, 1971.

Halle, Morris and Samuel Jay Keyser. *English Stress: Its Form, Its Growth, and Its Role in Verse.* New York: Harper & Row, 1971.

Halpern, Martin. "On the Two Chief Metrical Modes in English." *PMLA* 77 (1962): 177-86.

Hartman, Charles O. *English Metrics: A Hypertext Tutorial and Reference.* New London: Connecticut College, 1995. A tutorial and reference work available for both the DOS computers and the Macintosh.

————.*Free Verse: An Essay on Prosody.* Princeton: Princeton University Press, 1980; reprint, Evanston: Northwestern University Press, 1996.

Hass, Robert. *Twentieth Century Pleasures: Prose on Poetry.* New York: The Ecco Press, 1984.

Hemphill, George, ed. *Discussions of Poetry: Rhythm and Sound.* Boston: D. C. Heath, 1961.

Hobsbaum, Philip. *Metre, Rhythm and Verse Form.* London: Routledge, 1996.

Holder, Alan. *Rethinking Meter.* Lewisburg, Pa.: Bucknell University Press, 1995.

Hollander, John. *Melodious Guile: Fictive Pattern in Poetic Language.* New Haven: Yale University Press, 1988.

————. *Vision and Resonance: Two Senses of Poetic Form.* 2nd ed. New Haven: Yale University Press, 1985.

Hornsby, Roger A. *Reading Latin Poetry.* Norman: University of Oklahoma Press, 1967.

Ing, Catherine. *Elizabethan Lyrics: A Study of the Development of English Metrics and their Relation to Poetic Effect.* London: Chatto & Windus, 1951; reprint, 1969.

Jakobson, Roman. "Closing Statement: Linguistics and Poetics." In *Style in Language.* Ed. T. A. Sebeok. Cambridge, Mass.: MIT Press, 1960.

Justice, Donald. "Meters and Memory." *Antaeus* 30-31 (1978): 314-20.

Kiparsky, Paul. "The Role of Linguistics in a Theory of Poetry." *Daedalus* 102 (1973): 231-44.

————. "The Rhythmic Structure of English Verse." *Poetics I,* ns 6 (1977): 111-53.

Kiparsky, Paul and Gilbert Youmans, eds. *Rhythm and Meter.* Vol. 7 of *Phonetics and Phonology.* 7 vols. San Diego: Academic Press, 1989.

Leithauser, Brad. "Metrical Illiteracy." *The New Criterion* 1.5 (1983): 41-46.

Lewis, C. S. "On Metre." *Selected Literary Essays.* Ed. Walter Hooper. Cambridge: Cambridge University Press, 1969.

McAuley, James. *Versification: A Short Introduction.* East Lansing: Michigan State University Press, 1966.

McCorkle, James, ed. *Conversant Essays: Contemporary Poets on Poetry.* Detroit: Wayne State University Press, 1990. See Section Two, "Questions of Form," with essays by Timothy Steele, Charles O. Hartman, Denise Levertov, Luz Maria Umpierre, Mark Rudman, Brad Leithauser, Dana Gioia, Alice Fulton, and Nathaniel Mackey.

Mayor, J. B. *Chapters on English Metre.* 2nd ed. Cambridge: Cambridge University Press, 1901; reprint, New York: AMS, 1969.

Nabokov, Vladimir. *Notes on Prosody.* Princeton: Princeton University Press, 1964.

Nims, John Frederick. *Western Wind: An Introduction to Poetry.* New York: Random House, 1974.

Olson, Charles. *Projective Verse.* New York: Totem Press, 1959.

Omond, T. S. *English Metrists: Being a Sketch of English Prosodical Criticism from Elizabethan Times to the Present Day.* Oxford: Clarendon Press, 1921.

————. *A Study of Metre.* London: Grant Richards, 1903.

Pike, Kenneth L. *The Intonation of American English.* Ann Arbor: University of Michigan Press, 1956.

Preminger, Alex and T. V. F. Brogan, eds. *The New Princeton Encyclopedia of Poetry and Poetics.* Princeton: Princeton University Press, 1993.

Raven, David. *Greek Metre: An Introduction.* 2nd ed. London: Faber, 1968.

Richards, I. A. *Practical Criticism: A Study of Literary Judgment.* 2nd ed. New York: Harcourt, Brace, 1948.

Saintsbury, George. *A History of English Prosody from the Twelfth Century to the Present Day.* London: Macmillan, 1908–10. 3 vols.; reprint, New York: Russell & Russell, 1961.

Schipper, Jakob. *A History of English Versification.* Oxford: Clarendon Press, 1910; reprint, New York: AMS, 1971.

Shapiro, Alan. *In Praise of the Impure: Poetry and the Ethical Imagination: Essays, 1980-1991.* Evanston: TriQuarterly Books, Northwestern University Press, 1993. See part 2 on meter and free verse.

Shapiro, Karl and Robert Beum. *A Prosody Handbook.* New York: Harper and Row, 1965.

Sievers, Eduard. "Old Germanic Metrics and Old English Metrics." *Essential Articles for the Study of Old English Poetry.* Eds. Jess B. Bessinger Jr. and Stanley J. Kahrl. Hamden, Conn.: Archon, 1968.

Steele, Timothy. *Missing Measures: Modern Poetry and the Revolt Against Meter.* Fayetteville: University of Arkansas Press, 1990.

————. "On Meter." *Hellas* 1.2 (1990): 289-310.

Stewart, George R. *The Technique of English Verse.* New York: Holt, Rinehart & Winston, 1930; reprint, Port Washington, N. Y.: Kennikat, 1966.

Tarlinskaja, Marina G. *English Verse: Theory and History.* The Hague: Mouton, 1976.

————. "Rhythm and Meaning: 'Rhythmical Figures' in English Iambic Pentameter, Their Grammar, and Their Links with Semantics." *Style* 21.1 (1987): 1-35.

Thompson, John. *The Founding of English Metre.* New York: Columbia University Press, 1961; reprint, 1988.

Trager, George L. and Henry Lee Smith, Jr. *An Outline of English Structure.* Norman: University of Oklahoma Press, 1951.

Turco, Lewis. *The Book of Forms.* New York: E. P. Dutton, 1968.

————. *The New Book of Forms: A Handbook of Poetics.* Hanover, N.H.: University Press of New England, 1986.

Turner, Frederick and Ernst Pöppel. "The Neural Lyre: Poetic Meter, the Brain and Time." *Poetry* 142 (August 1983): 277-309.

West, M. L. *Greek Metre.* Oxford: Oxford University Press, 1982.

Williams, Miller. *Patterns of Poetry: An Encyclopedia of Forms.* Baton Rouge: Louisiana State University Press, 1986.

Wimsatt, W. K., ed. *Versification: Major Language Types*. New York: New York University Press, 1972.

Wimsatt, W. K. and Monroe Beardsley. "The Concept of Meter: An Exercise in Abstraction." *PMLA* 74 (1959): 585-98.

Winters, Yvor. "The Audible Reading of Poetry." *The Function of Criticism*. Denver: Alan Swallow, 1957.

———. "The Influence of Meter on Poetic Convention." *In Defense of Reason*. Chicago: Alan Swallow, 1947.

Woods, Susanne. *Natural Emphasis: English Versification from Chaucer to Dryden*. San Marino, Calif.: Huntington Library Press, 1985.

Wrinn, Mary J. J. *The Hollow Reed*. New York: Harper & Brothers, 1935.

Yeats, William Butler. "A General Introduction for my Work." *Essays and Introductions*. New York: MacMillan, 1961.

CONTRIBUTORS

EAVAN BOLAND is the author of many books of poetry, including *In a Time of Violence, Outside History: Selected Poems 1980-1990,* and *An Origin Like Water: Collected Poems 1967-1987,* as well as a prose work, *Object Lessons: The Life of the Woman and the Poet in Our Time,* all published by W. W. Norton. She lives in Dublin, reviews regularly for the *Irish Times,* and teaches for part of the year at Stanford University.

ANNIE FINCH is author of the poetry collections *Catching the Mermother* (Aralia, 1995) and *The Encyclopedia of Scotland* (1982) and a book on poetics, *The Ghost of Meter: Culture and Prosody in American Free Verse* (Michigan, 1993). She is editor of *Beyond New Formalism: Contemporary Essays on Poetic Form and Narrative* (1996) and *A Formal Feeling Comes: Poems in Form by Contemporary Women* (1994), both from Story Line Press. Her poems appear widely and she teaches at Miami University in Ohio.

DANA GIOIA has published two volumes of verse with Graywolf Press, *Daily Horoscope* (1986) and *The Gods of Winter* (1991). He is also the author of *Can Poetry Matter?: Essays on Poetry and American Culture* (1992). His recently published translation of Seneca's tragedy, The *Madness of Hercules,* appeared in the Johns Hopkins Roman Drama series. Gioia lives in Santa Rosa, California, and is a full-time writer and reviewer.

RACHEL HADAS is professor of English at the Newark campus of Rutgers University and author of eleven books of poetry, essays, and translations. Her memoir, *The Double Legacy,* recently appeared from Faber & Faber, and her translations of elegies by Tibullus and of Seneca's tragedy *Oedipus* have recently been published in collections of Latin lyric and Roman drama. Hadas's awards include Guggenheim and Ingram Merrill fellowships and an award in literature from the American Academy-Institute of Arts and Letters.

CHARLES O. HARTMAN is author of four books of poetry, most recently *Glass Enclosure* (Wesleyan, 1995) and, with Hugh Kenner, *Sentences* (Sun & Moon, 1995), a long poem with "computer interventions." His critical work includes *Free Verse: An Essay on Prosody* (Princeton, 1980; Northwestern, 1996), *Jazz Text: Voice and Improvisation in Poetry, Jazz, and Song* (Princeton, 1991), and *English Metrics,* a reference work available on computers. He is professor of English and poet-in-residence at Connecticut College.

ROBERT HASS is the author of several books of poems, including *Field Guide* (1973), which won the Yale Series for Younger Poets, as well as *Praise* (1979), *Human Wishes* (1989), and *Sun Under Wood* (1996), all published by Ecco Press. He won the National Book Critics Circle Award for his volume of essays, *Twentieth Century Pleasures* (Ecco Press, 1984). He teaches English at the University of California at Berkeley and also currently serves as the Poet Laureate of the United States.

MARGARET HOLLEY directs the creative writing program at Bryn Mawr College. Her critical study, *The Poetry of Marianne Moore, A Study in Voice and Value,* was published by Cambridge University Press in 1988. Her first book of poems, *The Smoke Tree,* won the Bluestem Award in 1991, and her second, *Morning Star,* was published by Copper Beech Press in 1992. She lives with her husband, Peter Sparks, in West Chester, Pennsylvania.

JOHN FREDERICK NIMS has written about meter in his *Western Wind: An Introduction to Poetry* and his *The Harper Anthology of Poetry,* as well as in his *Sappho to Valéry: Poems in Translation* (Arkansas) and in *A Local Habitation: Essays on Poetry* (Michigan).

In his eight books of poems, he writes, he has, "amid the iambs, resorted to our many meters, from free verse to syllabic haiku to the galliambics of Catullus and the glyconic-pherecratic grid of Pindar's first Olympian ode."

DAVID J. ROTHMAN was educated at Harvard, University of Utah, and New York University where he received his Ph.D. in 1992 with a dissertation entitled *The Whitmanian Poets and the Origin of Open Form*. His essays in literature and social science appear in *Hellas, The Eighteenth Century: Theory and Interpretation, Restoration, Society,* and *Political Communication*. His poetry has been published in *The Atlantic, Poetry, Kenyon Review, Gettysburg Review,* and elsewhere. He lives in Crested Butte, Colorado, with his wife Emily and son Jacob.

TIMOTHY STEELE has recently published two collections of verse, *Sapphics and Uncertainties: Poems 1970-1986* (Arkansas, 1995) and *The Color Wheel* (Johns Hopkins, 1994). He has published as well a book of critical scholarship, *Missing Measures: Modern Poetry and the Revolt against Meter* (Arkansas, 1990). Among his honors are a Guggenheim Fellowship and the Peter I. B. Lavan Younger Poets Award from the Academy of American Poets. He is a professor of English at California State University, Los Angeles.

LEWIS PUTNAM TURCO was the winner in 1986 of the Melville Cane Memorial Award of the Poetry Society of America for his *Visions and Revisions of American Poetry* (Arkansas). His *The Book of Forms: A Handbook of Poetics* appeared in 1968 (Dutton) and *The New Book of Forms* in 1986 (New England). He is currently at work on *The Oxford Handbook of Literary Forms*. His recent books of poetry are *The Shifting Web: New and Selected Poems* (Arkansas, 1989) and *Emily Dickinson: Woman of Letters* (SUNY Press, 1993). He is professor of English and poet-in-residence at SUNY-Oswego.

ROBERT WALLACE is a graduate of Harvard and Cambridge, and since 1965 has taught at a university in Cleveland, Ohio. He was editor and publisher of *Light Year* and most recently is coauthor, with Michelle Boisseau, of the textbook *Writing Poems* (4th ed.,

1996). *The Common Summer: New & Selected Poems* appeared in 1989 from Carnegie Mellon University Press and an essay, "Reconstructing Contemporary Poetry," in *AWP Chronicle* in 1995.

BARRY WELLER is professor of English at the University of Utah and editor of *Western Humanities Review*. He has also coedited scholarly editions of Lord Byron's plays (Oxford) and Elizabeth Cary's *The Tragedy of Mariam* (University of California), the earliest original play in English by a woman. His essays on Montaigne, Shakespeare, Behn, Equiano, Shelley, Dickens, and other topics, appear in such journals as *English Literary History, Kenyon Review, Modern Language Notes,* and *New Literary History.*

RICHARD WILBUR served as the poet laureate of the United States in 1987–88, and during the latter year was awarded his second Pulitzer Prize for *New and Collected Poems* (Harcourt, Brace & Jovanovich). His first Pulitzer was awarded in 1957 for *Things of This World.* Among his many translations are Racine's *Andromache* and *Phaedra,* and seven verse comedies from Molière, most recently *Amphitryon* (1995).

SUSANNE WOODS is the author of a number of essays on English Renaissance poetry and poetics, and of *Natural Emphasis: English Versification from Chaucer to Dryden* (1985). She is also a general editor of the Oxford University Press series *Women Writers in English 1350-1850,* for which she edited *The Poems of Aemilia Lanyer.* She taught at Brown University, where she founded the Brown University Women Writers Project, and for five years was Dean of Franklin and Marshall University, where she is now professor of English.

INDEX OF
PROPOSAL DISCUSSIONS

INDEX OF AUTHORS